SOCIAL WELFARE

FIGHTING POVERTY AND HOMELESSNESS

D1307017

ISSN 1937-3295

SOCIAL WELFARE
FIGHTING POVERTY AND HOMELESSNESS

Melissa J. Doak

INFORMATION PLUS® REFERENCE SERIES
Formerly Published by Information Plus, Wylie, Texas

Detroit • New York • San Francisco • New Haven, Conn • Waterville, Maine • London

Social Welfare: Fighting Poverty and Homelessness

Melissa J. Doak
Paula Kepos, Series Editor

Project Editors: Kathleen J. Edgar, Elizabeth Manar

Rights Acquisition and Management: Margaret Abendroth, Edna Shy

Composition: Evi Abou-El-Seoud, Mary Beth Trimper

Manufacturing: Cynde Lentz

For product information and technology assistance, contact us at
Gale Customer Support, 1-800-877-4253.
For permission to use material from this text or product,
submit all requests online at **www.cengage.com/permissions.**
Further permissions questions can be e-mailed to
permissionrequest@cengage.com

Cover photograph: Image copyright Sharon Day, 2009. Used under license from Shutterstock.com.

While every effort has been made to ensure the reliability of the information presented in this publication, Gale, a part of Cengage Learning, does not guarantee the accuracy of the data contained herein. Gale accepts no payment for listing; and inclusion in the publication of any organization, agency, institution, publication, service, or individual does not imply endorsement of the editors or publisher. Errors brought to the attention of the publisher and verified to the satisfaction of the publisher will be corrected in future editions.

Gale
27500 Drake Rd.
Farmington Hills, MI 48331-3535

ISBN-13: 978-0-7876-5103-9 (set)
ISBN-13: 978-1-4144-3382-0

ISBN-10: 0-7876-5103-6 (set)
ISBN-10: 1-4144-3382-4

ISSN 1937-3295

This title is also available as an e-book.
ISBN-13: 978-1-4144-5765-9 (set)
ISBN-10: 1-4144-5765-0 (set)
Contact your Gale sales representative for ordering information.

Printed in the United States of America
1 2 3 4 5 6 7 13 12 11 10 09

TABLE OF CONTENTS

PREFACE

Social Welfare: Fighting Poverty and Homelessness is part of the *Information Plus Reference Series*. The purpose of each volume of the series is to present the latest facts on a topic of pressing concern in modern American life. These topics include the most controversial and studied social issues in the twenty-first century: abortion, capital punishment, care of senior citizens, crime, the environment, health care, immigration, minorities, national security, women, youth, and many more. Even though this series is written especially for high school and undergraduate students, it is an excellent resource for anyone in need of factual information on current affairs.

By presenting the facts, it is the intention of Gale, Cengage Learning, to provide its readers with everything they need to reach an informed opinion on current issues. To that end, there is a particular emphasis in this series on the presentation of scientific studies, surveys, and statistics. These data are generally presented in the form of tables, charts, and other graphics placed within the text of each book. Every graphic is directly referred to and carefully explained in the text. The source of each graphic is presented within the graphic itself. The data used in these graphics are drawn from the most reputable and reliable sources, such as from the various branches of the U.S. government and from major independent polling organizations. Every effort was made to secure the most recent information available. Readers should bear in mind that many major studies take years to conduct and that additional years often pass before the data from these studies are made available to the public. Therefore, in many cases the most recent information available in 2009 is dated from 2006 or 2007. Older statistics are sometimes presented as well, if they are of particular interest and no more-recent information exists.

Even though statistics are a major focus of the *Information Plus Reference Series*, they are by no means its only content. Each book also presents the widely held positions and important ideas that shape how the book's subject is discussed in the United States. These positions are explained in detail and, where possible, in the words of their proponents. Some of the other material to be found in these books includes historical background, descriptions of major events related to the subject, relevant laws and court cases, and examples of how these issues play out in American life. Some books also feature primary documents or have pro and con debate sections that provide the words and opinions of prominent Americans on both sides of a controversial topic. All material is presented in an even-handed and unbiased manner; readers will never be encouraged to accept one view of an issue over another.

HOW TO USE THIS BOOK

Aid for the poor has long been a controversial topic in the United States. Most Americans agree that society should help those who have fallen on hard times, but there are many different opinions as to how this is best accomplished. The 1990s were a time of particularly heavy debate about this issue, resulting in major changes to the U.S. welfare system in 1996 with the introduction of the Personal Responsibility and Work Opportunity Reconciliation Act, which required recipients to work in exchange for time-limited assistance. In this book both the old and the new welfare systems are examined, and their differences are highlighted. The volume also describes those who make use of the welfare system, why they use it, and what they get out of it.

Social Welfare: Fighting Poverty and Homelessness consists of seven chapters and three appendixes. Each chapter is devoted to a particular aspect of social welfare. For a summary of the information covered in each chapter, please see the synopses provided in the Table of Contents at the front of the book. Chapters generally begin with an overview of the basic facts and background information on the chapter's topic, then proceed to examine subtopics of particular interest. For example, Chapter 4, Characteristics of the Homeless, begins with an overview of the estimates of homelessness by examining several types of surveys and studies that have been conducted. The chapter then profiles the homeless, such as their gender and race, their family structure, their age, and their military background. Next, the duration and recurrence of homelessness and where the homeless live are examined. Then the chapter looks at the trends in homeless, including poverty estimates and profiled cities. The chapter then details the employment of the homeless, such as day labor and shadow work. It concludes with a discussion about the challenges of exiting homelessness. Readers can find their way through a chapter by looking for the section and subsection headings, which are clearly set off from the text. They can also refer to the book's extensive Index if they already know what they are looking for.

Statistical Information

The tables and figures featured throughout *Social Welfare: Fighting Poverty and Homelessness* will be of particular use to readers in learning about this topic. These tables and figures represent an extensive collection of the most recent and valuable statistics on social welfare, as well as related issues—for example, graphics cover the amount of money spent each year for various government welfare programs, the demographics of poverty, the role of child support payments in preventing poverty, and the number of people without health insurance in the United States. Gale, Cengage Learning, believes that making this information available to readers is the most important way to fulfill the goal of this book: to help readers understand the issues and controversies surrounding social welfare and reach their own conclusions.

Each table or figure has a unique identifier appearing above it for ease of identification and reference. Titles for the tables and figures explain their purpose. At the end of each table or figure, the original source of the data is provided.

To help readers understand these often complicated statistics, all tables and figures are explained in the text. References in the text direct readers to the relevant statistics. Furthermore, the contents of all tables and figures are fully indexed. Please see the opening section of the Index at the back of this volume for a description of how to find tables and figures within it.

Appendixes

Besides the main body text and images, *Social Welfare: Fighting Poverty and Homelessness* has three appen-

dixes. The first is the Important Names and Addresses directory. Here, readers will find contact information for a number of government and private organizations that can provide further information on aspects of social welfare. The second appendix is the Resources section, which can also assist readers in conducting their own research. In this section the author and editors of *Social Welfare: Fighting Poverty and Homelessness* describe some of the sources that were most useful during the compilation of this book. The final appendix is the Index.

ADVISORY BOARD CONTRIBUTIONS

The staff of Information Plus would like to extend its heartfelt appreciation to the Information Plus Advisory Board. This dedicated group of media professionals provides feedback on the series on an ongoing basis. Their comments allow the editorial staff who work on the project to continually make the series better and more user-friendly. The staff's top priorities are to produce the highest-quality and most useful books possible, and the Advisory Board's contributions to this process are invaluable.

The members of the Information Plus Advisory Board are:

- Kathleen R. Bonn, Librarian, Newbury Park High School, Newbury Park, California

- Madelyn Garner, Librarian, San Jacinto College, North Campus, Houston, Texas

- Anne Oxenrider, Media Specialist, Dundee High School, Dundee, Michigan

- Charles R. Rodgers, Director of Libraries, Pasco-Hernando Community College, Dade City, Florida

- James N. Zitzelsberger, Library Media Department Chairman, Oshkosh West High School, Oshkosh, Wisconsin

COMMENTS AND SUGGESTIONS

The editors of the *Information Plus Reference Series* welcome your feedback on *Social Welfare: Fighting Poverty and Homelessness*. Please direct all correspondence to:

Editors
Information Plus Reference Series
27500 Drake Rd.
Farmington Hills, MI 48331-3535

CHAPTER 1
POVERTY IN THE UNITED STATES

THE FEDERAL DEFINITION OF POVERTY

The federal government began measuring poverty in 1959. During the 1960s President Lyndon B. Johnson (1908–1973) declared a national war on poverty. Researchers realized that few statistical tools were available to measure the number of Americans who continued to live in poverty in one of the most affluent nations in the world. To fight this "war," it had to be determined who was poor and why.

During the early 1960s Mollie Orshansky (1915–2006) of the Social Security Administration suggested that the poverty income level be defined as the income sufficient to purchase a minimally adequate amount of goods and services. The necessary data for defining and pricing a full market basket of goods was not available then, nor is it available now. However, Orshansky noted that in 1955 the U.S. Department of Agriculture (USDA) had published the Household Food Consumption Survey, which showed that the average family of three or more people spent approximately one-third of its after-tax income on food. She multiplied the USDA's 1961 economy food plan (a no-frills food basket meeting the then-recommended dietary allowances) by three.

Basically, this defined a poor family as any family or person whose after-tax income was not sufficient to purchase a minimally adequate diet if one-third of the income was spent on food. Differences were allowed for size of family, gender of the head of the household, and whether it was a farm or nonfarm family. The threshold (the level at which poverty begins) for a farm family was set at 70% of a nonfarm household. (The difference between farm and nonfarm households was eliminated in 1982.)

The poverty guidelines set by the U.S. Department of Health and Human Services (HHS) are based on the poverty thresholds as established by the U.S. Census Bureau. The poverty thresholds are updated each year to reflect inflation. People with incomes below the applicable threshold are classified as living below the poverty level.

The poverty guidelines vary by family size and composition. In 2009 a family of four earning $21,200 or less annually was considered impoverished. (See Table 1.1.) A person living alone who earned less than $10,400 was considered poor, as was a family of eight members making less than $35,600. The poverty level is considerably higher in Alaska and Hawaii, where the cost of living is higher than in the contiguous 48 states and the District of Columbia.

The poverty guidelines set by the HHS are important because various government agencies use them as the basis for eligibility to key assistance programs. The HHS uses the poverty guidelines to determine Community Services Block Grants, Low-Income Home Energy Assistance Block Grants, and Head Start allotments. The guidelines are also the basis for funding the USDA's Supplemental Nutrition Assistance Program (formerly the Food Stamp Program), National School Lunch Program, and Special Supplemental Food Program for Women, Infants, and Children. The U.S. Department of Labor uses the guidelines to determine funding for the Job Corps and other employment and training programs under the Workforce Investment Act of 1998. Some state and local governments choose to use the federal poverty guidelines for some of their own programs, such as state health insurance programs and financial guidelines for child support enforcement.

THE HISTORICAL EFFORT
TO REDUCE POVERTY

Since the late 1950s Americans have seen some successes and some failures in the battle against poverty. For the total population in 1960, 22.2%, or 39.9 million people, lived below the poverty level. (See Table 1.2.) After an initial decline through the 1960s and 1970s, the poverty rate began to increase during the early 1980s, coinciding with a downturn in household and family incomes for all Americans. The poverty rate rose steadily until it reached an 18-year high of 15.2% in 1983, a year during which the country

TABLE 1.1

Department of Health and Human Services poverty guidelines, 2008–09

Size of family unit	100 Percent of poverty	110 Percent of poverty	125 Percent of poverty	150 Percent of poverty	175 Percent of poverty	185 Percent of poverty	200 Percent of poverty
1	$10,400	$11,440	$13,000	$15,600	$18,200	$19,240	$20,800
2	$14,000	$15,400	$17,500	$21,000	$24,500	$25,900	$28,000
3	$17,600	$19,360	$22,000	$26,400	$30,800	$32,560	$35,200
4	$21,200	$23,320	$26,500	$31,800	$37,100	$39,220	$42,400
5	$24,800	$27,280	$31,000	$37,200	$43,400	$45,880	$49,600
6	$28,400	$31,240	$35,500	$42,600	$49,700	$52,540	$56,800
7	$32,000	$35,200	$40,000	$48,000	$56,000	$59,200	$64,000
8	$35,600	$39,160	$44,500	$53,400	$62,300	$65,860	$71,200

Notes: For optional use in federal fiscal year 2008 and mandatory use in federal fiscal year 2009.
For all states (except Alaska and Hawaii) and for the District of Columbia
For family units with more than 8 members, add $3,600 for each additional person at 100% of poverty; $3,960 at 110 %; $4,500 at 125%; $5,400 at 150%; $6,300 at 175%; $6,660 at 185% and $7,200 at 200% of poverty.

SOURCE: "2008/2009 HHS Poverty Guidelines," U.S. Department of Health and Human Services, Administration for Children and Families, June 4, 2008, http://liheap.ncat.org/profiles/povertytables/FY2009/popstate.htm (accessed December 15, 2008)

was climbing out of a serious economic recession. The percentage of Americans living in poverty then began dropping, falling to 12.8% in 1989. After that, however, the percentage increased again, reaching 15.1% in 1993. It then dropped to 11.3% in 2000; however, because the nation's economy slowed, the poverty rate rose again to 12.5% in 2007. Sharon Parrott of the Center on Budget and Policy Priorities (CBPP) explains in *Recession Could Cause Large Increases in Poverty and Push Millions into Deep Poverty* (November 2, 2008, http://www.cbpp.org/files/11-24-08pov .pdf) that the poverty rate will undoubtedly rise again due to the severe economic recession that began in 2008. Figure 1.1 provides a graphic representation of the number of poor people and the poverty rates between 1959 and 2007.

Analysts believe the overall decline in poverty from 1960 to 2007 was due to both the growth in the economy and to the success of some of the antipoverty programs instituted in the late 1960s; yet not all demographic subcategories have experienced the same level of change. For example, in *Income, Poverty, and Health Insurance Coverage in the United States: 2007* (August 2008, http://www.census.gov/prod/ 2008pubs/p60-235.pdf), Carmen DeNavas-Walt, Bernadette D. Proctor, and Jessica C. Smith of the Census Bureau note that the poverty rate of those 65 years of age and older has improved dramatically from 24.6% in 1970 to 9.7% in 2007. (See Figure 1.2.) For related children under 18 years of age in African-American families, the improvement from 41.5% in 1970 to 33.6% in 2007 shows that antipoverty programs still have not reached many people in need.

RATIO OF INCOME TO POVERTY LEVELS

For purposes of analysis, the Census Bureau uses income-to-poverty ratios that are calculated by dividing income by the respective poverty threshold for each family size. The resulting number is then tabulated on a scale that includes three categories: poor, near-poor, and nonpoor. Poor people have a poverty ratio below 1.00. People above the poverty level are divided into two groups: the near-poor and the nonpoor. The near-poor have a poverty ratio between 1.00 and 1.24 (100% to 124% of the poverty level), and the nonpoor have an income-to-poverty ratio of 1.25 (125% of the poverty level) and above.

In 2007, 12.5% of the total population had income-to-poverty ratios under 1.00; in other words, 37.3 million people in the United States had incomes below the poverty threshold, and 17% were classified as poor or near-poor. (See Table 1.3.) Children were disproportionately poor. Children were the most likely to be poor (18%), and nearly one out of four (23.8%) children were poor or near-poor. Young adults aged 18 to 24 were the next most likely to be poor (17.3%), and 22.2% were poor or near-poor. More than one out of five (20.8%) families with children under six years of age had income-to-poverty ratios below 1.00; over one out of four (27.1%) of these families had income-to-poverty ratios below 1.25.

HOW ACCURATE IS THE POVERTY LEVEL?

Almost every year since the Census Bureau first defined the poverty level observers have been concerned about its accuracy. Since the early 1960s, when Orshansky defined the estimated poverty level based on a family's food budget, living patterns have changed and food costs have become a smaller percentage of family spending. For example, the U.S. Bureau of Labor Statistics (BLS) reports in the news release "Consumer Expenditures in 2007" (November 25, 2008, http://www.bls.gov/news.release/pdf/cesan.pdf) that the average family spent $6,133 (12.4%) of its total expenditures on food. By contrast, housing accounted for $16,920 (34.1%) of family spending. Based on these changes in buying patterns, should the amount spent on food be multiplied by a factor of eight instead of three? Or should the poverty level be based on housing or other factors? What about geographical differences in the cost of living?

TABLE 1.2

Poverty status of people and people in families, 1960–2007

[Numbers in thousands]

	All people			All families			People in families — Families with female householder no husband present			Unrelated individuals		
		Below poverty level			Below poverty level			Below poverty level			Below poverty level	
Year	Total	Number	Percent	Total	Number	Percent	Total	Number	Percent	Total	Number	Percent
All races												
2007	298,699	37,276	12.5	245,443	26,509	10.8	43,961	13,478	30.7	51,740	10,189	19.7
2006	296,450	36,460	12.3	245,199	25,915	10.6	43,223	13,199	30.5	49,884	9,977	20.0
2005	293,135	36,950	12.6	242,389	26,068	10.8	42,244	13,153	31.1	49,526	10,425	21.1
2004	290,617	37,040	12.7	240,754	26,544	11.0	42,053	12,832	30.5	48,609	9,926	20.4
2003	287,699	35,861	12.5	238,903	25,684	10.8	41,311	12,413	30.0	47,594	9,713	20.4
2002	285,317	34,570	12.1	236,921	24,534	10.4	40,529	11,657	28.8	47,156	9,618	20.4
2001	281,475	32,907	11.7	233,911	23,215	9.9	39,261	11,223	28.6	46,392	9,226	19.9
2000	278,944	31,581	11.3	231,909	22,347	9.6	38,375	10,926	28.5	45,624	8,653	19.0
1999	276,208	32,791	11.9	230,789	23,830	10.3	38,580	11,764	30.5	43,977	8,400	19.1
1998	271,059	34,476	12.7	227,229	25,370	11.2	39,000	12,907	33.1	42,539	8,478	19.9
1997	268,480	35,574	13.3	225,369	26,217	11.6	38,412	13,494	35.1	41,672	8,687	20.8
1996	266,218	36,529	13.7	223,955	27,376	12.2	38,584	13,796	35.8	40,727	8,452	20.8
1995	263,733	36,425	13.8	222,792	27,501	12.3	38,908	14,205	36.5	39,484	8,247	20.9
1994	261,616	38,059	14.5	221,430	28,985	13.1	37,253	14,380	38.6	38,538	8,287	21.5
1993	259,278	39,265	15.1	219,489	29,927	13.6	37,861	14,636	38.7	38,038	8,388	22.1
1992	256,549	38,014	14.8	217,936	28,961	13.3	36,446	14,205	39.0	36,842	8,075	21.9
1991	251,192	35,708	14.2	212,723	27,143	12.8	34,795	13,824	39.7	36,845	7,773	21.1
1990	248,644	33,585	13.5	210,967	25,232	12.0	33,795	12,578	37.2	36,056	7,446	20.7
1989	245,992	31,528	12.8	209,515	24,066	11.5	32,525	11,668	35.9	35,185	6,760	19.2
1988	243,530	31,745	13.0	208,056	24,048	11.6	32,164	11,972	37.2	34,340	7,070	20.6
1987	240,982	32,221	13.4	206,877	24,725	12.0	31,893	12,148	38.1	32,992	6,857	20.8
1986	238,554	32,370	13.6	205,459	24,754	12.0	31,152	11,944	38.3	31,679	6,846	21.6
1985	236,594	33,064	14.0	203,963	25,729	12.6	30,878	11,600	37.6	31,351	6,725	21.5
1984	233,816	33,700	14.4	202,288	26,458	13.1	30,844	11,831	38.4	30,268	6,609	21.8
1983	231,700	35,303	15.2	201,338	27,933	13.9	30,049	12,072	40.2	29,158	6,740	23.1
1982	229,412	34,398	15.0	200,385	27,349	13.6	28,834	11,701	40.6	27,908	6,458	23.1
1981	227,157	31,822	14.0	198,541	24,850	12.5	28,587	11,051	38.7	27,714	6,490	23.4
1980	225,027	29,272	13.0	196,963	22,601	11.5	27,565	10,120	36.7	27,133	6,227	22.9
1979	222,903	26,072	11.7	195,860	19,964	10.2	26,927	9,400	34.9	26,170	5,743	21.9
1978	215,656	24,497	11.4	191,071	19,062	10.0	26,032	9,269	35.6	24,585	5,435	22.1
1977	213,867	24,720	11.6	190,757	19,505	10.2	25,404	9,205	36.2	23,110	5,216	22.6
1976	212,303	24,975	11.8	190,844	19,632	10.3	24,204	9,029	37.3	21,459	5,344	24.9
1975	210,864	25,877	12.3	190,630	20,789	10.9	23,580	8,846	37.5	20,234	5,088	25.1
1974	209,362	23,370	11.2	190,436	18,817	9.9	23,165	8,462	36.5	18,926	4,553	24.1
1973	207,621	22,973	11.1	189,361	18,299	9.7	21,823	8,178	37.5	18,260	4,674	25.6
1972	206,004	24,460	11.9	189,193	19,577	10.3	21,264	8,114	38.2	16,811	4,883	29.0
1971	204,554	25,559	12.5	188,242	20,405	10.8	20,153	7,797	38.7	16,311	5,154	31.6
1970	202,183	25,420	12.6	186,692	20,330	10.9	19,673	7,503	38.1	15,491	5,090	32.9
1969	199,517	24,147	12.1	184,891	19,175	10.4	17,995	6,879	38.2	14,626	4,972	34.0
1968	197,628	25,389	12.8	183,825	20,695	11.3	18,048	6,990	38.7	13,803	4,694	34.0
1967	195,672	27,769	14.2	182,558	22,771	12.5	17,788	6,898	38.8	13,114	4,998	38.1
1966	193,388	28,510	14.7	181,117	23,809	13.1	17,240	6,861	39.8	12,271	4,701	38.3
1965	191,413	33,185	17.3	179,281	28,358	15.8	16,371	7,524	46.0	12,132	4,827	39.8
1964	189,710	36,055	19.0	177,653	30,912	17.4	(NA)	7,297	44.4	12,057	5,143	42.7
1963	187,258	36,436	19.5	176,076	31,498	17.9	(NA)	7,646	47.7	11,182	4,938	44.2
1962	184,276	38,625	21.0	173,263	33,623	19.4	(NA)	7,781	50.3	11,013	5,002	45.4
1961	181,277	39,628	21.9	170,131	34,509	20.3	(NA)	7,252	48.1	11,146	5,119	45.9
1960	179,503	39,851	22.2	168,615	34,925	20.7	(NA)	7,247	48.9	10,699	4,928	46.1

SOURCE: Adapted from "Table 2. Poverty Status of People by Family Relationship, Race, and Hispanic Origin: 1959 to 2007," in *Historical Poverty Tables—Current Population Survey* U.S. Census Bureau, August 26, 2008, http://www.census.gov/hhes/www/poverty/histpov/perindex.html (accessed December 15, 2008)

The proportion of family income spent on food is not the only change in family budgets since the 1950s. In families headed by two parents, both parents are far more likely to be working than they were a generation ago. There is also a much greater likelihood that a single parent, usually the mother, will be heading the family. Child care costs, which were of little concern during the 1950s, have become a major issue for working mothers and single parents in the twenty-first century.

Critics of the current poverty calculations tend to believe that the poverty levels are set too low, because they are based on a 50-year-old concept of American life that does not reflect the economic and social realities of the twenty-first century. Food has become a shrinking proportion of the household budget as costs for things such as housing, health care, and transportation have skyrocketed. Jared Bernstein and Arloc Sherman note in *Poor Measurement: New Census Report on Measuring Poverty Raises Concerns* (March 28,

FIGURE 1.1

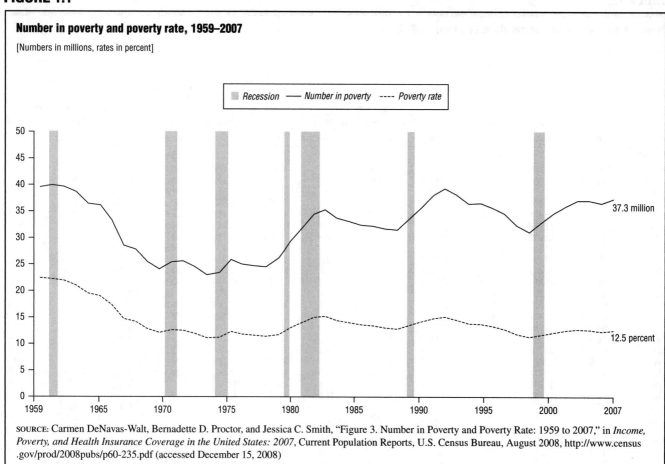

Number in poverty and poverty rate, 1959–2007

[Numbers in millions, rates in percent]

Legend: Recession — Number in poverty ---- Poverty rate

37.3 million

12.5 percent

SOURCE: Carmen DeNavas-Walt, Bernadette D. Proctor, and Jessica C. Smith, "Figure 3. Number in Poverty and Poverty Rate: 1959 to 2007," in *Income, Poverty, and Health Insurance Coverage in the United States: 2007*, Current Population Reports, U.S. Census Bureau, August 2008, http://www.census .gov/prod/2008pubs/p60-235.pdf (accessed December 15, 2008)

2006, http://epi.3cdn.net/3ef4568efe79adcc13_i2m6bhr3k .pdf) that most critics feel the poverty level should be raised, probably to about 130% to 150% of the current levels.

Some are concerned because the poverty threshold is different for elderly and nonelderly Americans. When the poverty threshold was first established, it was thought that older people did not need as much food. Therefore, the value of their basic food needs was lower. Consequently, when this figure was multiplied by three to get the poverty rate, it was naturally lower than the rate for nonelderly people. (The U.S. government, however, uses the poverty rate for nonelderly Americans when determining the eligibility for welfare services for all people, including the elderly.) Critics point out that even though the elderly might eat less than younger people, they have greater needs in other areas, which are not considered when their food needs are simply multiplied by three. Probably the most notable difference between the needs of the elderly and nonelderly is in the area of health care. The BLS (2008, http://www.bls.gov/cex/2007/Standard/age.pdf) finds that even though the total population interviewed spent $2,853 (5.7%) of their annual expenditure on health care, those over 65 years of age spent $ 4,631 (12.7%). Critics feel the poverty level should be the same for everyone, regardless of their age.

In *Measuring Poverty: A New Approach* (1995), the National Research Council's Panel on Poverty and Family Assistance raises several important issues regarding poverty thresholds or measurement of need. It recommends that new thresholds be developed using consumer expenditure data to represent a budget for basic needs: food, clothing, shelter (including utilities), and a small allowance for miscellaneous needs. This budget would be adjusted to reflect the needs of different family types and geographic differences in costs.

In June 2004 the Committee on National Statistics met to research alternative methods for measuring poverty, as recommended by the Panel on Poverty and Family Assistance. The committee recommended adopting a new poverty measure, taking into account the current dollar value of food, clothing, shelter, and utilities, as well as taxes, the value of food stamps and other near-cash benefits, and child support payments. In addition, the committee recommended adjusting the new poverty measure based not only on inflation but also on data on yearly consumer expenditures. John Iceland, the rapporteur for the committee, notes in "The CNSTAT Workshop on Experimental Poverty Measures, June 2004" (*Focus*, vol. 23, no. 3, Spring 2005), "The reasoning here is that CE [consumer expenditure] based calculations will allow the thresholds to retain their social significance for longer periods of time than absolute thresholds."

FIGURE 1.2

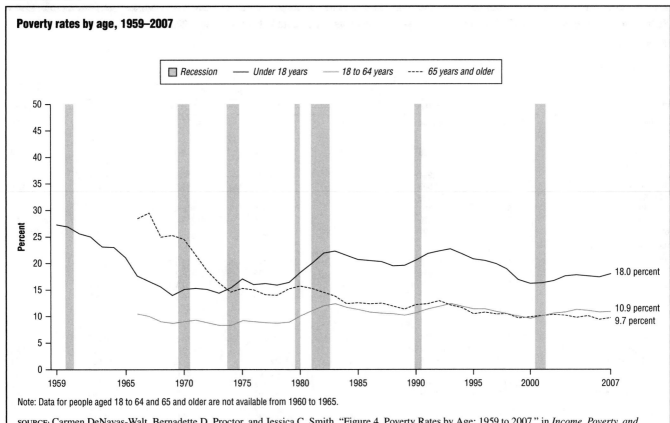

Poverty rates by age, 1959–2007

Note: Data for people aged 18 to 64 and 65 and older are not available from 1960 to 1965.

SOURCE: Carmen DeNavas-Walt, Bernadette D. Proctor, and Jessica C. Smith, "Figure 4. Poverty Rates by Age: 1959 to 2007," in *Income, Poverty, and Health Insurance Coverage in the United States: 2007*, Current Population Reports, U.S. Census Bureau, August 2008, http://www.census.gov/prod/2008pubs/p60-235.pdf (accessed December 15, 2008)

Testifying in 2008 before the Subcommittee on Income Security and Family Support of the House Ways and Means Committee, Rebecca M. Blank (July 17, 2008, http://www.brookings.edu/~/media/Files/rc/testimonies/2008/0717_poverty_blank/0717_poverty_blank.pdf) of the Brookings Institution addressed the inadequacy of the current poverty measures by arguing that the measures "are numbers without any valid conceptual basis." She indicated that food costs a smaller percentage of American household budgets in 2008 than it did when the poverty measure was developed and that threshold numbers should not be based on the cost of a single commodity. In addition, noncash assistance is not counted in the poverty measure, and therefore, "a cash income-based definition of family resources is highly insensitive to many of our nation's most effective anti-poverty programs." Blank suggested that the definition of the poverty threshold should be updated to reflect modern realities facing low-income families.

INCOME AND POVERTY
How Should Income Be Defined?

The Panel on Poverty and Family Assistance also recommended in 1995 that family resources be redefined to reflect the net amount available to buy goods and services in that budget for basic needs. Some critics point out that

the definition of income used to set the poverty figure is not accurate because it does not include the value of all welfare services as income. If the value of these services were counted as income, they believe the proportion of Americans considered to be living in poverty would be lower.

In the 1990s the Census Bureau developed several experimental methods of estimating income for evaluating poverty levels, but the bureau has had considerable difficulty determining the value of many of these subsidies. For example, it first tried to consider Medicare and Medicaid at full market value (this meant taking the total amount of money that the government spent on medical care for a particular group and then dividing it by the number of people in that group). The value was often greater than the actual earnings of the low-income family, which meant that even though the family's total earnings may not have been enough to cover food and housing, adding the market value of Medicare or Medicaid to its earnings put the family above the poverty threshold.

This did not make much sense, so the Census Bureau began trying a fungible value (giving equivalent value to units) for Medicare and Medicaid. When the bureau measures a household's income, Medicare and Medicaid are given no value if the earners cannot cover the cost of housing

TABLE 1.3

People with income below specified ratios of their poverty thresholds, by selected characteristics, 2007

[Numbers in thousands]

| Characteristic | Total | Income-to-poverty ratio | | | | | |
| | | Under 0.50 | | Under 1.00 | | Under 1.25 | |
		Number	Percent	Number	Percent	Number	Percent
All people	298,699	15,586	5.2	37,276	12.5	50,876	17.0
Age							
Under 18 years	73,996	5,768	7.8	13,324	18.0	17,645	23.8
18 to 24 years	28,398	2,495	8.8	4,901	17.3	6,306	22.2
25 to 34 years	40,146	2,234	5.6	4,930	12.3	6,704	16.7
35 to 44 years	42,132	1,600	3.8	3,971	9.4	5,494	13.0
45 to 54 years	43,935	1,498	3.4	3,722	8.5	4,929	11.2
55 to 59 years	18,371	552	3.0	1,471	8.0	1,947	10.6
60 to 64 years	14,931	529	3.5	1,402	9.4	1,935	13.0
65 years and older	36,790	909	2.5	3,556	9.7	5,916	16.1
Race* and Hispanic origin							
White	239,133	10,120	4.2	25,120	10.5	35,407	14.8
White, not Hispanic	196,583	6,724	3.4	16,032	8.2	22,416	11.4
Black	37,665	4,215	11.2	9,237	24.5	11,557	30.7
Asian	13,257	552	4.2	1,349	10.2	1,868	14.1
Hispanic (any race)	45,933	3,779	8.2	9,890	21.5	14,086	30.7
Family status							
In families	245,443	10,376	4.2	26,509	10.8	36,707	15.0
Householder	77,908	3,064	3.9	7,623	9.8	10,551	13.5
Related children under 18	72,792	5,396	7.4	12,802	17.6	17,036	23.4
Related children under 6	24,543	2,347	9.6	5,101	20.8	6,644	27.1
Unrelated subfamilies	1,516	389	25.7	577	38.1	679	44.8
Unrelated individuals	51,740	4,821	9.3	10,189	19.7	13,490	26.1
Male	25,447	2,195	8.6	4,348	17.1	5,707	22.4
Female	26,293	2,627	10.0	5,841	22.2	7,784	29.6

*Federal surveys now give respondents the option of reporting more than one race. Therefore, two basic ways of defining a race group are possible. A group such as Asian may be defined as those who reported Asian and no other race (the race-alone or single-race concept) or as those who reported Asian regardless of whether they also reported another race (the race-alone-or-in-combination concept). This table shows data using the first approach (race alone). The use of the single-race population does not imply that it is the preferred method of presenting or analyzing data. The Census Bureau uses a variety of approaches. About 2.6 percent of people reported more than one race in Census 2000. Data for American Indians and Alaska Natives, Native Hawaiians and Other Pacific Islanders, and those reporting two or more races are not shown separately.

Note: Details may not sum to totals because of rounding.

SOURCE: Carmen DeNavas-Walt, Bernadette D. Proctor, and Jessica C. Smith, "Table 4. People with Income below Specified Ratios of Their Poverty Thresholds by Selected Characteristics: 2007," in *Income, Poverty, and Health Insurance Coverage in the United States: 2007*, Current Population Reports, U.S. Census Bureau, August 2008, http://www.census.gov/prod/2008pubs/p60–235.pdf (accessed December 15, 2008)

and food. However, if the family can cover the cost of food and shelter, the bureau calculates the difference between the household income and the amount needed to meet basic housing and food costs. It then values the health services at this difference (up to the amount of the market value of the medical benefits). Even though this is complicated, the formula is believed to give a fair value to these services. Similar problems have developed in trying to determine the value of housing subsidies, school lunches, and other benefits.

Still other observers point out that most income definitions do not include assets and liabilities. Perhaps the poor household has some assets, such as a home or a car, that could be converted into income. One experimental definition of income includes capital gains on earnings, although it seems to make little difference because approximately 90% of all capital gains are earned by those in the upper fifth of the earnings scale. Michael Sherraden of Washington University in St. Louis indicates in "Building Assets to Fight Poverty" (*Shelterforce Online*, no. 110, March–April 2000) that including assets generally means little, because the overwhelming majority of poor families have few financial assets.

Another major issue is the question of income before and after income taxes. Even though the Tax Reform Act of 1986 removed most poor households from the federal income tax rolls, many poor households still pay state and local taxes. Naturally, some critics claim, the taxes paid to local and state governments are funds that are no longer available for feeding and housing the family and, therefore, should not be counted as income.

Growing Income Inequality

The Census Bureau has released a number of studies showing a change in the distribution of wealth and earnings in the United States. This change has resulted in an increase in the gap between the rich and the poor. Unlike many short-term economic changes that are often the product of normal economic cycles of growth and recession, these changes seem to indicate fundamental changes in American society.

Chye-Ching Huang and Chad Stone of the CBPP explain in "Average Income in 2006 up $60,000 for Top 1 Percent of

TABLE 1.4

Household income dispersion, selected years, 1967–2007

[Income in 2007 CPI-U-RS adjusted dollars]

Measures of income dispersion	2007	2002	1997	1992[a]	1987[b]	1982	1977	1972[c]	1967[d]
Household income at selected percentiles									
10th percentile limit	12,162	12,240	11,870	10,859	10,890	10,441	10,915	10,456	8,847
20th percentile limit	20,291	20,649	19,836	18,244	18,857	17,329	17,871	17,951	16,283
50th (median)	50,233	48,878	47,665	44,359	45,502	41,613	42,300	42,980	38,771
80th percentile limit	100,000	96,831	92,097	83,990	84,441	75,093	74,800	73,133	64,265
90th percentile limit	136,000	131,518	125,796	112,287	111,401	99,031	95,402	93,965	81,634
95th percentile limit	177,000	172,883	163,005	143,374	141,299	123,958	118,434	117,700	103,128
Household income ratios of selected percentiles									
90th/10th	11.18	10.75	10.60	10.34	10.23	9.49	8.74	8.99	9.23
95th/20th	8.72	8.37	8.22	7.86	7.49	7.15	6.63	6.56	6.33
95th/50th	3.52	3.54	3.42	3.23	3.11	2.98	2.80	2.74	2.66
80th/50th	1.99	1.98	1.93	1.89	1.86	1.80	1.77	1.70	1.66
80th/20th	4.93	4.69	4.64	4.60	4.48	4.33	4.19	4.07	3.95
20th/50th	0.40	0.42	0.42	0.41	0.41	0.42	0.42	0.42	0.42
Mean household income of quintiles									
Lowest quintile	11,551	11,514	11,385	10,506	10,706	9,881	10,394	10,120	8,683
Second quintile	29,442	29,274	28,464	26,325	27,210	25,006	25,584	26,139	24,060
Third quintile	49,968	49,330	47,886	44,351	45,492	41,392	42,323	42,658	38,415
Fourth quintile	79,111	77,596	74,169	68,083	68,763	61,561	62,010	61,240	53,747
Highest quintile	167,971	165,669	158,128	131,921	130,768	112,907	110,579	109,944	96,725
Shares of household income of quintiles									
Lowest quintile	3.4	3.5	3.6	3.8	3.8	4.0	4.2	4.1	4.0
Second quintile	8.7	8.8	8.9	9.4	9.6	10.0	10.2	10.4	10.8
Third quintile	14.8	14.8	15.0	15.8	16.1	16.5	16.9	17.0	17.3
Fourth quintile	23.4	23.3	23.2	24.2	24.3	24.5	24.7	24.5	24.2
Highest quintile	49.7	49.7	49.4	46.9	46.2	45.0	44.0	43.9	43.6
Summary measures									
Gini index of income inequality	0.463	0.462	0.459	0.433	0.426	0.412	0.402	0.401	0.397
Mean logarithmic deviation of income	0.532	0.514	0.484	0.416	0.414	0.401	0.364	0.370	0.380
Theil	0.391	0.398	0.396	0.323	0.31	0.287	0.276	0.279	0.287
Atkinson									
e=0.25	0.095	0.095	0.094	0.080	0.077	0.072	0.069	0.070	0.071
e=0.50	0.185	0.186	0.183	0.160	0.155	0.146	0.139	0.140	0.143
e=0.75	0.281	0.279	0.272	0.242	0.238	0.226	0.213	0.216	0.220[d]

[a]Implementation of 1990 census population controls.
[b]Implementation of a new Current Population Survey American Savings Education Council (CPS ASEC) processing system.
[c]Full implementation of 1970 census-based sample design.
[d]Implementation of a new CPS ASEC processing system.
Note: CPI-U-RS is Consumer Price Index research series for urban consumers.

SOURCE: Adapted from Carmen DeNavas-Walt, Bernadette D. Proctor, and Jessica C. Smith, "Table A-3. Selected Measures of Household Income Dispersion: 1967 to 2007," in *Income, Poverty, and Health Insurance Coverage in the United States: 2007*, Current Population Reports, U.S. Census Bureau, August 2008, http://www.census.gov/prod/2008pubs/p60–235.pdf (accessed December 15, 2008)

Households, Just $430 for Bottom 90 Percent" (October 22, 2008, http://www.cbpp.org/files/3-27-08tax2.pdf) that according to economists Thomas Piketty and Emmanuel Saez, the growing inequality in income in the United States began in 1976. The economists' analysis of Internal Revenue Service data shows that in 2006 the wealthiest 1% of American society earned 20% of the nation's income, the highest proportion since 1928. Census data show that in 2007 the income differences between income quintiles were close to record highs, with only the top fifth having increased its percentage of the nation's income since the 1980s. (See Table 1.4.) In 2007 the quintile of households with the highest incomes received 49.7% of the national income, about the same as that received by the other 80% of the population combined. The lowest quintile received only 3.4% of the national income in 2007.

Why Is the Income Gap Growing?

Many reasons exist to explain the growing inequality, although observers disagree about which are more important. One reason is that the proportion of the elderly population, who are likely to earn less, is growing. According to the Census Bureau, 24.1 million of 116.8 million households, or 20.6%, were headed by a householder 65 years of age or older in 2007. (See Table 1.5; a household may consist of a single individual or a group of related or unrelated people living together, whereas a family consists of related individuals.) The median (the middle value—half are higher and half are lower) household income of households headed by a person aged 65 years or older was $28,305, the lowest of any age group.

TABLE 1.5

Income and earnings summary measures by selected characteristics, 2006 and 2007

[Income in 2007 dollars]

Characteristic	2006		2007		Percentage change in real median income (2007 less 2006)
	Number (thousands)	Median income (dollars) Estimate	Number (thousands)	Median income (dollars) Estimate	Estimate
Households					
All households	**116,011**	**49,568**	**116,783**	**50,233**	**1.3**
Type of household					
Family households	78,425	61,593	77,873	62,359	1.2
Married-couple	58,945	71,694	58,370	72,785	1.5
Female householder, no husband present	14,416	32,721	14,404	33,370	2
Male householder, no wife present	5,063	48,414	5,100	49,839	2.9
Nonfamily households	37,587	29,908	38,910	30,176	0.9
Female householder	20,249	24,553	21,038	24,294	−1.1
Male householder	17,338	36,624	17,872	36,767	0.4
Race[a] and Hispanic origin of householder					
White	94,705	52,111	95,112	52,115	—
White, not Hispanic	82,675	53,910	82,785	54,920	1.9
Black	14,354	32,876	14,551	33,916	3.2
Asian	4,454	66,060	4,494	66,103	0.1
Hispanic (any race)	12,973	38,853	13,339	38,679	−0.4
Age of householder					
Under 65 years	92,282	56,279	92,671	56,545	0.5
15 to 24 years	6,662	31,815	6,554	31,790	−0.1
25 to 34 years	19,435	50,559	19,225	51,016	0.9
35 to 44 years	22,779	62,119	22,448	62,124	—
45 to 54 years	24,140	66,714	24,536	65,476	−1.9
55 to 64 years	19,266	56,141	19,909	57,386	2.2
65 years and older	23,729	28,587	24,113	28,305	−1.0
Nativity of householder					
Native born	100,603	50,466	101,104	50,946	1
Foreign born	15,408	45,190	15,680	44,230	−2.1
Naturalized citizen	7,210	52,899	7,469	52,092	−1.5
Not a citizen	8,198	40,617	8,211	37,637	−7.3
Earnings of full-time, year-round workers					
Men with earnings	63,055	43,460	62,984	45,113	3.8
Women with earnings	44,663	33,437	45,613	35,102	5
Per capita income[b]					
Total[a]	**296,824**	**$27,100**	**299,106**	**26,804**	**−1.1**
White	237,892	28,610	239,399	28,325	−1.0
White, not Hispanic	196,252	31,294	196,768	31,051	−0.8
Black	37,369	18,410	37,775	18,428	0.1
Asian	13,194	31,339	13,268	29,901	−4.6
Hispanic (any race)	44,854	15,858	46,026	15,603	−1.6

—Represents or rounds to zero.

[a]Federal surveys now give respondents the option of reporting more than one race. Therefore, two basic ways of defining a race group are possible. A group such as Asian may be defined as those who reported Asian and no other race (the race-alone or single-race concept) or as those who reported Asian regardless of whether they also reported another race (the race-alone-or-in-combination concept). This table shows data using the first approach (race alone). The use of the single-race population does not imply that it is the preferred method of presenting or analyzing data. The Census Bureau uses a variety of approaches. About 2.6 percent of people reported more than one race in Census 2000. Data for American Indians and Alaska Natives, Native Hawaiians and Other Pacific Islanders, and those reporting two or more races are not shown separately in this table.

[b]The data shown in this section are per capita incomes and their respective confidence intervals. Per capita income is the mean income computed for every man, woman, and child in a particular group. It is derived by dividing the total income of a particular group by the total population in that group (excluding patients or inmates in institutional quarters).

SOURCE: Adapted from Carmen DeNavas-Walt, Bernadette D. Proctor, and Jessica C. Smith, "Table 1. Income and Earnings Summary Measures by Selected Characteristics: 2006 and 2007," in *Income, Poverty, and Health Insurance Coverage in the United States: 2007*, Current Population Reports, U.S. Census Bureau, August 2008, http://www.census.gov/prod/2008pubs/p60–235.pdf (accessed December 15, 2008)

In addition, more people than in previous years were living in nonfamily situations (either alone or with non-relatives). In 2007, 38.9 million of 116.8 million households, or 33.3%, were nonfamily households. (See Table 1.5.) These nonfamily households earned a median income of $30,176, compared to the $62,359 median income of family households.

The increase in the number of households headed by females and the increased labor force participation of women have also contributed to growing income inequality in the United States. In 2007, 14.4 million of 77.9 million family households, or 18.5%, were headed by women, and 21 million of 38.9 million nonfamily households, or 54%, were headed by women. (See Table 1.5.) Female-headed households typically earn significantly less than other types of households. In female-headed family households in 2007, females earned only 67% of what male-headed family households earned ($33,370 and $49,839, respectively) and female nonfamily householders earned only 66.1% of male nonfamily householders ($24,294 and $36,767, respectively).

(See Table 1.5.) On average, female full-time workers earned 77.5% of what male full-time workers earned in 2007. (See Table 1.6.)

In *The Changing Shape of the Nation's Income Distribution* (June 2000, http://www.census.gov/prod/2000pubs/

TABLE 1.6

Median earnings in the past 12 months of workers by sex and women's earnings as a percentage of men's earnings, by selected characteristics, 2007

[In 2007 inflation-adjusted dollars]

Selected characteristic	Median earnings (dollars)		Women's earnings as a percentage of men's earnings
	Men	Women	
	Estimate	Estimate	Estimate
Race and Hispanic origin			
Full-time, year-round workers 16 years and older with earnings	44,255	34,278	77.5
White alone	47,113	35,542	75.4
White alone, not Hispanic	50,139	36,398	72.6
Black alone	35,652	31,035	87.1
American Indian and Alaska Native alone	34,833	28,837	82.8
Asian alone	51,174	40,664	79.5
Native Hawaiian and other Pacific Islander alone	36,624	29,835	81.5
Some other race alone	28,462	24,801	87.1
Two or more races	40,353	32,976	81.7
Hispanic (any race)	29,239	25,454	87.1
Educational attainment			
Population 25 years and older with earnings	40,481	27,276	67.4
Less than high school graduate	22,602	14,202	62.8
High school graduate (includes equivalency)	32,435	21,219	65.4
Some college or associate's degree	41,035	27,046	65.9
Bachelor's degree	57,397	38,628	67.3
Graduate or professional degree	77,219	50,937	66.0
Industry			
Full-time, year-round civilian workers 16 years and older with earnings	44,627	34,393	77.1
Agriculture, forestry, fishing, and hunting	27,854	23,621	84.8
Mining	55,533	47,146	84.9
Construction	38,823	36,593	94.3
Manufacturing	45,954	32,535	70.8
Wholesale trade	45,767	36,187	79.1
Retail trade	35,721	25,959	72.7
Transportation and warehousing	46,052	37,145	80.7
Utilities	60,617	45,539	75.1
Information	58,964	43,614	74.0
Finance and insurance	71,422	39,390	55.2
Real estate and rental and leasing	43,314	36,959	85.3
Professional, scientific, and technical services	75,320	47,292	62.8
Management of companies and enterprises	76,630	47,715	62.3
Administrative and support and waste management services	31,706	28,973	91.4
Educational services	47,308	40,100	84.8
Health care and social assistance	50,258	33,477	66.6
Arts, entertainment, and recreation	35,953	30,293	84.3
Accommodation and food services	25,611	20,708	80.9
Other services (except public administration)	35,504	26,166	73.7
Public administration	54,545	41,936	76.9
Class of worker*			
Full-time, year-round civilian workers 16 years and older with earnings	44,627	34,393	77.1
Employee of private company workers	42,215	32,035	75.9
Self-employed in own incorporated business workers	61,549	41,395	67.3
Private not-for-profit wage and salary workers	46,420	37,918	81.7
Local government workers	47,915	39,729	82.9
State government workers	48,778	38,584	79.1
Federal government workers	57,377	50,329	87.7
Self-employed in own unincorporated business workers	38,564	25,003	64.8

*Data from unpaid family workers are excluded from this table.

SOURCE: Alemayehu Bishaw and Jessica Semega, "Table 7. Median Earnings in the Past 12 Months of Workers by Sex and Women's Earnings As a Percentage of Men's Earnings by Selected Characteristics for the United States: 2007," in *Income, Earnings, and Poverty Data From the 2007 American Community Survey*, U.S. Census Bureau, August 2008, http://www.census.gov/prod/2008pubs/acs-09.pdf (accessed December 13, 2008)

p60-204.pdf), Arthur F. Jones Jr. and Daniel H. Weinberg of the Census Bureau note that other factors contribute to the growing income gap, including the decline in the influence of unions and the changing occupational structure, in general, from better-paying manufacturing positions to lower-paying service jobs. Robert J. Gordon and Ian Dew-Becker of the National Bureau of Economic Research argue in "Controversies about the Rise of American Inequality: A Survey" (May 2008, http://papers.nber.org/papers/w13982) that the declining real value of the minimum wage has contributed to income inequality, particularly for female workers, who are more likely than males to work for minimum wages; among men, the decline of unions has contributed to growing income inequality. They also highlight the increasing disparity in incomes in the wealthiest 10% of the population. In addition, DeNavas-Walt, Proctor, and Hill Lee indicate that the proportion of low-wage workers who receive employer-based health insurance and pension benefits dropped significantly between 1987 and 2007.

HOMELESSNESS

Homelessness is a complex social problem. According to the National Coalition for the Homeless, in the fact sheet "How Many People Experience Homelessness?" (June 2008, http://www.nationalhomeless.org/publications/facts/How_Many.pdf), approximately 3.5 million people, 1.4 million of them children, lack a place to sleep at some time during the year. Social researchers (educators, sociologists, economists, and political scientists), who have studied homelessness for decades, have determined that homelessness is caused by a combination of poverty, misfortune, illness, and behavior.

What Does It Mean to Be Homeless?

During a period of growing concern about homelessness in the mid-1980s, the first major piece of federal legislation aimed specifically at helping the homeless was adopted: the Stewart B. McKinney Homeless Assistance Act of 1987 (also known as the McKinney-Vento Homeless Assistance Act). Part of the act officially defined a homeless person as:

1. An individual who lacks a fixed, regular, and adequate nighttime residence; and

2. An individual who has a primary nighttime residence that is:

A. A supervised publicly or privately operated shelter designed to provide temporary living accommodations (including welfare hotels, congregate shelters, and transitional housing for the mentally ill);

B. An institution that provides a temporary residence for individuals intended to be institutionalized; or

C. A public or private place not designed for, or ordinarily used as, a regular sleeping accommodation for human beings.

The government's definition of a homeless person focuses on whether a person is housed. Broader definitions of homelessness take into account whether a person has a home. For example, Martha Burt et al. report in *Helping America's Homeless: Emergency Shelter or Affordable Housing?* (2001) that as late as 1980 the Census Bureau identified people who lived alone and did not have a "usual home elsewhere"—in other words, a larger family—as homeless. In this sense the term *home* describes living within a family, rather than having a roof over one's head.

Burt et al. also state that homeless people themselves, when interviewed in the 1980s and 1990s, drew a distinction between having a house and having a home. Even when homeless people had spent significant periods of time in a traditional shelter, such as an apartment or rented room, if they felt those houses were transitional or insecure, they identified themselves as having been homeless while living there. According to Burt et al., these answers "reflect how long they have been without significant attachments to people."

Burt et al. and other homeless advocates disagree with the narrow government definition of a homeless person, which focuses on a person's sleeping arrangements. They assert that the definition should be broadened to include groups of people who, while they may have somewhere to live, do not really have a home in the conventional sense. Considerable debate has resulted over expanding the classification to include people in situations such as the following:

- People engaging in prostitution who spend each night in a different hotel room, paid for by clients
- Children in foster or relative care
- People living in stable but inadequate housing (e.g., having no plumbing or heating)
- People doubled up in conventional dwellings for the short term
- People in hotels paid for by vouchers to the needy
- Elderly people living with family members because they cannot afford to live elsewhere

Official definitions are important because total counts of the homeless influence levels of funding authorized by Congress for homeless programs. With the availability of federal funds since the passage of the McKinney-Vento Homeless Assistance Act, institutional constituencies have formed that advocate for additional funding, an effort in which more expansive definitions are helpful.

Causes of Homelessness

In 2008 the U.S. Conference of Mayors, a nonpartisan organization of cities with populations higher than 30,000, surveyed the mayors of major cities on the extent and causes of urban homelessness. Three-quarters (72%) of the mayors cited lack of affordable housing as a major cause of family homelessness, whereas 52% said poverty and 44% said unemployment were major causes of family homelessness. (See Figure 1.3.) Over two-thirds (68%) of mayors surveyed cited substance abuse as a major cause of homelessness among single adults and unaccompanied youth; 60% cited lack of affordable housing and 48% cited mental illness as major causes of homelessness among these individuals. (See Figure 1.4.) Mayors also cited low-paying jobs, domestic violence, and family disputes as major causes of homelessness among families and single adults and unaccompanied youth.

As evident in the findings of the Conference of Mayors survey, homelessness is a complex social problem arising from three fundamental and interacting causes: lack of means, medical conditions, and behavioral problems.

COUNTING THE HOMELESS
Methodology

An accurate count of the U.S. homeless population has proved to be challenging for statisticians. The most formidable obstacle is the nature of homelessness itself. Typically, researchers contact people in their homes using in-person or telephone surveys to obtain information regarding income, education levels, household size, ethnicity, and other demographic data. Because homeless people cannot be counted at

FIGURE 1.3

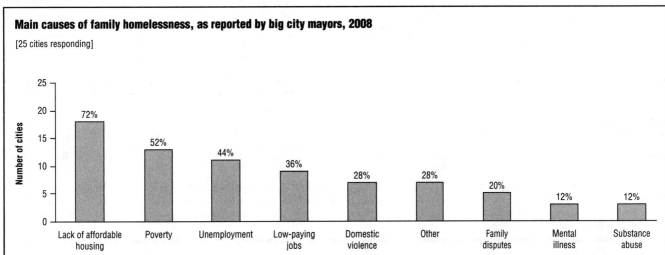

Main causes of family homelessness, as reported by big city mayors, 2008

[25 cities responding]

SOURCE: "Exhibit 2.6. Causes of Family Homelessness," in *Hunger and Homelessness Survey: A Status Report on Hunger and Homelessness in America's Cities, A 25-City Survey*, U.S. Conference of Mayors, December 2008, http://www.usmayors.org/pressreleases/documents/hungerhomelessnessreport_121208.pdf (accessed January 4, 2009)

FIGURE 1.4

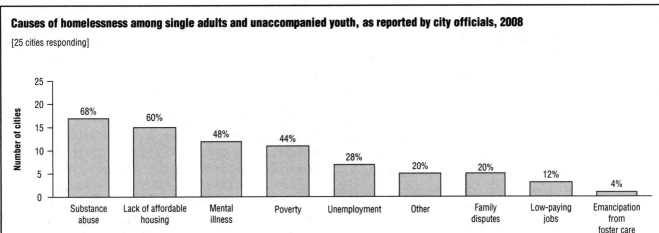

Causes of homelessness among single adults and unaccompanied youth, as reported by city officials, 2008

[25 cities responding]

SOURCE: "Exhibit 2.7. Causes of Homelessness among Single Adults and Unaccompanied Youth," in *Hunger and Homelessness Survey: A Status Report on Hunger and Homelessness in America's Cities, A 25-City Survey*, U.S. Conference of Mayors, December 2008, http://www.usmayors.org/pressreleases/documents/hungerhomelessnessreport_121208.pdf (accessed January 4, 2009)

TABLE 1.7

Common methods for collecting planning information

Method	Usual places to find people for study	Usual period of data collection and of estimate	Probable complexity of data collected
Full counts and other non-probability methods			
Analysis of agency records	Specific agency	Varies; usually not done to develop a population estimate	Whatever the agency routinely records in its case documents
Simple count, involving significant amounts of data by observation or from minimal agency records	Shelters, streets	1 night; point-in-time estimate	Enumeration+very simple population characteristics (gender, adult/child,race)
Simple count with brief interview	Shelters, meal programs, streets	1 night; point-in-time estimate	Enumeration+basic information as reported by respondent
Screener, counts and brief interviews for anyone screened in, plus unduplication using unique identifiers	Service agencies of all types	Several weeks or months; point-in-time and period prevalence estimate	Enumeration+basic information as reported by respondent
Complete enumeration through multiple agency search and referral followed by extensive interview (also unduplication)	Service agencies and key informants	Several weeks or months; point-in-time and period prevalence estimate	Usually extensive
Probability-based methods			
Block probability with substantial interview	Streets	Several weeks or months; point-in-time estimate	Usually extensive
Other probability approaches	Abandoned buildings, conventional housing in poor neighborhoods	Several days or weeks; point-in-time estimate	Enumeration+basic information as reported by respondent
Service-based random sampling	Usually homeless assistance programs	Several weeks, months, or years; point-in-time estimate	Usually extensive
Shelter and other service tracking systems that allow unduplication across all services in a jurisdiction over time	Service agencies	On going; point-in-time or period prevalence for periods of any length	Whatever the system collects, but usually simple data for administrative purposes
Other interesting methods			
Surveys of the housed population	At home	Multi-year; produces period prevalence for periods asked about	Basic information as reported by respondent
Longitudinal studies	Shelters, soup kitchens, streets	Multi-year; does not produce a population estimate	Extensive information, collected from the same person at several points in time

SOURCE: Martha R. Burt, "Table 3. Common Methods for Collecting Planning Information," in "Demographics and Geography: Estimating Needs," in *Practical Lessons: The 1998 Symposium on Homelessness Research*, edited by Linda B. Fosburg and Deborah L. Dennis, U.S. Department of Housing and Urban Development and the U.S. Department of Health and Human Services, August 1999, http://aspe.os.dhhs.gov/progsys/homeless/symposium/1-demograp .htm (accessed December 15, 2008)

home, researchers have been forced to develop new methods for collecting data on these transient groups. (See Table 1.7.)

Counting each and every person without a home would be the most accurate way to establish the number of homeless people. However, such a count is almost impossible. In *Homeless Count Methodologies: An Annotated Bibliography* (February 1999), Anita Drever discusses other methods. One way to estimate the number of homeless people is to search records at homeless service provider locations. Alternatively, a sampling of those records combined with projections, called probability-based methods, can be used to count the number of homeless. Another way to count the homeless is to count the number of homeless at one particular time in one particular place. This snapshot method estimates the number of homeless at any one time. Longitudinal studies are a way to estimate the proportion of people in a population who may become homeless at some point in their life. These studies follow individuals over a period of time to determine if they become homeless.

As Table 1.7 reveals, methods vary in scope and design. Different designs will produce different results even if the

intention is the same—namely to accurately enumerate the homeless population. For example, Table 1.8 shows the results of surveys conducted by the Association of Gospel Rescue Missions (AGRM) in 2007 and 2008 of people who use their services. The data presented are based on the snapshot method—counts of a population at a point in time. The AGRM counted all people receiving homeless services during one specific night in each year at its rescue missions around the country. The 2008 results were based on data received from 137 rescue missions, approximately half the number of missions operated by the AGRM in North America.

By contrast, Martha Burt et al. conducted a study in 1996 that sampled 76 geographical areas selected by the Urban Institute as being representative of all service providers in the United States and published their findings in *Homelessness: Programs and the People They Serve—Findings of the National Survey of Homeless Assistance Providers and Clients* (December 1999, http://www.huduser.org/publications/ homeless/homeless_tech.html). The researchers then compared their results by demographic characteristics to the total population as enumerated by the U.S. census. The male-to-female ratios in the AGRM study are quite different from

TABLE 1.8

Demographic overview of the homeless population, 2007 and 2008

	2008	2007
Gender		
Male	74%	76%
Female	26%	24%
Age groups*		
Under 18	12%	12%
18–25	9%	9%
26–35	18%	17%
36–45	26%	26%
46–65	31%	31%
65+	4%	5%
Race/ethnic groups*		
Caucasian	46%	47%
African-American	35%	36%
Hispanic	11%	10%
Asian	2%	1%
Native American	5%	6%
Women/children/families*		
Couples	15%	16%
Women with children	66%	55%
Men with children	5%	5%
Intact families	14%	24%
Other information		
Veterans—male	18%	21%
Veterans—female	3%	3%
Served in Korea	4%	5%
Served in Vietnam	33%	42%
Served in Persian Gulf	15%	14%
Homeless less than one year	60%	61%
Never before homeless	33%	35%
Homeless once previously	24%	25%
Homeless twice previously	18%	18%
Homeless 3+ times previously	25%	22%
More than 6-month resident	73%	72%
Victim of physical violence in last 12 months	18%	20%
Lost government benefits in last 12 months	15%	18%
Prefer spiritual emphasis in services	76%	80%
Comes to the mission daily for assistance	77%	76%
In long-term rehab—male	31%	35%
In long-term rehab—female	28%	35%

*Figures may not add up to 100% because of rounding

SOURCE: "Snapshot Survey of the Homeless Statistical Comparison," in *Women with Children Hit Hardest by Slow Economy*, Association of Gospel Rescue Missions, November 2008, http://www.agrm.org/pdf/snapshot_national_2008.pdf (accessed December 15, 2008)

Burt et al.'s study, with the AGRM finding that males made up approximately three-quarters (74% in 2008) of the homeless population (see Table 1.8), whereas Burt et al.'s study showed that males were just over two-thirds (68% in 1996) of the homeless population. Both studies show that males outnumbered females among the homeless, but the proportions are different.

Counting the Homeless for the U.S. Census

The official U.S. census, which takes place at 10-year intervals, is intended to count everyone in the United States. The results of the census are critical in determining how much federal money goes into different programs and to various regions of the country. Representation of the population in Congress is also based on the census. Because the Census Bureau counts people in their homes, counting the homeless presents special challenges.

In "The 1990 Census Shelter and Street Night Enumeration" (March 1992, http://www.amstat.org/sections/srms/proceedings/papers/1992_029.pdf), Diane F. Barrett, Irwin Anolik, and Florence H. Abramson of the Census Bureau indicate that census officials, on what was known as Shelter and Street Night (S-Night), counted homeless people found in shelters, emergency shelters, shelters for abused women, shelters for runaway and neglected youth, low-cost motels, Young Men's Christian Associations and Young Women's Christian Associations, and subsidized units at motels. Additionally, they counted people found in the early morning hours sleeping in abandoned buildings, bus and train stations, all-night restaurants, parks, and vacant lots. The results of this count were released the following year in the Census Bureau publication "Count of Persons in Selected Locations Where Homeless Persons Are Found." Homeless advocates criticized the methods and results as inadequate and charged that they provided a low estimate of homeless people in the United States. According to Annetta C. Smith and Denise I. Smith of the Census Bureau, in *Emergency and Transitional Shelter Population: 2000* (October 2001, http://www.census.gov/prod/2001pubs/censr01-2.pdf), the Census Bureau responded by emphasizing that S-Night "should not be used as a count of people experiencing homelessness." S-Night results were not a reflection of the prevalence of homelessness over a given year, but a count of homeless people identified during a single night, a snapshot, like the census itself.

The National Law Center on Homelessness and Poverty alleged that the methodology of the S-Night count was unconstitutional. In 1992 the law center, the Conference of Mayors, the cities of Baltimore, Maryland, and San Francisco, California, 15 local homeless organizations, and seven homeless people (the plaintiffs) filed suit in the federal district court in Washington, D.C. They charged the Census Bureau with excluding segments of the homeless population in the 1990 population count by not counting those in hidden areas and by not allocating adequate funds for S-Night.

In its suit, the law center cited an internal Census Bureau memorandum that stated, in part, "We know we will miss people by counting the 'open' rather than 'concealed' (two studies showed that about two-thirds of the street population sleep concealed)." Studies funded by the Census Bureau indicated that up to 70% of the homeless street population in Los Angeles, California, were missed, as were 32% in New Orleans, Louisiana, 47% in New York City, New York, and 69% in Phoenix, Arizona. Advocates were greatly concerned that this underrepresentation would negatively affect the funding of homeless initiatives.

In 1994 the district court dismissed the case, ruling that the plaintiffs' case was without merit. The court ruled that failure to count all the homeless was not a failure to perform a constitutional duty, because the Constitution does not give individuals a right to be counted or a right to a perfectly accurate census. The court stated that the "methods used by the Bureau on S-Night were reasonably designed to count as nearly as practicable all those people residing in the United States and, therefore, easily pass constitutional muster." In *National Law Center on Homelessness and Poverty v. Michael Kantor* (No. 94-5312 [1996]), the U.S. Court of Appeals upheld the district court's finding.

For the 2000 census, the Census Bureau undertook a special operation, called Service-Based Enumeration (SBE). From March 27 to March 29, 2000, census workers focused solely on counting the homeless population at the locations where they were the most likely to be found. On specific nights, counts of those staying in emergency and transitional shelters, of homeless people taking advantage of soup kitchens, and of those staying in outdoor locations were done.

The SBE methods were considered an improvement over the methods used in the 1990 census. Homeless citizens and advocates alike expected to see an increase in the number of homeless people reported by the Census Bureau in the 2000 census as compared to the count reported for the 1990 census. Expectations that the higher population counts would translate into higher funding levels for services to the homeless were also raised.

In 2001 the Census Bureau reported that it would not be releasing a specific homeless count because of the liability issues raised after the 1990 census. The Census Bureau stated that it would have only one category showing the number of people tabulated at "emergency and transitional shelters." The people who were counted at domestic violence shelters, family crisis centers, soup kitchens, mobile food vans, and targeted nonsheltered outdoor locations (i.e. street people, car dwellers, etc.) during the March 2000 SBE night were to be included in the category of "other non-institutional group quarters population." This category was overly inclusive; it included, for instance, students living in college dormitories. The homeless portion of the category could not be extracted.

As a result of this Census Bureau decision, Smith and Smith reported on people sleeping in shelters rather than on all homeless people. Census Bureau officials said the homeless people they did find during the exhaustive, three-day SBE count were included in total population figures for states, counties, and municipalities. Researchers voiced concern that the numbers teased from these data sets would be flawed.

People involved in the receipt or delivery of services to the homeless were worried that their programs would suffer from the lack of SBE night information. A detailed homeless count was thought to be essential for city officials and advocacy groups to plan budgets for shelters and other homeless outreach programs. To complicate matters, homeless program funding for most cities was already strained.

Only Estimates Are Available

The actual number of homeless people is unknown. Most organizations consider the Urban Institute study *America's Homeless II: Populations and Services* (February 1, 2000, http://www.urban.org/Presentations/AmericasHomelessII/toc.htm) to be the most authoritative estimate. This study estimates that 3.5 million people were homeless at some point during 1996.

After the 2000 census, Congress directed the U.S. Department of Housing and Urban Development (HUD) to conduct periodic surveys of representative communities to get a better idea of the extent of the problem nationally. In 2008 the department published *Second Annual Homeless Assessment Report to Congress* (March 2008, http://www.hudhre.info/documents/2ndHomelessAssessmentReport.pdf). This survey found that on a single night in January 2006, 427,971 homeless people were in shelters and another 331,130 were unsheltered. (See Table 1.9.) These numbers were much higher than the numbers released by the Census Bureau after the 2000 count. HUD reported that 155,623 people, or 21 percent of the total

TABLE 1.9

Total number of homeless persons on a single January night in 2005 and 2006

	January 2006		January 2005*		Change	
	#	%	#	%	#	%
Sheltered	427,971	56.4%	418,165	54.8%	9,806	2.3%
Unsheltered	331,130	44.6%	344,845	45.2%	−3,715	−3.9%
Total	**759,101**	**100%**	**763,010**	**100%**	**−3,909**	**−0.5%**

Note: These counts include homeless persons in CoCs located throughout the 50 states as well as U.S. Territories and the Commonwealth of Puerto Rico.
*The first Annual Homeless Assessment Report (February 2007) reported 754,147 homeless persons in total. This estimate excluded 8,863 homeless persons (or 2,799 sheltered and 6,064 unsheltered homeless persons) in the U.S. Territories and the Commonwealth of Puerto Rico.

SOURCE: "Exhibit 2–1. Total Number of Homeless Persons on a Single January Night in 2005 and 2006," in *The Second Annual Homeless Assessment Report to Congress*, U.S. Department of Housing and Urban Development, Office of Community Planning and Development, March 2008, http://www.hudhre.info/documents/2ndHomelessAssessmentReport.pdf (accessed December 18, 2008)

homeless population, were chronically homeless (homeless for a year or more) in 2006.

PUBLIC INTEREST IN HOMELESSNESS

Interest in and attitudes toward homelessness in the United States have changed over time. The mid- to late 1980s was a period of relatively high concern about homelessness. In 1986 the American public demonstrated concern over the plight of the homeless by initiating the Hands across America fund-raising effort. Some 6 million people locked hands across 4,152 miles (6,682 km) to form a human chain across the country, bringing an outpouring of national attention and concern to the issue. That same year the comedians Robin Williams (1952–), Whoopi Goldberg (1955–), and Billy Crystal (1947–) hosted the HBO comedy special *Comic Relief* to help raise money for the homeless. The show was a success and became an annual event. Magazines, art shows, books, and songs turned the nation's attention toward homelessness. Well-funded research studies came out by the dozens. The country was awash in statistical information regarding the homeless. All these activities pointed to the widely held belief that people became homeless because of circumstances outside their control.

By 2009, however, national concern about homelessness had faded. One could only see *Comic Relief* in reruns. The annual fund-raiser ran out of steam in 1996 except for a revival show two years later. After that, there was no resurgence of public interest in the homeless problem, even though the problem remained, and the Conference of Mayors reported in 2008 that the demand for services continued to increase.

In "The Real Face of Homelessness" (*Time*, January 20, 2003), Joel Stein explores a change in the national mood about homelessness. This change in national mood corresponded with efforts to criminalize homelessness. For example, a campaign was launched in Philadelphia, Pennsylvania, to discourage giving money to panhandlers. In Orlando, Florida, people could be jailed for sleeping on the sidewalk. In San Francisco, Proposition N ("Care Not Cash") reduced county housing support payments from $395 to $59 a month. In Dallas, Texas, the homeless complained that they were issued vagrancy tickets.

However, as a result of the economic recession and the housing crisis that began in 2008, localities across the country began to report a huge surge in homelessness, even among populations previously considered middle class. Public concern about homelessness may be on the increase as the housing crisis intensifies. Wendy Koch reports in "Homelessness up as Families on the Edge Lose Hold" (*USA Today*, April 6, 2009) that around the country homelessness is up sharply and the demand for homeless services such as shelter requests is up dramatically. She quotes Nancy Radner, the head of the Chicago Alliance to End Homelessness,

who said, "We're getting requests from people earning more than $30,000 a year, even $65,000. That's unprecedented."

Treating the Homeless as Criminals

Government attempts to criminalize homelessness continue. Betsy Streisand reports in "Homeless Sprawl" (*U.S. News & World Report*, December 10, 2006) that Los Angeles, the homeless capital of the nation, attempted to enforce a law that would prohibit people from sleeping on the streets and sidewalks. The city was stopped when the American Civil Liberties Union sued. The U.S. Ninth Circuit Court of Appeals ruled that in a city without enough shelter beds, the law amounted to cruel and unusual punishment. In "OK, Sister, Drop That Sandwich!: Cities Fight Panhandling by Outlawing Food Giveaways in Parks" (*Newsweek*, November 6, 2006), Matthew Philips explains that in Orlando, Florida, city lawmakers have passed ordinances making it illegal to feed large groups of people in public parks—making not only homelessness but also helping the homeless illegal. According to Forrest Norman, in "Proposed Ordinance Targeting Shantytown Pulled" (*Daily Business Review*, January 9, 2007), an ordinance in Miami, Florida, that would make it illegal for homeless people to sleep on vacant city-owned lots missed emergency passage in December 2006 by only one vote and was pulled from the agenda in January because city commissioners "needed more time to consider the ordinance" due to community support of the targeted shantytown. In "Lacey to Revisit Homeless Ordinance" (*The Olympian*, January 20, 2009), Christian Hill indicates that in 2009 the city council of Olympia, Washington, debated an ordinance that would require churches to house homeless people indoors, rather than in tents. Hill notes in "Lawmaker Pens Homeless Bill" (*The Olympian*, February 5, 2009) that in response, the state representative Brendan Williams (1968–) introduced legislation in the Washington House of Representatives that would limit localities' ability to impose regulations on churches who shelter homeless people.

Addressing Homelessness Is a Low Priority

When asked, Americans in the twenty-first century state they continue to be troubled by the existence of homelessness. According to "Americans Say Homelessness in U.S. Is a Serious Problem" (February 26, 2005, http://www.ipsos-na.com/news/pressrelease.cfm?id=2580), a survey of adults by the Associated Press/Ipsos-Public Affairs, nine out of 10 adults considered homelessness a serious problem. However, only half (56%) of adults surveyed believed chronic homelessness is caused by external circumstances, and more than a third (38%) believed homeless people are responsible for their homelessness. In *Economic Anxiety Surges in Past Year* (March 28, 2008, http://www.gallup.com/poll/105802/Economic-Anxiety-Surges-Past-Year.aspx), Lydia Saad of the Gallup Organization indicates that in January 2008, 38% of Americans said they worried about hunger and homelessness a great deal and 35% said they worried about it a fair amount. Only 26% said they were worried only a little or not at all. Dennis Jacobe of the Gallup Organization explains in *Americans on Housing Aid: Unfair but Necessary* (February 25, 2009, http://www.gallup.com/poll/116101/Americans-Housing-Aid-Unfair-Necessary.aspx) that in 2009, 51% of Americans believed that providing government assistance to homeowners who could not pay their mortgage was unfair, but 59% believed such aid was necessary nonetheless. When the question was phrased another way and Americans were asked about "giving aid to homeowners who are in danger of losing their homes to foreclosure," and thus potentially facing homelessness, nearly two-thirds (64%) of Americans said they were in favor of the plan.

Research studies, once so plentiful, were outdated by 2009, but some well-funded research centers and organizations continued to study the homeless population. Their studies are used throughout this book.

HOMELESS SERVICES

A substantial number of organizations provide services to homeless people across the country. Faith-based organizations have been providing assistance to the needy throughout history, including programs for the homeless. Many secular nonprofits (organizations with no religious affiliation) also provide such assistance. Since 1987, with the passage of the McKinney-Vento Homeless Assistance Act, federal funding targeted to help homeless people has been available. According to HUD, in "Homelessness Prevention Fund (Formula)" (March 30, 2009, http://www.hud.gov/recovery/homeless-prevention.cfm), the American Recovery and Reinvestment Act of 2009 created a Homelessness Prevention Fund of $1.5 billion that provides assistance to families who are facing or experiencing homelessness. The funds can be used for short- or medium-term rental assistance and housing relocation and stabilization services. In the press release "President's 2010 Budget Proposal Boosts Affordable Housing and Homelessness Assistance" (February 26, 2009, http://www.endhome

lessness.org/content/article/detail/2182), the National Alliance to End Homelessness notes that President Barack Obama's (1961–) proposed 2010 budget would increase HUD funding by 20%, including $1 billion for the National Housing Trust Fund to rehabilitate affordable housing projects and substantial increases for other homeless programs.

In *Second Annual Homeless Assessment Report to Congress*, HUD states that it counted the number of beds for homeless people available in emergency and transitional assistance programs in 2006. There were 206,877 year-round beds available in emergency shelters—95,301 available for families and 111,576 for individuals. (See Table 1.10.) An additional 21,769 beds were available during certain months of the year (winter months in the North and summer months in the South), and 55,047 overflow beds (beds made available during unanticipated emergencies) and voucher beds (beds provided in a motel or hotel) were available as well. In that same year, there were 103,743 family beds available in transitional housing and 95,966 individual beds in transitional housing. HUD notes that Permanent Supportive Housing contributed another 196,626 beds—87,275 for members of families and 109,351 for individuals. In 2006, 56.4% of all homeless people surveyed were sheltered and 43.6% were not sheltered. (See Table 1.11.)

HUD compares the demographics of the sheltered homeless population to the poor population of the United States in general. It finds that while males make up 39.6% of the poor population in 2006, they make up 68.3% of the sheltered homeless population. (See Table 1.12.) Even though male and female children were equally likely to be poor in 2006, 53% of sheltered homeless children were male, compared to 47% who were female. Non-Hispanic whites accounted for 45.4% of the entire population, but only 33.7% of the homeless population. African-Americans were overrepresented among the homeless population; 23.2% of the poor population was African-American, whereas 43.7% of the sheltered homeless population was African-American. In addition, veterans and disabled adults were disproportionately homeless.

TABLE 1.10

Number of emergency and transitional beds in homeless assistance system nationwide, 2006

	Year-round units/beds				Other beds	
	Family units	Family beds	Individual beds	Total year-round beds	Seasonal beds	Overflow/voucher
Emergency shelters						
Current inventory	28,745	95,301	111,576	206,877	21,769	55,047
Transitional housing						
Current inventory	32,802	103,743	95,966	199,709	—	—
Total						
Total inventory	61,547	199,044	207,542	406,586	21,769	55,047

SOURCE: "Exhibit 4-2. Number of Emergency and Transitional Beds in Homeless Assistance System Nationwide," in *The Second Annual Homeless Assessment Report to Congress*, U.S. Department of Housing and Urban Development, Office of Community Planning and Development, March 2008, http://www.hudhre.info/documents/2ndHomelessAssessmentReport.pdf (accessed December 18, 2008)

TABLE 1.11

Homeless individuals and persons in families on a single January night, 2005 and 2006

	January 2006			January 2005		
	Number	% of sheltered or unsheltered homeless persons	% of all homeless persons (n=759,101)	Number	%of sheltered or unsheltered homeless persons	% of all homeless person (n=763,010)
Sheltered homeless persons						
Individuals and persons in households without children	224,293	52.4%	29.6%	216,448	51.8%	28.4%
Persons in households with children*	203,678	47.6%	26.8%	201,717	48.2%	26.4%
Total	**427,971**	**100%**	**56.4%**	**418,165**	**100%**	**54.8%**
Unsheltered homeless persons						
Individuals and persons in households without children	228,287	68.9%	30.1%	227,579	66.0%	29.8%
Persons in households with children	102,843	31.1%	13.5%	117,266	34.0%	15.4%
Total	**331,130**	**100%**	**43.6%**	**344,845**	**100%**	**45.2%**

*This category includes unaccompanied adults and youth as well as multiple adult households without children.
n = Sample size.

SOURCE: "Exhibit 2–3. Homeless Individuals and Persons in Families on a Single January Night," in *The Second Annual Homeless Assessment Report to Congress*, U.S. Department of Housing and Urban Development, Office of Community Planning and Development, March 2008, http://www.hudhre.info/documents/2ndHomelessAssessmentReport.pdf (accessed December 18, 2008)

Special Populations

Many homeless assistance programs are open to anyone who wants to use them, but other programs are designed to serve only specific groups of people. The population served may be defined in several different ways: for example, men by themselves, women by themselves, households with children, youth by themselves, battered women, or veterans. In 2006 only 26.4% of beds in assistance programs accepted mixed household types, 38.1% were for households and individuals without children, 33.3% were for households with children, and 1.9% were for unaccompanied youth.

(See Table 1.13.) After meeting the basic needs of food, shelter, and health care, some homeless programs provided for other special needs. When an emergency shelter had a specific focus, it was most likely to offer shelter to victims of domestic violence (15.6% of beds in emergency shelters and 8.8% of beds in transitional housing). Other special populations served included veterans and people with the human immunodeficiency syndrome/acquired immunodeficiency syndrome (HIV/AIDS). Most beds (83.4%) in emergency shelters or transitional housing were for the general population.

TABLE 1.12

Demographic characteristics of sheltered homeless persons compared to the U.S. and poverty populations, January 1 to June 30, 2006

Characteristic	% of all sheltered homeless pop.	% U.S. poverty pop.	% of U.S. pop.
Gender of adults[a]			
Female	31.7%	60.4%	51.7%
Male	68.3%	39.6%	48.3%
Gender of children[a]			
Female	47.0%	49.4%	48.8%
Male	53.0%	50.5%	51.2%
Ethnicity[b]			
Non-Hispanic/non-Latino	75.3%	75.5%	85.5%
Hispanic/Latino	24.7%	24.5%	14.5%
Race			
White, Non-Hispanic/non-Latino	33.7%	45.4%	66.8%
White, Hispanic/Latino[c]	12.8%	13.1%	7.9%
Black or African-American	43.7%	23.2%	12.1%
Asian	.6%	3.8%	4.3%
American Indian or Alaska Native	2.3%	1.5%	0.8%
Native Hawaiian or other Pacific Islander	.4%	0.2%	0.1%
Some other race (alone)	0.0%	10.3%	6.0%
Multiple races	6.6%	2.5%	1.9%
Age[a]			
Under 1	2.1%	2.4%	1.4%
1 to 5	7.6%	10.7%	7.0%
6 to 12	6.8%	12.9%	9.7%
13 to 17	3.4%	8.9%	7.3%
18 to 30	20.5%	23.7%	17.2%
31 to 50	41.2%	22.4%	29.6%
51 to 61	12.9%	8.2%	13.2%
62 and older	3.0%	10.8%	14.7%
Unknown	2.7%	—	—
Persons by household size[d]			
1 person	73.0%	35.3%	45.4%
2 people	6.3%	5.2%	2.4%
3 people	9.3%	13.5%	12.3%
4 people	5.7%	17.2%	19.1%
5 or more people	5.7%	28.6%	20.8%
Veteran (adults)[e]	14.3%	5.5%	11.2%
Disabled (adults)[e]	38.4%	29.6%	16.8%

[a] Age is calculated based on a person's first time in shelter during the covered time period. A child is defined as a person age 17 or under, and an adult is defined as a person age 18 or older.
[b] A substantial number of records were missing ethnicity information (25.0 percent).
[c] It is not possible to identify other race-Hispanic/Latino categories (e.g., Black, Hispanic/Latino) because the aggregate race data provided by communities are not broken out by these categories. Non-white Hispanic/Latinos are included within the other race categories.
[d] If a person is part of more than one household over the study period, the household size reflects the size of the first household in which the person presented during the covered time period. If household size changed during the program episode (i.e., a household member left the program early or joined later), household size for each person reflects household size on the day that person entered the program.
[e] Veteran status and whether a person had a disabling condition are recorded only for adults in HMIS. The percentage calculations shown indicate the percent of homeless adults with this characteristic. A substantial number of records were missing information on disability status (42.8 percent) and veteran status (20.1 percent). The percentage calculations include only persons whose disability and veteran status was recorded.

SOURCE: "Exhibit 3–4. Demographic Characteristics of Sheltered Homeless Persons in January 1 to June 30, 2006 Period Compared to the U.S. and Poverty Populations," in *The Second Annual Homeless Assessment Report to Congress*, U.S. Department of Housing and Urban Development, Office of Community Planning and Development, March 2008, http://www.hudhre.info/documents/2ndHomelessAssessmentReport.pdf (accessed December 18, 2008)

TABLE 1.13

Year-round beds in emergency shelters and transitional housing by household and subpopulation type, 2006

	Emergency shelters		Transitional housing		Total	
	Number	Percent	Number	Percent	Number	Percent
Household type						
Persons in households without children	76,405	36.9%	78,593	39.4%	154,998	38.1%
Persons in households with children	60,905	29.4%	74,408	37.3%	135,313	33.3%
Unaccompanied youth	4,463	2.2%	3,351	1.7%	7,814	1.9%
Mixed household types	64,577	31.2%	42,738	21.4%	107,315	26.4%
Total*	**206,877**	**100.0%**	**199,709**	**100.0%**	**406,586**	**100.0%**
Homeless subpopulation						
Domestic violence victims only	32,196	15.6%	17,585	8.8%	49,781	12.2%
Veterans only	1,795	0.9%	9,912	5.0%	11,707	2.9%
Persons with HIV/AIDS only	2,277	1.1%	3,695	1.9%	5,972	1.5%
General population	170,609	82.5%	168,517	84.4%	339,126	83.4%
Total	**206,877**	**100.0%**	**199,709**	**100.0%**	**406,586**	**100.0%**

*There were 523 emergency shelter programs and 573 transitional housing programs with missing household type information.

SOURCE: "Exhibit 4–4. Year-Round Beds by Household and Subpopulation Type," in *The Second Annual Homeless Assessment Report to Congress*, U.S. Department of Housing and Urban Development, Office of Community Planning and Development, March 2008, http://www.hudhre.info/documents/ 2ndHome lessAssessmentReport.pdf (accessed December 18, 2008)

CHAPTER 2
WHO ARE THE POOR?

CHARACTERISTICS OF THE POOR

Carmen DeNavas-Walt, Bernadette D. Proctor, and Jessica C. Smith of the U.S. Census Bureau state in *Income, Poverty, and Health Insurance Coverage in the United States: 2007* (August 2008, http://www.census.gov/prod/2008pubs/p60-235.pdf) that in 2007, 12.5% of the total population had income-to-poverty ratios under 1.00; in other words, 37.3 million people in the United States were poor. Another 4.5% had income-to-poverty ratios between 1.00 and 1.25, meaning that 17% of the U.S. population was poor or near-poor. Children under 18 years of age and young adults 18 to 24 years old were the most likely to be poor (18% and 17.3%, respectively) or near-poor (23.8% and 22.2%, respectively). Young children suffer disproportionately from poverty and deprivation. In 2007 one out of five (20.8%) children under the age of six were poor, and more than one out of four (27.1%) children under the age of six were poor or near-poor. Almost one out of 10 (9.6%) children this age were desperately poor, living in families with income-to-poverty ratios of under 0.50.

Race and Ethnicity

Historically, poverty rates have been consistently lower for whites than for minorities in the United States. According to DeNavas-Walt, Proctor, and Smith, in 1959, 18.1% (28.5 million) of all whites lived below the poverty level, whereas 55.1% (9.9 million) of African-Americans did. By 1970 the rate of poverty of white Americans had declined to 9.9%, where it remained for about the next 10 years. The poverty rate for African-Americans was still almost triple that of whites in 1970, at 33.5%. By 2000, a year in which the U.S. economy was strong, only 9.5% of whites (21.6 million) lived in poverty, whereas 22.5% (8 million) of all African-Americans did.

In 2007 African-Americans and Hispanics continued to be disproportionately affected by poverty. In that year, 8.2% of non-Hispanic whites were poor, compared to 24.5% of

African-Americans and 21.5% of Hispanics. (See Table 2.1.) Even more African-American and Hispanic children suffered from poverty. In 2006 one-third (33%) of African-Americans under the age of 18 and 37% of Hispanics under the age of 18 were poor, compared to only 10% of non-Hispanic white children in the same age group. (See Table 2.2.) Only 4% of non-Hispanic white children were desperately poor, compared to 16% of African-American children and 10% of Hispanic children.

DeNavas-Walt, Proctor, and Smith indicate that the overall Asian and Pacific Islander poverty rate in 2007 was 10.2% (or 1.3 million people). The rate was substantially lower than it was in 1987, the first year that the Census Bureau kept statistics on Asians and Pacific Islanders, when 16.1% lived below the poverty level.

Median (the middle value—half are higher and half are lower) household income reflects the disparity in poverty levels between different groups. In 2007 Asian-Americans and non-Hispanic whites had the highest median incomes, at $66,935 and $55,096, respectively. (See Table 2.3.) African-Americans ($34,001), Native Americans ($35,343), and Hispanics ($40,766) had the lowest median household incomes.

Age

CHILD POVERTY. DeNavas-Walt, Proctor, and Smith note that young adults and children under 18 years of age were the most likely to be poor in 2007. The child poverty rate, at 18%, was significantly higher than the poverty rate for adults under the age of 65 (10.9%) in 2007. Very young children were at the greatest risk of being poor. According to Sylvia A. Allegretto, in "Child Poverty: U.S. Leads Industrialized Nations with Appallingly High Rates" (*People's Weekly World Newspaper*, July 27, 2006), the United States has the highest rate of child poverty among the eight richest nations in the world—and its public assistance policies do little to reduce child poverty.

TABLE 2.1

People and families in poverty, by selected characteristics, 2006 and 2007

[Numbers in thousands]

Characteristic	2006			2007			Change in poverty (2007 less 2006)[a]	
		Below poverty			Below poverty			
	Total	Number	Percentage	Total	Number	Percentage	Number	Percentage
People								
Total	296,450	36,460	12.3	298,699	37,276	12.5	816	0.2
Family status								
In families	245,199	25,915	10.6	245,443	26,509	10.8	594	0.2
Householder	78,454	7,668	9.8	77,908	7,623	9.8	−45	—
Related children under 18	72,609	12,299	16.9	72,792	12,802	17.6	504	0.6
Related children under 6	24,204	4,830	20.0	24,543	5,101	20.8	271	0.8
In unrelated subfamilies	1,367	567	41.5	1,516	577	38.1	9	−3.4
Reference person	567	229	40.4	609	222	36.5	−7	−3.9
Children under 18	719	323	44.9	819	332	40.5	9	−4.4
Unrelated individuals	49,884	9,977	20.0	51,740	10,189	19.7	212	−0.3
Male	24,674	4,388	17.8	25,447	4,348	17.1	−40	−0.7
Female	25,210	5,589	22.2	26,293	5,841	22.2	252	—
Race[b] and Hispanic origin								
White	237,619	24,416	10.3	239,133	25,120	10.5	704	0.2
White, not Hispanic	196,049	16,013	8.2	196,583	16,032	8.2	19	—
Black	37,306	9,048	24.3	37,665	9,237	24.5	189	0.3
Asian	13,177	1,353	10.3	13,257	1,349	10.2	−4	−0.1
Hispanic (any race)	44,784	9,243	20.6	45,933	9,890	21.5	647	0.9
Age								
Under 18 years	73,727	12,827	17.4	73,996	13,324	18.0	497	0.6
18 to 64 years	186,688	20,239	10.8	187,913	20,396	10.9	157	—
65 years and older	36,035	3,394	9.4	36,790	3,556	9.7	162	0.2
Nativity								
Native born	259,199	30,790	11.9	261,456	31,126	11.9	336	—
Foreign born	37,251	5,670	15.2	37,243	6,150	16.5	480	1.3
Naturalized citizen	14,534	1,345	9.3	15,050	1,426	9.5	81	0.2
Not a citizen	22,716	4,324	19.0	22,193	4,724	21.3	400	2.2
Region								
Northeast	54,072	6,222	11.5	53,952	6,166	11.4	−56	−0.1
Midwest	65,411	7,324	11.2	65,403	7,237	11.1	−87	−0.1
South	107,902	14,882	13.8	109,545	15,501	14.2	619	0.4
West	69,065	8,032	11.6	69,799	8,372	12.0	340	0.4
Metropolitan status								
Inside metropolitan statistical areas.	249,092	29,283	11.8	251,023	29,921	11.9	638	0.2
Inside principal cities	95,138	15,336	16.1	96,731	15,983	16.5	646	0.4
Outside principal cities	153,954	13,947	9.1	154,292	13,938	9.0	−8	—
Outside metropolitan statistical areas[c]	47,357	7,177	15.2	47,676	7,355	15.4	178	0.3
Work experience								
Total, 16 years and older	231,800	24,896	10.7	233,885	25,297	10.8	401	0.1
All workers	157,352	9,181	5.8	158,468	9,089	5.7	−92	−0.1
Worked full-time, year-round	107,734	2,906	2.7	108,617	2,768	2.5	−138	−0.1
Not full-time, year-round	49,618	6,275	12.6	49,851	6,320	12.7	45	—
Did not work at least one week	74,448	15,715	21.1	75,417	16,208	21.5	493	0.4

In 2007 children living with a female householder were particularly likely to live in poverty. Over four out of 10 (42%) of these children lived in poverty, compared to only 8% of children living with married parents. (See Table 2.2.) Younger children living with single mothers were even more likely to be poor. Over half (52.7%) of children aged five and under in female-householder parents were poor, compared to 37.4% of children aged six to 17. Half (50%) of African-American children and 47% of Hispanic children living in female-householder families were poor, compared to 33% of non-Hispanic white children living in female-householder families.

Not only are children overrepresented among the poor but also they arguably suffer more from the deprivations of poverty than do adults. Childhood poverty is a matter of great concern because strong evidence suggests that food insecurity and lack of good medical care caused by poverty can limit a child's physical and cognitive development. In addition, poverty is the largest predictor of child abuse and neglect. In fact, the Children's Defense Fund argues in *America's Cradle to the Prison Pipeline, Summary Report* (November 2007, http://www.childrensdefense.org/child-research-data-publi cations/data/cradle-prison-pipeline-summary-report.pdf) that poverty is the driving force behind what it calls the

TABLE 2.1

[Numbers in thousands]

| Characteristic | 2006 | | | 2007 | | | Change in poverty | |
| | Total | Below poverty | | Total | Below poverty | | (2007 less 2006)[a] | |
		Number	Percentage		Number	Percentage	Number	Percentage
Families								
Total	78,454	7,668	9.8	77,908	7,623	9.8	−45	—
Type of family								
Married-couple	58,964	2,910	4.9	58,395	2,849	4.9	−61	−0.1
Female householder, no husband present	14,424	4,087	28.3	14,411	4,078	28.3	−9	—
Male householder, no wife present	5,067	671	13.2	5,103	696	13.6	25	0.4

—Represents or rounds to zero.

[a]Details may not sum to totals because of rounding.

[b]Federal surveys now give respondents the option of reporting more than one race. Therefore, two basic ways of defining a race group are possible. A group such as Asian may be defined as those who reported Asian and no other race (the race-alone or single-race concept) or as those who reported Asian regardless of whether they also reported another race (the race-alone-or-in-combination concept). This table shows data using the first approach (race alone). The use of the single-race population does not imply that it is the preferred method of presenting or analyzing data. The Census Bureau uses a variety of approaches. About 2.6 percent of people reported more than one race in Census 2000. Data for American Indians and Alaska Natives, Native Hawaiians and other Pacific Islanders, and those reporting two or more races are not shown separately.

[c]The "outside metropolitan statistical areas" category includes both micropolitan statistical areas and territory outside of metropolitan and m icropolitan statistical areas.

SOURCE: Carmen DeNavas-Walt, Bernadette D. Proctor, and Jessica C. Smith, "Table 3. People and Families in Poverty by Selected Characteristics: 2006 and 2007," in *Income, Poverty, and Health Insurance Coverage in the United States: 2007*, Current Population Reports, U.S. Census Bureau, August 2008, http://www.census.gov/prod/2008pubs/p60-235.pdf (accessed December 15, 2008)

"Cradle to Prison Pipeline," a life cycle in which "so many poor and minority youths are and will remain trapped in a trajectory that leads to marginalized lives, imprisonment and premature death." In addition, the National Center for Children in Poverty states in "Children's Mental Health: Facts for Policymakers" (November 2006, http://www.nccp.org/publications/pdf/text_687.pdf) that children in poverty are more likely to suffer from mental health problems than are other children.

POVERTY AMONG THE ELDERLY. In contrast with children, senior citizens are underrepresented among the poor. Nearly one out of 10 (9.7%) adults aged 65 and older were poor, up slightly from 9.4% the year before. (See Table 2.1.) From 1959 to 2007 the number of people 65 years and older living in poverty dropped significantly, from about 35% to 9.7%. (See Figure 1.2 in Chapter 1.) Most observers credit Social Security for the sharp decline in poverty among the elderly. In contrast to children, senior citizens are now underrepresented among the poor.

Urban Areas

People living in inner cities are the most likely to suffer from poverty. In 2007, 16.5% of people living in inner cities lived below the poverty line. (See Table 2.1.) Only 9% of people who lived in suburban areas—inside metropolitan statistical areas but outside principle cities—lived below the poverty line. In rural areas the poverty rate was also high—15.4%.

Family Status

In 2007 people living in families (10.8%) were much less likely than people living in unrelated subfamilies (38.1%) or in households with unrelated individuals (19.7%) to suffer from poverty. (See Table 2.1.) However, there was a major variation in the poverty rate between different family structures. Whereas one out of every 10 (10.8%) families in the United States was living in poverty in 2007, families headed by married couples had the lowest poverty rate (4.9%). More than a quarter (28.3%) of all families with a female householder (no husband present) were living in poverty. Male households were also more likely than married-couple families to be in poverty (13.6%), but they were much less likely than female householders to have incomes below the poverty line. Single parents were much more likely to have household incomes below the poverty line if they did not work full time. (See Figure 2.1.)

SINGLE-PARENT FAMILIES. An increasing number of children are being raised by one parent, usually the mother. The proportion of single-parent families steadily increased between 1970 and the early 1990s, whereas the proportion of married-couple families continued to decline. Since then, the structure of U.S. households and families has remained relatively stable. According to the Census Bureau, in "Families by Presence of Own Children under 18: 1950 to Present" (February 25, 2009, http://www.census.gov/population/www/socdemo/hh-fam.html), in 1970 single-parent families with children under the age of 18 made up 6.4% of the total number of families, whereas married-couple families accounted for 49.6%. By 1990 the number of single-parent families had increased to 11.7%, and married-couple families had decreased to 37.1%. In 2008 single-parent families had risen slightly to 13.5%, whereas married-couple families had dropped to 32.3%. Table 2.4 shows that in 2007 there were almost three times as many single female-headed families (14.4 million) as there were single male-headed families (5.1 million).

TABLE 2.2

Percentage of all children and related children living below selected poverty levels by selected characteristics, 1980–2006

Characteristic	1980	1981	1982	1983	1984	1985	1986	1987	1988	1989	1990	1991	1992	1993	1994	1995	1996	1997	1998	1999	2000	2001	2002	2003	2004	2005	2006
Below 100% poverty																											
All children[b]	18.0	20.0	22.0	22.0	22.0	21.0	21.0	20.0	20.0	20.0	21.0	22.0	22.0	23.0	22.0	21.0	21.0	20.0	19.0	17.0	16.0	16.0	17.0	18.0	18.0	18.0	17.0
Gender																											
Male	—	—	—	—	—	—	—	20.0	20.0	20.0	21.0	21.0	22.0	23.0	21.0	20.0	20.0	20.0	18.0	17.0	16.0	16.0	17.0	18.0	18.0	17.0	17.0
Female	—	—	—	—	—	—	—	20.0	19.0	20.0	21.0	22.0	23.0	23.0	22.0	21.0	21.0	20.0	19.0	17.0	16.0	16.0	17.0	18.0	18.0	18.0	18.0
Age																											
Ages 0–5	—	—	—	—	—	—	—	23.0	22.0	23.0	24.0	25.0	26.0	26.0	25.0	24.0	23.0	22.0	21.0	19.0	18.0	18.0	19.0	20.0	20.0	20.0	20.0
Ages 6–17	—	—	—	—	—	—	—	19.0	18.0	18.0	19.0	20.0	20.0	21.0	20.0	19.0	19.0	19.0	18.0	16.0	15.0	15.0	16.0	16.0	17.0	16.0	16.0
Race and Hispanic origin[c]																											
White, non-Hispanic	12.0	13.0	14.0	15.0	14.0	13.0	13.0	12.0	11.0	12.0	12.0	13.0	13.0	14.0	13.0	11.0	11.0	11.0	11.0	9.0	9.0	10.0	—	—	—	—	—
White-alone, non-Hispanic	—	—	—	—	—	—	—	—	—	—	—	—	—	—	—	—	—	—	—	—	—	—	9.4	9.8	10.5	10.0	10.0
Black	42.0	45.0	48.0	47.0	47.0	44.0	43.0	45.0	44.0	44.0	45.0	46.0	47.0	46.0	44.0	42.0	40.0	37.0	37.0	33.0	31.0	30.0	—	—	—	—	—
Black-alone	—	—	—	—	—	—	—	—	—	—	—	—	—	—	—	—	—	—	—	—	—	—	32.0	34.0	34.0	35.0	33.0
Hispanic[d]	33.0	36.0	40.0	38.0	39.0	40.0	38.0	40.0	38.0	36.0	38.0	40.0	40.0	41.0	42.0	40.0	40.0	37.0	34.0	30.0	28.0	28.0	29.0	30.0	29.0	28.0	27.0
Region																											
Northeast	—	—	—	—	—	—	—	17.0	16.0	16.0	18.0	20.0	20.0	21.0	20.0	19.0	19.0	20.0	19.0	16.0	15.0	15.0	15.0	15.0	16.0	16.0	16.0
Midwest	—	—	—	—	—	—	—	19.0	16.0	19.0	19.0	20.0	20.0	20.0	19.0	17.0	16.0	15.0	15.0	17.0	13.0	13.0	13.0	15.0	17.0	16.0	16.0
South	—	—	—	—	—	—	—	24.0	24.0	23.0	24.0	24.0	26.0	25.0	24.0	24.0	23.0	22.0	20.0	19.0	18.0	19.0	19.0	20.0	20.0	20.0	19.0
West	—	—	—	—	—	—	—	19.0	20.0	20.0	20.0	22.0	22.0	23.0	23.0	22.0	23.0	22.0	21.0	18.0	17.0	16.0	17.0	18.0	18.0	18.0	17.0
Related children[a]																											
Children in all families, total	18.0	20.0	21.0	22.0	21.0	20.0	20.0	20.0	19.0	19.0	20.0	21.0	22.0	22.0	21.0	20.0	20.0	19.0	18.0	17.0	16.0	16.0	16.0	17.0	17.0	17.0	17.0
Related children ages 0–5	20.0	22.0	23.0	25.0	23.0	23.0	22.0	22.0	22.0	22.0	23.0	24.0	26.0	26.0	25.0	24.0	23.0	22.0	21.0	18.0	18.0	18.0	19.0	20.0	20.0	20.0	20.0
Related children ages 6–17	17.0	18.0	20.0	20.0	20.0	19.0	19.0	18.0	17.0	17.0	18.0	20.0	19.0	20.0	20.0	18.0	18.0	18.0	17.0	16.0	15.0	15.0	15.0	16.0	16.0	16.0	15.0
White, non-Hispanic	11.0	12.0	14.0	14.0	13.0	12.0	12.0	11.0	11.0	11.0	12.0	12.0	12.0	13.0	12.0	11.0	10.0	11.0	10.0	9.0	9.0	9.0	—	—	—	—	—
White-alone, non-Hispanic	—	—	—	—	—	—	—	—	—	—	—	—	—	—	—	—	—	—	—	—	—	—	9.0	9.0	10.0	10.0	10.0
Black	42.0	45.0	47.0	46.0	46.0	43.0	43.0	44.0	43.0	43.0	44.0	46.0	46.0	46.0	43.0	42.0	40.0	37.0	36.0	33.0	31.0	30.0	—	—	—	—	—
Black-alone	—	—	—	—	—	—	—	—	—	—	—	—	—	—	—	—	—	—	—	—	—	—	32.0	34.0	33.0	34.0	33.0
Hispanic[d]	33.0	35.0	39.0	38.0	39.0	40.0	37.0	39.0	37.0	36.0	38.0	40.0	39.0	40.0	41.0	39.0	40.0	36.0	34.0	30.0	28.0	27.0	28.0	30.0	29.0	28.0	27.0
Children in married-couple families, total	—	—	—	—	—	—	—	10.0	10.0	10.0	10.0	11.0	11.0	12.0	11.0	10.0	10.0	10.0	9.0	9.0	8.0	8.0	9.0	9.0	9.0	9.0	8.0
Related children ages 0–5	—	—	—	—	—	—	—	12.0	11.0	12.0	12.0	12.0	13.0	13.0	12.0	11.0	12.0	11.0	10.0	9.0	9.0	9.0	10.0	10.0	10.0	10.0	9.0
Related children ages 6–17	—	—	—	—	—	—	—	10.0	9.0	9.0	10.0	10.0	10.0	11.0	10.0	9.0	9.0	9.0	9.0	8.0	8.0	7.0	8.0	8.0	8.0	8.0	8.0
White, non-Hispanic	—	—	—	—	—	—	—	7.0	6.0	7.0	7.0	7.0	7.0	8.0	7.0	6.0	5.0	5.0	5.0	5.0	5.0	5.0	—	—	—	—	—
White-alone, non-Hispanic	—	—	—	—	—	—	—	—	—	—	—	—	—	—	—	—	—	—	—	—	—	—	5.0	5.0	5.0	5.0	4.0
Black	—	—	—	—	—	—	—	18.0	17.0	18.0	18.0	15.0	18.0	18.0	15.0	13.0	14.0	13.0	12.0	11.0	9.0	10.0	—	—	—	—	—
Black-alone	—	—	—	—	—	—	—	—	—	—	—	—	—	—	—	—	—	—	—	—	—	—	12.0	11.0	13.0	13.0	12.0
Hispanic[d]	—	—	—	—	—	—	—	27.0	25.0	25.0	27.0	29.0	29.0	30.0	30.0	28.0	29.0	26.0	23.0	22.0	21.0	20.0	21.0	21.0	21.0	20.0	19.0
Children in female-householder families, no husband present, total	51.0	52.0	56.0	55.0	54.0	54.0	54.0	54.0	53.0	51.0	53.0	56.0	55.0	54.0	53.0	50.0	49.0	49.0	46.0	42.0	40.0	39.0	40.0	42.0	42.0	43.0	42.0
Related children ages 0–5	65.0	66.0	67.0	68.0	65.0	66.0	65.0	66.0	64.0	62.0	66.0	66.0	66.0	64.0	64.0	62.0	59.0	59.0	55.0	51.0	50.0	49.0	49.0	53.0	53.0	53.0	52.7
Related children ages 6–17	46.0	47.0	51.0	50.0	49.0	48.0	50.0	48.0	48.0	46.0	47.0	50.0	49.0	49.0	47.0	45.0	35.0	45.0	42.0	39.0	36.0	35.0	36.0	37.0	37.0	38.0	37.4
White, non-Hispanic	—	—	—	—	—	—	—	38.0	37.0	36.0	40.0	41.0	40.0	39.0	38.0	34.0	35.0	37.0	33.0	29.0	28.0	29.0	—	—	—	—	—
White-alone, non-Hispanic	—	—	—	—	—	—	—	—	—	—	—	—	—	—	—	—	—	—	—	—	—	—	29.0	31.0	32.0	33.0	33.0
Black	65.0	52.0	56.0	55.0	54.0	67.0	67.0	67.0	65.0	63.0	65.0	68.0	67.0	66.0	63.0	62.0	58.0	55.0	55.0	52.0	49.0	47.0	—	—	—	—	—
Black-alone	—	—	—	—	—	—	—	—	—	—	—	—	—	—	—	—	—	—	—	—	—	—	48.0	50.0	49.0	50.0	50.0
Hispanic[d]	65.0	52.0	56.0	54.0	54.0	72.0	67.0	70.0	70.0	64.0	68.0	69.0	66.0	66.0	68.0	66.0	67.0	63.0	60.0	52.0	50.0	49.0	48.0	51.0	52.0	50.0	47.0

TABLE 2.2

Percentage of all children and related children living below selected poverty levels by selected characteristics, 1980–2006 [CONTINUED]

Characteristic	1980	1981	1982	1983	1984	1985	1986	1987	1988	1989	1990	1991	1992	1993	1994	1995	1996	1997	1998	1999	2000	2001	2002	2003	2004	2005	2006
Below 50% poverty																											
All children[b]	—	—	—	—	—	—	—	9.0	9.0	8.0	9.0	10.0	10.0	10.0	10.0	9.0	9.0	9.0	8.0	7.0	7.0	7.0	7.0	8.0	8.0	8.0	8.0
Gender																											
Male	—	—	—	—	—	—	—	9.0	9.0	8.0	9.0	10.0	10.0	10.0	10.0	8.0	8.0	9.0	8.0	7.0	7.0	7.0	7.0	8.0	8.0	7.0	8.0
Female	—	—	—	—	—	—	—	9.0	9.0	9.0	9.0	10.0	11.0	10.0	10.0	9.0	10.0	9.0	8.0	7.0	6.0	7.0	7.0	8.0	8.0	8.0	8.0
Age																											
Ages 0–5	—	—	—	—	—	—	—	10.0	11.0	10.0	11.0	12.0	13.0	12.0	12.0	11.0	11.0	10.0	10.0	8.0	8.0	8.0	8.0	10.0	9.0	9.0	9.0
Ages 6–17	—	—	—	—	—	—	—	9.0	8.0	7.0	8.0	9.0	9.0	9.0	9.0	7.0	8.0	8.0	7.0	7.0	6.0	7.0	6.0	7.0	7.0	7.0	7.0
Race and Hispanic Origin[c]																											
White, non-Hispanic	—	—	—	—	—	—	—	5.0	5.0	4.0	5.0	5.0	6.0	6.0	5.0	4.0	5.0	5.0	4.0	4.0	4.0	4.0	—	—	—	—	—
White-alone, non-Hispanic	—	—	—	—	—	—	—	—	—	—	—	—	—	—	—	—	—	—	—	—	—	—	4.0	4.0	5.0	4.0	4.0
Black	—	—	—	—	—	—	—	23.0	25.0	23.0	23.0	26.0	27.0	26.0	24.0	21.0	21.0	20.0	18.0	15.0	15.0	16.0	—	—	—	—	—
Black-alone[d]	—	—	—	—	—	—	—	—	—	—	—	—	—	—	—	—	—	—	—	—	—	—	15.0	18.0	17.0	17.0	16.0
Hispanic[d]	—	—	—	—	—	—	—	15.0	16.0	13.0	14.0	15.0	16.0	15.0	17.0	16.0	15.0	16.0	14.0	11.0	10.0	11.0	11.0	11.0	10.0	12.0	10.0
Region																											
Northeast	—	—	—	—	—	—	—	7.0	7.0	6.0	8.0	9.0	9.0	10.0	9.0	9.0	10.0	10.0	8.0	6.0	6.0	7.0	6.0	7.0	8.0	8.0	6.0
Midwest	—	—	—	—	—	—	—	9.0	8.0	9.0	9.0	9.0	10.0	9.0	9.0	7.0	7.0	6.0	6.0	6.0	6.0	6.0	6.0	7.0	7.0	7.0	7.0
South	—	—	—	—	—	—	—	12.0	12.0	11.0	11.0	12.0	13.0	12.0	12.0	10.0	11.0	10.0	9.0	7.0	8.0	8.0	8.0	9.0	9.0	9.0	9.0
West	—	—	—	—	—	—	—	6.0	8.0	6.0	6.0	8.0	8.0	8.0	9.0	8.0	8.0	9.0	8.0	6.0	6.0	6.0	6.0	8.0	7.0	7.0	7.0
Related children[a]																											
Children in all families, total	7.0	7.0	9.0	9.0	9.0	8.0	8.0	9.0	9.0	8.0	8.0	9.0	10.0	10.0	9.0	8.0	8.0	8.0	8.0	6.0	6.0	7.0	7.0	7.0	7.0	7.0	7.0
Related children ages 0–5	—	—	—	—	—	—	—	10.0	10.0	10.0	10.0	11.0	12.0	12.0	12.0	10.0	11.0	10.0	9.0	8.0	8.0	8.0	8.0	10.0	9.0	9.0	9.0
Related children ages 6–17	—	—	—	—	—	—	—	8.0	8.0	7.0	7.0	8.0	9.0	8.0	8.0	7.0	7.0	8.0	7.0	6.0	6.0	6.0	6.0	6.0	6.0	6.0	6.0
White, non-Hispanic	—	—	—	—	—	—	—	5.0	4.0	4.0	4.0	5.0	5.0	5.0	4.0	3.0	4.0	4.0	4.0	3.0	3.0	3.0	—	—	—	—	—
White-alone, non-Hispanic	—	—	—	—	—	—	—	—	—	—	—	—	—	—	—	—	—	—	—	—	—	—	3.0	4.0	4.0	4.0	4.0
Black	17.0	21.0	23.0	23.0	23.0	22.0	23.0	23.0	24.0	22.0	22.0	25.0	27.0	26.0	23.0	20.0	20.0	20.0	17.0	15.0	15.0	16.0	—	—	—	—	—
Black-alone[d]	—	—	—	—	—	—	—	—	—	—	—	—	—	—	—	—	—	—	—	—	—	—	15.0	18.0	17.0	17.0	16.0
Hispanic[d]	17.0	21.0	23.0	23.0	23.0	22.0	23.0	16.0	16.0	13.0	14.0	14.0	15.0	14.0	17.0	16.0	14.0	16.0	13.0	11.0	9.0	10.0	11.0	11.0	10.0	12.0	10.0
Children in married-couple families, total	—	—	—	—	—	—	—	3.0	3.0	3.0	3.0	3.0	3.0	3.0	3.0	3.0	3.0	3.0	3.0	2.0	2.0	2.0	2.0	2.0	3.0	2.0	2.0
Related children ages 0–5	—	—	—	—	—	—	—	3.0	3.0	3.0	3.0	4.0	4.0	4.0	4.0	3.0	3.0	3.0	3.0	2.0	2.0	3.0	3.0	3.0	3.0	3.0	3.0
Related children ages 6–17	—	—	—	—	—	—	—	3.0	3.0	2.0	2.0	3.0	3.0	3.0	3.0	3.0	3.0	3.0	2.0	2.0	2.0	2.0	2.0	2.0	2.0	2.0	2.0
White, non-Hispanic	—	—	—	—	—	—	—	2.0	2.0	2.0	2.0	2.0	2.0	2.0	2.0	1.0	2.0	1.0	2.0	1.0	2.0	2.0	—	—	—	—	—
White-alone, non-Hispanic	—	—	—	—	—	—	—	—	—	—	—	—	—	—	—	—	—	—	—	—	—	—	2.0	1.0	2.0	1.0	1.0
Black	—	—	—	—	—	—	—	6.0	7.0	4.0	4.0	6.0	7.0	7.0	6.0	3.0	3.0	5.0	3.0	3.0	3.0	3.0	—	—	—	—	—
Black-alone[d]	—	—	—	—	—	—	—	—	—	—	—	—	—	—	—	—	—	—	—	—	—	—	3.0	4.0	4.0	5.0	3.0
Hispanic[d]	—	—	—	—	—	—	—	7.0	7.0	6.0	7.0	8.0	9.0	7.0	9.0	9.0	7.0	7.0	5.0	5.0	4.0	5.0	5.0	5.0	4.0	5.0	5.0
Children in female-householder families, no husband present, total	—	—	—	—	—	—	—	28.0	29.0	26.0	28.0	29.0	30.0	29.0	28.0	24.0	26.0	26.0	23.0	20.0	19.0	20.0	20.0	22.0	22.0	22.0	21.0
Related children ages 0–5	—	—	—	—	—	—	—	36.0	38.0	34.0	37.0	37.0	39.0	36.0	37.0	34.0	35.0	34.0	31.0	27.0	28.0	28.0	28.0	31.0	31.0	29.0	30.0
Related children ages 6–17	—	—	—	—	—	—	—	25.0	25.0	22.0	22.0	25.0	26.0	25.0	24.0	19.0	22.0	22.0	19.0	17.0	15.0	17.0	16.0	17.0	18.0	19.0	17.0
White, non-Hispanic	—	—	—	—	—	—	—	19.0	18.0	16.0	19.0	19.0	20.0	19.0	18.0	13.0	18.0	17.0	15.0	13.0	12.0	13.0	—	—	—	—	—
White-alone, non-Hispanic	—	—	—	—	—	—	—	—	—	—	—	—	—	—	—	—	—	—	—	—	—	—	12.0	15.0	15.0	15.0	16.0
Black	—	—	—	—	—	—	—	38.0	38.0	36.0	37.0	40.0	41.0	40.0	36.0	32.0	33.0	31.0	29.0	25.0	24.0	27.0	—	—	—	—	—
Black-alone[d]	—	—	—	—	—	—	—	—	—	—	—	—	—	—	—	—	—	—	—	—	—	—	25.0	27.0	27.0	26.0	26.0
Hispanic[d]	—	—	—	—	—	—	—	32.0	39.0	30.0	32.0	31.0	31.0	30.0	36.0	33.0	34.0	36.0	32.0	27.0	25.0	26.0	26.0	25.0	28.0	28.0	23.0

TABLE 2.2

Percentage of all children and related children living below selected poverty levels by selected characteristics, 1980–2006 [CONTINUED]

Characteristic	1980	1981	1982	1983	1984	1985	1986	1987	1988	1989	1990	1991	1992	1993	1994	1995	1996	1997	1998	1999	2000	2001	2002	2003	2004	2005	2006
Below 150% poverty																											
All children[b]	—	—	—	—	—	—	—	31.0	30.0	31.0	31.0	33.0	33.0	34.0	33.0	32.0	32.0	31.0	30.0	28.0	27.0	28.0	28.0	29.0	28.0	28.0	29.0
Gender																											
Male	—	—	—	—	—	—	—	31.0	30.0	31.0	31.0	32.0	33.0	34.0	33.0	32.0	31.0	30.0	29.0	28.0	27.0	27.0	28.0	29.0	28.0	28.0	28.0
Female	—	—	—	—	—	—	—	31.0	30.0	31.0	32.0	33.0	34.0	34.0	33.0	33.0	33.0	31.0	30.0	29.0	27.0	28.0	28.0	29.0	28.0	28.0	29.0
Age																											
Ages 0–5	—	—	—	—	—	—	—	33.0	34.0	34.0	35.0	36.0	38.0	38.0	37.0	36.0	35.0	34.0	32.0	31.0	29.0	30.0	31.0	32.0	32.0	32.0	32.0
Ages 6–17	—	—	—	—	—	—	—	29.0	28.0	28.0	30.0	31.0	31.0	32.0	31.0	31.0	30.0	29.0	28.0	28.0	25.0	26.0	27.0	27.0	27.0	27.0	27.0
Race and Hispanic origin[c]																											
White, non-Hispanic	—	—	—	—	—	—	—	21.0	20.0	20.0	21.0	22.0	22.0	22.0	22.0	20.0	20.0	20.0	18.0	18.0	16.0	17.0	—	—	—	—	—
White-alone, non-Hispanic	—	—	—	—	—	—	—	—	—	—	—	—	—	—	—	—	—	—	—	—	—	—	17.0	18.0	18.0	17.0	18.0
Black	—	—	—	—	—	—	—	58.0	57.0	58.0	58.0	60.0	60.0	61.0	58.0	57.0	56.0	52.0	52.0	48.0	46.0	46.0	—	—	—	—	—
Black-alone[d]	—	—	—	—	—	—	—	—	—	—	—	—	—	—	—	—	—	—	—	—	—	—	48.0	49.0	48.0	49.0	48.0
Hispanic[d]	—	—	—	—	—	—	—	56.0	54.0	55.0	56.0	59.0	58.0	60.0	59.0	59.0	58.0	56.0	53.0	50.0	47.0	47.0	47.0	48.0	47.0	46.0	46.0
Region																											
Northeast	—	—	—	—	—	—	—	25.0	25.0	25.0	27.0	28.0	29.0	29.0	29.0	29.0	29.0	28.0	28.0	26.0	23.0	25.0	25.0	25.0	23.0	25.0	25.0
Midwest	—	—	—	—	—	—	—	29.0	27.0	28.0	29.0	30.0	30.0	30.0	30.0	27.0	26.0	24.0	25.0	23.0	22.0	23.0	23.0	25.0	26.0	25.0	27.0
South	—	—	—	—	—	—	—	35.0	35.0	36.0	36.0	37.0	38.0	39.0	36.0	36.0	35.0	34.0	32.0	31.0	30.0	31.0	31.0	32.0	31.0	31.0	32.0
West	—	—	—	—	—	—	—	31.0	31.0	32.0	31.0	34.0	34.0	35.0	36.0	35.0	35.0	34.0	33.0	31.0	29.0	28.0	30.0	30.0	30.0	29.0	29.0
Related children[a]																											
Children in all families, total	29.0	32.0	34.0	34.0	32.0	32.0	30.0	30.0	30.0	30.0	31.0	32.0	33.0	33.0	32.0	32.0	31.0	30.0	29.0	28.0	26.0	27.0	27.0	28.0	28.0	28.0	28.0
Related children ages 0–5	—	—	—	—	—	—	—	33.0	34.0	34.0	34.0	36.0	37.0	38.0	37.0	35.0	35.0	33.0	32.0	30.0	29.0	30.0	31.0	31.0	31.0	31.0	32.0
Related children ages 6–17	—	—	—	—	—	—	—	29.0	28.0	28.0	29.0	30.0	30.0	31.0	30.0	30.0	29.0	28.0	27.0	27.0	25.0	25.0	26.0	27.0	26.0	26.0	26.0
White, non-Hispanic	—	—	—	—	—	—	—	20.0	20.0	20.0	21.0	21.0	21.0	22.0	21.0	19.0	19.0	19.0	18.0	17.0	16.0	17.0	—	—	—	—	—
White-alone, non-Hispanic	—	—	—	—	—	—	—	—	—	—	—	—	—	—	—	—	—	—	—	—	—	—	17.0	17.0	17.0	17.0	17.0
Black	57.0	62.0	63.0	62.0	61.0	59.0	57.0	57.0	56.0	57.0	57.0	60.0	60.0	61.0	58.0	56.0	56.0	51.0	52.0	48.0	45.0	46.0	—	—	—	—	—
Black-alone[d]	—	—	—	—	—	—	—	—	—	—	—	—	—	—	—	—	—	—	—	—	—	—	48.0	48.0	48.0	49.0	48.0
Hispanic[d]	—	—	—	—	—	—	—	56.0	54.0	54.0	55.0	58.0	58.0	60.0	58.0	59.0	57.0	56.0	52.0	49.0	47.0	46.0	47.0	48.0	47.0	46.0	46.0
Children in married-couple families, total	—	—	—	—	—	—	—	20.0	19.0	20.0	20.0	21.0	21.0	22.0	21.0	20.0	20.0	19.0	18.0	17.0	16.0	17.0	18.0	18.0	17.0	17.0	17.0
Related children ages 0–5	—	—	—	—	—	—	—	22.0	23.0	23.0	22.0	24.0	24.0	25.0	23.0	21.0	22.0	21.0	20.0	19.0	18.0	19.0	20.0	20.0	20.0	20.0	20.0
Related children ages 6–17	—	—	—	—	—	—	—	19.0	17.0	18.0	19.0	19.0	20.0	20.0	19.0	19.0	19.0	17.0	17.0	17.0	15.0	16.0	16.0	17.0	16.0	16.0	16.0
White, non-Hispanic	—	—	—	—	—	—	—	15.0	14.0	14.0	15.0	15.0	15.0	15.0	15.0	13.0	13.0	12.0	11.0	11.0	10.0	11.0	—	—	—	—	—
White-alone, non-Hispanic	—	—	—	—	—	—	—	—	—	—	—	—	—	—	—	—	—	—	—	—	—	—	11.0	11.0	10.0	10.0	10.0
Black	—	—	—	—	—	—	—	32.0	30.0	33.0	32.0	32.0	33.0	35.0	28.0	26.0	28.0	24.0	26.0	21.0	21.0	21.0	—	—	—	—	—
Black-alone[d]	—	—	—	—	—	—	—	—	—	—	—	—	—	—	—	—	—	—	—	—	—	—	25.0	22.0	23.0	23.0	23.0
Hispanic[d]	—	—	—	—	—	—	—	46.0	45.0	45.0	47.0	50.0	49.0	51.0	49.0	50.0	48.0	47.0	43.0	41.0	39.0	39.0	40.0	41.0	40.0	39.0	37.0
Children in female-householder families, no husband present, total	—	—	—	—	—	—	—	67.0	67.0	66.0	67.0	69.0	68.0	68.0	67.0	65.0	65.0	64.0	62.0	60.0	57.0	57.0	57.0	58.0	58.0	59.0	59.0
Related children ages 0–5	—	—	—	—	—	—	—	77.0	77.0	75.0	77.0	78.0	79.0	77.0	78.0	75.0	74.0	74.0	71.0	68.0	67.0	66.0	65.0	68.0	68.0	69.0	69.0
Related children ages 6–17	—	—	—	—	—	—	—	63.0	63.0	62.0	62.0	64.0	63.0	63.0	62.0	60.0	60.0	60.0	58.0	56.0	53.0	54.0	53.0	54.0	53.0	54.0	55.0
White, non-Hispanic	—	—	—	—	—	—	—	53.0	53.0	53.0	54.0	55.0	54.0	53.0	53.0	49.0	50.0	52.0	48.0	45.0	44.0	46.0	—	—	—	—	—
White-alone, non-Hispanic	—	—	—	—	—	—	—	—	—	—	—	—	—	—	—	—	—	—	—	—	—	—	45.0	46.0	46.0	47.0	48.0
Black	57.0	62.0	63.0	62.0	61.0	59.0	57.0	79.0	79.0	77.0	77.0	81.0	79.0	80.0	78.0	76.0	75.0	72.0	72.0	71.0	66.0	66.0	—	—	—	—	—
Black-alone[d]	—	—	—	—	—	—	—	—	—	—	—	—	—	—	—	—	—	—	—	—	—	—	65.0	67.0	66.0	67.0	68.0
Hispanic[d]	—	—	—	—	—	—	—	81.0	81.0	79.0	80.0	81.0	80.0	81.0	81.0	82.0	81.0	78.0	76.0	71.0	70.0	66.0	66.0	68.0	68.0	67.0	67.0

TABLE 2.2

TABLE 2.2

Percentage of all children and related children living below selected poverty levels by selected characteristics, 1980–2006 [CONTINUED]

Characteristic	1980	1981	1982	1983	1984	1985	1986	1987	1988	1989	1990	1991	1992	1993	1994	1995	1996	1997	1998	1999	2000	2001	2002	2003	2004	2005	2006
Below 200% poverty																											
All children[b]	—	—	—	—	—	—	—	41.0	41.0	41.0	42.0	44.0	44.0	45.0	44.0	43.0	43.0	41.0	40.0	39.0	38.0	38.0	38.0	39.0	39.0	39.0	39.0
Gender																											
Male	—	—	—	—	—	—	—	41.0	41.0	41.0	43.0	44.0	44.0	45.0	44.0	43.0	43.0	41.0	40.0	39.0	38.0	38.0	38.0	39.0	39.0	39.0	39.0
Female	—	—	—	—	—	—	—	41.0	41.0	42.0	42.0	44.0	45.0	45.0	44.0	44.0	44.0	42.0	41.0	38.0	38.0	38.0	38.0	40.0	40.0	39.0	39.0
Age																											
Ages 0–5	—	—	—	—	—	—	—	44.0	45.0	45.0	46.0	48.0	48.0	50.0	48.0	47.0	47.0	45.0	43.0	42.0	41.0	42.0	42.0	42.0	43.0	42.0	43.0
Ages 6–17	—	—	—	—	—	—	—	40.0	39.0	39.0	41.0	42.0	42.0	43.0	42.0	42.0	42.0	40.0	39.0	38.0	36.0	37.0	37.0	38.0	38.0	37.0	37.0
Race and Hispanic origin[c]																											
White, non-Hispanic	—	—	—	—	—	—	—	31.0	31.0	30.0	32.0	33.0	33.0	33.0	32.0	31.0	31.0	30.0	28.0	27.0	26.0	27.0	—	—	—	—	—
White-alone, non-Hispanic	—	—	—	—	—	—	—	—	—	—	—	—	—	—	—	—	—	—	—	—	—	—	26.0	26.0	27.0	26.0	26.0
Black	—	—	—	—	—	—	—	68.0	67.0	68.0	68.0	70.0	71.0	72.0	68.0	68.0	68.0	64.0	64.0	61.0	59.0	57.0	—	—	—	—	—
Black-alone[d]	—	—	—	—	—	—	—	—	—	—	—	—	—	—	—	—	—	—	—	—	—	—	60.0	61.0	61.0	61.0	60.0
Hispanic[d]	—	—	—	—	—	—	—	68.0	66.0	67.0	70.0	72.0	71.0	73.0	72.0	73.0	72.0	69.0	67.0	64.0	63.0	62.0	62.0	63.0	62.0	61.0	61.0
Region																											
Northeast	—	—	—	—	—	—	—	34.0	34.0	35.0	36.0	38.0	39.0	39.0	38.0	38.0	39.0	38.0	37.0	35.0	33.0	34.0	34.0	34.0	33.0	34.0	34.0
Midwest	—	—	—	—	—	—	—	39.0	38.0	38.0	40.0	41.0	42.0	41.0	41.0	37.0	37.0	36.0	34.0	33.0	31.0	33.0	33.0	34.0	36.0	35.0	36.0
South	—	—	—	—	—	—	—	46.0	46.0	47.0	48.0	49.0	49.0	50.0	48.0	48.0	48.0	46.0	43.0	42.0	42.0	42.0	42.0	44.0	43.0	43.0	42.0
West	—	—	—	—	—	—	—	42.0	43.0	42.0	43.0	45.0	45.0	46.0	47.0	46.0	47.0	44.0	44.0	42.0	41.0	40.0	40.0	41.0	42.0	41.0	40.0
Related children[a]																											
Children in all families, total	—	—	—	—	—	—	—	40.0	41.0	41.0	42.0	43.0	44.0	44.0	43.0	43.0	43.0	41.0	40.0	38.0	37.0	38.0	38.0	39.0	39.0	38.0	39.0
Related children ages 0–5	—	—	—	—	—	—	—	44.0	45.0	45.0	45.0	47.0	48.0	49.0	48.0	46.0	46.0	45.0	43.0	41.0	41.0	41.0	41.0	42.0	42.0	42.0	43.0
Related children ages 6–17	—	—	—	—	—	—	—	39.0	38.0	39.0	40.0	41.0	41.0	42.0	41.0	41.0	41.0	39.0	38.0	37.0	35.0	36.0	36.0	37.0	37.0	37.0	37.0
White, non-Hispanic	—	—	—	—	—	—	—	30.0	30.0	30.0	31.0	33.0	32.0	32.0	32.0	30.0	30.0	29.0	27.0	26.0	25.0	26.0	—	—	—	—	—
White-alone, non-Hispanic	—	—	—	—	—	—	—	—	—	—	—	—	—	—	—	—	—	—	—	—	—	—	25.0	26.0	26.0	25.0	26.0
Black	—	—	—	—	—	—	—	68.0	67.0	68.0	68.0	70.0	71.0	72.0	68.0	68.0	68.0	64.0	64.0	60.0	59.0	57.0	—	—	—	—	—
Black-alone[d]	—	—	—	—	—	—	—	—	—	—	—	—	—	—	—	—	—	—	—	—	—	—	59.0	61.0	60.0	61.0	60.0
Hispanic[d]	—	—	—	—	—	—	—	68.0	66.0	67.0	69.0	72.0	70.0	72.0	72.0	73.0	72.0	69.0	66.0	64.0	62.0	61.0	62.0	62.0	62.0	60.0	61.0
Children in married-couple families, total	—	—	—	—	—	—	—	30.0	30.0	30.0	31.0	33.0	32.0	33.0	32.0	31.0	31.0	29.0	28.0	27.0	26.0	27.0	27.0	27.0	27.0	27.0	27.0
Related children ages 0–5	—	—	—	—	—	—	—	34.0	35.0	34.0	34.0	36.0	35.0	36.0	35.0	33.0	34.0	33.0	31.0	29.0	29.0	30.0	30.0	30.0	31.0	30.0	30.0
Related children ages 6–17	—	—	—	—	—	—	—	29.0	28.0	28.0	30.0	31.0	31.0	31.0	30.0	30.0	30.0	27.0	27.0	26.0	25.0	25.0	25.0	26.0	26.0	25.0	25.0
White, non-Hispanic	—	—	—	—	—	—	—	24.0	25.0	24.0	25.0	26.0	25.0	25.0	25.0	23.0	23.0	21.0	20.0	18.0	19.0	19.0	—	—	—	—	—
White-alone, non-Hispanic	—	—	—	—	—	—	—	—	—	—	—	—	—	—	—	—	—	—	—	—	—	—	19.0	19.0	18.0	18.0	18.0
Black	—	—	—	—	—	—	—	46.0	44.0	46.0	45.0	46.0	47.0	50.0	42.0	39.0	43.0	38.0	39.0	35.0	36.0	33.0	—	—	—	—	—
Black-alone[d]	—	—	—	—	—	—	—	—	—	—	—	—	—	—	—	—	—	—	—	—	—	—	36.0	36.0	36.0	36.0	35.0
Hispanic[d]	—	—	—	—	—	—	—	60.0	58.0	60.0	62.0	65.0	64.0	65.0	64.0	66.0	65.0	63.0	59.0	58.0	55.0	54.0	56.0	56.0	56.0	54.0	53.0
Children in female-householder families, no husband present, total	—	—	—	—	—	—	—	77.0	76.0	77.0	77.0	78.0	79.0	78.0	78.0	76.0	76.0	75.0	73.0	72.0	69.0	70.0	69.0	70.0	71.0	71.0	72.0
Related children ages 0–5	—	—	—	—	—	—	—	85.0	85.0	84.0	85.0	86.0	87.0	86.0	87.0	84.0	84.0	83.0	80.0	80.0	78.0	79.0	76.0	78.0	79.0	80.0	80.0
Related children ages 6–17	—	—	—	—	—	—	—	73.0	73.0	73.0	73.0	74.0	74.0	74.0	73.0	72.0	73.0	72.0	70.0	68.0	66.0	66.0	66.0	67.0	67.0	67.0	68.0
White, non-Hispanic	—	—	—	—	—	—	—	65.0	65.0	66.0	67.0	66.0	67.0	66.0	66.0	61.0	64.0	64.0	61.0	59.0	56.0	59.0	—	—	—	—	—
White-alone, non-Hispanic	—	—	—	—	—	—	—	—	—	—	—	—	—	—	—	—	—	—	—	—	—	—	58.0	59.0	60.0	59.0	61.0
Black	—	—	—	—	—	—	—	86.0	86.0	85.0	86.0	88.0	88.0	88.0	85.0	87.0	85.0	83.0	82.0	82.0	79.0	77.0	—	—	—	—	—
Black-alone[d]	—	—	—	—	—	—	—	—	—	—	—	—	—	—	—	—	—	—	—	—	—	—	76.0	78.0	79.0	79.0	79.0
Hispanic[d]	—	—	—	—	—	—	—	89.0	87.0	87.0	89.0	87.0	88.0	89.0	90.0	88.0	89.0	86.0	84.0	82.0	82.0	80.0	79.0	80.0	80.0	80.0	80.0

TABLE 2.2

Percentage of all children and related children living below selected poverty levels by selected characteristics, 1980–2006 [CONTINUED]

— Not available.

[a]A related child is a person ages 0–17 who is related to the householder by birth, marriage, or adoption, but is not the householder or the householder's spouse.

[b]Includes children not related to the householder.

[c]For race and Hispanic-origin data in this table: From 1980 to 2002, following the 1977 OMB standards for collecting and presenting data on race, the Current Population Survey (CPS) asked respondents to choose one race from the following: White, Black, American Indian or Alaskan Native, or Asian or Pacific Islander. The Census Bureau also offered an "Other" category. Beginning in 2003, following the 1997 OMB standards for collecting and presenting data on race, the CPS asked respondents to choose one or more races from the following: White, Black, Asian, American Indian or Alaska Native, and Native Hawaiian or Other Pacific Islander. All race groups discussed in this table from 2002 onward refer to people who indicated only one racial identity within the racial categories presented. People who responded to the question on race by indicating only one race are referred to as the race-alone population. The use of the race-alone population in this table does not imply that it is the preferred method of presenting or analyzing data. Data from 2002 onward are not directly comparable with data from earlier years. Data on race and Hispanic origin are collected separately. Persons of Hispanic origin may be of any race.

[d]Persons of Hispanic origin may be of any race.

Note: The 2004 data have been revised to reflect a correction to the weights in the 2005 Annual Social and Economic Supplement. Data for 1999, 2000, and 2001 use Census 2000 population controls. Data for 2000 onward are from the expanded Current Population Survey sample. The poverty level is based on money income and does not include noncash benefits, such as food stamps. Poverty thresholds reflect family size and composition and are adjusted each year using the annual average Consumer Price Index level. The average poverty threshold for a family of four was $20,614 in 2006. The levels shown here are derived from the ratio of the family's income to the family's poverty threshold.

SOURCE: "Table ECON1.A. Child Poverty: Percentage of All Children and Related Children Ages 0–17 Living below Selected Poverty Levels by Selected Characteristics, 1980–2006," in *America's Children in Brief: Key National Indicators of Well-Being, 2008,* Federal Interagency Forum on Child and Family Statistics, 2008, http://www.childstats.gov/americaschildren/tables.asp (accessed December 23, 2008)

TABLE 2.3

Median household income in the past 12 months by race and Hispanic origin, 2007

[In 2007 inflation-adjusted dollars]

Race and Hispanic origin	Median household income (dollars) Estimate
All households	**50,740**
White alone	53,714
White alone, not Hispanic	55,096
Black alone	34,001
American Indian and Alaska Native alone	35,343
Asian alone	66,935
Native Hawaiian and other Pacific Islander alone	55,273
Some other race alone	40,755
Two or more races	44,626
Hispanic (any race)	40,766

Note: Data are limited to the household population and are subject to sampling variability.

SOURCE: Alemayehu Bishaw and Jessica Semega, "Table 1. Median Household Income in the Past 12 Months by Race and Hispanic Origin: 2007," in *Income, Earnings, and Poverty Data from the 2007 American Community Survey*, U.S. Census Bureau, August 2008, http://www.census.gov/prod/2008pubs/acs-09.pdf (accessed December 13, 2008)

One factor in the rise of single-parent families is the rise in the divorce rate. Jason Fields of the Census Bureau indicates in *America's Families and Living Arrangements: 2003* (November 2004, http://www.census.gov/prod/2004pubs/p20-553.pdf) that in 1970 only 3.5% of men and 5.7% of women were separated or divorced. By 2007, 8.9% of men and 11.5% of women were divorced and had not remarried. (See Table 2.5.) The percentage of divorced women is consistently higher than the percentage of divorced men because divorced men are more likely to remarry, whereas divorced women are more likely to raise the children. As Table 2.6 shows, six out of 10 (61.4%) custodial parents in 2005 were women.

Another reason for the rise in single-parent families is the rise in people who never marry yet still have children. In "Marital Status of the Population 15 Years Old and over, by Sex and Race: 1950 to Present" (February 25, 2009, http://www.census.gov/population/www/socdemo/hh-fam.html), the Census Bureau indicates that the percentage of males aged 15 and older who had never married rose from 28.1% in 1970

FIGURE 2.1

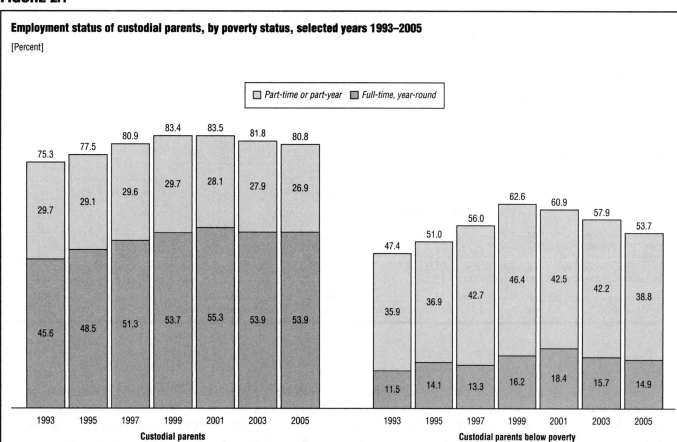

Employment status of custodial parents, by poverty status, selected years 1993–2005

[Percent]

SOURCE: Timothy S. Grall, "Figure 2. Employment Status of Custodial Parents by Poverty Status: 1993–2005," in *Custodial Mothers and Fathers and Their Child Support: 2005*, Current Population Reports, U.S. Census Bureau, August 2007, http://www.census.gov/prod/2007pubs/p60-234.pdf (accessed December 21, 2008)

TABLE 2.4

Households by type and selected characteristics, 2007

[Numbers in thousands]

		Family households				Nonfamily households		
	Total	Total	Married couple	Male householder	Female householder	Total	Male householder	Female householder
All households	116,011	78,425	58,945	5,063	14,416	37,587	17,338	20,249
Size of household								
One member	31,132	—	—	—	—	31,132	13,528	17,604
Two members	38,580	33,296	25,216	2,131	5,949	5,284	2,976	2,307
Three members	18,808	18,054	11,926	1,578	4,550	753	521	232
Four members	16,172	15,929	12,868	777	2,284	244	191	52
Five members	7,202	7,095	5,745	356	993	107	77	31
Six members	2,702	2,656	2,134	136	386	46	31	15
Seven or more members	1,415	1,394	1,056	84	254	21	14	7
Nunber of nonrelatives in household								
No nonrelatives	105,712	74,580	58,183	3,825	12,572	31,132	13,528	17,604
One nonrelative	8,648	3,364	622	1,018	1,724	5,284	2,976	2,307
Two nonrelatives	1,079	326	88	152	86	753	521	232
Three or more nonrelatives	573	155	52	69	35	418	313	105
Race of householder								
White alone	94,705	64,091	50,729	3,806	9,556	30,614	14,138	16,476
Black alone	14,354	9,272	4,358	864	4,050	5,081	2,249	2,832
Asian alone	4,454	3,346	2,754	223	369	1,109	540	569
All remaining single races and all race combinations	2,498	1,715	1,103	170	441	783	411	372
Hispanic origin of householder								
Hispanic[a]	12,973	10,152	6,762	945	2,445	2,821	1,590	1,231
White alone, Non-Hispanic	82,675	54,632	44,327	2,921	7,384	28,043	12,686	15,357
Other non-Hispanic	20,363	13,641	7,855	1,198	4,588	6,723	3,062	3,661
White alone or combination householder								
White alone or in combination with one or more other races	95,946	64,935	51,311	3,878	9,746	31,011	14,359	16,652
Other	20,065	13,490	7,634	1,185	4,670	6,576	2,979	3,597
Black alone or combination householder								
Black alone or in combination with one or more other races	14,709	9,502	4,489	882	4,132	5,207	2,312	2,894
Other	101,302	68,922	54,456	4,182	10,284	32,380	15,026	17,354
Asian alone or combination householder								
Asian alone or in combination with one or more other races	4,664	3,489	2,858	239	392	1,175	572	603
Other	111,347	74,936	56,087	4,824	14,025	36,412	16,766	19,646
Marital status of householder								
Married, spouse present	58,945	58,945	58,945	—	—			
Married, spouse absent[b]	1,979	833	—	281	552	1,147	695	451
Widowed	11,716	2,606	—	419	2,186	9,110	1,849	7,261
Divorced	17,204	6,632	—	1,600	5,032	10,572	5,152	5,420
Separated[c]	3,563	1,999	—	358	1,641	1,564	903	661
Never married	22,604	7,410	—	2,404	5,006	15,194	8,738	6,456

Dash ("—") represents or rounds to zero.

[a]Hispanics may be of any race.

[b]In past reports: married spouse absent—other (excluding separated).

[c]In past reports: married spouse absent—separated.

SOURCE: Adapted from "Table H1. Households by Type and Tenure of Householder for Selected Characteristics: 2007," in *America's Families and Living Arrangements: 2007*, U.S. Census Bureau, July 2008, http://www.census.gov/population/www/socdemo/hh-fam/cps2007.html (accessed December 21, 2008)

to 33.5% in 2008, whereas the percentage of females aged 15 and older who had never married rose from 22.1% in 1970 to 26.8% in 2008. The proportion of those who have never married has increased as young adults delay the age at which they marry. Between 1970 and 2008 the median age at first marriage rose from 20.8 years to 25.6 years for women, and from 23.2 years to 27.4 years for men. In addition, the proportion of all households that were unmarried-partner heterosexual households steadily rose between 1996 and 2008, from 2.9% to 5.9% of all households. Nearly half (45.4%) of these households have children. (See Table 2.7.)

Single-parent women were more likely than single-parent men to have never been married. In 2007, 43% of

TABLE 2.5

Marital status of the population 18 years old and over by sex, race, and Hispanic origin, selected years 1990–2007

[In millions, except percent (181.8 represents 181,800,000)]

Marital status, race, and Hispanic origin	Total				Male				Female			
	1990	2000	2005	2007	1990	2000	2005	2007	1990	2000	2005	2007
Total[a]	181.8	201.8	217.2	222.6	86.9	96.9	104.8	107.8	95.0	104.9	112.3	114.8
Never married	40.4	48.2	53.9	56.1	22.4	26.1	29.6	30.9	17.9	22.1	24.3	25.3
Married[b]	112.6	120.1	127.4	129.7	55.8	59.6	63.3	64.6	56.7	60.4	64.0	65.1
Widowed	13.8	13.7	13.8	13.9	2.3	2.6	2.7	2.7	11.5	11.1	11.1	11.2
Divorced	15.1	19.8	22.1	22.8	6.3	8.5	9.2	9.6	8.8	11.3	12.9	13.2
Percent of total	100.0	100.0	100.0	100.0	100.0	100.0	100.0	100.0	100.0	100.0	100.0	100.0
Never married	22.2	23.9	24.8	25.2	25.8	27.0	28.2	28.6	18.9	21.1	21.6	22.0
Married[b]	61.9	59.5	58.6	58.2	64.3	61.5	60.4	59.9	59.7	57.6	56.9	56.7
Widowed	7.6	6.8	6.4	6.2	2.7	2.7	2.6	2.5	12.1	10.5	9.9	9.8
Divorced	8.3	9.8	10.2	10.3	7.2	8.8	8.8	8.9	9.3	10.8	11.5	11.5
White, total[c]	155.5	168.1	177.5	181.3	74.8	81.6	86.6	88.7	80.6	86.6	90.9	92.5
Never married	31.6	36.0	39.7	41.2	18.0	20.3	22.6	23.5	13.6	15.7	17.0	17.6
Married[b]	99.5	104.1	108.3	109.8	49.5	51.8	54.0	54.9	49.9	52.2	54.2	54.9
Widowed	11.7	11.5	11.5	11.5	1.9	2.2	2.3	2.3	9.8	9.3	9.2	9.3
Divorced	12.6	16.5	18.1	18.8	5.4	7.2	7.6	8.1	7.3	9.3	10.4	10.7
Percent of total	100.0	100.0	100.0	100.0	100.0	100.0	100.0	100.0	100.0	100.0	100.0	100.0
Never married	20.3	21.4	22.3	22.7	24.1	24.9	26.1	26.5	16.9	18.1	18.7	19.1
Married[b]	64.0	62.0	61.0	60.5	66.2	63.5	62.4	61.8	61.9	60.3	59.7	59.3
Widowed	7.5	6.8	6.5	6.4	2.6	2.7	2.6	2.5	12.2	10.8	10.2	10.0
Divorced	8.1	9.8	10.2	10.4	7.2	8.8	8.8	9.1	9.0	10.7	11.5	11.6
Black, total[c]	20.3	24.0	25.2	26.1	9.1	10.7	11.2	11.7	11.2	13.3	13.9	14.3
Never married	7.1	9.5	10.2	10.5	3.5	4.3	4.7	4.9	3.6	5.1	5.5	5.6
Married[b]	9.3	10.1	10.3	10.8	4.5	5.0	5.0	5.3	4.8	5.1	5.2	5.5
Widowed	1.7	1.7	1.7	1.7	0.3	0.3	0.3	0.3	1.4	1.4	1.4	1.4
Divorced	2.1	2.8	2.9	3.1	0.8	1.1	1.1	1.1	1.3	1.7	1.8	1.9
Percent of total	100.0	100.0	100.0	100.0	100.0	100.0	100.0	100.0	100.0	100.0	100.0	100.0
Never married	35.1	39.4	40.6	40.4	38.4	40.2	42.0	41.9	32.5	38.3	39.5	39.1
Married[b]	45.8	42.1	41.0	41.4	49.2	46.7	45.5	45.5	43.0	38.3	37.4	38.1
Widowed	8.5	7.0	6.6	6.6	3.7	2.8	2.7	2.9	12.4	10.5	10.0	9.6
Divorced	10.6	11.5	11.7	11.5	8.8	10.3	9.8	9.7	12.0	12.8	13.3	13.0
Asian, total[c]	(NA)	(NA)	9.4	10.2	(NA)	(NA)	4.5	4.9	(NA)	(NA)	4.9	5.4
Never married	(NA)	(NA)	2.3	2.7	(NA)	(NA)	1.3	1.5	(NA)	(NA)	1.0	1.2
Married[b]	(NA)	(NA)	6.2	6.7	(NA)	(NA)	2.9	3.2	(NA)	(NA)	3.3	3.5
Widowed	(NA)	(NA)	0.4	0.4	(NA)	(NA)	0.1	0.1	(NA)	(NA)	0.3	0.4
Divorced	(NA)	(NA)	0.5	0.4	(NA)	(NA)	0.2	0.1	(NA)	(NA)	0.3	0.3
Percent of total	100.0	100.0	100.0	100.0	100.0	100.0	100.0	100.0	100.0	100.0	100.0	100.0
Never married	(NA)	(NA)	24.8	26.5	(NA)	(NA)	29.7	31.0	(NA)	(NA)	20.3	22.5
Married[b]	(NA)	(NA)	65.6	65.5	(NA)	(NA)	64.7	65.2	(NA)	(NA)	66.5	65.6
Widowed	(NA)	(NA)	4.3	4.0	(NA)	(NA)	1.3	1.2	(NA)	(NA)	6.7	6.6
Divorced	(NA)	(NA)	5.3	4.0	(NA)	(NA)	4.1	2.7	(NA)	(NA)	6.4	5.2
Hispanic, total[d]	13.6	21.1	27.5	29.6	6.7	10.4	14.1	15.3	6.8	10.7	13.4	14.3
Never married[b]	3.7	5.9	8.6	9.3	2.2	3.4	5.2	5.6	1.5	2.5	3.4	3.7
Married[b]	8.4	12.7	15.6	17.0	4.1	6.2	7.8	8.5	4.3	6.5	7.8	8.4
Widowed	0.5	0.9	1.0	1.0	0.1	0.2	0.2	0.2	0.4	0.7	0.8	0.8
Divorced	1.0	1.6	2.2	2.3	0.4	0.7	0.9	0.9	0.6	1.0	1.3	1.4
Percent of total	100.0	100.0	100.0	100.0	100.0	100.0	100.0	100.0	100.0	100.0	100.0	100.0
Never married	27.2	28.0	31.3	31.4	32.1	32.3	36.7	36.7	22.5	23.4	25.6	25.7
Married[b]	61.7	60.2	57.0	57.3	60.9	59.7	55.6	55.7	62.4	60.7	58.7	58.8
Widowed	4.0	4.2	3.7	3.5	1.5	1.6	1.5	1.5	6.5	6.5	6.1	5.7
Divorced	7.0	7.6	7.9	7.8	5.5	6.4	6.3	6.1	8.5	9.3	9.7	9.7
Non-Hispanic white, total[c, d]	(NA)	(NA)	151.9	153.7	(NA)	(NA)	73.4	74.4	(NA)	(NA)	78.5	79.3
Never married	(NA)	(NA)	31.8	32.7	(NA)	(NA)	17.8	18.4	(NA)	(NA)	13.9	14.3
Married[b]	(NA)	(NA)	93.5	93.8	(NA)	(NA)	46.6	46.8	(NA)	(NA)	47.0	47.1
Widowed	(NA)	(NA)	10.6	10.6	(NA)	(NA)	2.1	2.0	(NA)	(NA)	8.5	8.5
Divorced	(NA)	(NA)	16.0	16.7	(NA)	(NA)	6.8	7.2	(NA)	(NA)	9.2	9.4

single mothers and 24.3% of single fathers had never been married. (See Table 2.8.) In 2007 African-American children were far more likely to live with a single parent than were white or Hispanic children. In that year, 53.2% of African-American children lived with one parent. (See Table 2.9.) Nearly half (49.7%) of all African-American children lived only with their mothers and 3.5% lived only with their fathers. Thirty percent of Hispanic children lived with one parent. In 2007, 24.5% of Hispanic children lived only with their mothers and 2.1% lived

TABLE 2.5

Marital status of the population 18 years old and over by sex, race, and Hispanic origin, selected years 1990–2007 [CONTINUED]

[In millions, except percent (181.8 represents 181,800,000)]

Marital status, race, and Hispanic origin	Total				Male				Female			
	1990	2000	2005	2007	1990	2000	2005	2007	1990	2000	2005	2007
Percent of total	**100.0**	**100.0**	**100.0**	**100.0**	**100.0**	**100.0**	**100.0**	**100.0**	**100.0**	**100.0**	**100.0**	**100.0**
Never married	(NA)	(NA)	20.9	21.3	(NA)	(NA)	24.3	24.7	(NA)	(NA)	17.7	18.1
Married[b]	(NA)	(NA)	61.5	61.0	(NA)	(NA)	63.5	62.9	(NA)	(NA)	59.7	58.9
Widowed	(NA)	(NA)	6.9	6.9	(NA)	(NA)	2.8	2.7	(NA)	(NA)	10.8	10.8
Divorced	(NA)	(NA)	10.6	10.8	(NA)	(NA)	9.3	9.7	(NA)	(NA)	11.7	11.9

NA = Not available.
[a]Includes persons of other races not shown separately.
[b]Includes persons who are married with spouse present, married with spouse absent, and separated.
[c]Beginning 2005, data represent persons who selected this race group only and exclude persons reporting more than one race. The Current Population Survey (CPS) in 1990 and 2000 only allowed respondents to report one race group.
[d]Hispanic persons may be any race.
Notes: As of March. Persons 18 years old and over. Excludes members of Armed Forces except those living off post or with their families on post.

SOURCE: "Table 55. Marital Status of the Population by Sex, Race, and Hispanic Origin: 1990 to 2007," in *The 2009 Statistical Abstract*, U.S. Census Bureau, December 2008, http://www.census.gov/prod/2008pubs/09statab/pop.pdf (accessed January 4, 2009)

only with their fathers. Of all non-Hispanic white children, 18.9% lived with one parent in 2007. In that year, 15.3% of all non-Hispanic white children lived with only their mothers and 3.6% lived only with their fathers.

In 2007 a higher percentage of African-American children than non-Hispanic white children or Hispanic children lived with neither parent. In that year, 818,000 (6.6%) African-American children, 537,000 (3.6%) Hispanic children, and 1 million (2.5%) non-Hispanic white children lived with neither parent. (See Table 2.9.) In part, this is because African-American children are more likely than children from other racial groups to live with grandparents without the presence of either parent.

CHILD SUPPORT. Child support is becoming an increasingly important source of income for single mothers because of the time limits now in place for receiving cash assistance. In 2005, 61.4% of custodial mothers and 36.4% of custodial fathers had child support awards. (See Table 2.6.) However, less than half of all custodial parents received all child support payments due them (43.1% of custodial fathers and 47.3% of custodial mothers). Almost a quarter of all custodial mothers (22.5%) and over a quarter of custodial fathers (25.7%) due child support payments received none at all.

Child support is often not enough to keep custodial mothers and their children out of poverty. According to the Census Bureau, between 1993 and 2001 the percent of custodial parents and their children living below the poverty level declined from 33.3% to 23.4%, and then remained statistically unchanged from 2001 to 2005. (See Figure 2.2.) However, the poverty rate among custodial mothers (27.7%) remained significantly higher than the poverty rate among custodial fathers (11.1%) in 2005.

The Census Bureau further breaks down whether custodial parents received their child support payments by whether their families were below the poverty level in 2005. A lower proportion of custodial parents with incomes below the poverty level (51.4%) received child support payments in 2005 than did all custodial parents (65.2%). (See Table 2.10.) In addition, a lower proportion of the poor custodial parents (39.6%) than all custodial parents (46.9%) received the full amount of child support due them.

The average amount of child support due to custodial mothers in 2005 was $5,176; they actually received an average of $3,579. (See Table 2.6.) The average amount of child support due to custodial fathers in 2005 was $4,471; they actually received an average of $2,797. According to the Census Bureau (December 18, 2008, http://www.census.gov/compendia/statab/tables/09s0549.pdf), the mean (average) total income of custodial parents who received no child support payments in 2005 was $25,961, among those who received at least some of the support due them was $25,626, and among those with no support agreements was $29,787.

By Race

The poverty rate differs among racial and ethnic groups. DeNavas-Walt, Proctor, and Smith find that in 2007 non-Hispanic whites had the lowest rate, at 8.2%, followed by Asian-Americans, at 10.2%. In contrast, more than one out of five (21.5%) Hispanics and one out of four (24.5%) African-Americans lived in poverty. In addition, African-Americans and Hispanics were much more likely to be desperately poor or have incomes below 0.50 of the poverty level. Over one out of 10 (11.2%) African-Americans and 8.2% of Hispanics were desperately poor in 2007. Non-Hispanic whites (3.4%) and Asian-Americans (4.2%) had much lower rates of desperate poverty.

TABLE 2.6

Demographic characteristics of custodial parents by award status and payments received, 2005

[Numbers in thousands]

Characteristic	Total	With child support agreements or awards									
		Total	Percent	Due child support payments in 2005							
				Total	Average due	Average received	Percent received	Received all payments		Did not receive payments	
								Total	Percent	Total	Percent
All custodial parents											
Total	13,605	7,802	57.3	6,809	$5,584	$3,643	65.2	3,192	46.9	1,550	22.8
Sex											
Male	2,199	800	36.4	678	$4,471	$2,797	62.6	292	43.1	174	25.7
Female	11,406	7,002	61.4	6,131	$5,176	$3,579	69.1	2,900	47.3	1,377	22.5
Age											
Under 30 years	3,194	1,613	50.5	1,352	$4,063	$2,296	56.5	532	39.3	343	25.4
30 to 39 years	4,841	2,982	61.6	2,668	$5,238	$3,322	63.4	1,198	44.9	680	25.5
40 years and over	5,571	3,207	57.6	2,789	$6,652	$4,603	69.2	1,461	52.4	528	18.9
Race and ethnicity[a]											
White alone	9,493	5,748	60.5	5,038	$5,893	$4,041	68.6	2,475	49.1	1,032	20.5
White alone, not Hispanic	7,570	4,783	63.2	4,167	$6,010	$4,146	69.0	2,096	50.3	825	19.8
Black alone	3,431	1,699	49.5	1,484	$4,514	$2,250	49.8	584	39.4	457	30.8
Hispanic (any race)	2,146	1,062	49.5	949	$5,529	$3,535	63.9	421	44.4	226	23.8
Current marital status[b]											
Married	3,007	1,895	63.0	1,703	$5,507	$3,864	70.2	793	46.6	395	23.2
Divorced	4,795	3,098	64.6	2,727	$6,212	$4,246	68.4	1,451	53.2	560	20.5
Separated	1,506	750	49.8	638	$6,205	$3,623	58.4	255	40.0	158	24.8
Never married	4,130	1,975	47.8	1,663	$4,412	$2,486	56.3	671	40.3	418	25.1
Educational attainment											
Less than high school diploma	2,062	975	47.3	791	$5,019	$2,429	48.4	309	39.1	228	28.8
High school graduate	4,880	2,780	57.0	2,457	$5,022	$3,043	60.6	1,070	43.5	603	24.5
Less than 4 years of college	4,568	2,813	61.6	2,482	$5,561	$3,750	67.4	1,192	48.0	556	22.4
Bachelor's degree or more	2,096	1,235	58.9	1,079	$7,326	$5,651	77.1	620	57.5	163	15.1
Selected characteristics											
Family income below 2005 poverty level	3,406	1,796	52.7	1,502	$4,756	$2,446	51.4	595	39.6	412	27.4
Worked full-time, year-round	7,331	4,294	58.6	3,825	$5,756	$3,782	65.7	1,887	49.3	861	22.5
Public assistance program participation[c]	4,273	2,402	56.2	2,032	$4,556	$2,437	53.5	780	38.4	566	27.9
With one child	7,792	4,058	52.1	3,523	$5,128	$3,519	68.6	1,722	48.9	744	21.1
With two or more children	5,813	3,744	64.4	3,287	$6,072	$3,775	62.2	1,470	44.7	806	24.5
Child had contact with other parent in 2005	9,154	5,700	62.3	5,008	$5,674	$4,108	72.4	2,654	53.0	879	17.6

[a]Includes those reporting one race alone and not in combination with any other race.
[b]Excludes 200,000 with marital status of widowed.
[c]Received either Medicaid, food stamps, public housing or rent subsidy, Temporary Assistance for Needy Families (TANF) or general assistance.
Note: Parents living with own children under 21 years of age whose other parent is not living in the home.

SOURCE: Timothy S. Grall, "Table 2. Demographic Characteristics of Custodial Parents by Award Status and Payments Received: 2005," in *Custodial Mothers and Fathers and Their Child Support: 2005*, Current Population Reports, U.S. Census Bureau, August 2007, http://www.census.gov/prod/2007pubs/ p60–234.pdf (accessed December 21, 2008).

Work Experience

The probability of a family living in poverty is influenced by three primary factors: the size of the family, the number of workers, and the characteristics of the wage earners. As the number of wage earners in a family increases, the probability of poverty declines. The likelihood of a second wage earner is greatest in families headed by married couples.

In 2006 most Americans aged 16 and older worked at some point during the year (158.6 million of 231 million, or 68.6%). (See Table 2.11.) About 6.2% of all Americans who worked lived in poverty, compared to 20.7% of those who did not work that year. The rate of poverty was higher for those who worked only 26 weeks or less (18.4%) than for those who worked 27 weeks or more (5.1%).

Most poor children live in families in which one or more adults work. However, millions of working parents are not able to earn enough to lift their families out of poverty—even those who work full time all year.

Education

Not surprisingly, poverty rates drop sharply as years of schooling rise. In *Income, Earnings, and Poverty Data*

TABLE 2.7

Opposite-sex unmarried couples, by age, race, marital status, and presence of biological children, 2007

[Numbers in thousands]

	Total		Unmarried partner households[a]		Other couples[b]	
All opposite sex unmarried couples	Population	%	Population	%	Population	%
Total	**6,445**	**100.0**	**5,200**	**100.0**	**1,245**	**100.0**
Male's age						
15–24 years	1,212	17.6	881	16.9	331	26.6
25–29 years	1,340	19.8	1,079	20.7	261	20.9
30–34 years	870	14.0	736	14.2	134	10.8
35–39 years	689	11.6	549	10.6	140	11.3
40–44 years	659	10.7	557	10.7	103	8.2
45–49 years	499	8.6	416	8.0	82	6.6
50–54 years	448	7.1	384	7.4	64	5.1
55–64 years	432	6.7	358	6.9	74	5.9
65 years and over	296	3.8	240	4.6	56	4.5
Female's age						
15–24 years	1,755	25.4	1,289	24.8	467	37.5
25–29 years	1,264	19.1	1,056	20.3	208	16.7
30–34 years	740	12.6	621	11.9	119	9.6
35–39 years	631	10.7	535	10.3	96	7.7
40–44 years	565	9.8	464	8.9	101	8.1
45–49 years	538	8.7	439	8.4	99	8.0
50–54 years	362	5.7	296	5.7	66	5.3
55–64 years	382	5.2	329	6.3	53	4.2
65 years and over	208	2.9	171	3.3	36	2.9
Race difference[c]						
Both white non-Hispanic	3,937	56.9	3,239	62.3	699	56.1
Both black non-Hispanic	632	8.6	518	10.0	114	9.2
Both other non-Hispanic	205	4.6	136	2.6	69	5.5
Both Hispanic	715	11.7	524	10.1	191	15.3
Neither Hispanic, different race groups	425	8.2	361	6.9	64	5.2
One is Hispanic, one is non-Hispanic	531	10.0	422	8.1	109	8.7
Couple's marital status						
Both are never married	3,212	48.5	2,519	48.4	692	55.6
Man is ever married, woman is never married	674	10.9	556	10.7	117	9.4
Woman is ever married, man is never married	768	12.6	641	12.3	127	10.2
Both are ever married	1,792	28.0	1,483	28.5	308	24.8
Presence of biological children						
No biological children	3,940	54.6	3,190	61.4	750	60.2
At least one biological child under 18 of either partner	2,505	45.4	2,009	38.6	495	39.8

[a]Includes couples where one is the householder, and the other is reported as the unmarried partner on the relationship to householder item.
[b]Including couples where neither is reported as the unmarried partner of the householder on the relationship to householder item.
[c]Hispanics may be of any race.

SOURCE: "Table UC4. Opposite Sex Unmarried Couples: 2007," in *America's Families and Living Arrangements: 2007*, U.S. Census Bureau, July 2008, http://www.census.gov/population/www/socdemo/hh-fam/cps2007.html (accessed December 21, 2008)

from the *2007 American Community Survey* (August 2008, http://www.census.gov/prod/2008pubs/acs-09.pdf), Alemayehu Bishaw and Jessica Semega of the Census Bureau note that in 2007 the median income for men aged 25 and older who had not completed high school was $22,602; for women it was only $14,202, 62.8% of what their male peers earned. Male high school graduates earned a median of $32,435, whereas females earned $21,219, 65.4% of what males earned. Men with a four-year college degree earned a median of $57,397, whereas women earned $38,628, 67.3% of what males earned. Ayana Douglas-Hall and Michelle Chau of the National Center for Children in Poverty report in "Parents' Low Education Leads to Low Income, Despite Full-Time Employment" (November 2007, http://nccp.org/publications/pub_786.html) that most children who live in low-income or poor families have

parents without any college education, and that full-time employment does not protect families from low earnings.

GOVERNMENT ASSISTANCE

With few exceptions, the demand for welfare assistance increased sharply in the 1990s. However, because of decreased funding and welfare reform measures that gave states more flexibility in dispersing benefits, a smaller proportion of eligible families actually received benefits. In the fact sheet "A Decade of Welfare Reform: Facts and Figures—Assessing the New Federalism" (June 2006, http://www.urban.org/UploadedPDF/900980_welfarereform.pdf), the Urban Institute explains that the number of eligible families enrolled in welfare programs decreased from 80% in 1996 to 48% in 2002. Some were ineligible because they had assets such as

TABLE 2.8

Single-parent family groups with own children under 18, by marital status and demographic characteristics, 2007

[Numbers in thousands]

	All one-parent unmarried family groups		Maintained by father										Maintained by mother									
			Total		Never married		Divorced		Separated*		Widowed		Total		Never married		Divorced		Separated*		Widowed	
	N	%	N	%	N	%	N	%	N	%	N	%	N	%	N	%	N	%	N	%	N	%
All family groups	11,707	100.0	1,742	100.0	423	24.3	908	52.1	314	18.0	97	5.6	9,965	100.0	4,288	43.0	3,446	34.6	1,866	18.7	365	3.7
Region																						
Northeast	2,132	18.2	297	100.0	84	28.3	132	44.6	62	21.0	18	6.1	1,835	100.0	831	45.3	553	30.2	382	20.8	69	3.8
Midwest	2,503	21.4	381	100.0	92	24.2	217	57.0	53	14.0	18	4.7	2,122	100.0	957	45.1	804	37.9	281	13.2	79	3.7
South	4,600	39.3	601	100.0	141	23.5	303	50.5	125	20.9	31	5.1	3,999	100.0	1,740	43.5	1,357	33.9	756	18.9	146	4.0
West	2,472	21.1	463	100.0	105	22.8	255	55.0	73	15.7	30	6.5	2,009	100.0	759	37.8	732	36.4	448	22.3	70	3.5
Size of family group																						
Two members	5,251	44.9	978	100.0	281	28.7	499	51.0	156	15.9	43	4.4	4,273	100.0	2,142	50.1	1,394	32.6	593	13.9	144	3.4
Three members	3,850	32.9	542	100.0	103	19.0	299	55.2	103	19.0	36	6.7	3,309	100.0	1,220	36.9	1,295	39.2	678	20.5	115	3.5
Four members	1,665	14.2	161	100.0	19	11.6	82	50.9	45	28.2	15	9.2	1,505	100.0	579	38.5	509	33.8	356	23.6	61	4.0
Five members	600	5.1	39	100.0	12	31.6	16	42.7	8	20.4	2	5.2	562	100.0	213	37.9	158	28.1	159	28.3	32	5.7
Six or more members	340	2.9	23	100.0	8	36.7	11	49.4	3	11.1	1	2.9	317	100.0	134	42.2	90	28.2	81	25.4	13	4.2
Age of reference person																						
Under 20 years	290	2.5	3	100.0	3	100.0	—	—	—	—	—	—	287	100.0	266	92.7	6	2.2	15	5.1	—	—
20–24 years	1,206	10.3	80	100.0	76	94.5	2	2.4	2	3.1	—	—	1,125	100.0	940	83.6	56	5.0	125	11.1	4	0.4
25–29 years	1,846	15.8	158	100.0	91	57.7	42	26.4	23	14.9	2	1.0	1,689	100.0	1,092	64.7	297	17.6	281	16.6	19	1.1
30–34 years	1,834	15.7	220	100.0	87	39.8	86	38.9	43	19.4	4	1.9	1,614	100.0	770	47.7	486	30.1	337	20.9	22	1.3
35–39 years	2,093	17.9	342	100.0	75	22.0	178	52.2	64	18.6	25	7.2	1,751	100.0	544	31.1	743	42.4	426	24.3	38	2.2
40–44 years	2,040	17.4	377	100.0	46	12.1	244	64.8	67	17.9	20	5.2	1,663	100.0	379	22.8	888	53.4	315	18.9	81	4.9
45–54 years	2,045	17.5	469	100.0	40	8.5	295	62.8	99	21.1	36	7.7	1,576	100.0	263	16.7	845	53.7	337	21.4	130	8.3
55+ years	353	3.0	93	100.0	4	4.8	61	66.3	16	16.9	11	12.0	261	100.0	34	13.0	125	47.8	32	12.2	70	27.0
Family status																						
Family income under																						
$10,000	1,886	16.1	121	100.0	42	34.7	53	44.0	18	15.2	7	6.1	1,765	100.0	988	56.0	350	19.8	380	21.5	47	2.7
$10,000 to $14,999	1,167	10.0	97	100.0	41	42.3	30	30.9	21	21.4	5	5.4	1,070	100.0	516	48.2	282	26.3	239	22.4	33	3.1
$15,000 to $19,999	1,066	9.1	85	100.0	30	35.6	34	40.5	17	20.4	3	3.5	981	100.0	465	47.3	276	28.1	211	21.5	29	3.0
$20,000 to $24,999	966	8.3	108	100.0	38	35.5	42	39.2	22	20.1	6	5.2	858	100.0	392	45.7	287	33.5	151	17.6	28	3.3
$25,000 to $29,999	976	8.3	139	100.0	45	32.3	66	47.4	21	15.1	7	5.2	837	100.0	316	37.8	338	40.3	160	19.2	23	2.7
$30,000 to $39,999	1,631	13.9	305	100.0	74	24.4	152	49.8	61	20.1	17	5.7	1,326	100.0	496	37.4	539	40.6	238	18.0	53	4.0
$40,000 to $49,999	1,101	9.4	227	100.0	49	21.8	124	54.7	43	18.8	11	4.7	874	100.0	291	33.3	403	46.1	135	15.5	44	5.1
$50,000 to $74,999	1,551	13.2	328	100.0	51	15.6	218	66.3	44	13.3	15	4.7	1,222	100.0	391	32.0	566	46.3	190	15.6	75	6.1
$75,000 to $99,999	640	5.5	128	100.0	21	16.1	63	49.5	33	25.7	11	8.8	513	100.0	196	38.3	212	41.3	83	16.2	22	4.3
$100,000 and over	722	6.2	204	100.0	31	15.1	125	61.1	35	17.0	14	6.7	518	100.0	237	45.7	193	37.3	77	15.0	10	2.0
Poverty status																						
Below poverty level	3,619	30.9	249	100.0	90	36.2	96	38.5	49	19.6	14	5.7	3,370	100.0	1,761	52.3	767	22.8	736	21.8	105	3.1
At or above poverty level	8,088	69.1	1,492	100.0	333	22.3	812	54.4	265	17.8	83	5.5	6,596	100.0	2,527	38.3	2,679	40.6	1,130	17.1	259	3.9

TABLE 2.8

Single-parent family groups with own children under 18, by marital status and demographic characteristics, 2007 [CONTINUED]

[Numbers in thousands]

	All one-parent unmarried family groups		Maintained by father										Maintained by mother									
			Total		Never married		Divorced		Separated*		Widowed		Total		Never married		Divorced		Separated*		Widowed	
	N	%	N	%	N	%	N	%	N	%	N	%	N	%	N	%	N	%	N	%	N	%
Number of own children under 18																						
One own child under 18	6,504	55.6	1,146	100.0	311	27.1	586	51.2	189	16.5	60	5.2	5,358	100.0	2,470	46.1	1,859	34.7	803	15.0	226	4.2
Two own children under 18	3,510	30.0	457	100.0	89	19.5	249	54.5	94	20.5	26	5.6	3,052	100.0	1,209	39.6	1,117	36.6	642	21.0	85	2.8
Three own children under 18	1,241	10.6	115	100.0	19	16.6	56	49.1	28	24.0	12	10.2	1,126	100.0	435	38.6	358	31.8	293	26.0	41	3.6
Four or more own children under 18	453	3.9	23	100.0	4	16.5	16	67.3	4	16.2	—	—	429	100.0	174	40.6	112	26.1	129	30.0	14	3.3
Own children in specified age groups																						
Children in two or more age groups	4,255	36.3	411	100.0	65	15.8	217	52.7	94	22.9	35	8.5	3,844	100.0	1,459	37.9	1,348	35.1	889	23.1	148	3.9
Families with children 12–17 only	2,849	24.3	632	100.0	72	11.4	414	65.5	103	16.3	43	6.8	2,217	100.0	536	24.2	1,144	51.6	398	18.0	140	6.3
Families with children 6–11 only	2,228	19.0	425	100.0	108	25.3	218	51.3	80	18.9	19	4.4	1,803	100.0	745	41.3	694	38.5	307	17.0	57	3.2
Families with children 3–5 only	1,116	9.5	140	100.0	80	57.3	34	24.5	26	18.3	—	—	976	100.0	631	64.7	188	19.3	140	14.3	17	1.8
Families with children under 3 only	1,260	10.8	134	100.0	98	73.6	24	18.2	11	8.2	—	—	1,126	100.0	918	81.5	72	6.4	133	11.8	3	0.3
Under 6 only	2,745	23.4	292	100.0	189	64.8	64	22.0	38	13.1	—	—	2,453	100.0	1,760	71.7	328	13.4	336	13.7	30	1.2
Some under 6, some 6–17	1,671	14.3	117	100.0	27	23.3	54	46.5	26	22.4	9	7.8	1,554	100.0	781	50.3	378	24.3	371	23.9	24	1.5
6–17 only	7,291	62.3	1,333	100.0	206	15.5	789	59.2	250	18.7	88	6.6	5,958	100.0	1,747	29.3	2,741	46.0	1,159	19.5	311	5.2

Dash ("—") represents or rounds to zero.

Note: "Own children" exclude ever-married children under 18 years.

*Includes 'married spouse absent'

SOURCE: "Table FG6. One-Parent Unmarried Family Groups with Own Children under 18, by Marital Status of the Reference Person: 2007," in *America's Families and Living Arrangements: 2007*, U.S. Census Bureau, July 2008, http://www.census.gov/population/www/socdemo/hh-fam/cps2007.html (accessed December 21, 2008)

TABLE 2.9

Living arrangements of children and marital status of parents, by age, sex, race, Hispanic origin, and selected characteristics, 2007

[Numbers in thousands]

	Living with both parents			Living with mother only					Living with father only					Living with neither parent
	Total	Married to each other	Not married to each other	Married spouse absent	Widowed	Divorced	Separated	Never married	Married spouse absent	Widowed	Divorced	Separated	Never married	No parent present
All children	73,746	49,999	2,154	830	572	5,663	2,648	6,945	132	136	1,283	311	526	2,545
Total	**73,746**	**49,999**	**2,154**	**830**	**572**	**5,663**	**2,648**	**6,945**	**132**	**136**	**1,283**	**311**	**526**	**2,545**
Age of child														
Under 1 year	4,072	2,733	386	25	2	64	73	617	2	2	8	3	35	122
1–2 years	8,217	5,729	521	100	11	199	229	1,088	7	2	38	12	91	190
3–5 years	12,256	8,493	474	137	51	606	403	1,504	18	4	96	36	121	312
6–8 years	11,937	8,153	294	157	66	846	442	1,236	18	12	177	56	86	393
9–11 years	11,837	8,065	192	150	120	1,122	488	924	31	35	235	48	69	357
12–14 years	12,455	8,385	171	130	122	1,328	476	851	25	30	319	69	65	484
15–17 years	12,971	8,440	116	132	201	1,497	536	726	32	50	409	87	59	687
Race														
White alone	56,223	41,557	1,599	462	361	4,290	1,669	2,928	103	97	1,067	247	301	1,544
Black alone	11,310	4,136	329	268	161	961	786	3,501	12	28	142	48	175	764
Asian alone	2,953	2,516	60	37	22	53	66	87	10	6	24	2	6	63
All remaining single races and all race combinations	3,259	1,790	167	64	28	359	127	429	7	5	50	15	45	173
Race														
Hispanic*	15,113	9,907	650	268	106	960	797	1,569	29	20	118	45	105	537
White alone, Non-Hispanic	42,261	32,218	1,010	252	268	3,435	944	1,556	76	77	962	211	207	1,046
All remaining single races and all race combinations, non-hispanic	16,372	7,874	494	310	198	1,268	907	3,819	27	39	203	56	215	962
Race														
White alone or in combination with one or more other races	58,400	42,815	1,689	493	380	4,516	1,761	3,217	109	100	1,094	257	328	1,641
Other	15,346	7,184	465	338	193	1,147	886	3,728	23	36	189	54	198	904
Race														
Black alone or in combination with one or more other races	12,375	4,596	383	284	167	1,081	857	3,757	12	28	148	53	191	818
Other	61,371	45,403	1,771	546	405	4,582	1,791	3,188	120	108	1,135	259	335	1,727
Race														
Asian alone or in combination with one or more other races	3,569	2,993	79	40	23	86	78	123	11	6	32	7	9	80
Other	70,177	47,006	2,075	790	549	5,577	2,569	6,822	121	130	1,251	304	518	2,465
Highest education of either parent														
Less than 9th grade	2,332	1,535	87	58	33	127	154	274	11	5	21	15	13	—
9th to 12th grade, no diploma	5,622	2,384	290	145	91	464	459	1,505	18	11	103	50	103	—
High school graduate	17,463	9,940	814	330	154	1,767	852	2,619	57	69	477	139	247	—
Some college or AA degree	20,278	13,544	702	192	149	2,093	850	2,109	16	15	415	69	123	—
Bachelor's degree	15,321	13,219	215	71	106	871	251	332	22	30	158	19	27	—
Prof. or graduate degree	10,185	9,379	45	35	39	341	82	106	9	6	109	20	13	—
No parents present	2,545	—	—	—	—	—	—	—	—	—	—	—	—	2,545

TABLE 2.9

Living arrangements of children and marital status of parents, by age, sex, race, Hispanic origin, and selected characteristics, 2007 [CONTINUED]

[Numbers in thousands]

	Living with both parents			Living with mother only					Living with father only					Living with neither parent
	Total	Married to each other	Not married to each other	Married spouse absent	Widowed	Divorced	Separated	Never married	Married spouse absent	Widowed	Divorced	Separated	Never married	No parent present
Presence of adults other than parents														
Other relatives only	16,011	8,696	296	283	184	1,345	649	2,260	32	34	229	75	130	1,797
Non relatives only	3,165	361	69	37	34	763	207	699	7	18	208	31	196	535
Both relatives and non relatives	864	217	34	33	20	110	40	132	5	4	31	5	24	211
No other relatives or non relatives	53,705	40,725	1,755	477	334	3,445	1,752	3,854	88	80	816	200	176	2
Poverty status														
Below 100% of poverty	13,098	3,981	952	397	196	1,561	1,160	3,389	28	18	162	50	128	1,077
100% to 199% of poverty	15,823	9,172	630	243	118	1,668	821	1,995	50	39	273	81	175	559
200% of poverty and above	44,825	36,846	572	190	259	2,434	667	1,561	54	80	849	180	224	909
100 percent of poverty														
Below 100% of poverty	13,098	3,981	952	397	196	1,561	1,160	3,389	28	18	162	50	128	1,077
100% of poverty and above	60,647	46,018	1,202	433	377	4,102	1,488	3,556	104	119	1,122	261	399	1,468
125 percent of poverty														
Below 125% of poverty	17,292	6,045	1,157	477	222	2,068	1,481	4,099	33	21	220	72	161	1,237
125% of poverty and above	56,453	43,954	997	353	351	3,595	1,166	2,846	99	115	1,064	239	365	1,309

Dash "—" represents or rounds to zero.
Note: Excludes children in group quarters, and those who are a family reference person or spouse.
*Hispanics may be of any race.

SOURCE: "C3. Living Arrangements of Children under 18 Years and Marital Status of Parents, by Age, Sex, Race, and Hispanic Origin and Selected Characteristics of the Child for All Children: 2007," in *America's Families and Living Arrangements: 2007*, U.S. Census Bureau, July 2008, http://www.census.gov/population/www/socdemo/hh-fam/cps2007.html (accessed December 21, 2008)

FIGURE 2.2

Poverty status of custodial parents, 1993–2005

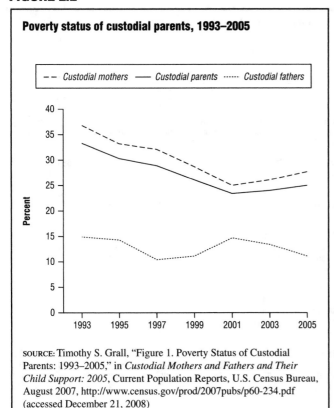

SOURCE: Timothy S. Grall, "Figure 1. Poverty Status of Custodial Parents: 1993–2005," in *Custodial Mothers and Fathers and Their Child Support: 2005*, Current Population Reports, U.S. Census Bureau, August 2007, http://www.census.gov/prod/2007pubs/p60-234.pdf (accessed December 21, 2008)

a car or a savings account that brought them above permitted limits. Others did not know they were eligible for benefits, and some knew they were eligible but chose not to accept benefits or thought the effort was not worth the amount of benefits they would receive.

The economic recession that began in 2008 may increase the number of people receiving means-tested benefits. The American Recovery and Reinvestment Act, signed by President Barack Obama (1961–) on February 17, 2009, contained provisions for a $5 billion contingency fund for Temporary Assistance to Needy Families programs under which states can receive up to 80% of the cost of spending increases in fiscal years 2009 and 2010. The act also allocates an additional $500 million to support participation in the Supplemental Nutrition Assistance Program (SNAP). The act authorized an increase in SNAP benefits to families of up to 113.6% of the value of the Thrifty Food Plan (a plan that serves as the basis for maximum food stamp allotments).

Who Receives Benefits?

The Census Bureau reports that in 2006, 77.1 million people (26% of the total U.S. population) lived in households that received some form of means-tested assistance—assistance based on earning below a certain amount. (See Table 2.12.) In 2006 approximately 36.5 million people were living below the poverty level. (See Table 2.13.) Of those living in poverty, 24.7 million (67.8%) were receiving some form of means-tested aid.

Certain types of households were more likely than others to receive means-tested assistance in 2006. Almost nine out of 10 (86%) poor families with children under 18 years of age received government assistance. (See Table 2.13.) Poor families headed by a single mother were the most likely to receive government assistance; 89.6% of these families received some form of government assistance. In fact, more than two out of three (69.6%) of all families (not just those in poverty) with children headed by a single mother received some form of means-tested assistance in 2006. (See Table 2.12.) In comparison, about half (48.8%) of families headed by a single father received means-tested assistance in that year.

In 2006 a slightly higher proportion of females (27.5%) than males (24.4%) lived in a household that received means-tested assistance or welfare benefits of any kind. (See Table 2.12.) About 41.6 million females received program assistance during 2006, compared to 35.5 million males. Among those living below the poverty level, 14.2 million women, or 69.5% of females living below the poverty line, received benefits during some part of the year, compared to 10.5 million males, or 65.6% of males living below the poverty line. (See Table 2.13.)

One reason for the larger percentage of females receiving assistance is that women are more likely to live in a family without a spouse present. Bishaw and Semega indicate that another reason is that women, on average, earned approximately 77.5% of what men earned in 2007. Age may also play a role in the higher number of women in poverty; there are far more elderly women then men. Another reason is that fewer single mothers participate in the workforce permanently and full time than do single fathers. In *Custodial Mothers and Fathers and Their Child Support: 2005* (August 2007, http://www.census.gov/prod/2007pubs/p60-234.pdf), Timothy S. Grall of the Census Bureau reports that even though 78.6% of custodial mothers worked in 2005, only 50.1% of them worked full-time year-round, whereas 73.7% of custodial fathers held full-time, full-year jobs. Grall suggests one reason that might be part of the cause of this disparity: Custodial mothers were more likely than custodial fathers to have two or more children living with them (44.2% and 35%, respectively).

African-Americans and Hispanics were more likely than Asian-Americans and non-Hispanic whites to receive some form of means-tested assistance in 2004. The Census Bureau reports in "Program Participation Status of Household-Poverty Status of People" (August 29, 2006, http://pubdb3.census.gov/macro/032005/pov/new26_002.htm) that 49.6% of Hispanics, 46.7% of African-Americans, 23.3% of Asian-Americans, and 17.6% of non-Hispanic whites lived in households receiving some form of means-tested assistance.

TABLE 2.10

Custodial parents, by child support award status, payments received, and demographic characteristics, 2005

[Numbers in thousands]

Characteristic	Total	With child support agreements or awards									
		Total	Percent	Due child support payments in 2005							
				Total	Average due	Average received	Percent received	Received all payments		Did not receive payments	
								Total	Percent	Total	Percent
All custodial parents											
Total	13,605	7,802	57.3	6,809	$5,584	$3,643	65.2	3,192	46.9	1,550	22.8
Sex											
Male	2,199	800	36.4	678	$4,471	$2,797	62.6	292	43.1	174	25.7
Female	11,406	7,002	61.4	6,131	$5,176	$3,579	69.1	2,900	47.3	1,377	22.5
Age											
Under 30 years	3,194	1,613	50.5	1,352	$4,063	$2,296	56.5	532	39.3	343	25.4
30 to 39 years	4,841	2,982	61.6	2,668	$5,238	$3,322	63.4	1,198	44.9	680	25.5
40 years and over	5,571	3,207	57.6	2,789	$6,652	$4,603	69.2	1,461	52.4	528	18.9
Race and ethnicity[a]											
White alone	9,493	5,748	60.5	5,038	$5,893	$4,041	68.6	2,475	49.1	1,032	20.5
White alone, not Hispanic	7,570	4,783	63.2	4,167	$6,010	$4,146	69.0	2,096	50.3	825	19.8
Black alone	3,431	1,699	49.5	1,484	$4,514	$2,250	49.8	584	39.4	457	30.8
Hispanic (any race)	2,146	1,062	49.5	949	$5,529	$3,535	63.9	421	44.4	226	23.8
Current marital status[b]											
Married	3,007	1,895	63.0	1,703	$5,507	$3,864	70.2	793	46.6	395	23.2
Divorced	4,795	3,098	64.6	2,727	$6,212	$4,246	68.4	1,451	53.2	560	20.5
Separated	1,506	750	49.8	638	$6,205	$3,623	58.4	255	40.0	158	24.8
Never married	4,130	1,975	47.8	1,663	$4,412	$2,486	56.3	671	40.3	418	25.1
Educational attainment											
Less than high school diploma	2,062	975	47.3	791	$5,019	$2,429	48.4	309	39.1	228	28.8
High school graduate	4,880	2,780	57.0	2,457	$5,022	$3,043	60.6	1,070	43.5	603	24.5
Less than 4 years of college	4,568	2,813	61.6	2,482	$5,561	$3,750	67.4	1,192	48.0	556	22.4
Bachelor's degree or more	2,096	1,235	58.9	1,079	$7,326	$5,651	77.1	620	57.5	163	15.1
Selected characteristics											
Family income below 2005 poverty level	3,406	1,796	52.7	1,502	$4,756	$2,446	51.4	595	39.6	412	27.4
Worked full-time, year-round	7,331	4,294	58.6	3,825	$5,756	$3,782	65.7	1,887	49.3	861	22.5
Public assistance program participation[c]	4,273	2,402	56.2	2,032	$4,556	$2,437	53.5	780	38.4	566	27.9
With one child	7,792	4,058	52.1	3,523	$5,128	$3,519	68.6	1,722	48.9	744	21.1
With two or more children	5,813	3,744	64.4	3,287	$6,072	$3,775	62.2	1,470	44.7	806	24.5
Child had contact with other parent in 2005	9,154	5,700	62.3	5,008	$5,674	$4,108	72.4	2,654	53.0	879	17.6

[a]Includes those reporting one race alone and not in combination with any other race.
[b]Excludes 200,000 with marital status of widowed.
[c]Received either Medicaid, food stamps, public housing or rent subsidy, Temporary Assistance for Needy Families (TANF) or general assistance.
Note: Parents living with own children under 21 years of age whose other parent is not living in the home.

SOURCE: Timothy S. Grall, "Table 2. Demographic Characteristics of Custodial Parents by Award Status and Payments Received: 2005," in *Custodial Mothers and Fathers and Their Child Support: 2005*, Current Population Reports, U.S. Census Bureau, August 2007, http://www.census.gov/prod/2007pubs/p60–234 .pdf (accessed December 21, 2008)

Among those with incomes below the poverty line, 79.9% of African-Americans, 79.6% of Hispanics, 55% of non-Hispanic whites, and 53.8% of Asian-Americans received benefits. The lower proportion of non-Hispanic whites living below the poverty line who receive means-tested benefits may be due to the fact that a lower proportion of non-Hispanic whites live in desperate poverty than do others.

Nearly four out of 10 (39.3%) children under 18 years old lived in households that received means-tested assistance at some time during 2006. (See Table 2.12.) Approx-imately one out of six (17.3%) people aged 65 and older received assistance.

Only 19.9% of those living in families headed by married couples received assistance in 2006. (See Table 2.12.) Well over half (56.8%) of individuals in female-headed families with no spouse present received benefits. In contrast, only a little over a third (37.3%) of those living in families headed by single male received means-tested benefits. The highest rate of assistance was provided to families headed by women with children under the age of six (75.9%).

TABLE 2.11

Poverty status and work experience of people in families and unrelated individuals, 2006

[Numbers in thousands]

Poverty status and work experience	Total persons	In married-couple families				In families maintained by women			In families maintained by men			Unrelated individuals
		Husbands	Wives	Related children under 18	Other relatives	Householder	Related children under 18	Other relatives	Householder	Related children under 18	Other relatives	
Total												
All people[a]	231,033	58,408	58,927	5,906	18,452	14,405	2,235	11,352	5,031	518	5,287	50,511
With labor force activity	158,563	46,025	38,056	2,107	12,382	10,253	587	7,325	3,974	147	3,508	34,199
1 to 26 weeks	13,334	1,359	3,075	1,308	2,608	778	341	950	193	86	325	2,312
27 weeks or more	145,229	44,666	34,981	800	9,774	9,476	246	6,375	3,782	61	3,182	31,887
With no labor force activity	72,470	12,383	20,872	3,799	6,070	4,151	1,648	4,027	1,057	371	1,779	16,312
At or above poverty level												
All people[a]	206,167	55,535	56,013	5,584	17,700	10,321	1,551	9,585	4,353	449	4,765	40,311
With labor force activity	148,685	44,519	37,286	2,047	12,134	8,110	468	6,744	3,620	142	3,292	30,324
1 to 26 weeks	10,883	1,234	2,842	1,258	2,503	311	266	796	137	83	276	1,177
27 weeks or more	137,802	43,285	34,444	789	9,631	7,799	202	5,948	3,483	59	3,015	29,146
With no labor force activity	57,482	11,016	18,727	3,536	5,565	2,211	1,083	2,841	733	307	1,474	9,987
Below poverty level												
All people[a]	24,866	2,873	2,914	323	752	4,083	684	1,767	678	70	522	10,200
With labor force activity	9,878	1,506	770	60	247	2,143	119	582	354	5	216	3,875
1 to 26 weeks	2,451	125	233	49	105	467	76	154	56	3	49	1,134
27 weeks or more	7,427	1,380	537	11	142	1,677	43	428	299	2	167	2,741
With no labor force activity	14,988	1,367	2,144	262	505	1,940	565	1,186	323	64	306	6,325
Rate[b]												
All people[a]	10.8	4.9	4.9	5.5	4.1	28.3	30.6	15.6	13.5	13.4	9.9	20.2
With labor force activity	6.2	3.3	2.0	2.9	2.0	20.9	20.3	7.9	8.9	3.7	6.2	11.3
1 to 26 weeks	18.4	9.2	7.6	3.8	4.0	60.0	22.2	16.2	28.9	3.9	15.1	49.1
27 weeks or more	5.1	3.1	1.5	1.4	1.5	17.7	17.6	6.7	7.9	(c)	5.3	8.6
With no labor force activity	20.7	11.0	10.3	6.9	8.3	46.7	34.3	29.4	30.6	17.3	17.2	38.8

[a]Data on families include people in primary families and family households with unrelated individuals.
[b]Number below the poverty level as a percent of the total.
[c]Data not shown where base is less than 80,000.

SOURCE: "Table 6. People in Families and Unrelated Individuals: Poverty Status and Work Experience, 2006," in *A Profile of the Working Poor, 2006,* U.S. Department of Labor, Bureau of Labor Statistics, August 2008, http://www.bls.gov/cps/cpswp2006.pdf (accessed December 21, 2008)

TABLE 2.12

Program participation status of household for all income levels, 2006

[Numbers in thousands]

All races	Total	In household that received means-tested assistance		In household that received means-tested assistance excluding school lunch		In household that received means-tested cash assistance		In household that received food stamps		In household which one or more persons were covered by Medicaid		Lived in public or authorized housing	
		Number	Percent	Number	Percent	Number	Percent	Number	Percent	Number	Percent	Number	Percent
All income levels													
Both sexes													
Total[a]	**296,450**	**77,058**	**26.0**	**67,738**	**22.8**	**17,056**	**5.8**	**21,780**	**7.3**	**60,453**	**20.4**	**10,250**	**3.5**
Under 18 years	73,727	28,988	39.3	24,340	33.0	5,111	6.9	9,421	12.8	22,638	30.7	3,773	5.1
18 to 24 years	28,405	7,706	27.1	7,072	24.9	1,605	5.7	2,275	8.0	6,331	22.3	1,095	3.9
25 to 34 years	39,868	10,948	27.5	9,723	24.4	1,977	5.0	3,186	8.0	8,778	22.0	1,283	3.2
35 to 44 years	42,762	10,149	23.7	8,494	19.9	2,093	4.9	2,502	5.9	7,663	17.9	1,000	2.3
45 to 54 years	43,461	8,000	18.4	7,193	16.5	2,342	5.4	1,879	4.3	6,311	14.5	931	2.1
55 to 59 years	18,221	2,812	15.4	2,677	14.7	1,074	5.9	711	3.9	2,222	12.2	353	1.9
60 to 64 years	13,970	2,235	16.0	2,167	15.5	907	6.5	566	4.1	1,814	13.0	370	2.7
65 years and over	36,035	6,221	17.3	6,072	16.8	1,947	5.4	1,241	3.4	4,696	13.0	1,444	4.0
65 to 74 years	18,998	3,253	17.1	3,159	16.6	1,033	5.4	684	3.6	2,551	13.4	644	3.4
75 years and over	17,037	2,968	17.4	2,913	17.1	914	5.4	557	3.3	2,145	12.6	800	4.7
Male													
Total	**145,486**	**35,475**	**24.4**	**31,078**	**21.4**	**7,535**	**5.2**	**9,347**	**6.4**	**27,888**	**19.2**	**4,053**	**2.8**
Under 18 years	37,643	14,653	38.9	12,286	32.6	2,537	6.7	4,726	12.6	11,435	30.4	1,925	5.1
18 to 24 years	14,422	3,488	24.2	3,149	21.8	718	5.0	947	6.6	2,797	19.4	409	2.8
25 to 34 years	20,024	4,668	23.3	4,206	21.0	810	4.0	1,093	5.5	3,780	18.9	382	1.9
35 to 44 years	21,181	4,465	21.1	3,798	17.9	880	4.2	978	4.6	3,432	16.2	295	1.4
45 to 54 years	21,296	3,748	17.6	3,338	15.7	998	4.7	782	3.7	2,947	13.8	367	1.7
55 to 59 years	8,879	1,274	14.3	1,209	13.6	490	5.5	276	3.1	988	11.1	147	1.7
60 to 64 years	6,599	932	14.1	900	13.6	396	6.0	188	2.9	757	11.5	126	1.9
65 years and over	15,443	2,248	14.6	2,193	14.2	705	4.6	357	2.3	1,752	11.3	402	2.6
65 to 74 years	8,739	1,307	15.0	1,273	14.6	411	4.7	237	2.7	1,057	12.1	216	2.5
75 years and over	6,703	941	14.0	919	13.7	294	4.4	120	1.8	695	10.4	185	2.8
Female													
Total	**150,964**	**41,582**	**27.5**	**36,660**	**24.3**	**9,521**	**6.3**	**12,433**	**8.2**	**32,566**	**21.6**	**6,197**	**4.1**
Under 18 years	36,085	14,335	39.7	12,054	33.4	2,573	7.1	4,694	13.0	11,203	31.0	1,848	5.1
18 to 24 years	13,982	4,217	30.2	3,923	28.1	887	6.3	1,328	9.5	3,535	25.3	686	4.9
25 to 34 years	19,843	6,280	31.6	5,517	27.8	1,167	5.9	2,093	10.5	4,997	25.2	901	4.5
35 to 44 years	21,582	5,684	26.3	4,696	21.8	1,213	5.6	1,524	7.1	4,230	19.6	705	3.3
45 to 54 years	22,166	4,252	19.2	3,855	17.4	1,344	6.1	1,097	4.9	3,364	15.2	564	2.5
55 to 59 years	9,342	1,538	16.5	1,468	15.7	584	6.3	435	4.7	1,234	13.2	206	2.2
60 to 64 years	7,371	1,303	17.7	1,267	17.2	511	6.9	378	5.1	1,057	14.3	244	3.3
65 years and over	20,593	3,973	19.3	3,879	18.8	1,242	6.0	884	4.3	2,944	14.3	1,042	5.1
65 to 74 years	10,259	1,947	19.0	1,886	18.4	622	6.1	447	4.4	1,494	14.6	428	4.2
75 years and over	10,334	2,026	19.6	1,994	19.3	620	6.0	437	4.2	1,450	14.0	614	5.9

TABLE 2.12

Program participation status of household for all income levels, 2006 [CONTINUED]

[Numbers in thousands]

All races	Total	In household that received means-tested assistance		In household that received means-tested assistance excluding school lunch		In household that received means-tested cash assistance		In household that received food stamps		In household which one or more persons were covered by Medicaid		Lived in public or authorized housing	
		Number	Percent	Number	Percent	Number	Percent	Number	Percent	Number	Percent	Number	Percent
Household relationship													
Total[a]	**296,450**	**77,058**	**26.0**	**67,738**	**22.8**	**17,056**	**5.8**	**21,780**	**7.3**	**60,453**	**20.4**	**10,250**	**3.5**
65 years and over	36,035	6,221	17.3	6,072	16.8	1,947	5.4	1,241	3.4	4,696	13.0	1,444	4.0
In families[b]	245,199	67,272	27.4	58,257	23.8	14,221	5.8	18,471	7.5	53,271	21.7	7,516	3.1
Householder	78,454	18,711	23.8	16,366	20.9	4,296	5.5	5,192	6.6	14,709	18.7	2,398	3.1
Under 65 years	66,065	16,793	25.4	14,516	22.0	3,612	5.5	4,837	7.3	13,167	19.9	2,196	3.3
65 years and over	12,389	1,918	15.5	1,849	14.9	684	5.5	355	2.9	1,542	12.4	202	1.6
Related children under 18 years[e]	72,609	28,343	39.0	23,774	32.7	4,942	6.8	9,202	12.7	22,096	30.4	3,738	5.1
Under 6 years	24,204	9,918	41.0	9,072	37.5	1,685	7.0	3,628	15.0	8,483	35.0	1,472	6.1
6 to 17 years	48,404	18,426	38.1	14,702	30.4	3,257	6.7	5,574	11.5	13,613	28.1	2,266	4.7
Own children 18 years and over[d]	23,279	6,377	27.4	5,840	25.1	1,944	8.4	1,525	6.6	5,340	22.9	574	2.5
In married-couple families[f]	187,788	37,434	19.9	32,267	17.2	6,161	3.3	6,573	3.5	29,661	15.8	1,782	0.9
Husbands[f]	58,964	9,333	15.8	8,173	13.9	1,771	3.0	1,572	2.7	7,333	12.4	513	0.9
Under 65 years	48,064	8,127	16.9	6,993	14.6	1,389	2.9	1,404	2.9	6,373	13.3	379	0.8
65 years and over	10,900	1,205	11.1	1,180	10.8	382	3.5	168	1.5	960	8.8	134	1.2
Wives[f]	58,964	9,333	15.8	8,173	13.9	1,771	3.0	1,572	2.7	7,333	12.4	513	0.9
Under 65 years	50,557	8,447	16.7	7,303	14.4	1,464	2.9	1,463	2.9	6,642	13.1	420	0.8
65 years and over	8,407	886	10.5	870	10.3	307	3.7	109	1.3	690	8.2	93	1.1
Related children under 18 years[e]	51,366	14,356	27.9	11,894	23.2	1,599	3.1	2,887	5.6	11,193	21.8	648	1.3
Under 6 years	17,563	5,087	29.0	4,566	26.0	471	2.7	1,131	6.4	4,306	24.5	262	1.5
6 to 17 years	33,803	9,268	27.4	7,328	21.7	1,128	3.3	1,756	5.2	6,887	20.4	386	1.1
Own children 18 years and over[d]	14,616	2,963	20.3	2,690	18.4	734	5.0	374	2.6	2,519	17.2	81	0.6
In families with male householder, no spouse present	14,188	5,289	37.3	4,565	32.2	1,215	8.6	1,323	9.3	4,148	29.2	511	3.6
Householder	5,067	1,787	35.3	1,559	30.8	413	8.2	457	9.0	1,401	27.7	191	3.8
Under 65 years	4,631	1,648	35.6	1,429	30.9	359	7.7	432	9.3	1,284	27.7	184	4.0
65 years and over	436	139	31.9	130	29.8	55	12.6	25	5.7	118	27.0	7	1.5
Related children under 18 years[e]	3,827	1,867	48.8	1,507	39.4	287	7.5	488	12.8	1,391	36.3	162	4.2
Under 6 years	1,253	742	59.3	693	55.3	123	9.8	248	19.8	647	51.6	72	5.8
6 to 17 years	2,574	1,125	43.7	814	31.6	164	6.4	240	9.3	744	28.9	90	3.5
Own children 18 years and over[d]	1,517	459	30.3	440	29.0	159	10.5	95	6.3	402	26.5	52	3.4
In families with female householder, no spouse present	43,223	24,549	56.8	21,425	49.6	6,795	15.7	10,575	24.5	19,462	45.0	5,223	12.1
Householder	14,424	7,592	52.6	6,634	46.0	2,112	14.6	3,163	21.9	5,975	41.4	1,694	11.7
Under 65 years	12,589	6,908	54.9	5,987	47.6	1,842	14.6	2,977	23.6	5,416	43.0	1,616	12.8
65 years and over	1,834	684	37.3	647	35.3	269	14.7	186	10.1	560	30.5	78	4.2
Related children under 18 years[e]	17,416	12,121	69.6	10,373	59.6	3,056	17.5	5,827	33.5	9,512	54.6	2,928	16.8
Under 6 years	5,389	4,088	75.9	3,813	70.8	1,091	20.3	2,248	41.7	3,530	65.5	1,137	21.1
6 to 17 years	12,027	8,033	66.8	6,559	54.5	1,965	16.3	3,578	29.8	5,982	49.7	1,791	14.9
Own children 18 years and over[d]	7,146	2,955	41.3	2,709	37.9	1,051	14.7	1,056	14.8	2,419	33.9	441	6.2
In unrelated subfamilies[c]	1,367	830	60.7	748	54.7	212	15.5	289	21.1	733	53.6	14	1.1
Under 18 years	719	448	62.3	403	56.0	129	18.0	173	24.1	397	55.2	7	1.0
Under 6 years	220	155	70.8	150	68.5	49	22.4	72	32.6	148	67.5	4	1.7
6 to 17 years	499	293	58.6	252	50.5	80	16.1	102	20.4	249	49.8	4	0.7
18 years and over	648	381	58.8	345	53.2	83	12.8	115	17.8	336	51.9	7	1.1

TABLE 2.12

Program participation status of household for all income levels, 2006 [CONTINUED]

[Numbers in thousands]

All races	Total	In household that received means-tested assistance		In household that received means-tested assistance excluding school lunch		In household that received means-tested cash assistance		In household that received food stamps		In household which one or more persons were covered by Medicaid		Lived in public or authorized housing	
		Number	Percent	Number	Percent	Number	Percent	Number	Percent	Number	Percent	Number	Percent
Unrelated individuals[d]	49,884	8,956	18.0	8,733	17.5	2,673	5.4	3,021	6.1	6,449	12.9	2,720	5.5
Male	24,674	4,156	16.8	3,990	16.2	1,213	4.9	1,337	5.4	3,063	12.4	1,031	4.2
Under 65 years	21,252	3,502	16.5	3,337	15.7	1,034	4.9	1,210	5.7	2,606	12.3	779	3.7
Living alone	10,629	1,166	11.0	1,166	11.0	464	4.4	459	4.3	776	7.3	515	4.8
65 years and over	3,422	654	19.1	653	19.1	180	5.3	126	3.7	457	13.4	252	7.4
Living alone	2,947	555	18.8	555	18.8	135	4.6	106	3.6	370	12.6	246	8.4
Female	25,210	4,801	19.0	4,743	18.8	1,459	5.8	1,684	6.7	3,386	13.4	1,689	6.7
Under 65 years	16,805	3,075	18.3	3,017	18.0	1,020	6.1	1,226	7.3	2,274	13.5	863	5.1
Living alone	9,687	1,573	16.2	1,573	16.2	649	6.7	721	7.4	1,053	10.9	708	7.3
65 years and over	8,404	1,726	20.5	1,726	20.5	439	5.2	458	5.4	1,112	13.2	826	9.8
Living alone	7,950	1,627	20.5	1,627	20.5	406	5.1	438	5.5	1,023	12.9	819	10.3

Notes: People who lived with someone (a nonrelative or a relative) who received aid themselves. Not every person tallied here received the aid themselves.
[a]Universe: All people except unrelated individuals under age 15 (such as foster children). Since the Current Population Survey asks income questions only to people age 15 and over, if a child under age 15 is not part of a family by birth, marriage, or adoption, we do not know their income and cannot determine whether or not they are poor. Those people are excluded from the totals so as not to affect the percentages.
[b]People in families: People who are related to the householder by birth, marriage, or adoption. People who are related to each other but not to the householder are counted elsewhere (usually as unrelated subfamilies).
[c]People in unrelated subfamilies: People who are not related to the householder, but who are related to each other, either as a married couple or as a parent-child relationship with an unmarried child under 18.
[d]Unrelated individuals: People who are not in primary families (the householder's family) or unrelated subfamilies.
[e]People in families with related children: People living in a family where at least one member is a related child—a person under 18 who is related to the householder but is not the householder or spouse.
[f]In married-couple families the householder may be either the husband or the wife.
[g]Own children: Sons and daughters, including stepchildren and adopted children, of the householder.

SOURCE: "Pov26. Program Participation Status of Household—Poverty Status of People: 2006, All Races—All Income Levels," in *Current Population Survey, 2007 Annual Social and Economic Supplement,* U.S. Census Bureau, 2007, http://pubdb3.census.gov/macro/032007/pov/new26_001_01.htm (accessed January 12, 2009)

TABLE 2.13

Program participation status of household for persons below poverty level, 2006

[Numbers in thousands]

All races	Total	In household that received means-tested assistance		In household that received means-tested assistance excluding school luch		In household that received means-tested cash assistance		In household that received food stamps		In household which one or more persons were covered by Medicaid		Lived in public or authorized housing	
		Number	Percent	Number	Percent	Number	Percent	Number	Percent	Number	Percent	Number	Percent
Below poverty level													
Both sexes													
Total[a]	36,460	24,705	67.8	22,568	61.9	7,126	19.5	13,707	37.6	19,897	54.6	6,009	16.5
Under 18 years	12,827	10,975	85.6	9,835	76.7	2,815	21.9	6,478	50.5	9,016	70.3	2,677	20.9
18 to 24 years	5,047	2,647	52.4	2,472	49.0	666	13.2	1,434	28.4	2,140	42.4	660	13.1
25 to 34 years	4,920	3,410	69.3	3,136	63.7	893	18.2	1,879	38.2	2,775	56.4	733	14.9
35 to 44 years	4,049	2,791	68.9	2,497	61.7	837	20.7	1,497	37.0	2,183	53.9	573	14.1
45 to 54 years	3,399	2,009	59.1	1,860	54.7	766	22.5	1,048	30.8	1,553	45.7	489	14.4
55 to 59 years	1,468	821	55.9	778	53.0	356	24.3	433	29.5	631	43.0	187	12.8
60 to 64 years	1,357	683	50.3	660	48.6	294	21.7	359	26.4	551	40.6	197	14.5
65 years and over	3,394	1,369	40.4	1,329	39.2	498	14.7	579	17.1	1,047	30.9	494	14.6
65 to 74 years	1,636	729	44.6	706	43.1	293	17.9	332	20.3	587	35.8	240	14.6
75 years and over	1,757	640	36.4	624	35.5	205	11.6	246	14.0	461	26.2	254	14.5
Male													
Total	16,000	10,491	65.6	9,537	59.6	2,916	18.2	5,680	35.5	8,422	52.6	2,329	14.6
Under 18 years	6,491	5,515	85.0	4,946	76.2	1,376	21.2	3,252	50.1	4,530	69.8	1,359	20.9
18 to 24 years	2,151	1,006	46.8	921	42.8	260	12.1	542	25.2	771	35.8	208	9.7
25 to 34 years	1,951	1,132	58.0	1,042	53.4	283	14.5	530	27.1	905	46.4	170	8.7
35 to 44 years	1,659	1,007	60.7	905	54.6	303	18.2	516	31.1	783	47.2	134	8.1
45 to 54 years	1,518	851	56.1	781	51.5	281	18.5	398	26.3	642	42.3	191	12.6
55 to 59 years	623	339	54.4	320	51.4	155	24.9	167	26.9	259	41.5	77	12.4
60 to 64 years	587	263	44.7	253	43.0	123	20.9	123	20.9	216	36.9	68	11.5
65 years and over	1,020	379	37.1	368	36.1	136	13.3	151	14.8	316	30.9	122	12.0
65 to 74 years	604	246	40.8	240	39.8	99	16.4	106	17.5	209	34.5	80	13.2
75 years and over	416	132	31.8	128	30.8	36	8.8	45	10.8	107	25.7	43	10.3
Female													
Total	20,460	14,214	69.5	13,031	63.7	4,210	20.6	8,027	39.2	11,475	56.1	3,680	18.0
Under 18 years	6,335	5,460	86.2	4,889	77.2	1,440	22.7	3,225	50.9	4,486	70.8	1,318	20.8
18 to 24 years	2,896	1,641	56.7	1,551	53.6	406	14.0	891	30.8	1,369	47.3	452	15.6
25 to 34 years	2,969	2,278	76.7	2,094	70.5	611	20.6	1,350	45.5	1,869	63.0	563	19.0
35 to 44 years	2,390	1,784	74.6	1,592	66.6	535	22.4	981	41.0	1,401	58.6	439	18.4
45 to 54 years	1,881	1,158	61.6	1,079	57.4	484	25.7	650	34.6	911	48.5	297	15.8
55 to 59 years	845	482	57.0	458	54.2	201	23.8	266	31.5	372	44.0	110	13.1
60 to 64 years	770	420	54.6	407	52.9	171	22.2	236	30.6	335	43.5	129	16.8
65 years and over	2,373	991	41.7	961	40.5	362	15.3	428	18.0	732	30.8	371	15.6
65 to 74 years	1,032	483	46.8	465	45.1	194	18.8	226	21.9	378	36.6	160	15.5
75 years and over	1,342	508	37.9	496	37.0	168	12.5	201	15.0	354	26.4	211	15.7

TABLE 2.13

Program participation status of household for persons below poverty level, 2006 [CONTINUED]

[Numbers in thousands]

All races / Household relationship	Total	In household that received means-tested assistance		In household that received means-tested assistance excluding school lunch		In household that received means-tested cash assistance		In household that received food stamps		In household which one or more persons were covered by Medicaid		Lived in public or authorized housing	
		Number	Percent	Number	Percent	Number	Percent	Number	Percent	Number	Percent	Number	Percent
Total[a]	**36,460**	**24,705**	**67.8**	**22,568**	**61.9**	**7,126**	**19.5**	**13,707**	**37.6**	**19,897**	**54.6**	**6,009**	**16.5**
65 years and over	3,394	1,369	40.4	1,329	39.2	498	14.7	579	17.1	1,047	30.9	494	14.6
In families[b]	25,915	20,105	77.6	18,063	69.7	5,430	21.0	11,465	44.2	16,317	63.0	4,632	17.9
Householder	7,668	5,626	73.4	5,118	66.7	1,639	21.4	3,215	41.9	4,594	59.9	1,397	18.2
Under 65 years	6,916	5,310	76.8	4,824	69.8	1,524	22.0	3,069	44.4	4,345	62.8	1,331	19.2
65 years and over	752	316	42.0	294	39.1	115	15.3	146	19.5	249	33.1	67	8.9
Related children under 18 years[e]	12,299	10,581	86.0	9,466	77.0	2,693	21.9	6,300	51.2	8,661	70.4	2,656	21.6
Under 6 years	4,830	4,126	85.4	3,854	79.8	1,004	20.8	2,538	52.5	3,568	73.9	1,089	22.6
6 to 17 years	7,468	6,455	86.4	5,612	75.1	1,689	22.6	3,762	50.4	5,094	68.2	1,566	21.0
Own children 18 years and over[g]	1,843	1,306	70.9	1,195	64.9	488	26.5	774	42.0	1,048	56.8	286	15.5
In married-couple families[f]	10,755	7,388	68.7	6,464	60.1	1,425	13.2	3,334	31.0	5,792	53.9	788	7.3
Husbands[f]	2,910	1,749	60.1	1,554	53.4	392	13.5	782	26.9	1,370	47.1	201	6.9
Under 65 years	2,419	1,612	66.7	1,420	58.7	340	14.0	716	29.6	1,256	51.9	171	7.1
65 years and over	492	137	27.8	134	27.2	53	10.7	66	13.4	114	23.1	30	6.0
Wives[f]	2,910	1,749	60.1	1,554	53.4	392	13.5	782	26.9	1,370	47.1	201	6.9
Under 65 years	2,547	1,668	65.5	1,476	57.9	354	13.9	746	29.3	1,300	51.0	186	7.3
65 years and over	363	82	22.5	78	21.6	39	10.6	35	9.8	70	19.2	15	4.2
Related children under 18 years[e]	4,182	3,372	80.6	2,917	69.8	520	12.4	1,544	36.9	2,661	63.6	350	8.4
Under 6 years	1,659	1,329	80.1	1,203	72.5	177	10.6	594	35.8	1,108	66.8	142	8.6
6 to 17 years	2,522	2,044	81.0	1,714	68.0	343	13.6	949	37.6	1,553	61.6	208	8.3
Own children 18 years and over[g]	513	340	66.3	291	56.6	96	18.7	170	33.2	251	48.9	30	5.9
In families with male householder, no spouse present	1,961	1,407	71.7	1,261	64.3	396	20.2	718	36.6	1,084	55.3	223	11.3
Householder	671	465	69.3	426	63.4	128	19.1	239	35.6	364	54.3	73	10.9
Under 65 years	627	439	70.0	403	64.4	118	18.8	228	36.3	342	54.5	71	11.4
65 years and over	44	26	60.0	22	50.3	10	23.5	11	25.5	22	50.3	2	4.0
Related children under 18 years[e]	776	630	81.2	558	71.9	157	20.2	312	40.2	495	63.8	101	13.0
Under 6 years	332	268	80.9	254	76.4	72	21.7	160	48.2	230	69.2	47	14.3
6 to 17 years	444	362	81.5	304	68.4	85	19.0	152	34.3	266	59.9	54	12.1
Own children 18 years and over[g]	160	97	60.3	93	57.8	51	31.8	60	37.4	86	53.4	26	16.3
In families with female house-holder, no spouse present	13,199	11,310	85.7	10,338	78.3	3,609	27.3	7,413	56.2	9,440	71.5	3,622	27.4
Householder	4,087	3,412	83.5	3,138	76.8	1,118	27.4	2,195	53.7	2,860	70.0	1,123	27.5
Under 65 years	3,814	3,239	84.9	2,981	78.1	1,057	27.7	2,117	55.5	2,728	71.5	1,083	28.4
65 years and over	273	172	63.2	158	57.8	61	22.4	78	28.7	132	48.4	40	14.7
Related children under 18 years[e]	7,341	6,579	89.6	5,991	81.6	2,016	27.5	4,444	60.5	5,505	75.0	2,204	30.0
Under 6 years	2,839	2,529	89.1	2,397	84.4	755	26.6	1,784	62.8	2,230	78.5	900	31.7
6 to 17 years	4,502	4,050	90.0	3,594	79.8	1,261	28.0	2,661	59.1	3,275	72.7	1,304	29.0
Own children 18 years and over[g]	1,169	869	74.3	812	69.4	341	29.1	544	46.5	711	60.8	229	19.6
In unrelated subfamilies[c]	567	470	82.9	451	79.4	148	26.1	233	41.1	443	78.1	14	2.5
Under 18 years	323	272	84.2	260	80.6	97	30.2	144	44.6	256	79.4	7	2.1
Under 6 years	126	108	86.1	104	82.8	38	30.1	59	46.9	104	82.5	4	2.9
6 to 17 years	197	164	83.0	156	79.2	60	30.2	85	43.2	153	77.5	3	1.7
18 years and over	245	198	81.2	190	77.9	51	20.8	89	36.5	187	76.4	7	2.9

TABLE 2.13

Program participation status of household for persons below poverty level, 2006 [CONTINUED]

[Numbers in thousands]

All races	Total	In household that received means-tested assistance		In household that received means-tested assistance excluding school luch		In household that received means-tested cash assistance		In household that received food stamps		In household which one or more persons were covered by Medicaid		Lived in public or authorized housing	
		Number	Percent	Number	Percent	Number	Percent	Number	Percent	Number	Percent	Number	Percent
Unrelated individuals[d]	9,977	4,130	41.4	4,054	40.6	1,548	15.5	2,008	20.1	3,137	31.4	1,363	13.7
Male	4,388	1,718	39.2	1,672	38.1	632	14.4	819	18.7	1,333	30.4	530	12.1
Under 65 years	3,945	1,534	38.9	1,489	37.7	567	14.4	754	19.1	1,183	30.0	441	11.2
Living alone	1,537	634	41.3	634	41.3	286	18.6	349	22.7	475	30.9	286	18.6
65 years and over	443	184	41.5	183	41.2	65	14.6	65	14.7	151	34.0	89	20.1
Living alone	365	157	43.0	157	43.0	53	14.5	58	15.8	130	35.5	86	23.5
Female	5,589	2,412	43.2	2,382	42.6	916	16.4	1,189	21.3	1,804	32.3	834	14.9
Under 65 years	3,985	1,766	44.3	1,737	43.6	680	17.1	909	22.8	1,347	33.8	526	13.2
Living alone	1,785	932	52.2	932	52.2	439	24.6	561	31.4	665	37.3	440	24.7
65 years and over	1,604	645	40.2	645	40.2	235	14.7	280	17.5	457	28.5	307	19.1
Living alone	1,482	607	40.9	607	40.9	219	14.8	266	17.9	423	28.5	302	20.4

Notes: People who lived with someone (a nonrelative or a relative) who received aid. Not every person tallied here received the aid themselves.

aUniverse: All people except unrelated individuals under age 15 (such as foster children). Since the Current Population Survey asks income questions only to people age 15 and over, if a child under age 15 is not part of a family by birth, marriage, or adoption, we do not know their income and cannot determine whether or not they are poor. Those people are excluded from the totals so as not to affect the percentages.

bPeople in families: People who are related to the householder by birth, marriage, or adoption. People who are related to each other but not to the householder are counted elsewhere (usually as unrelated subfamilies).

cPeople in unrelated subfamilies: People who are not related to the householder, but who are related to each other, either as a married couple or as a parent-child relationship with an unmarried child under 18.

dUnrelated individuals: People who are not in primary families (the householder's family) or unrelated subfamilies.

ePeople in families with related children: People living in a family where at least one member is a related child—a person under 18 who is related to the householder but is not the householder or spouse.

fIn married-couple families the householder may be either the husband or the wife.

gOwn children: Sons and daughters, including stepchildren and adopted children, of the householder.

SOURCE: "Pov26: Program Participation Status of Household—Poverty Status of People: 2006, All Races—Below Poverty Level," in *Current Population Survey, 2007 Annual Social and Economic Supplement*, U.S. Census Bureau, 2007, http://pubdb3.census.gov/macro/032007/pov/new26_002_01.htm (accessed January 12, 2009)

Entering and Exiting Poverty

For most poor Americans poverty is not a static condition. Some people near the poverty level improve their economic status within two years or less, whereas others at near-poverty levels become poor through economic catastrophes, such as an illness or job loss. Most data collected by the Census Bureau reflect a single point in time—in other words, showing how many people are in poverty or participating in a means-tested government program in a certain month. These surveys, however, do not reflect the dynamic nature of poverty for individual people and families.

The Census Bureau collects longitudinal information (measurements over time for specific individuals or families) about poverty and government program participation rates in its Survey of Income and Program Participation (SIPP). This makes it possible to measure the movement of individuals and families into and out of poverty (entry and exit rates) and the duration of poverty spells (the number of months in poverty for those who were not poor during the first interview month, but who became poor at some point during the study) as well as the length of time individuals and families use government programs.

In *Dynamics of Economic Well-Being, Poverty 1996–1999* (July 2003, http://www.census.gov/prod/2003pubs/p70-91.pdf), John Iceland of the Census Bureau uses data from the 1996 SIPP panel to examine poverty in the period from January 1996 through December 1999. He focuses on monthly measures of poverty and distinguishes between short- and long-term poverty. Some highlights of the survey include:

- More than one out of three people (34.2%) were poor for at least two months in the four years between 1996 and 1999.

- About 2% of the population were chronically poor. That is, they were poor during all 48 months from January 1996 through December 1999.

- Nonelderly adults were more likely to exit poverty than children and the elderly.

- Children had the highest entry rates into poverty and, along with retirement-age adults, had a low exit rate.

- More than half of all poverty spells lasted two to four months, whereas 11.9% lasted more than 21 months.

RACE AND AGE. Iceland notes that of the poor in 1996, non-Hispanic whites (57.1%) were more likely to have left poverty by 1999 than either African-Americans (42.4%) or Hispanics (41.6%). Also, non-Hispanic whites were less likely to have entered poverty by 1999 than African-Americans or Hispanics.

The elderly (often on fixed incomes) and children were less likely to exit poverty than were people of other ages. About 32.4% of the elderly and 47.9% of children under 18 years of age who were poor in 1996 were able to escape poverty by 1999. Adults 18 to 64 years of age were the most likely to escape—53.9% moved out of poverty. However, only 3.3% of the elderly entered poverty by 1999, compared to 4.5% of children under 18 years of age.

FAMILY STATUS. According to Iceland, poor families headed by married couples were much more likely than other poor family types to have left poverty by 1999, underscoring how having two potential wage earners in a family helps protect a family from poverty. Of the poor families headed by married couples in 1996, 59.7% were able to escape poverty by 1999. Only 39.4% of the poor families of other types recovered from poverty by 1996. Families headed by married couples were also significantly less likely to have entered poverty by 1999. With at least two adults in the household, these families are more likely to have at least one person working than a family headed by a single person.

Having a Job Does Not Guarantee Escape from Poverty

The working poor are those people who participated in the labor force for at least 27 weeks (either working or looking for work) and who lived in families with incomes below the official poverty level. Over 7.4 million workers in 2006 (5.1% of individuals aged 16 and older in the labor force) found that their jobs did not provide enough income to keep them out of poverty. (See Table 2.14.)

In 2006, 3.9 million working women and 3.6 million working men had incomes below the poverty level. (See Table 2.14.) Therefore, working women had a higher poverty rate (5.8%) than working men (4.5%). Even though nearly three-quarters of the working poor were white (5.3 million of 7.4 million workers, or 71.3%), African-American and Hispanic workers continued to experience poverty while employed at more than twice the rates of whites. African-Americans (9.7%) and Hispanics (9.8%) with at least 27 weeks in the labor force had a far higher poverty rate than whites (4.5%) or Asian-Americans (3.8%). Younger workers were more likely to be in poverty than older workers. Much of the reason for this is that many younger workers are still in school and work at part-time or entry-level jobs that often do not pay well.

In general, the lower the educational level, the higher the risk of poverty among workers. Among workers in the labor force for at least 27 weeks in 2006, those with less than a high school diploma had a much higher poverty rate (13.8%) than high school graduates (6.3%). (See Table 2.15.) Far lower poverty rates were reported for workers with an associate's degree (4.4%) or a four-year college degree (1.4%). African-American and Hispanic workers, regardless of education levels, had higher poverty rates than white workers.

TABLE 2.14

Poverty status of people in the labor force for 27 weeks or more, by age, sex, race, and Hispanic origin, 2006

[Numbers in thousands]

Age and sex	Total	White	Black or African-American	Asian	Hispanic or Latino ethnicity	Below poverty level Total	White	Black or African-American	Asian	Hispanic or Latino ethnicity	Rate[a] Total	White	Black or African-American	Asian	Hispanic or Latino ethnicity
Total, 16 years and older	**145,229**	**118,915**	**16,437**	**6,624**	**19,985**	**7,427**	**5,295**	**1,601**	**251**	**1,956**	**5.1**	**4.5**	**9.7**	**3.8**	**9.8**
16 to 19 years	4,128	3,461	440	65	620	432	320	91	4	91	10.5	9.2	20.7	b	14.7
20 to 24 years	13,299	10,743	1,706	436	2,420	1,480	1,079	306	39	266	11.1	10.0	17.9	8.9	11.0
25 to 34 years	31,831	25,212	4,012	1,704	6,259	2,196	1,515	527	72	689	6.9	6.0	13.1	4.2	11.0
35 to 44 years	34,617	27,815	4,184	1,859	5,267	1,674	1,212	333	59	546	4.8	4.4	8.0	3.2	10.4
45 to 54 years	34,977	28,926	3,866	1,536	3,528	1,050	710	243	59	241	3.0	2.5	6.3	3.8	6.8
55 to 64 years	20,618	17,658	1,812	843	1,496	498	388	81	14	102	2.4	2.2	4.4	1.7	6.8
65 years and older	5,759	5,100	417	182	396	96	71	22	3	21	1.7	1.4	5.2	1.9	5.3
Men, 16 years and older	**78,457**	**65,533**	**7,648**	**3,552**	**12,177**	**3,564**	**2,726**	**547**	**147**	**1,187**	**4.5**	**4.2**	**7.2**	**4.1**	**9.7**
16 to 19 years	2,054	1,701	229	38	360	201	129	55	4	51	9.8	7.6	24.0	b	14.1
20 to 24 years	7,185	5,926	822	214	1,498	668	520	98	17	167	9.3	8.8	11.9	8.0	11.2
25 to 34 years	17,740	14,397	1,921	930	4,021	1,064	829	147	49	441	6.0	5.8	7.7	5.3	11.0
35 to 44 years	18,951	15,618	1,911	1,019	3,191	821	657	99	30	325	4.3	4.2	5.2	3.0	10.2
45 to 54 years	18,433	15,513	1,778	811	1,999	528	358	111	37	130	2.9	2.3	6.3	4.6	6.5
55 to 64 years	10,894	9,507	789	441	873	231	197	23	5	57	2.1	2.1	3.0	1.2	6.6
65 years and older	3,200	2,870	197	100	235	52	36	13	3	15	1.6	1.3	6.7	3.0	6.3
Women, 16 years and older	**66,772**	**53,382**	**8,790**	**3,072**	**7,808**	**3,863**	**2,569**	**1,054**	**104**	**769**	**5.8**	**4.8**	**12.0**	**3.4**	**9.8**
16 to 19 years	2,074	1,760	211	27	261	232	190	36	—	40	11.2	10.8	17.0	—	15.5
20 to 24 years	6,114	4,816	884	222	922	812	559	208	22	99	13.3	11.6	23.5	9.7	10.7
25 to 34 years	14,090	10,816	2,090	774	2,238	1,132	687	379	23	247	8.0	6.3	18.1	2.9	11.0
35 to 44 years	15,666	12,197	2,273	840	2,075	854	555	233	29	221	5.4	4.6	10.3	3.5	10.6
45 to 54 years	16,544	13,413	2,088	725	1,529	522	352	132	21	111	3.2	2.6	6.3	2.9	7.3
55 to 64 years	9,724	8,151	1,023	403	623	268	191	57	9	44	2.8	2.3	5.6	2.3	7.1
65 years and older	2,558	2,230	220	82	161	44	35	8	—	6	1.7	1.6	3.8	0.5	3.8

[a]Number below the poverty level as a percent of the total in the labor force for 27 weeks or more.
[b]Data not shown where base is less than 80,000.
Note: Estimates for the race groups shown (white, black or African-American, and Asian) do not sum to totals because data are not presented for all races. Persons whose ethnicity is identified as Hispanic or Latino may be of any race. Dash represents or rounds to zero.

SOURCE: "Table 2. People in the Labor Force for 27 Weeks or More: Poverty Status by Age, Sex, Race, and Hispanic or Latino Ethnicity, 2006," in A Profile of the Working Poor, 2006, U.S. Department of Labor, Bureau of Labor Statistics, August 2008, http://www.bls.gov/cps/cpswp2006.pdf (accessed December 21, 2008)

TABLE 2.15

Poverty status by educational attainment, race and Hispanic origin, and sex, 2006

[Numbers in thousands]

Educational attainment, race, and Hispanic or Latino ethnicity	Total	Men	Women	Below poverty level Total	Men	Women	Rate[a] Total	Men	Women
Total, 16 years and older	**145,229**	**78,457**	**66,772**	**7,427**	**3,564**	**3,863**	**5.1**	**4.5**	**5.8**
Less than a high school diploma	16,229	10,358	5,870	2,241	1,309	932	13.8	12.6	15.9
Less than 1 year of high school	5,028	3,429	1,599	764	515	248	15.2	15.0	15.5
1–3 years of high school	9,167	5,691	3,476	1,238	672	565	13.5	11.8	16.3
4 years of high school, no diploma	2,034	1,239	795	239	121	118	11.8	9.8	14.8
High school graduates, no college[b]	43,273	24,361	18,911	2,718	1,238	1,479	6.3	5.1	7.8
Some college or associate degree	41,261	20,315	20,946	1,827	705	1,122	4.4	3.5	5.4
Some college, no degree	27,667	13,993	13,674	1,381	521	860	5.0	3.7	6.3
Associate degree	13,594	6,322	7,272	446	184	262	3.3	2.9	3.6
Bachelor's degree and higher[c]	44,466	23,422	21,044	642	312	330	1.4	1.3	1.6
White, 16 years and older	**118,915**	**65,533**	**53,382**	**5,295**	**2,726**	**2,569**	**4.5**	**4.2**	**4.8**
Less than a high school diploma	13,225	8,742	4,482	1,672	1,061	611	12.6	12.1	13.6
Less than 1 year of high school	4,331	3,051	1,280	661	463	198	15.3	15.2	15.4
1–3 years of high school	7,354	4,726	2,628	859	517	342	11.7	10.9	13.0
4 years of high school, no diploma	1,540	966	575	152	80	72	9.9	8.3	12.5
High school graduates, no college[b]	35,165	20,169	14,996	1,841	879	961	5.2	4.4	6.4
Some college or associate degree	33,698	16,973	16,724	1,276	537	740	3.8	3.2	4.4
Some college, no degree	22,482	11,643	10,839	982	408	574	4.4	3.5	5.3
Associate degree	11,216	5,330	5,886	295	129	166	2.6	2.4	2.8
Bachelor's degree and higher[c]	36,828	19,648	17,179	506	249	256	1.4	1.3	1.5
Black or African-American, 16 years and older	**16,437**	**7,648**	**8,790**	**1,601**	**547**	**1,054**	**9.7**	**7.2**	**12.0**
Less than a high school diploma	1,933	1,014	919	421	156	265	21.8	15.4	28.9
Less than 1 year of high school	275	151	123	51	23	27	18.4	15.2	22.3
1–3 years of high school	1,315	672	643	299	100	199	22.7	14.9	30.9
4 years of high school, no diploma	343	190	153	72	33	39	21.0	17.1	25.7
High school graduates, no college[b]	5,863	2,940	2,923	711	264	446	12.1	9.0	15.3
Some college or associate degree	5,222	2,184	3,038	399	95	305	7.6	4.3	10.0
Some college, no degree	3,634	1,542	2,092	295	63	232	8.1	4.1	11.1
Associate degree	1,587	642	946	105	32	73	6.6	5.0	7.7
Bachelor's degree and higher[c]	3,420	1,510	1,910	70	32	38	2.0	2.1	2.0
Asian, 16 years and older	**6,624**	**3,552**	**3,072**	**251**	**147**	**104**	**3.8**	**4.1**	**3.4**
Less than a high school diploma	563	283	281	57	33	24	10.1	11.7	8.4
Less than 1 year of high school	267	124	143	25	12	13	9.4	9.8	9.0
1–3 years of high school	204	112	92	25	17	8	12.3	14.8	9.1
4 years of high school, no diploma	93	46	46	7	4	2	7.3	(d)	(d)
High school graduates, no college[b]	1,229	674	555	76	46	30	6.2	6.8	5.5
Some college or associate degree	1,201	598	603	62	39	23	5.1	6.5	3.8
Some college, no degree	744	403	342	43	26	17	5.8	6.5	5.1
Associate degree	457	196	261	18	13	5	4.0	6.6	2.1
Bachelor's degree and higher[c]	3,631	1,997	1,633	56	29	27	1.5	1.4	1.7
Hispanic or Latino ethnicity, 16 years and older	**19,985**	**12,177**	**7,808**	**1,956**	**1,187**	**769**	**9.8**	**9.7**	**9.8**
Less than a high school diploma	6,795	4,783	2,012	1,123	761	361	16.5	15.9	18.0
Less than 1 year of high school	3,473	2,508	965	587	419	168	16.9	16.7	17.4
1–3 years of high school	2,739	1,883	856	451	288	163	16.5	15.3	19.1
4 years of high school, no diploma	582	392	190	84	54	30	14.5	13.9	15.8
High school graduates, no college[b]	6,087	3,701	2,386	548	298	251	9.0	8.0	10.5
Some college or associate degree	4,498	2,343	2,155	222	96	126	4.9	4.1	5.8
Some college, no degree	3,170	1,735	1,435	174	77	97	5.5	4.4	6.8
Associate degree	1,328	608	720	48	19	29	3.6	3.2	4.0
Bachelor's degree and higher[c]	2,605	1,350	1,255	63	32	31	2.4	2.4	2.5

[a]Number below the poverty level as a percent of the total in the labor force for 27 weeks or more.
[b]Includes persons with a high school diploma or the equivalent.
[c]Includes persons with bachelor's, master's, professional, or doctoral degrees.
[d]Data not shown where base is less than 80,000.
Note: Estimates for the race groups shown (white, black or African-American, and Asian) do not sum to totals because data are not presented for all races. Persons whose ethnicity is identified as Hispanic or Latino may be of any race.

SOURCE: "Table 3. People in the Labor Force for 27 Weeks or More: Poverty Status by Educational Attainment, Race, Hispanic or Latino Ethnicity, and Sex, 2006," in *A Profile of the Working Poor, 2006*, U.S. Department of Labor, Bureau of Labor Statistics, August 2008, http://www.bls.gov/cps/cpswp2006.pdf (accessed December 21, 2008)

Women had a higher poverty rate than men at all educational levels and among all race and ethnic groups. The highest poverty rate (28.9%) was for African-American women workers without a high school diploma.

In 2006 working families headed by married couples without children were less likely than other family types to be poor (1.1%). (See Table 2.16.) The presence of children under the age of 18 increased the married-couple poverty

TABLE 2.16

Poverty status of families, by presence of related children and work experience of family members, 2006

[Numbers in thousands]

Characteristic	Total families	At or above poverty level	Below poverty level	Rate*
Total primary families	**65,388**	**61,429**	**3,960**	**6.1**
With related children under 18 years	36,459	33,033	3,426	9.4
Without children	28,929	28,396	533	1.8
With one member in the labor force	27,559	24,156	3,403	12.3
With two or more members in the labor force	37,829	37,273	557	1.5
With two members	31,948	31,428	520	1.6
With three or more members	5,881	5,845	36	.6
Married-couple families	49,703	48,058	1,645	3.3
With related children under 18 years	26,502	25,120	1,382	5.2
Without children	23,200	22,937	263	1.1
With one member in the labor force	16,764	15,500	1,264	7.5
Husband	12,436	11,415	1,022	8.2
Wife	3,710	3,499	211	5.7
Relative	618	586	31	5.1
With two or more members in the labor force	32,938	32,557	381	1.2
With two members	28,007	27,644	362	1.3
With three or more members	4,932	4,913	19	.4
Families maintained by women	11,273	9,333	1,940	17.2
With related children under 18 years	7,655	5,883	1,772	23.2
Without children	3,618	3,450	168	4.6
With one member in the labor force	8,107	6,292	1,815	22.4
Householder	6,675	5,109	1,565	23.5
Relative	1,432	1,182	250	17.5
With two or more members in the labor force	3,166	3,041	125	3.9
Families maintained by men	4,412	4,038	374	8.5
With related children under 18 years	2,302	2,030	272	11.8
Without children	2,111	2,008	102	4.8
With one member in the labor force	2,687	2,364	324	12.0
Householder	2,230	1,978	252	11.3
Relative	457	386	71	15.6
With two or more members in the labor force	1,725	1,674	51	2.9

*Number below the poverty level as a percent of the total in the labor force for 27 weeks or more.
Note: Data relate to primary families with at least one member in the labor force for 27 weeks or more.

SOURCE: "Table 5. Primary Families: Poverty Status, Presence of Related Children, and Work Experience of Family Members in the Labor Force for 27 Weeks or More, 2006," in *A Profile of the Working Poor, 2006*, U.S. Department of Labor, Bureau of Labor Statistics, August 2008, http://www.bls.gov/cps/cpswp 2006.pdf (accessed December 21, 2008).

rate to 5.2%, reflecting the added monetary burdens of raising children and the decreased likelihood that a family will have two adults working full time. Single women with children were the most likely to be living in poverty (23.2%), although a significant portion of single men with children were among the working poor (11.8%).

In a family headed by a married couple, a greater likelihood exists that two members of the family are working than exists in a single-parent family. Two-income families are rarely poor. Only 1.2% of families headed by married couples with two or more wage earners were poor in 2006. (See Table 2.16.) In *A Profile of the Working Poor, 2006* (August 2008, http://www.bls.gov/cps/cpswp2006.pdf), the Bureau of Labor Statistics states that of the 3.9 million working-poor families, 1.9 million (48.9%) were families maintained by women. Working women who were the sole supporters of their families had the highest poverty rate: 22.4%.

Several factors affect the poverty status of working families: the size of the family, the number of workers in the family, the characteristics of the workers, and various labor market problems. The addition of a child puts a financial strain on the family and increases the chances that a parent might have to stay home to care for the child. Even though a child in a single-parent family may work, children are usually employed for low pay and at part-time jobs. In addition, the more education a person has, the more his or her job is likely to pay. Single mothers are more likely to have less education than married women with children.

Finally, the labor market plays a major role in whether a working family lives in poverty. Three major labor market problems contributed to poverty among workers in 2006: unemployment, low earnings, and involuntary part-time employment. Only 0.7% of workers who did not suffer from any of these problems were poor in 2006. (See Table 2.17.) By contrast, 22.3% of low-paid workers were in poverty. Unemployment accounted for the poverty of 7.2% of workers, and involuntary part-time work for 2.4%. However, it was the combination of two or more factors that had the

TABLE 2.17

Poverty status and labor market problems of full-time wage and salary workers, 2006

[Numbers in thousands]

Labor market problems	Total	At or above poverty level	Below poverty level	Rate[a]
Total, full-time wage and salary workers	114,265	110,285	3,980	3.5
No unemployment, involuntary part-time employment, or low earnings[b]	94,359	93,708	652	.7
Unemployment only	5,467	5,071	396	7.2
Involuntary part-time employment only	2,530	2,468	62	2.4
Low earnings only	8,547	6,641	1,906	22.3
Unemployment and involuntary part-time employment	941	867	75	7.9
Unemployment and low earnings	1,262	760	501	39.7
Involuntary part-time employment and low earnings	790	582	208	26.4
Unemployment, involuntary part-time employment, and low earnings	369	188	181	49.0
Unemployment (alone or with other problems)	8,039	6,886	1,153	14.3
Involuntary part-time employment (alone or with other problems)	4,631	4,105	526	11.4
Low earnings (alone or with other problems)	10,968	8,171	2,797	25.5

[a]Number below the poverty level as a percent of the total in the labor force for 27 weeks or more.
[b]The low-earnings threshold in 2006 was $296.72 per week.

SOURCE: "Table 8. People in the Labor Force for 27 Weeks or More: Poverty Status and Labor Market Problems of Full-Time Wage and Salary Workers, 2006," in *A Profile of the Working Poor, 2006*, U.S. Department of Labor, Bureau of Labor Statistics, August 2008, http://www.bls.gov/cps/cpswp2006.pdf (accessed December 21, 2008)

most devastating effect on families. Among workers who experienced unemployment, low earnings, and involuntary part-time employment, 49% were in poverty.

Duration of Program Spells

In *Dynamics of Economic Well-Being: Participation in Government Programs, 2001 through 2003—Who Gets Assistance* (October 2006, http://www.census.gov/prod/2006pubs/p70-108.pdf), a Census Bureau report using SIPP data that focuses on the use of government assistance programs by families and individuals, Tracy A. Loveless and Jan Tin of the Census Bureau examine the use of government programs over the survey period. Some highlights of the survey include:

• In 2003 one out of five (20%) people took part in one or more major aid program (Housing Assistance, Supplemental Security Income [SSI], Temporary Assistance for Needy Families [TANF]/general assistance, food stamps, or Medicaid) for at least one month. (See Figure 2.3.)

• More individuals participated in Medicaid (16% for at least one month in 2003) than in any other single aid program.(See Figure 2.3.)

• In an average month in 2003, 50.8% of people in poverty received benefits, compared to only 9.7% of people who were not poor. (See Figure 2.4.)

• In 2003, 48% of all households headed by a single female participated in a major means-tested program for at least one month, compared to 25.7% of single-

male households and 13.7% of married-couple households. (See Figure 2.5.)

• Adults who had not graduated from high school were more likely than high school graduates to participate in means-tested programs in an average month in 2003 (25.6% and 11.7%, respectively). (See Figure 2.6.)

The length of time people received assistance, referred to as a spell, differed by program. As Figure 2.7 shows, the average number of months for receiving any means-tested assistance between January 2001 and December 2003 was 7.2 months. The spell length for TANF/general assistance (4.9 months) was shorter than that for food stamps (7.7 months) and Medicaid (7.6 months). The spell length for SSI was longest (15 months).

Table 2.18 gives more detail about the characteristics of people by the length of time they participated in major means-tested programs between 2001 and 2003. Among racial and ethnic groups, non-Hispanic whites (7 months), Hispanics (7.2 months), and African-Americans (7.5 months) had similar median durations of participation in means-tested programs, whereas Asians and Pacific Islanders (3.9 months) had a significantly lower median duration of program participation. Adults who had not graduated from high school had a longer median duration of participation (7.4 months) than did high school graduates (5.6 months) or those with at least some college (3.9 months), reflecting the increased economic opportunities of those with higher educational attainments.

Families had a longer median duration of participation in major means-tested programs than did households

FIGURE 2.3

Program participation rates for major means-tested programs, 2001, 2002, and 2003

[Percent of noninstitutionalized civilian population]

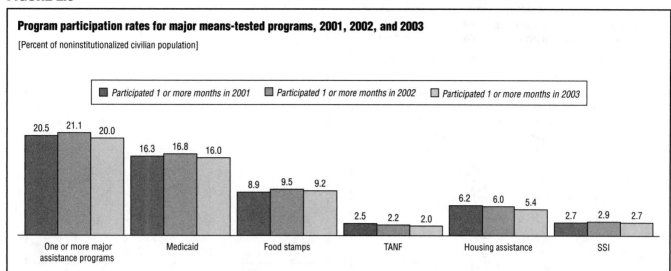

Notes: TANF is Temporary Assistance for Needy Families. SSI is Supplemental Security Income.

SOURCE: Tracy A. Loveless and Jan Tin, "Figure 4. Program Participation Rates for Major Means-Tested Programs: 2001, 2002, and 2003," in *Dynamics of Economic Well-Being: Participation in Government Programs, 2001 through 2003, Who Gets Assistance?* Current Population Reports, U.S. Census Bureau, October 2006, http://www.census.gov/prod/2006pubs/p70-108.pdf (accessed January 4, 2009)

FIGURE 2.4

Average monthly participation rates in major means-tested programs by poverty status, 2001, 2002 and 2003

[Percent of noninstitutionalized civilian population]

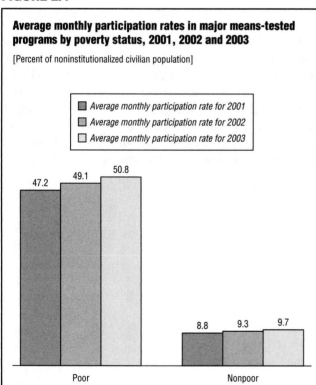

SOURCE: Tracy A. Loveless and Jan Tin, "Figure 7. Average Monthly Participation Rates in Major Means-Tested Programs by Poverty Status: 2001, 2002, and 2003," in *Dynamics of Economic Well-Being: Participation in Government Programs, 2001 through 2003, Who Gets Assistance?* Current Population Reports, U.S. Census Bureau, October 2006, http://www.census.gov/prod/2006pubs/p70-108.pdf (accessed January 4, 2009)

FIGURE 2.5

Program participation for one or more months in major means-tested programs by family type, 2001, 2002, and 2003

[Percent of noninstitutionalized civilian population]

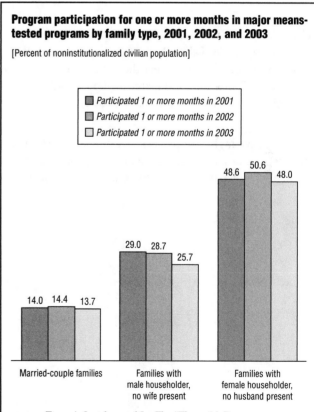

SOURCE: Tracy A. Loveless and Jan Tin, "Figure 14. Program Participation for 1 or More Months in Major Means-Tested Programs by Family Type: 2001, 2002, and 2003," in *Dynamics of Economic Well-Being: Participation in Government Programs, 2001 through 2003, Who Gets Assistance?* Current Population Reports, U.S. Census Bureau, October 2006, http://www.census.gov/prod/2006pubs/p70-108.pdf (accessed January 4, 2009)

FIGURE 2.6

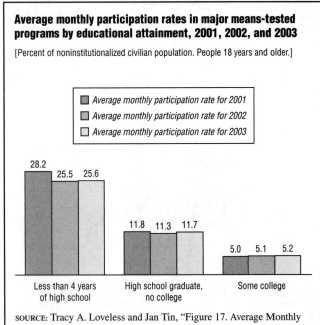

Average monthly participation rates in major means-tested programs by educational attainment, 2001, 2002, and 2003

[Percent of noninstitutionalized civilian population. People 18 years and older.]

- ■ Average monthly participation rate for 2001
- ■ Average monthly participation rate for 2002
- ■ Average monthly participation rate for 2003

28.2 25.5 25.6

11.8 11.3 11.7

5.0 5.1 5.2

Less than 4 years of high school | High school graduate, no college | Some college

SOURCE: Tracy A. Loveless and Jan Tin, "Figure 17. Average Monthly Participation Rates in Major Means-Tested Programs by Educational Attainment: 2001, 2002, and 2003," in *Dynamics of Economic Well-Being: Participation in Government Programs, 2001 through 2003, Who Gets Assistance?* Current Population Reports, U.S. Census Bureau, October 2006, http://www.census.gov/prod/2006pubs/p70-108.pdf (accessed January 4, 2009)

FIGURE 2.7

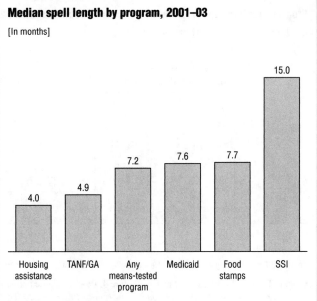

Median spell length by program, 2001–03

[In months]

15.0

4.0 4.9 7.2 7.6 7.7

Housing assistance | TANF/GA | Any means-tested program | Medicaid | Food stamps | SSI

Notes: TANF is Temporary Assistance for Needy Families. GA is government assistance. SSI is Supplemental Security Income.

SOURCE: Tracy A. Loveless and Jan Tin, "Figure 20. Median Spell Length by Program: January 2001–December 2003," in *Dynamics of Economic Well-Being: Participation in Government Programs, 2001 through 2003, Who Gets Assistance?* Current Population Reports, U.S. Census Bureau, October 2006, http://www.census.gov/prod/2006pubs/p70-108.pdf (accessed January 4, 2009)

of unrelated individuals (7.2 months and 5.2 months, respectively). (See Table 2.18.) Among families, those headed by single females spent the longest time in these programs (7.7 months), compared to households headed by single males (7.3 months) and married couples (6.9 months).

Not surprisingly, people who were not employed full time and families with incomes under the poverty line had the longest median durations of participation in means-tested programs. Those who were employed full time spent a median of 3.8 months in these programs, compared to 6.6 months for those employed part time and 7.2 months for those who were either unemployed or not in the labor force. (See Table 2.18.) Families under the poverty line spent a median of 10 months participating in means-tested programs, whereas families with incomes above the poverty line spent a median of only six months in these programs.

TABLE 2.18

Median spell length in major means-tested programs, by program and selected characteristics, 2001–03

[In months]

Characteristic	Any means-tested programs[a] Median	TANF/GA Median	Supplemental Security Income Median	Food stamps Median	Medicaid Median	Housing assistance[b] Median
All recipients[c]	7.2	4.9	15.0	7.7	7.6	4.0
Race and Hispanic origin[d]						
White	7.1	4.0	15.0	7.4	7.6	3.9
Not Hispanic	7.0	4.0	11.7	7.5	7.6	3.9
Black	7.5	6.5	11.8	8.6	7.9	7.5
Asian or Pacific Islander	3.9	11.4	(X)	7.1	7.0	3.7
Hispanic	7.2	4.0	22.3	7.0	7.7	3.9
Not Hispanic	7.2	5.4	11.9	7.8	7.6	4.0
Age[e]						
Under 18 years	7.9	6.3	11.3	8.8	9.7	7.0
18 to 64 years	5.4	4.0	15.0	7.1	7.4	3.9
65 years and older	4.0	(B)	15.7	19.8	4.9	7.9
Sex						
Men	7.0	5.7	15.2	7.2	7.7	3.9
Women	7.3	4.4	12.0	8.2	7.6	5.0
Educational attainment (people 18 and older)						
Less than high school graduate	7.4	4.3	19.7	10.2	7.7	7.2
High school graduate, no college	5.6	3.9	16.2	7.0	7.2	3.9
Some college	3.9	3.9	7.9	5.2	5.0	3.8
Disability status (people 15 to 64 years old)						
With a work disability	7.8	4.0	19.3	11.6	9.3	7.6
With no work disability	4.5	4.0	7.8	6.5	7.1	3.8
Residence						
Metropolitan	7.1	5.9	11.9	7.6	7.6	4.0
Central city	7.1	6.9	11.9	7.8	7.6	4.4
Noncentral city	7.2	5.6	13.4	7.3	7.6	3.9
Nonmetropolitan	7.4	3.8	19.0	7.9	7.9	3.9
Region						
Northeast	7.2	7.2	15.6	9.0	7.6	4.0
Midwest	7.3	5.3	11.7	7.7	7.8	7.3
South	7.2	3.8	12.9	8.0	7.6	3.9
West	7.0	5.1	11.5	6.1	7.6	3.9
Family status						
In families	7.2	4.9	11.5	7.6	7.7	4.0
In married-couple families	6.9	3.9	11.5	6.0	7.3	3.8
In families with a female householder, no husband present	7.7	5.8	11.3	8.8	9.9	7.6
In families with a male householder, no wife present	7.3	3.8	15.7	8.4	7.8	3.8
Unrelated individuals	5.2	4.6	(X)	9.5	7.6	3.9
Employment and labor force status (people 18 and older)						
Employed full-time[f]	3.8	3.7	3.9	3.9	3.9	3.7
Employed part-time	6.6	3.7	11.6	6.3	7.3	4.0
Unemployed	7.2	3.9	(B)	8.4	7.5	5.1
Not in labor force	7.2	4.7	19.0	11.4	7.5	7.3

TABLE 2.18

Median spell length in major means-tested programs, by program and selected characteristics, 2001–03 [CONTINUED]

[In months]

Characteristic	Any means-tested programs[a] Median	TANF/GA Median	Supplemental Security Income Median	Food stamps Median	Medicaid Median	Housing assistance[b] Median
Family income-to-poverty ratio[g]						
Under 1.00	10.0	5.9	(X)	11.5	11.4	7.6
1.00 and over	6.0	3.9	11.3	5.8	7.3	3.8

(X) Not applicable. (B) The sample size is too small for analysis.

[a]Major means-tested programs include Temporary Assistance for Needy Families (TANF), General Assistance (GA), Supplemental Security Income (SSI), food stamps, Medicaid, and housing assistance.

[b]Median duration cannot be computed when more than half of the spells are continuing in the last month of data collection. (This situation is especially likely to occur for elderly recipients whose incomes from other sources are unlikely to rise over time.)

[c]Median duration for each program is derived only for those who begin participating in each program at the start of the survey, while those who are already in the program at the start of the survey are excluded from the analysis.

[d]Hispanics may be any race.

[e]Age, educational attainment, and other variables are measured at the time the spells begin, except that, for those who are already on programs at the start of the survey, these characteristics are measured at the first interview.

[f]Full-time and part-time employment reflects the average employment status.

[g]Family income-to-poverty threshold ratio reflects the monthly poverty status. A ratio of under 1.00 indicates that a person is in poverty, whereas a ratio of higher than or equal to 1.00 indicates that a person is not in poverty.

SOURCE: Tracy A. Loveless and Jan Tin, "Table A-7. Median Duration of Participation in Major Means-Tested Programs by Program: 2001–2003," in *Dynamics of Economic Well-Being: Participation in Government Programs, 2001 through 2003, Who Gets Assistance?* Current Population Reports, U.S. Census Bureau, October 2006, http://www.census.gov/prod/2006pubs/p70-108.pdf (accessed January 4, 2009)

CHAPTER 3
PUBLIC PROGRAMS TO FIGHT POVERTY

There are many methods that the federal government and the states use to combat poverty. There are a variety of programs that provide assistance to those in or at risk of poverty. These are often referred to as welfare. Some of these programs, such as Temporary Aid for Needy Families (TANF), are designed to help people improve their situation so they will no longer be poor. The Supplemental Security Income program provides assistance to people who have conditions that make it difficult for them to earn a living. A number of programs, including the Supplemental Nutrition Assistance Program and Medicaid, are designed to help those in poverty meet their basic needs for food, shelter, and medical care (these programs are discussed in Chapter 7). Besides welfare programs, the government has established programs and policies such as the minimum wage and unemployment compensation that are intended to help people avoid poverty in the first place.

The most far-reaching welfare law is the Personal Responsibility and Work Opportunity Reconciliation Act (PRWORA). First enacted in 1996 and renewed since, the PRWORA replaced a welfare system based primarily on the Aid to Families with Dependent Children (AFDC) program with one centered on TANF. Critics of the AFDC felt that the system produced welfare dependency rather than temporary assistance to help recipients move into a job and off welfare. TANF was specifically designed to limit the amount of time individuals could receive benefits and require them to work. The intention of the law was to reduce the number of people receiving welfare by bringing them into the workforce and out of poverty. The PRWORA also changed some other welfare programs to place greater emphasis on these priorities. In "Policy Basics: An Introduction to TANF" (March 19, 2009 http://www.cbpp.org/files/1-22-02tanf2.pdf), Liz Schott of the Center on Budget and Policy Priorities (CBPP) notes that additional work requirements for TANF recipients put in place by the Deficit Reeducation Act of 2005 further reduced the TANF caseload.

According to the U.S. Department of Health and Human Services (HHS), the welfare caseload fell from a monthly average of 4.4 million families during fiscal year (FY) 1996 to an average of 1.9 million families during FY 2006, a drop of 57%. (See Table 3.1.) This represents the largest welfare caseload decline in history. Observers agreed that some of the decline was the result of a strong economy in which unemployment was around 4%, rather than welfare reform. For example, a study conducted by the City University of New York and cited by the HHS in *Temporary Assistance for Needy Families Program (TANF): Fourth Annual Report to Congress* (April 2002, http://www.acf.hhs.gov/programs/ofa/data-reports/ar2001/indexar.htm) attributes 60% of the reductions in caseloads to welfare reform and 20% to the effects of a robust economy.

Critics of the PRWORA question if the reduction in welfare caseloads is really a good thing. They are concerned that the current system causes former welfare recipients—without adequate health care, child care, and affordable housing—to slip through the cracks of the welfare system into destitution and homelessness. For example, in states in which living wage jobs are unavailable, the poor population may simply be moved from welfare into low-wage work and deeper into poverty. In the fact sheet "TANF at 10: Program Results Are More Mixed Than Often Understood" (August 17, 2006, http://www.cbpp.org/files/8-17-06tanf.pdf), Sharon Parrott and Arloc Sherman of the CBPP note that the share of poor children who received TANF benefits dropped from 62% in 1995 to 31% in 2003, a decrease of 50%. Parrott and Sherman state, "More than half—57%—of the caseload decline during the first decade of welfare reform reflects a decline in the extent to which TANF programs serve families that are poor enough to qualify, rather than to a reduction in the number of families who are poor enough to qualify for aid."

In addition, Sheila Zedlewski of the Urban Institute notes in "The Role of Welfare during a Recession" (December

TABLE 3.1

Trends in the cash welfare caseload, 1960–2006

	Cash welfare caseload (Numbers in thousands)			Children in families receiving cash welfare as a percent of	
Year	Families	Recipients	Children	All children	Children in poverty
1960	791	3,012	2,330	3.4	12.1
1961	873	3,363	2,598	3.7	14.3
1962	939	3,704	2,844	4.0	15.7
1963	963	3,945	2,957	4.1	17.4
1964	1,010	4,195	3,145	4.3	18.6
1965	1,060	4,422	3,321	4.5	21.5
1966	1,096	4,546	3,434	4.7	26.5
1967	1,220	5,014	3,771	5.2	31.2
1968	1,410	5,702	4,274	5.9	37.8
1969	1,696	6,689	4,973	6.9	49.7
1970	2,207	8,462	6,212	8.6	57.7
1971	2,763	10,242	7,435	10.4	68.5
1972	3,048	10,944	7,905	11.1	74.9
1973	3,148	10,949	7,903	11.2	79.9
1974	3,219	10,847	7,805	11.2	75.0
1975	3,481	11,319	8,071	11.8	71.2
1976	3,565	11,284	7,982	11.8	76.2
1977	3,568	11,015	7,743	11.6	73.9
1978	3,517	10,551	7,363	11.2	72.8
1979	3,509	10,312	7,181	11.0	68.0
1980	3,712	10,774	7,419	11.5	63.2
1981	3,835	11,079	7,527	11.7	59.2
1982	3,542	10,358	6,903	10.8	49.6
1983	3,686	10,761	7,098	11.1	50.1
1984	3,714	10,831	7,144	11.2	52.3
1985	3,701	10,855	7,198	11.3	54.4
1986	3,763	11,038	7,334	11.5	56.0
1987	3,776	11,027	7,366	11.5	56.4
1988	3,749	10,915	7,329	11.4	57.8
1989	3,798	10,992	7,419	11.5	57.9
1990	4,057	11,695	7,911	12.1	57.9
1991	4,497	12,930	8,715	13.2	59.8
1992	4,829	13,773	9,303	13.9	59.9
1993	5,012	14,205	9,574	14.1	60.0
1994	5,033	14,161	9,568	13.9	61.7
1995	4,791	13,418	9,135	13.1	61.5
1996	4,434	12,321	8,600	12.3	58.7
1997	3,740	10,376	NA	NA	NA
1998	3,050	8,347	6,320	8.9	46.1
1999	2,578	6,924	5,109	7.2	40.9
2000	2,303	6,143	4,479	6.1	38.1
2001	2,192	5,717	4,195	5.7	35.3
2002	2,187	5,609	4,119	5.6	33.6
2003	2,180	5,490	4,063	5.5	31.3
2004	2,153	5,342	3,969	5.4	30.2
2005	2,061	5,028	3,756	5.1	28.9
2006	1,908	4,591	3,457	4.7	26.7

Note: For 2000 through 2006 the cash welfare caseload includes families receiving assistance under the Temporary Assistance for Needy Families (TANF) program and under "Separate State Programs (SSPs)" funded with TANF dollars.

SOURCE: Adapted from "Table 7.8. Trends in the Cash Welfare Caseload, Selected Years 1936 to 1960 and 1960–2006," in *The Green Book*, U.S. House of Representatives Committee on Ways and Means, 2008, http://waysandmeans.house.gov/media/pdf/110/tanf.pdf (accessed January 11, 2009)

2008, http://www.urban.org/UploadedPDF/411809_role_of_welfare.pdf), that "changes to welfare have significantly curtailed the role that the Temporary Assistance for Needy Families (TANF) program can play in cushioning the current recession." She recommends that Congress consider increasing funds available to the program and relaxing the work-participation requirements in response to the recession that began in 2008. The administration of President Barack Obama (1961–) responded to the economic crisis by passing the American Recovery and Reinvestment Act, signed into law on February 17, 2009. Sharon Parrott of the CBPP states in "Despite Critics' Over-heated Rhetoric, the Economic Recovery Bill Does Not Undermine Welfare Reform" (February 17, 2009, http://www.cbpp.org/files/2-17-09tanf.pdf) that the recovery legislation does provide additional TANF resources through an emergency contingency fund to states to help them assist poor families during the crisis while leaving the basic principles of TANF in place.

THE PERSONAL RESPONSIBILITY AND WORK OPPORTUNITY RECONCILIATION ACT
Title I: Block Grants

Under the PRWORA, each state receives a single block grant (a lump sum of money). The amount of money available under TANF is actually shrinking. Federal funding for this TANF block grant was reduced from $16.4 billion per FY 1996 through June 30, 2004, to $16 billion per FYs 2006 through 2010. TANF is due to be reauthorized in 2010. Gene Falk of the Congressional Research Service points out in *Temporary Assistance for Needy Families (TANF) Block Grant: FY2007 Budget Proposals* (March 3, 2006, http://www.nationalaglawcenter.org/assets/crs/RS22385.pdf) that in constant dollars, federal welfare spending has steadily decreased since 2001.

States have considerable control over how they implement the programs covered by the block grant, but the act requires that:

- Families on welfare for five cumulative years no longer receive further cash assistance. States can set shorter time limits and can exempt up to 20% of their caseload from the time limits.

- To count toward meeting the work requirement, a state must require individuals to participate in employment (public or private), on-the-job training, community service, work experience, vocational training (up to 12 months), or child care for other workers for at least 20 hours per week. State and local communities are responsible for the development of work, whether by creating community service jobs or by providing income subsidies or hiring incentives for potential employers.

- Unmarried parents under the age of 18 must live with an adult or with adult supervision and must participate in educational or job training to receive benefits. In addition, the law encourages second-chance homes to provide teen parents with the skills and support they need. The law also provides $50 million per year in new funding for state abstinence education activities that are geared toward discouraging teen pregnancy through abstinence rather than through birth control.

None of the block grant funds can be used for adults who have been on welfare for over five years or who do not work after receiving benefits for two years. However, states are given some flexibility in how they spend their TANF funds.

Title II: Supplemental Security Income

The PRWORA redefined the term *disability* for children who receive Supplemental Security Income (SSI). A child is considered disabled if he or she has a medically determinable physical or mental impairment that results in marked and severe functional limitations that have lasted or can be expected to last at least 12 months or that can be expected to cause death. The PRWORA removed "maladaptive behavior" as a medical criterion from the listing of impairments used for evaluating mental disabilities in children.

Title III: Child Support

To be eligible for federal funds, each state must operate a Child Support Enforcement program that meets federal guidelines. The state must establish centralized registries of child support orders and centers for the collection and disbursement of child support payments, and parents must sign their child support rights over to the state to be eligible for TANF benefits. The state must also establish enforcement methods, such as revoking the driver's and professional licenses of delinquent parents. The Administration for Children and Families (ACF) notes in the fact sheet "Office of Child Support Enforcement" (January 2009, http://www.acf.hhs.gov/opa/fact_sheets/cse_factsheet.html) that in FY 2007 the program handled 15.8 million cases and collected $25 billion at a cost of $3.7 billion.

To receive full benefits, a mother must cooperate with state efforts to establish paternity. She may be denied assistance if she refuses to disclose the father.

Title IV: Restricting Welfare and Public Benefits for Noncitizens

The PRWORA originally severely limited or banned benefits to most legal immigrants who entered the country on or after the date on which the bill became law. Ineligibility continued for a five-year period or until they attained citizenship. In addition, states had the option of withholding eligibility for Medicaid, TANF, and other social services from legal immigrants already residing in the United States.

Illegal immigrants no longer had any entitlement to benefit programs, such as TANF or Medicaid. They could receive emergency medical care, short-term disaster relief, immunizations, and treatment for communicable diseases (in the interest of public health). They could also use community services such as soup kitchens and shelters, some housing programs, and school lunches/breakfasts if their children were eligible for free public education. States have established programs to verify the legal residence of immigrants before paying benefits and may elect to deny Special Supplemental Food Program for Women, Infants, and Children (WIC) benefits and other child nutrition programs to illegal aliens.

The Balanced Budget Act of 1997 and the Noncitizen Technical Amendment Act of 1998 invested $11.5 billion to restore disability and health benefits to 380,000 legal immigrants who were in the United States before welfare reform became law on August 22, 1996. The Balanced Budget Act also extended the SSI and Medicaid eligibility period for refugees and people seeking asylum from five years after entry to seven years to give these residents more time to naturalize.

Title V: Child Protection

The PRWORA gave states the authority to use current federal funds to pay for foster care for children in child care institutions. It extended the enhanced federal match for statewide automated child welfare information systems through 1997 and appropriated $6 million per year (FYs 1996 to 2002) for a national random sample study of abused and neglected children.

Title VI: Child Care

The law required that states maintain spending for child care for low-income families at the level of FY 1994 or FY 1995, whichever was greater, to be eligible for federally matched funds. Mandatory funding was set at $13.9 billion through June 30, 2004, with states receiving an estimated $1.2 billion per year before matching began. The remainder of the funds was available for state matching at the Medicaid rate. Total federal and state expenditures on child care totaled $3.2 billion in 2000, an increase of 60% over 1999 ($2 billion). In the press release "The Next Phase of Welfare Reform: Implementing the Deficit Reduction Act of 2005" (December 2006, http://www.dhhs.gov/news/press/2002pres/welfare.html), the HHS explains that the Deficit Reduction Act of 2005, which reauthorized the PRWORA, provided for increased annual federal funding for child care by $1 billion by FY 2010.

As under previous laws, states must establish standards for the prevention and control of infectious diseases, such as immunization programs, and for building codes and physical safety in child care institutions. Child care workers must also receive minimal training in health and safety. However, many low-income people rely on informal sources of child care, including relatives and friends.

Pamela A. Holcomb et al. of the Urban Institute indicate in *Child Care Subsidies and TANF: A Synthesis of Three Studies on Systems, Policies, and Parents* (2006, http://www.urban.org/UploadedPDF/311302_synthesis.pdf) that despite increased federal funding for child care, the need outweighs the resources available under the law. As a result of more parents working while still on welfare or leaving welfare to work, the critical need for child care has become more pronounced. In *The Changing Role of Welfare in the Lives of Low-Income Families with Children* (August 2006, http://www.urban.org/UploadedPDF/ 311357_occa73.pdf), Pamela Loprest and Sheila Zedlewski report that only 21.4% of families who received TANF monies in 2002 received help paying for child care in that year. Even though the child care support system gives priority to families leaving welfare for work over other low-income families, only four out of 10 (40.8%) families that had recently stopped receiving TANF monies received help paying for child care.

Some states are considering cutting child care subsidies in response to the economic crisis that began in 2008. For example, the National Association of Child Care Resource and Referral Agencies reports in "Child Care Subsidy Is a

Lifeline, but It May Be Changing" (February 3, 2009, http://www.earlychildhoodfocus.org/) that in early 2009 Oregon Governor Ted Kulongoski (1940–) proposed reducing the eligibility for child care subsidies and increasing the co-payments of low-income families. In "Providers, Parents at Rally Decry Monroe County Cuts to Child Care Subsidies" (September 18, 2008, http://www.earlychildhoodfocus .org/), the organization reports that New York State also announced that effective September 1, 2008, the child care subsidies would be decreased. The American Recovery and Reinvestment Act included an additional $2 billion to be distributed to the states to fund the Child Care and Development Block Grant.

Title VII: Child Nutrition Programs

The PRWORA continued existing child nutrition programs, such as the school lunch and breakfast programs. However, maximum reimbursement was reduced for the Summer Food Service Program and for some institutional food programs. States were allowed to decide whether to include or exclude legal immigrants from these programs. According to the U.S. Department of Agriculture (USDA), in *FY 2009 Budget Summary and Annual Performance Plan* (2008, http://www.obpa.usda.gov/budsum/fy09budsum .pdf), the budget for Child Nutrition Programs rose from $14.7 billion in FY 2008 to $15.4 billion in FY 2009, an increase of $671 million. As part of the American Recovery and Reinvestment Act, the National School Lunch Program received an additional $100 million to distribute to states to pay for equipment needed by the program. Obama's proposed 2010 budget included an additional $1 billion per year for program reforms, such as improving access to the program and bettering the nutritional quality of school meals.

Title VIII: Supplemental Nutrition Assistance Program

In 2008 the Food Stamp Program changed its name to the Supplemental Nutrition Assistance Program (SNAP). The PRWORA reduced maximum benefits to the level of the Thrifty Food Plan (a plan that serves as the basis for maximum food stamp allotments), the index set by the USDA that reflects the amount of money needed to purchase food to meet minimal nutrition requirements. Benefits were indexed to the rate of inflation so that they increase as inflation rises.

The law also restructured the way certain expenses and earnings were counted in establishing eligibility for food stamps. Under the PRWORA, when recipients' benefits are calculated, their countable monthly income is reduced by several deductions, including a standard deduction, a deduction for excessively high shelter expenses, a dependent care deduction, and medical expenses for the elderly and disabled. These deductions raised food stamp allotments. The Farm Bill of 2008 increased the minimum monthly benefit from $10 to $14 and excluded education and retirement accounts from countable resources.

In response to the severe economic recession that began in 2008, President Obama signed the American Recovery and Reinvestment Act in February 2009. According to the USDA, in the memo "Economic Stimulus—Adjustments to the Maximum Supplemental Nutrition Assistance Program (SNAP) Monthly Allotments" (February 18, 2009, http://www.fns.usda.gov/fsp/rules/Memo/09/021809.pdf), the act increased SNAP benefits by 13.6% over the June value of the Thrifty Food Plan. Maximum monthly benefits for a family of four in the continental United States increased to $668; the maximum monthly allotment for a family of three increased to $526.

By law, all SNAP recipients who are 18 to 50 years old and without children (known as able-bodied adults without dependents [ABAWD]) must work at least part time or be limited to three months of assistance in a 36-month period. Recipients who were in a workfare program (a welfare program that usually requires recipients to perform public-service duties) for 30 days but lost their placement may qualify for an additional three months of food assistance. (This provision was revised to allow states to exempt 15% of ABAWD recipients from this restriction.)

Reauthorization of the PRWORA

Since 1996 many changes have been made to the PRWORA. The PRWORA was reauthorized through 2010 when President George W. Bush (1946–) signed the Deficit Reduction Act on February 8, 2006. This bill did not increase funding for TANF programs and further restricted eligibility requirements. The Communications Workers of America notes in the fact sheet "TANF Reauthorization" (March 2, 2006, http://www.cwa-legislative.org/fact-sheets/page.jsp?itemID=27482970) that the basic TANF block grant did not increase with inflation but remained capped at $16 billion. The reauthorization bill required 50% of TANF recipients to work in 2006, increasing by 5% each year to 70% in 2010. Funding for child care was set at $2 billion for each year between 2006 and 2010. Child support enforcement funding was reduced. Drug testing became required for every TANF applicant and recipient. Finally, the bill allowed TANF funds to be used to promote the value of marriage through public advertising and high school and adult classes and mentoring programs. The PRWORA will be up for reauthorization once again in 2010.

ELIGIBILITY FOR TANF AND BENEFIT PAYMENTS

Under TANF, states decide how much to aid a needy family. No federal guidelines exist for determining eligibility, and no requirement mandates that states aid all needy families. TANF does not require states to have a need standard or a gross income limit, as the AFDC did, but many states have based their TANF programs in part on their earlier practices.

The maximum benefit is the amount paid to a family with no countable income. (Federal law specifies what income counts toward figuring benefits and what income, such as child support, is to be disregarded by the state.) The maximum benefit is to be paid only to those families that comply with TANF's work requirements or other program requirements established by the state, such as parental and personal responsibility rules.

Even though most states vary benefits according to family size, some eliminate or restrict benefit increases due to the birth of a new child to a recipient already receiving benefits. Instead, benefits depend on family size at the time of enrollment in 16 states. Idaho pays a flat monthly grant that is the same regardless of family size. Wisconsin pays benefits based on work activity of the recipient and not on family size. Five states provide an increase in benefits to TANF families following the birth of an additional child.

Most states did not change their maximum benefits between July 1994 and January 2009, despite the major changes brought about by the PRWORA. When looking at the maximum benefits as a percent of the poverty guidelines, benefits have actually declined in many states. Overall, the maximum ADFC benefits in 1996 were 34.9% of the poverty level for a family of three; by 2006 they had fallen to 28.6%. (See Table 3.2.)

Many families receiving TANF benefits are also eligible for SNAP. A single benefit determination is made for both cash and food assistance. Even though the eligibility and benefit amounts for TANF are determined by the states, SNAP eligibility and benefit amounts are determined by federal law and are consistent in all states.

SNAP benefits, which are administered by the USDA, are not counted in determining the TANF cash benefit. However, TANF benefits are considered part of a family's countable income in determining SNAP benefits, which are reduced $0.30 for each dollar of countable income. Therefore, SNAP benefits are higher in states with lower TANF benefits and vice versa. As of July 2006, combined monthly benefits for a family of three were lowest in Mississippi ($558), Tennessee ($568), Arkansas ($582), Alabama ($589), and Texas ($595). (See Table 3.3.) Alaska ($1,191) and Hawaii ($1,057) had the highest combined benefit for a family of three. (Poverty guidelines are higher in these two states because of higher costs of living.) Other states that paid the most in benefits included Vermont ($904), Wisconsin ($910), New York ($922), and California ($945).

Who Gets TANF Benefits?

In 2003, the latest year for which detailed data are available as of mid-2009, an average of 3.7 million people, or 1.3% of the population, received TANF benefits each month. (See Table 3.4.) Some groups in the population were more likely to receive these benefits than others.

TABLE 3.2

Maximum AFDC/TANF benefit for a family of three by state, selected years 1981–2006

State	Maximum benefits for a family of three				Maximum benefits as a percent of the poverty guidelines for a family of three			
	1981	1988	1996	2006	1981	1988	1996	2006
Alabama	$118	$118	$164	$215	20.0%	14.6%	15.2%	15.5%
Alaska	571	779	923	923	77.4	77.2	68.3	53.4
Arizona	202	293	347	347	34.3	36.3	32.1	25.1
Arkansas	161	204	204	204	27.3	25.3	18.9	14.7
California	506	663	596	723	85.9	82.1	55.1	52.3
Colorado	379	356	356	356	64.3	44.1	32.9	25.7
Connecticut	498	623	636	636	84.5	77.2	58.8	46.0
Delaware	266	319	338	338	45.1	39.5	31.2	24.4
District of Columbia	286	379	415	407	48.5	46.9	38.4	29.4
Florida	195	275	303	303	33.1	34.1	28.0	21.9
Georgia	183	270	280	280	31.1	33.4	25.9	20.2
Hawaii	468	515	712	570	69.0	55.4	57.2	35.8
Idaho	305	304	317	309	51.8	37.6	29.3	22.3
Illinois	302	342	377	396	51.3	42.4	34.9	28.6
Indiana	255	288	288	288	43.3	35.7	26.6	20.8
Iowa	360	394	426	426	61.1	48.8	39.4	30.8
Kansas	353	427	429	429	59.9	52.9	39.7	31.0
Kentucky	188	218	262	262	31.9	27.0	24.2	18.9
Louisiana	173	190	190	240	29.4	23.5	17.6	17.3
Maine	301	416	418	485	51.1	51.5	38.6	35.1
Maryland	270	377	373	490	45.8	46.7	34.5	35.4
Massachusetts	379	539	565	618	64.3	66.7	52.2	44.7
Michigan	397	436	459	459	67.4	54.0	42.4	33.2
Minnesota	446	532	532	532	75.7	65.9	49.2	38.5
Mississippi	96	120	120	170	16.3	14.9	11.1	12.3
Missouri	248	282	292	292	42.1	34.9	27.0	21.1
Montana	259	359	438	375	44.0	44.5	40.5	27.1
Nebraska	350	364	364	364	59.4	45.1	33.7	26.3
Nevada	241	330	348	348	40.9	40.9	32.2	25.2
New Hampshire	326	496	550	625	55.3	61.4	50.8	45.2
New Jersey	360	424	424	424	61.1	52.5	39.2	30.7
New Mexico	220	264	389	389	37.3	32.7	36.0	28.1
New York	429	539	577	691	72.8	66.7	53.3	50.0
North Carolina	192	266	272	272	32.6	32.9	25.1	19.7
North Dakota	334	371	431	477	56.7	45.9	39.8	34.5
Ohio	263	309	341	410	44.6	38.3	31.5	29.6
Oklahoma	282	310	307	292	47.9	38.4	28.4	21.1
Oregon	321	412	460	471	54.5	51.0	42.5	34.0
Pennsylvania	332	402	421	421	56.4	49.8	38.9	30.4
Rhode Island	367	517	554	554	62.3	64.0	51.2	40.0
South Carolina	129	201	200	240	21.9	24.9	18.5	17.3
South Dakota	321	366	430	508	54.5	45.3	39.8	36.7
Tennessee	122	173	185	185	20.7	21.4	17.1	13.4
Texas	118	184	188	223	20.0	22.8	17.4	16.1
Utah	348	376	426	474	59.1	46.6	39.4	34.3
Vermont	518	629	636	665	87.9	77.9	58.8	48.1
Virginia	310	354	354	389	52.6	43.8	32.7	28.1
Washington	415	492	546	546	70.4	60.9	50.5	39.5
West Virginia	206	249	253	340	35.0	30.8	23.4	24.6
Wisconsin	444	517	517	673	75.4	64.0	47.8	48.7
Wyoming	315	360	360	340	53.5	44.6	33.3	24.6
Median state	305	360	377	396	51.8	44.6	34.9	28.6

SOURCE: "Table 7–22. Maximum Cash Welfare Benefits for a Family of Three by State, Selected Years, 1981–2006," in *The Green Book*, U.S. House of Representatives Committee on Ways and Means, 2008, http://waysandmeans.house.gov/media/pdf/110/tanf.pdf (accessed January 11, 2009)

Fully 3.4% of children under 18 years old received TANF benefits, compared to only 0.7% of adults aged 18 to 64 years and 0.1% of adults aged 65 and older. Women were more likely than men to receive TANF benefits (1.5% and 1.1%, respectively), reflecting their role as the primary caretakers of children.

A higher proportion of African-Americans (3.7%) received TANF benefits each month in 2003 than any other racial or ethnic group. (See Table 3.4.) Among other groups, 2.7% of Hispanics, 1.5% of Asians and Pacific Islanders, and 0.5% of non-Hispanic whites received benefits, on average, each month.

Single female-headed families were by far the most likely family group to receive TANF benefits each month in 2003. More than one out of 20 (5.6%) of these families received TANF benefits each month, compared to 1.3% of single male-headed families and 0.5% of married-couple families. (See Table 3.4.)

TABLE 3.3

Combined TANF cash welfare and food stamp benefits for a family of three, by state, July 2006

State	TANF maximum benefit	Food stamp benefit	Combined benefits	As a percent of the 2006 HHS poverty guidelines		
				TANF maximum benefit	Food stamp benefit	Combined benefits
Alabama	$215	$374	$589	15.5%	27.0%	42.6%
Alaska	923	268	1191	53.4	15.5	68.9
Arizona	347	335	682	25.1	24.2	49.3
Arkansas	204	378	582	14.7	27.3	42.1
California	723	222	945	52.3	16.0	68.3
Colorado	356	332	688	25.7	24.0	49.7
Connecticut	636	248	884	46.0	17.9	63.9
Delaware	338	337	675	24.4	24.4	48.8
District of Columbia	407	317	724	29.4	22.9	52.3
Florida	303	348	651	21.9	25.2	47.1
Georgia	280	355	635	20.2	25.7	45.9
Hawaii	570	487	1057	35.8	30.6	66.4
Idaho	309	346	655	22.3	25.0	47.3
Illinois	396	320	716	28.6	23.1	51.8
Indiana	288	352	640	20.8	25.4	46.3
Iowa	426	311	737	30.8	22.5	53.3
Kansas	429	310	739	31.0	22.4	53.4
Kentucky	262	360	622	18.9	26.0	45.0
Louisiana	240	367	607	17.3	26.5	43.9
Maine	485	293	778	35.1	21.2	56.2
Maryland	490	292	782	35.4	21.1	56.5
Massachusetts	618	253	871	44.7	18.3	63.0
Michigan	459	301	760	33.2	21.8	54.9
Minnesota	532	312	884	38.5	24.4	63.9
Mississippi	170	388	558	12.3	28.0	40.3
Missouri	292	351	643	21.1	25.4	46.5
Montana	375	326	701	27.1	23.6	50.7
Nebraska	364	330	694	26.3	23.9	50.2
Nevada	348	334	682	25.2	24.1	49.3
New Hampshire	625	251	876	45.2	18.1	63.3
New Jersey	424	312	736	30.7	22.6	53.2
New Mexico	389	322	711	28.1	23.3	51.4
New York	691	231	922	50.0	16.7	66.7
North Carolina	272	357	629	19.7	25.8	45.5
North Dakota	477	296	773	34.5	21.4	55.9
Ohio	410	316	726	29.6	22.8	52.5
Oklahoma	292	351	643	21.1	25.4	46.5
Oregon	471	297	768	34.0	21.5	55.5
Pennsylvania	421	312	733	30.4	22.6	53.0
Rhode Island	554	273	827	40.0	19.7	59.8
South Carolina	240	367	607	17.3	26.5	43.9
South Dakota	508	286	794	36.7	20.7	57.4
Tennessee	185	383	568	13.4	27.7	41.1
Texas	223	372	595	16.1	26.9	43.0
Utah	474	297	771	34.3	21.5	55.7
Vermont	665	239	904	48.1	17.3	65.3
Virginia	389	322	711	28.1	23.3	51.4
Washington	546	275	821	39.5	19.9	59.3
West Virginia	340	337	677	24.6	24.4	48.9
Wisconsin	673	237	910	48.7	17.1	65.8
Wyoming	340	337	677	24.6	24.4	48.9
Median state	396	322	716	28.6	23.3	51.8

Note: TANF = Temporary Assistance for Needy Families. HHS = Department of Health and Human Services.

SOURCE: "Table 7–24. Combined TANF Cash Welfare and Food Stamp Benefits for a Family of Three, by State, July 2006," in *The Green Book*, U.S. House of Representatives Committee on Ways and Means, 2008, http://waysandmeans.house.gov/media/pdf/110/tanf.pdf (accessed January 11, 2009)

Adults who had a high school education or less were much more likely than their better-educated peers to receive TANF in 2003, reflecting the difficulty of earning a living wage without some higher education. In that year 1.4% of adults who had not received a high school diploma received TANF assistance each month, compared to 0.5% of high school graduates and 0.2% of adults who had attended college. (See Table 3.4.)

Because TANF is designed to help those most in need, it is not surprising that most people who received TANF in 2003 were poor. In that year 6.1% of people below the poverty line received TANF assistance each month, compared to 0.5% of people who lived in families with incomes above the poverty line. (See Table 3.4.)

Most states have imposed a lifetime limit of five years for the receipt of TANF benefits for adults, although states

TABLE 3.4

Average monthly program participation rates for Temporary Assistance for Needy Families (TANF) or general assistance, by selected characteristics, 2001–03

Characteristic	Temporary Assistance for Needy Families(TANF)/General Assistance participation rates (in percent)		
	2001	2002	2003
Total number of recipients[a]	3,935	3,584	3,667
As percent of the population	1.4	1.3	1.3
Race and Hispanic origin[b]			
White	0.9	0.8	0.8
Not Hispanic	0.6	0.5	0.5
Black	4.2	3.8	3.7
Asian or Pacific Islander	2.0	1.8	1.5
Hispanic	2.9	2.7	2.7
Not Hispanic	1.2	1.1	1.1
Age			
Under 18 years	3.7	3.3	3.4
18 to 64 years	0.7	0.7	0.7
65 years and older	0.1	0.1	0.1
Sex			
Men	1.2	1.1	1.1
Women	1.6	1.5	1.5
Educational attainment (people 18 and older)			
Less than high school graduate	1.7	1.6	1.4
High school graduate, no college	0.6	0.5	0.5
Some college	0.3	0.2	0.2
Disability status (people 15 to 64 years old)			
With a work disability	2.1	1.6	1.5
With no work disability	0.6	0.6	0.7
Residence			
Metropolitan	1.4	1.3	1.3
Central city	2.5	2.3	2.3
Noncentral city	0.8	0.7	0.8
Nonmetropolitan	1.3	1.2	1.1
Region			
Northeast	1.6	1.4	1.5
Midwest	1.2	1.1	1.1
South	1.0	0.9	0.9
West	2.1	2.0	1.9
Family status			
In families	1.6	1.5	1.5
In married-couple families	0.5	0.5	0.5
In families with a female householder, no husband present	6.5	5.8	5.6
In families with a male householder, no wife present	1.4	1.1	1.3
Unrelated individuals	0.4	0.3	0.3
Employment and labor force status (people 18 and older)			
Employed full-time[c]	0.1	0.1	0.1
Employed part-time	0.7	0.5	0.5
Unemployed	3.2	2.7	2.6
Not in labor force	1.2	1.2	1.1

TABLE 3.4

Average monthly program participation rates for Temporary Assistance for Needy Families (TANF) or general assistance, by selected characteristics, 2001–03 [CONTINUED]

Characteristic	Temporary Assistance for Needy Families(TANF)/General Assistance participation rates (in percent)		
	2001	2002	2003
Marital status (people 18 and older)			
Married	0.3	0.3	0.3
Separated, divorced, or widowed	0.9	0.7	0.7
Never married	1.2	1.2	1.1
Family income-to-poverty ratio[d]			
Under 1.00	7.2	6.7	6.1
1.00 and over	0.4	0.4	0.5

[a]In thousands.
[b]Hispanics may be any race.
[c]Full-time and part-time employment reflect the monthly employment status.
[d]Family income-to-poverty threshold ratio reflects the monthly poverty status. A ratio of under 1.00 indicates that a person is in poverty, whereas a ratio of higher than or equal to 1.00 indicates that a person is not in poverty.

SOURCE: Tracy A. Loveless and Jan Tin, "Table A-2. Average Monthly Program Participation Rates for Temporary Assistance for Needy Families or General Assistance by Selected Characteristics: 2001–2003," in *Dynamics of Economic Well-Being: Participation in Government Programs, 2001 through 2003: Who Gets Assistance?* Current Population Reports, U.S. Census Bureau, October 2006, http://www.census.gov/prod/2006pubs/p70-108.pdf (accessed February 21, 2009)

are allowed to extend benefits for hardship cases or victims of domestic violence. Some states have set limits lower than 60 months. Families in which there is no adult head of household are exempt from time limits. The actual median (the middle value—half are higher and half are lower) amount of time recipients receive TANF benefits is much lower than the lifetime limit. Between 2001 and 2003 TANF recipients received benefits for a median of 4.9 months. (See Table 2.18 in Chapter 2.) Children under the age of 18 tended to received TANF for a longer period; they received benefits for a median of 6.3 months, compared to a median of 4 months for adults aged 18 to 64.

Asians and Pacific Islanders had a much higher median duration of participation in TANF than did other racial and ethnic groups. Between 2001 and 2003 Asians and Pacific Islanders had a median duration of 11.4 months, compared to 6.5 months for African-Americans and 4 months for Hispanics and non-Hispanic whites. (See Table 2.18 in Chapter 2.)

People in families headed by a single female had a higher median duration of participation in TANF than did other family types. Between 2001 and 2003 these families had a median duration of 5.8 months, compared to 3.9 months for married-couple families and 3.8 months in families headed by a single male. (See Table 2.18 in Chapter 2.)

Mothers

Mothers who had a birth in the last year were more likely than other mothers to participate in public assistance programs in 2004—24.8% of new mothers received Medicaid, 18.8% received food stamps, 12.1% received WIC, 4.4% received housing assistance, and 3.3% received TANF. (See Figure 3.1.) Fully a third (34.2%) of recent mothers participated in any public assistance program, compared to 19.9% of other mothers. Mothers who had a birth in the last year were also more likely than other mothers to participate in multiple programs. (See Figure 3.2.)

FIGURE 3.1

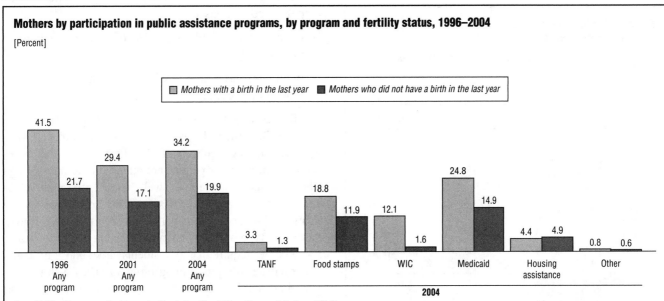

Mothers by participation in public assistance programs, by program and fertility status, 1996–2004

[Percent]

- Mothers with a birth in the last year
- Mothers who did not have a birth in the last year

Note: TANF = Temporary Assistance for Needy Families. WIC = Women, Infants and Children.

SOURCE: Jane Lawler Dye, "Figure 1. Mothers by Participation in Public Assistance Programs by Program and Fertility Status: 1996–2004," in *Participation of Mothers in Government Assistance Programs: 2004? Current Population Reports,* U.S. Census Bureau, May 2008, http://www.census.gov/prod/2008pubs/p70-116.pdf (accessed January 11, 2008)

In 2004 the rates of unmarried mothers who participated in public assistance programs were much higher than those of married mothers. A third (34.2%) of mothers who had a child in the last year participated in a public assistance program; however, married mothers had a participation rate of only 21.7%, compared to a participation rate of 64.2% among unmarried mothers. (See Table 3.5.) The participation rate of young married mothers aged 15 to 24 years was fairly high, at 44.8%, whereas the rate for older mothers aged 25 to 34 years was 17.5% and 35 to 44 years was 15%. By contrast, the participation rates for unmarried mothers remained well over 50% even in the oldest age group.

The participation rates varied by demographic characteristics. African-American mothers were the most likely to participate in public assistance programs. Nearly two-thirds (62.4%) of African-American women with a birth in the past year participated in a public assistance program, compared to 49.4% of Asian-Americans, 47.6% of Hispanics, and 23.9% of non-Hispanic whites. (See Table 3.6.)

Better-educated and more highly paid mothers were less likely than other mothers to participate in public assistance programs. Among mothers with a birth in the past year, those without a high school degree were the most likely to participate in public assistance programs (58.3%), whereas those with even some college were the least likely (19.7%). (See Table 3.6.) Recent mothers whose monthly family income was less than $500 participated in public assistance programs 72.4% of the time, whereas only 8.4% of mothers whose monthly income was $4,000 or more did. Women in poverty were more

likely to participate in public assistance programs than were other women. (See Figure 3.3.) As Table 3.7 shows, certain groups were more likely to receive government assistance than others. The most likely candidates for this assistance were young, poorly educated, unmarried, and African-American mothers with a birth in the last year.

TEEN MOTHERS. TANF contains provisions to encourage two-parent families and reduce out-of-wedlock births. Several provisions deal specifically with the reduction of births among teen mothers. According to Saul D. Hoffman, in *By the Numbers: The Public Costs of Adolescent Childbearing* (October 2006, http://www.thenationalcampaign.org/resources/pdf/pubs/BTN_Full.pdf), fewer than half of teens who become mothers while still in high school actually graduate, and only one out of 50 ever graduates from college. As a result, the National Campaign to Prevent Teen Pregnancy explains in the fact sheet "Teen Pregnancy and Education" (2009, http://www.thenationalcampaign.org/why-it-matters/pdf/education.pdf) that they have less education and fewer job skills than women who delay childbearing until their twenties.

Teen mothers have a much higher participation rate in major means-tested government programs than do mothers in other age groups. In 2004, 68% of unmarried mothers aged 15 to 24 who had a child in the last year received some form of government assistance, compared to 64.2% of all unmarried mothers who had a child in the last year. (See Table 3.5.)

The birth rate for unmarried teens is high, although it declined in the 1990s. (See Figure 3.4.) Between 1990 and

FIGURE 3.2

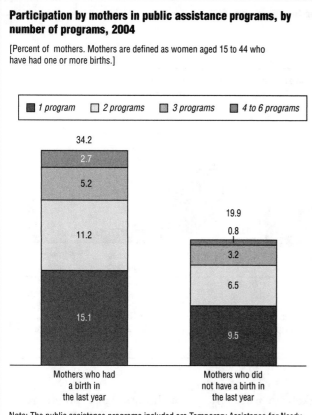

Participation by mothers in public assistance programs, by number of programs, 2004

[Percent of mothers. Mothers are defined as women aged 15 to 44 who have had one or more births.]

Legend: ■ 1 program □ 2 programs ▨ 3 programs ▦ 4 to 6 programs

Mothers who had a birth in the last year: 34.2 (15.1 + 11.2 + 5.2 + 2.7)

Mothers who did not have a birth in the last year: 19.9 (9.5 + 6.5 + 3.2 + 0.8)

Note: The public assistance programs included are Temporary Assistance for Needy Families (TANF), food stamps, Women, Infants and Children (WIC), Medicaid, housing assistance, and other (which includes general assistance and other welfare).

SOURCE: Jane Lawler Dye, "Figure 2. Participation in Public Assistance Programs by Number of Programs: 2004," in *Participation of Mothers in Government Assistance Programs: 2004*, U.S. Census Bureau, May 2008, http://www.census.gov/prod/2008pubs/p70-116.pdf (accessed January 11, 2008)

2006 the birth rate for 15- to 17-year-olds fell by 33%, from 30 births per 1,000 unmarried women to 20 births per 1,000 unmarried women. Births to teenagers represent a concern to society because teen mothers tend to have less education and less ability to support and care for their children. In addition, the National Campaign to Prevent Teen Pregnancy indicates in "Teen Pregnancy and Overall Child Well-Being" (2009, http://www.thenationalcampaign.org/why-it-matters/pdf/child_well-being.pdf) that compared to babies born to mothers who delay childbearing until their twenties, babies born to teen mothers are:

- More likely to be born prematurely and to be of low birth weight, and therefore at a higher risk for infant death, deafness, chronic respiratory problems, blindness, developmental disabilities, cerebral palsy, and hyperactivity, among other problems

- Less likely to display readiness for school

- More likely to repeat a grade or drop out of high school

- More likely to suffer from mental health problems such as anxiety, low self-esteem, or sadness

- Twice as likely as children of older mothers to be neglected or abused

- If male, twice as likely as sons of older mothers to be imprisoned

- If female, three times as likely as daughters of older mothers to become teen mothers themselves

To receive TANF benefits, states are required to submit plans detailing their efforts to reduce out-of-wedlock births, especially among teenagers. To be eligible for TANF benefits, unmarried minor parents are required to remain in high school or its equivalent as well as to live in an adult-supervised setting. One provision in the law allows for the creation of second-chance homes for teen parents and their children, a type of home that already existed in some states. These homes require that all residents either enroll in school or participate in a job-training program. They also provide parenting and life skills classes, counseling, and support services.

A performance bonus that is separate from the TANF block grant rewards states for reductions in births outside of marriage combined with a decline in the abortion rate. The George W. Bush administration promoted abstinence-only education programs as the best way to prevent teen pregnancy and provided grant money for states to implement abstinence-only education programs that stressed that teens should not be sexually active outside of marriage. This policy was controversial because many people believe that such programs are ineffective. The welfare-reform law directs the HHS to provide a strategy to prevent unmarried teen pregnancies and to ensure that 25% of the communities in the United States implement a teen pregnancy prevention program. The 2006 reauthorization of the PRWORA provided an additional $100 million per year from FYs 2006 to 2010 to fund "healthy marriage initiatives"—that is, a variety of activities designed to promote the value of marriage to the general population and teach interpersonal skills to help ensure the stability of marital relationships.

THE WELFARE-TO-WORK CONCEPT

TANF recipients are expected to participate in work activities while receiving benefits. After 24 months of assistance, states must require recipients to work at least part time to continue to receive cash benefits. States are permitted to exempt certain groups of people from the work-activity requirements, including parents of very young children (up to one year) and disabled adults. TANF defines the work activities that count when determining a state's work participation rate.

As part of their plans, states must require parents to work after two years of receiving benefits. In 2000 states were required to have 40% of all parents, and at least one adult in 90% of all two-parent families, engaged in a work activity for a minimum of 20 hours per week for single

TABLE 3.5

Program participation status of mothers 15 to 44 years old with a birth in the last year, by marital status and age, 1996, 2001 and 2004

[Numbers in thousands]

Marital status and age of mother	Total, 2004 Number	Total, 2004 Partici-pation rate[c]	Participants[a] Total Number	Participants[a] Total Percent	TANF	Food stamps	WIC	Medicaid	Housing assis-tance	Other[d]	Nonparticipants[b] Number	Nonparticipants[b] Percent	Participation rate[c] 1996[e]	Participation rate[c] 2001
Mothers who had a child in the last year	4,138	34.2	1,417	100.0	135	776	501	1,025	184	33	2,721	100.0	41.5	29.4
Now married[f]														
Total	2,919	21.7	634	44.7	16	272	282	360	28	10	2,285	84.0	27.7	18.2
15 to 24 years	518	44.8	232	16.4	10	98	103	138	10	5	286	10.5	55.4	41.7
25 to 34 years	1,742	17.5	304	21.5	6	117	128	180	17	5	1,438	52.8	21.7	12.9
35 to 44 years	659	15.0	99	7.0	—	58	52	43	—	—	560	20.6	15.2	14.8
Unmarried[g]														
Total	1,219	64.2	782	55.2	119	504	219	664	157	23	437	16.1	74.7	57.2
15 to 24 years	694	68.0	472	33.3	79	282	120	410	79	8	221	8.1	80.9	59.8
25 to 34 years	390	59.7	233	16.4	33	171	77	203	49	6	157	5.8	68.0	56.0
35 to 44 years	135	57.0	77	5.4	6	50	22	52	28	9	59	2.2	(B)	(B)
Mothers who did not have a child in the last year	30,435	19.9	6,070	100.0	385	3,631	502	4,523	1,499	181	24,365	100.0	21.7	17.1
Now married[f]														
Total	20,530	9.7	1,989	32.8	86	987	224	1,415	213	72	18,541	76.1	11.5	8.4
15 to 24 years	982	26.0	255	4.2	13	128	46	202	27	7	727	3.0	34.4	24.3
25 to 34 years	7,046	12.6	886	14.6	24	443	137	605	88	29	6,161	25.3	14.7	10.7
35 to 44 years	12,501	6.8	849	14.0	49	417	41	609	98	36	11,653	47.8	7.5	6.0
Unmarried[g]														
Total	9,905	41.2	4,081	67.2	299	2,644	278	3,108	1,286	110	5,824	23.9	44.2	34.2
15 to 24 years	1,630	57.1	930	15.3	109	606	137	729	219	23	700	2.9	63.5	48.6
25 to 34 years	3,522	45.8	1,613	26.6	85	1,096	122	1,181	559	37	1,908	7.8	50.1	37.9
35 to 44 years	4,753	32.4	1,538	25.3	105	942	19	1,198	508	50	3,215	13.2	33.1	26.4

— Represents or rounds to zero.

(B) Derived measure not shown when base is less than 75,000.

[a]Currently participating in or covered by one or more programs.

[b]Not currently participating in any program.

[c]Percent of mothers currently participating in or covered by one or more programs.

[d]Includes general assistance and other welfare.

[e]Data for 1996 in this report may vary from the report Fertility and Program Participation in the United States: 1996 (P70–82) due to the inclusion of additional assistance programs for consistency with 2004 data.

[f]Includes married, spouse present; married, spouse absent (excluding separated).

[g]Includes separated, divorced, widowed, and never married.

Note: TANF = Temporary Assistance for Needy Families. WIC = Women, Infants and Children.

SOURCE: Jane Lawler Dye, "Table 2. Program Participation Status of Mothers 15 to 44 Years Old with a Birth in the Last Year by Marital Status and Age: 1996, 2001, and 2004," in *Participation of Mothers in Government Assistance Programs: 2004*, Current Population Reports, U.S. Census Bureau, May 2008, http://www.census.gov/prod/2008pubs/p70–116.pdf (accessed January 11, 2008)

parents and 35 hours per week for at least one adult in two-parent families. This work requirement is becoming stricter. The 2006 reauthorization of the PRWORA required 50% of all single-parent TANF recipients to work in 2006, increasing by 5% each year to 70% in 2010.

TANF recipients required to work must spend a minimum number of hours per week engaged in one of the following activities:

- An unsubsidized job (no government help)
- A subsidized private job
- A subsidized public job
- Work experience
- On-the-job training
- Job search and job readiness (a usual maximum of six weeks total)
- Community service
- Vocational educational training (a 12-month maximum)
- Job skills training
- Education related to employment
- High school or a general equivalency diploma completion
- Providing child care for a community service participant

Additional provisions apply to young parents who are under the age of 20 and are either household heads or married

TABLE 3.6

Mothers 15 to 44 years old by participation status and selected characteristics, 2004

[Numbers in thousands]

Characteristic	Mothers who had a child in the last year						Mothers who did not have a child in the last year					
	Total		Participants[a]		Nonparticipants[b]		Total		Participants[a]		Nonparticipants[b]	
	Number	Participation rate[c]	Number	Percent	Number	Percent	Number	Participation rate[c]	Number	Percent	Number	Percent
Total	4,138	34.2	1,417	100.0	2,721	100.0	30,435	19.9	6,070	100.0	24,365	100.0
Race and Hispanic origin												
White	3,275	29.9	978	69.0	2,298	84.5	23,367	16.3	3,800	62.6	19,568	80.3
Non-Hispanic	2,388	23.9	570	40.2	1,818	66.8	18,355	13.5	2,486	41.0	15,869	65.1
Black	527	62.4	329	23.2	198	7.3	4,739	38.2	1,810	29.8	2,928	12.0
Asian	170	49.4	84	5.9	86	3.2	1,123	28.2	317	5.2	806	3.3
Hispanic (any race)	956	47.6	455	32.1	502	18.4	5,409	27.0	1,460	24.1	3,949	16.2
Nativity status												
Native[d]	3,557	33.7	1,198	84.5	2,359	86.7	27,138	19.8	5,360	88.3	21,777	89.4
Foreign born	581	37.7	219	15.5	362	13.3	3,297	21.5	710	11.7	2,587	10.6
Labor force status												
Had a job during last 4 months	2,303	23.7	545	38.5	1,758	64.6	22,094	15.1	3,338	55.0	18,757	77.0
No job last 4 months[e]	1,835	47.5	872	61.5	963	35.4	8,341	32.8	2,733	45.0	5,608	23.0
Unable to find work	57	(B)	49	3.5	7	0.3	451	57.6	260	4.3	191	0.8
Not able to work due to disability	35	(B)	28	2.0	7	0.3	851	76.3	649	10.7	202	0.8
Educational attainment												
Not a high school graduate	791	58.3	461	32.5	331	12.2	3,783	42.3	1,601	26.4	2,183	9.0
High school graduate	1,066	47.5	506	35.7	560	20.6	8,339	23.6	1,968	32.4	6,371	26.1
College, 1 or more years	2,281	19.7	450	31.8	1,831	67.3	18,312	13.7	2,501	41.2	15,811	64.9
Monthly family income[f]												
Less than $500	250	72.4	181	14.6	69	2.6	1,253	62.3	781	14.0	472	2.0
$500 to $1,499	612	67.0	410	33.2	202	7.6	3,650	57.2	2,087	37.5	1,563	6.6
$1,500 and over	3,016	21.4	645	52.2	2,370	89.7	24,520	11.0	2,695	48.4	21,825	91.5
$1,500 to $2,499	601	47.3	284	23.0	317	12.0	4,265	31.2	1,331	23.9	2,934	12.3
$2,500 to $3,999	724	30.2	219	17.7	505	19.1	5,569	13.6	758	13.6	4,811	20.2
$4,000 and over	1,691	8.4	142	11.5	1,548	58.6	14,686	4.1	605	10.9	14,081	59.0
Poverty level[f]												
Below poverty level	818	70.0	573	46.4	245	9.3	4,311	61.3	2,642	47.5	1,670	7.0
100 to 199 percent of poverty level	979	43.6	427	34.5	552	20.9	6,465	30.0	1,940	34.9	4,525	19.0
200 percent of poverty level or higher	2,080	11.3	236	19.1	1,844	69.8	18,647	5.3	981	17.6	17,665	74.0
Child support[g]												
Received payments	348	51.7	180	23.6	168	33.9	4,751	29.8	1,414	34.1	3,337	48.5
Did not receive payments	910	64.1	583	76.4	327	66.1	6,280	43.6	2,736	65.9	3,544	51.5
Type of residence												
Metropolitan	3,760	33.9	1,274	89.9	2,486	91.4	27,186	19.1	5,198	85.6	21,988	90.2
In central city	1,862	35.9	668	47.1	1,194	43.9	15,387	23.1	3,557	58.6	11,830	48.6
Not in central city	1,898	31.9	606	42.8	1,292	47.5	11,799	13.9	1,641	27.0	10,158	41.7
Nonmetropolitan	378	37.8	143	10.1	235	8.6	3,249	26.8	872	14.4	2,377	9.8

(B) Derived measure not shown when base is less than 75,000.
[a]Currently participating in or covered by one or more programs.
[b]Not currently participating in any program.
[c]Percent of mothers participating in or covered by one or more programs.
[d]Includes people born in U.S. outlying areas and abroad to parents who were U.S. citizens.
[e]Includes people not in the labor force.
[f]Percent distribution based only on families reporting income in the past 4 months. Average income for 4 months prior to the interview date.
[g]Data shown only for mothers whose children are under 21 years old and whose marital status is other than married, spouse present unless the spouse is a stepparent. Percent distribution based on this specified universe of mothers.

SOURCE: Jane Lawler Dye, "Table 4. Mothers 15 to 44 Years Old by Program Participation Status and Selected Characteristics: 2004," in *Participation of Mothers in Government Assistance Programs: 2004?* Current Population Reports, U.S. Census Bureau, May 2008, http://www.census.gov/prod/2008pubs/p70–116.pdf (accessed January 11, 2008)

and who lack a high school diploma. They are considered "engaged in work" if they either maintain satisfactory attendance in high school (no hours specified) or participate in education directly related to work (20 hours per week).

Education and Training

Reflecting a work-first philosophy, the 1996 welfare law limits the number of TANF recipients who may get work credit through participation in education and training. No

FIGURE 3.3

Selected employment, educational, and economic characteristics of mothers who had a birth in the last year by program participation status, 2004

[Percent with selected characteristics]

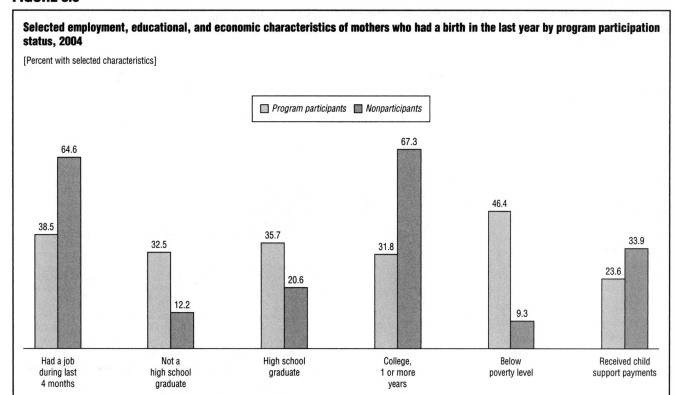

SOURCE: Jane Lawler Dye, "Figure 5. Selected Employment, Educational, and Economic Characteristics of Mothers Who Had a Birth in the Last Year by Program Participation Status: 2004," in *Participation of Mothers in Government Assistance Programs: 2004? Current Population Reports,* U.S. Census Bureau, May 2008, http://www.census.gov/prod/2008pubs/p70-116.pdf (accessed January 11, 2008)

more than 30% of TANF families who are counted as engaged in work may consist of people who are participating in vocational educational training. Vocational educational training is the only creditable work activity not explicitly confined to high school dropouts.

Finding and Creating Jobs for TANF Recipients

Job availability is one of the most difficult challenges that states face when moving recipients from welfare to work. Even though the national unemployment rate fell from a high of 7.5% in 1992 to 4% in 2000, it then began to rise again. The economic recession that began in 2008 further affected the unemployment rate. The Bureau of Labor Statistics (BLS) notes in the news release "Employment Situation Summary: March 2009" (April 3, 2009, http://www.bls.gov/news.re lease/pdf/empsit.pdf) that the rate reached 8.5% in March 2009. However, even when the national unemployment rate is low, unemployment in some areas of the country might be much higher, and the skill level of unemployed people may not match the skills required for available jobs. Welfare recipients often lack job skills and work experience. If suitable jobs cannot be found, states must create work-activity placements and may use TANF block grant funds to do so.

Welfare agencies have had to change their focus and train staff to function more as job developers and counselors than as caseworkers. They make an initial assessment

of recipients' skills as required by TANF. They may then develop personal responsibility plans for recipients, identifying what is needed (e.g., training, job-placement services, and support services) to move them into the workforce.

States have developed a variety of approaches to finding and creating job opportunities. Even though most rely on existing unemployment offices, many states have tried other options to help recipients find work:

- Collaboration with the business community to develop strategies that provide recipients with the skills and training employers want

- Use of several types of subsidies for employers who hire welfare recipients directly (subsidizing wages, providing tax credits to employers, and subsidizing workers' compensation and unemployment compensation taxes)

- Targeting state jobs for welfare recipients

- Financial encouragement for entrepreneurship and self-employment

- Creation of community service positions, often within city departments, such as parks and libraries (recipients usually participate in this workfare as a condition of continuing to receive benefits rather than wages)

The results of these efforts to find work for welfare recipients have been mixed. Karin Martinson and Pamela

TABLE 3.7

Odds of mothers receiving government assistance, by selected characteristics, 2004

Characteristic	Among mothers 15 to 44 years old	
	Percent[a]	Odds ratio
Total	21.7	
Current fertility status		
Birth last year	34.2	1.8***
No birth last year	19.9	(R)
Age		
Under 20 years	63.0	4.3***
21 to 24 years	47.2	4.4***
25 to 29 years	28.8	2.6***
30 to 34 years	20.4	2.0***
35 to 39 years	16.5	1.6***
40 to 44 years	12.2	(R)
Living arrangements		
No other person 18 years and older present	49.2	4.6***
Living with spouse and no other adult	9.9	(R)
Living with an unmarried partner and no other adult	38.5	2.0***
Other living arrangement	27.4	1.8***
Race and Hispanic origin		
White	17.9	
Non-Hispanic	14.7	
Black	40.6	
Asian	31.0	
Hispanic (any race)	30.1	
Race and Hispanic origin		
White non-Hispanic		(R)
Black non-Hispanic		2.2***
Asian non-Hispanic		1.9**
Hispanic		1.6***
Nativity status		
Native[b]	21.4	1.3
Foreign	23.9	(R)
Employment status		
Had a job during last 4 months	15.9	(R)
No job in last 4 months[c]	35.4	
Unable to find work	60.8	5.3***
Has a work-related disability	76.4	23.5***
Other reason for not working	29.8	2.7***
Educational attainment		
Not a high school graduate	45.1	2.8***
High school graduate	26.3	1.6***
College, 1 or more years	14.3	(R)

TABLE 3.7

Odds of mothers receiving government assistance, by selected characteristics, 2004 [CONTINUED]

Characteristic	Among mothers 15 to 44 years old	
	Percent[a]	Odds ratio
Child support[d]		
Received payments	31.3	2.3***
Did not receive payments	46.2	3.2***
Not in universe	11.6	(R)
Unweighted N	(NA)	12,720
Chi-square	(NA)	3,844
Degrees of freedom	(NA)	21

***Significant at .001 level.
**Significant at .01 level.
(R) Reference group.
(NA) Not available.
[a]Percent of mothers participating in or covered by one or more programs.
[b]Includes people born in U.S. outlying areas and abroad to parents who were U.S. citizens.
[c]Includes people not in the labor force.
[d]Data shown only for mothers whose children are under 21 years old and whose marital status is not married, spouse present unless the spouse present is a stepparent. Percent distribution based on this specified universe of mothers.

SOURCE: Jane Lawler Dye, "Table 5. Odds of Mothers Receiving Government Assistance: 2004," in *Participation of Mothers in Government Assistance Programs: 2004*, U.S. Census Bureau, May 2008, http://www.census.gov/prod/2008pubs/p70–116.pdf (accessed January 11, 2008)

A. Holcomb of the Urban Institute report in *Reforming Welfare: Institutional Change and Challenges* (July 2002, http://www.urban.org/UploadedPDF/310535_OP60.pdf) that TANF agencies have built a number of relationships with outside agencies to fulfill work program requirements, especially with nonprofit agencies; however, building partnerships with the for-profit business community occurred much less often. In addition, local TANF agencies rarely built partnerships with state agencies, but they did involve community-based nonprofit agencies, workforce development agencies, and occasionally other public agencies, such as the public school system, to find jobs for welfare recipients. However, not all local TANF agencies made even these connections. In addition, Parrott states that when the economy slows, such as it did beginning in 2008, fewer jobs exist for former welfare recipients.

Olivia A. Golden (1955–), the assistant secretary for children and families in the HHS under President Bill Clinton (1946–), writes about her thoughts concerning welfare reform in "Welfare Reform Mostly Worked" (*Orlando Sentinel*, July 24, 2005). In her words, the welfare-to-work model "mostly worked" in the sense that welfare caseloads have dropped and that most low-income parents are now working to support their families. However, even though welfare-to-work was successful, its very success brought about additional problems. She states, "In less than a decade, welfare has faded as a means of support for impoverished families. Many of these families are working long hours despite low wages, shrinking health-insurance coverage and serious trade-offs between work and decent care for their children. Yet, neither our politics nor our policies have adjusted to our success at bringing more of these parents into the labor force."

In *Assessing the New Federalism, Eight Years Later* (2005, http://www.urban.org/UploadedPDF/311198_ANF _EightYearsLater.pdf), Golden identifies many successes of the welfare-to-work policies, including the increase in the percentage of welfare recipients who worked rising from 22% in 1997 to 33% in 1999, while declining as a result of a weaker economy in the early twenty-first century; the rise in work activity among those most likely to use welfare, namely single mothers with a high school education or less; the finding that employers were willing to hire welfare recipients; the fact that most families that left welfare had at least one working adult; and that about one-third of former welfare recipients who worked had health insurance benefits. However, there were also some problems, including that roughly

FIGURE 3.4

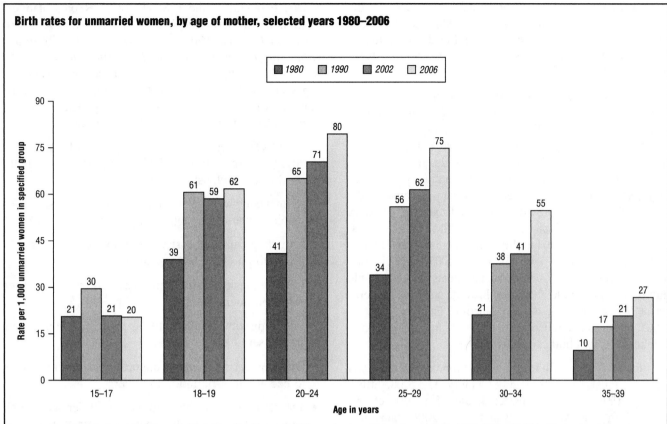

Birth rates for unmarried women, by age of mother, selected years 1980–2006

SOURCE: Joyce A. Martin et al., "Figure 6. Birth Rates for Unmarried Women by Age: United States, 1980, 1990, 2002, 2006," in *Births: Final Data for 2006*, National Vital Statistics Reports, vol. 57, no. 7, January 7, 2009, http://www.cdc.gov/nchs/data/nvsr/nvsr57/nvsr57_07.pdf (accessed January 11, 2009)

25% of those who left welfare were back on assistance two years later. The Urban Institute points out in *Jobs in an Uncertain Economy* (2009, http://www.urban.org/toolkit/issues/jobs.cfm) that low-income adults and public assistance recipients face multiple barriers to working that need to be addressed, such as a lack of basic skills and access to quality jobs, child care, and transportation.

Support Services Necessary for Moving Recipients to Work

CHILD CARE. The offer of affordable child care is one critical element in encouraging low-income mothers to seek and keep jobs. Holcomb et al. note that "child care is a key work support that can help those leaving cash assistance for work keep their jobs and avoid returning to welfare." The National Association of Child Care Resource and Referral Agencies shows in *Parents and the High Price of Child Care* (2008, http://issuu.com/naccrra/docs/parents-and-the-high-price-of-child-care-2008?mode=embed&layout=white) that in 2008 the average yearly cost for child care in a child care center for a four-year-old ranged from $4,475 in Arkansas to $10,787 in Massachusetts. For an infant, annual costs jumped to $5,231 in Arkansas and to $14,591 in Massachusetts.

The 1996 welfare reform law created a block grant to states for child care. The amount of the block grant was equivalent to what states received under the AFDC. However, states that maintain the amount that they spent for child care under the AFDC are eligible for additional matching funds. The block grant and the supplemental matching funds are referred to as the Child Care Development Fund (CCDF). In addition, states were given the option of transferring some of their TANF funds to the CCDF or spending them directly on child care services. In the fact sheet "Government Work Supports and Low-Income Families: Facts and Figures" (July 2006, http://www.urban.org/UploadedPDF/900981_work supports.pdf), the Urban Institute reports that the amount allocated for child care through the CCDF and TANF drawn from both federal and state funds tripled from $4 billion in 1996 to $12 billion in 2002. According to the Child Care Bureau of the HHS, in *Child Care and Development Fund (CCDF): Report to Congress for FY 2004 and FY 2005* (May 2008, http://www.acf.hhs.gov/programs/ccb/ccdf/rtc/rtc2004/rtc_2004_2005.pdf), in FYs 2004 and 2005 over $11 billion was available for child care programs. In "About the Child Care and Development Fund" (February 4, 2009, http://www.acf.hhs.gov/pro grams/ccb/ccdf/index.htm), the Administration for Children and Families indicates that in 2008 the federal government provided $5 billion to fund CCDF programs in the states. Even though some states cut the amount of money in their child care programs in response to the economic recession that began in 2008, the American Recovery and Reinvestment Act included an additional $2 billion to be distributed to the states specifically to fund the CCDF.

Because states may use TANF funds for child care, they have more flexibility than before to design child care programs, not only for welfare recipients but also for working-poor families who may need child care support to continue working and stay off welfare. States determine who is eligible for child care support, how much those parents will pay (often using a sliding fee scale), and the amount the state will reimburse providers of subsidized care. Children under the age of 13 are eligible for child care subsidies; depending on the state, families with incomes from 111% to 287% of the federal poverty level in 2005 were eligible, although few states guaranteed payments to all eligible families. For example, the Urban Institute notes in "Government Work Supports and Low-Income Families" that in 2005, 20 states either had waiting lists or had stopped taking applications for child care subsidies.

In "FY 2006 Child Care Development Fund Data Tables (Final Data, July 2008)" (July 31, 2008, http://www.acf.hhs.gov/programs/ccb/data/ccdf_data/06acf800/table1.htm), the ACF reports that in FY 2006 states provided child care subsidies to approximately 1.8 million low-income children in 1 million families. About 57% of the children were cared for in child care centers and 29% were cared for in licensed family child care homes. The remaining 14% of children were cared for in more informal settings, including arrangements with friends and relatives. Despite the dramatic increase in the provision of child care to low-income families, many eligible families were still not receiving assistance. About one out of five (18%) families received TANF assistance.

TRANSPORTATION AND ACCESS TO JOBS. According to the U.S. Department of Transportation (DOT), in "Use of TANF, WtW, and Job Access Funds for Transportation" (August 22, 2007, http://www.fta.dot.gov/printer_friendly/grants_financing_3715.html), transportation is another critical factor facing welfare recipients moving into a job. Recipients without a car must depend on public transportation. Yet, two out of three new jobs are in suburban areas, often outside the range of public transportation, whereas three out of four welfare recipients live in rural areas or central cities. Even when jobs are accessible to public transportation, many day care centers and schools are not. Some jobs require weekend or night shift work, when public transportation schedules are limited. Even for those recipients with cars, the expense of gas and repairs can deplete earnings.

To promote employment, the vehicle asset limits under TANF are broader than under the AFDC. Each state has the flexibility to determine its own vehicle asset level, but all states have chosen to increase the limit for the value of the primary automobile in the family beyond that set under the AFDC. In addition, the U.S. House of Representatives' Committee on Ways and Means indicates in *The Green Book: Background Material and Data on the Programs within the Jurisdiction of the Committee on Ways and Means* (2008, http://waysandmeans.house.gov/Documents.asp?section=2168) that in 2008, 29 states disregarded the value of at least one vehicle in the family. The remaining states excluded from $1,500 to $15,000 of the car's value.

The DOT notes that states use a variety of approaches to provide transportation for TANF recipients moving into the workforce, such as:

- Reimbursing work-related transportation expenses (automobile expenses or public transportation)

- Providing financial assistance in the form of loans or grants to purchase or lease an automobile

- Filling transit service gaps, such as new routes or extended hours

- Providing transit alternatives, such as vanpools or shuttle services

- Offering entrepreneurial opportunities for recipients to become transportation providers

- Transferring TANF funds to the Social Services Block Grant to develop the transportation infrastructure for the working poor in rural areas and inner cities

OTHER PUBLIC PROGRAMS TO FIGHT POVERTY

Unemployment Compensation

To qualify for unemployment compensation benefits, an unemployed person usually must have worked recently for a covered employer for some period of time and for a certain amount of pay. Almost all wage and salary workers and most of the civilian labor force are covered by unemployment insurance. Many of those not covered are people who are self-employed, agricultural or domestic workers, certain alien farm workers, and railroad workers (who have their own unemployment program). Unemployed people can receive up to 26 weeks of benefits, but that period can be extended during periods of high unemployment.

The severe recession that began in 2008 led to the expansion of unemployment compensation. On June 30, 2008, the Supplemental Appropriations Act of 2008 extended unemployment benefits for an additional 13 weeks. On November 21, 2008, the Unemployment Compensation Extension Act of 2008 extended the period of time individuals could receive compensation to an additional 20 weeks. Furthermore, the American Recovery and Reinvestment Act of 2009 extended the time during which individuals can file claims and be paid unemployment.

Unemployment compensation varies widely by state. Table 3.8 shows the percentages of unemployed receiving

TABLE 3.8

Unemployment compensation recipiency rates by state, third quarter 2008

State	Insured unemployment rate (%)	Total unemployment rate (%)	Covered employment* (in thousands)	Civilian labor force (in thousands)	Total unemployment (in thousands)
Alabama	2.0	5.4	1,888	2,184	117.3
Alaska	2.7	6.0	283	366	22.1
Arizona	2.1	5.8	2,583	3,116	180.1
Arkansas	2.8	4.7	1,149	1,386	64.7
California	3.2	7.6	15,239	18,522	1,405.3
Colorado	1.2	5.1	2,237	2,774	141.3
Connecticut	2.8	6.2	1,657	1,909	117.6
Delaware	2.5	4.7	411	448	21.2
District of Columbia	1.1	7.1	485	336	23.9
Florida	2.6	6.7	7,756	9,397	630.9
Georgia	2.1	6.4	3,956	4,921	314.7
Hawaii	2.1	4.4	593	666	29.5
Idaho	2.0	4.0	629	760	30.6
Illinois	2.4	7.1	5,689	6,768	477.4
Indiana	2.4	6.1	2,809	3,267	198.6
Iowa	1.6	4.0	1,446	1,689	67.3
Kansas	1.5	4.8	1,329	1,502	72.3
Kentucky	2.2	6.7	1,750	2,052	136.7
Louisiana	1.6	4.9	1,845	2,055	100.3
Maine	1.6	4.9	570	723	35.6
Maryland	2.0	4.5	2,392	3,038	136.4
Massachusetts	2.9	5.2	3,145	3,442	178.4
Michigan	3.5	8.6	4,002	4,982	429.3
Minnesota	1.6	5.7	2,609	2,960	168.6
Mississippi	2.4	7.9	1,107	1,334	105.6
Missouri	2.1	6.4	2,636	3,022	194.5
Montana	1.6	3.7	417	511	18.9
Nebraska	1.0	3.3	892	1,000	33.3
Nevada	3.1	7.0	1,247	1,409	98.2
New Hampshire	1.5	3.9	614	751	29.3
New Jersey	3.5	5.7	3,863	4,552	260.5
New Mexico	1.8	4.4	790	962	42.1
New York	2.4	5.5	8,394	9,686	535.3
North Carolina	2.7	6.7	3,984	4,610	310.8
North Dakota	0.8	3.1	331	380	11.8
Ohio	2.2	7.1	5,112	6,048	429.2
Oklahoma	1.2	3.8	1,504	1,751	66.3
Oregon	3.2	5.9	1,675	1,970	116.7
Pennsylvania	3.3	5.5	5,488	6,466	355.9
Puerto Rico	4.7	12.3	987	1,364	167.6
Rhode Island	3.2	8.4	454	577	48.5
South Carolina	2.9	7.4	1,845	2,178	160.6
South Dakota	0.4	2.9	376	451	13.2
Tennessee	2.0	6.8	2,683	3,061	209.4
Texas	1.2	5.1	10,171	11,798	604.7
Utah	1.1	3.6	1,180	1,393	49.7
Vermont	2.0	4.6	296	356	16.2
Virgin Islands	1.6		45		
Virginia	1.2	4.4	3,481	4,171	184.7
Washington	2.0	5.5	2,841	3,488	191.2
West Virginia	1.8	3.9	675	812	31.7
Wisconsin	2.7	4.6	2,698	3,101	143.3
Wyoming	0.8	3.0	269	295	8.8
United States	2.4	6.0	132,504	155,399	9,370.0

*Wages and covered employment lag the rest of the data summary information by 6 months.
Note: Blank cells appearing in any section of this report indicates that information is unavailable.

SOURCE: Adapted from "Labor Force Information by State (Levels in Thousands), for CYQ 2008.3," in *Unemployment Insurance Data Summary*, U.S. Department of Labor, Employment and Training Administration, 2008, http://workforcesecurity.doleta.gov/unemploy/content/data_stats/datasum08/DataSum_2008_3.pdf (accessed January 11, 2009)

benefits in each state during the third quarter of 2008. New Jersey (3.5%) and Michigan (3.5%) had the highest rates of those receiving unemployment compensation, and South Dakota (0.4%), North Dakota (0.8%), and Wyoming (0.8%) had the lowest rates.

The maximum a state may offer is 39 weeks of coverage (except for special programs), but all states provide up to 26 weeks of benefits, except Massachusetts and Washington, which offer 30 weeks. Benefits vary dramatically from state to state. In 2006 the average weekly benefits in Massachusetts ($366.33), New Jersey ($344.09), Rhode Island ($341.76), Minnesota ($333.47), and Colorado ($312.33) were significantly higher than those offered by Alabama ($183.76), Mississippi ($185.84), Louisiana ($191.12), Alaska ($197.63), and Arizona ($197.64). (See Table 3.9.)

TABLE 3.9

Amount and duration of weekly benefits for total unemployment under regular state programs, 2006

State or area	Average weekly benefit for total unemployment		Average weekly insured unemployment	Average actual duration (weeks)
	Amount[a] (dollars)	Percent of average weekly wages[b]		
Total	**277.20**	**34.3**	**2,475,634**	**15.2**
Alabama	183.76	27.0	26,726	11.3
Alaska	197.63	25.3	11,649	14.4
Arizona	197.64	25.9	25,007	14.6
Arkansas	243.98	39.7	27,899	13.7
California	289.07	31.2	340,772	16.6
Colorado	312.33	37.7	23,184	13.5
Connecticut	304.37	28.9	38,961	16.5
Delaware	251.08	28.3	7,822	17.2
District of Columbia	282.70	22.6	4,270	19.3
Florida	231.38	31.5	82,009	14.4
Georgia	255.57	33.3	52,529	11.0
Hawaii	365.09	51.7	6,223	13.1
Idaho	241.02	39.0	10,970	11.6
Illinois	291.67	33.4	124,030	17.3
Indiana	286.32	41.0	53,669	12.8
Iowa	281.97	43.0	24,139	12.5
Kansas	286.83	42.2	17,352	14.4
Kentucky	270.56	40.4	30,438	13.1
Louisiana	191.12	27.5	26,149	27.1
Maine	245.65	38.5	9,939	14.1
Maryland	273.68	32.0	33,677	14.8
Massachusetts	366.33	36.5	78,908	17.7
Michigan	293.66	36.4	148,683	14.5
Minnesota	333.47	41.3	46,126	15.3
Mississippi	185.84	31.6	22,147	16.9
Missouri	212.28	30.0	46,122	14.2
Montana	203.74	35.5	7,054	14.7
Nebraska	230.86	35.9	10,417	12.9
Nevada	274.02	35.8	18,756	13.3
New Hampshire	255.58	31.5	6,826	11.7
New Jersey	344.09	34.8	108,539	17.8
New Mexico	237.70	36.8	10,362	15.8
New York	277.41	26.0	177,823	17.9
North Carolina	265.08	37.1	74,989	13.7
North Dakota	254.84	43.0	3,447	11.0
Ohio	287.03	39.0	98,244	15.0
Oklahoma	233.23	36.4	14,463	15.1
Oregon	269.63	37.2	40,875	14.3
Pennsylvania	301.27	38.2	163,399	16.4
Rhode Island	341.76	44.6	12,034	15.2
South Carolina	222.80	34.1	37,027	13.4
South Dakota	218.51	38.3	2,220	11.4
Tennessee	215.70	30.3	40,282	13.6
Texas	271.04	33.5	104,963	14.2
Utah	274.22	41.3	8,158	14.8
Vermont	275.27	40.8	6,472	14.4
Virginia	255.67	31.0	30,625	12.5
Washington	322.13	39.4	51,985	13.8
West Virginia	230.52	37.6	12,920	14.2
Wisconsin	258.79	36.7	71,407	13.2
Wyoming	253.42	36.4	2,289	12.1
Outlying areas				
Puerto Rico	109.76	24.5	40,230	18.4
Virgin Islands	269.94	40.4	428	14.7

Notes: Except where noted, excludes data for federal employees and for ex-service members; includes data for state and local government employees where covered by state law after 1955. Totals do not necessarily equal the sum of rounded components.
[a]Includes dependents' allowances for states that provide such benefits.
[b]Based on average total weekly wage in current year.

SOURCE: Adapted from "Table 9.A2. Summary Data on State Programs, by State or Other Area, 2006," in *Annual Statistical Supplement, 2007*, Social Security Administration, April 2008, http://www.ssa.gov/policy/docs/statcomps/supplement/2007/9a.pdf (accessed January 11, 2009)

Unemployment insurance helps some workers avoid poverty, but is less likely to help low-wage workers. Falk notes in *The Potential Role of the Temporary Assistance for Needy Families (TANF) Block Grant in the Recession* (February 24, 2009, http://assets.opencrs.com/rpts/R40157_20090224.pdf) that in November 2008 unemployment insurance covered only 45% of unemployed people, and certain categories of low-wage workers, including part-time workers, contingent workers, and women workers, were even less likely to qualify for unemployment compensation if they lost their job. Falk cites a study that found that only 13% of people who were formerly drawing TANF benefits, entered the workforce, and then became unemployed, were able to draw unemployment benefits.

Howard Rosen of the Peterson Institute for International Economics argues in *Unemployment Insurance Is in Desperate Need of Modernization* (July 16, 2008, http://www.urban.org/UploadedPDF/411731_job_loss_rosen.pdf) that the system of unemployment insurance desperately needs to be modernized. He points out that the "replacement rate" of unemployment insurance (the amount of assistance as a percentage of the worker's wage) is only 36%, an amount insufficient to reduce poverty among low-income families who face layoffs. In addition, 30% of workers run out of benefits before finding new jobs. Only 22.4% of low-income workers who lose their jobs qualify for unemployment.

Unemployment hits some groups of workers harder than others. The unemployment rate of African-American and Hispanic workers is higher than that of non-Hispanic white and Asian-American workers. According to the BLS, in 2007 the unemployment rate for white male workers aged 16 and older was 4.2% and for Asian-American male workers of the same age it was 3.1%, compared to 9.1% for African-Americans and 5.3% for Hispanics. (See Table 3.10.) Single men and women have a higher unemployment rate than others. The unemployment rate for single women in 2007 was 7.2%, compared to 5% for widowed, divorced, or separated women and 2.8% for married women; the unemployment rate for single men in 2007 was 8.8%, compared to 5.2% of widowed, divorced, or separated men and 2.4% for married men.

Federal Minimum Wage

The federal minimum wage dates back to the passage of the Fair Labor Standards Act of 1938, which established basic national standards for minimum wages, overtime pay, and the employment of child workers. (The minimum wage is a cash wage only and does not include any fringe benefits. Consequently, the total compensation for minimum-wage workers is even lower than the total compensation for higher-paid workers, who generally receive some kind of benefits besides wages. Most minimum-wage workers do not receive any benefits.) The provisions of the act have been extended to cover many other areas of employment since 1938.

The first minimum wage instituted in 1938 was $0.25 an hour. (See Table 3.11.) Over the years, it gradually increased, reaching $4.25 in 1991. In July 1996 Congress passed legislation that raised the minimum wage to $5.15 in 1997 by means of two $0.45 increases. In July 2007 the minimum wage was raised to $5.85, in July 2008 it was raised to $6.55, and in July 2009 it was raised to $7.25.

Despite the minimum wage increases, a person working 40 hours a week for 50 weeks a year at minimum wage ($7.25 per hour) would gross $290 per week, or $14,500 per year, well below the poverty level for a family of three ($17,600 in 2009). (See Table 1.1 in Chapter 1.) For adults, this means that day laborers (those without a permanent job who look for a job every day) and those employed in service jobs for minimum wages will not be able to earn enough to escape poverty.

WHO WORKS FOR MINIMUM WAGE? Even though workers must receive at least the minimum wage for most jobs, there are some exceptions in which a person may be paid less than the minimum wage. Full-time students working on a part-time basis in the service and retail industries or at the students' academic institution, certain disabled people, and workers who are "customarily and regularly" tipped may receive less than the minimum wage. According to the BLS, in *Characteristics of Minimum Wage Workers: 2007* (March 24, 2008, http://www.bls.gov/cps/minwage2007.pdf), 267,000 people earned exactly the federal minimum wage in 2007, and nearly 1.5 million earned below the minimum.

The BLS also notes that in 2007, 1.2 million (72.2%) of the 1.7 million people who work for the minimum wage or below were employed in the service sector. Less than 1.2 million (68.4%) women aged 16 years and older were minimum-wage workers in 2007, compared to 546,000 (31.6%) men aged 16 years and older. (See Table 3.12.) White workers predominated among minimum-wage workers; 1.4 million (82.1%) minimum-wage workers were white, 246,000 (14.2%) were Hispanic, 205,000 (11.9%) were African-American, and 51,000 (2.9%) were Asian-American.

Supplemental Security Income

SSI is a means-tested income assistance program authorized in 1972 by Title XVI of the Social Security Act. The SSI program replaced the combined federal-state programs of Old Age Assistance, Aid to the Blind, and Aid to the Permanently and Totally Disabled in the 50 states and the District of Columbia. However, these programs still exist in the U.S. territories of Guam, Puerto Rico, and the Virgin Islands. Since the first payments in 1974, SSI has provided monthly cash payments to needy aged, blind, and disabled individuals who meet the eligibility requirements. States may supplement the basic federal SSI payment.

A number of requirements must be met to get financial benefits from SSI. First, a person must meet the program criteria for age, blindness, or disability. The aged, or elderly, are people 65 years and older. To be considered legally blind, a person must have vision of 20/200 or less in the better eye with the use of corrective lenses, have tunnel vision of 20 degrees or less (can only see a small area straight ahead), or have met state qualifications for the earlier Aid to the Blind program. A person is disabled if he or she cannot earn money at a job because of a physical or

TABLE 3.10

Unemployed persons by marital status, race and Hispanic origin, age, and sex, 2006 and 2007

Marital status, race, Hispanic or Latino ethnicity, and age	Men				Women			
	Thousands of persons		Unemployment rates		Thousands of persons		Unemployment rates	
	2006	2007	2006	2007	2006	2007	2006	2007
Total, 16 years and over	3,753	3,882	4.6	4.7	3,247	3,196	4.6	4.5
Married, spouse present	1,142	1,206	2.4	2.5	1,042	1,049	2.9	2.8
Widowed, divorced, or separated	545	544	5.2	5.3	709	724	4.9	5.0
Single (never married)	2,067	2,132	8.6	8.8	1,496	1,422	7.7	7.2
White, 16 years and over	2,730	2,869	4.0	4.2	2,271	2,274	4.0	4.0
Married, spouse present	896	965	2.2	2.4	839	830	2.7	2.6
Widowed, divorced, or separated	407	421	4.7	4.9	523	547	4.7	4.9
Single (never married)	1,428	1,483	7.5	7.8	909	897	6.4	6.3
Black or African American, 16 years and over	774	752	9.5	9.1	775	693	8.4	7.5
Married, spouse present	166	156	4.7	4.3	121	123	4.4	4.3
Widowed, divorced, or separated	105	92	8.3	7.5	155	135	6.4	5.7
Single (never married)	502	504	15.2	15.0	499	435	12.5	10.8
Asian, 16 years and over	110	119	3.0	3.1	95	110	3.1	3.4
Married, spouse present	49	54	2.2	2.2	55	61	2.9	3.1
Widowed, divorced, or separated	11	9	3.5	3.0	12	12	2.7	2.7
Single (never married)	49	56	4.9	5.2	29	37	3.8	4.4
Hispanic or Latino ethnicity, 16 years and over	601	695	4.8	5.3	480	525	5.9	6.1
Married, spouse present	201	247	3.0	3.5	177	191	4.5	4.7
Widowed, divorced, or separated	73	85	4.2	5.1	97	110	5.5	6.0
Single (never married)	327	363	7.8	8.3	206	224	8.2	8.3
Total, 25 years and over	2,426	2,538	3.5	3.6	2,221	2,198	3.7	3.6
Married, spouse present	1,088	1,152	2.4	2.5	955	959	2.7	2.7
Widowed, divorced, or separated	520	515	5.1	5.1	667	683	4.8	4.9
Single (never married)	819	871	6.1	6.3	599	556	5.7	5.2
White, 25 years and over	1,798	1,907	3.1	3.3	1,578	1,579	3.3	3.3
Married, spouse present	854	919	2.2	2.3	765	756	2.6	2.5
Widowed, divorced, or separated	389	401	4.6	4.8	494	516	4.5	4.7
Single (never married)	555	587	5.3	5.5	320	307	4.5	4.3
Black or African American, 25 years and over	473	457	7.0	6.6	505	453	6.5	5.8
Married, spouse present	156	149	4.5	4.1	113	113	4.2	4.1
Widowed, divorced, or separated	102	85	8.2	7.3	145	129	6.1	5.5
Single (never married)	214	222	10.6	10.5	247	211	9.2	7.7
Asian, 25 years and over	80	92	2.4	2.7	75	87	2.7	3.0
Married, spouse present	48	53	2.1	2.2	53	59	2.8	3.0
Widowed, divorced, or separated	11	9	3.4	2.8	10	12	2.3	2.7
Single (never married)	21	30	3.1	4.0	13	17	2.7	3.1
Hispanic or Latino ethnicity, 16 years and over	387	455	3.8	4.2	330	355	4.9	5.1
Married, spouse present	189	234	3.0	3.5	154	166	4.2	4.3
Widowed, divorced, or separated	67	77	4.1	4.9	91	100	5.3	5.7
Single (never married)	131	144	5.7	5.8	85	89	6.4	6.1

Note: Estimates for the above race groups (white, black or African American, and Asian) do not sum to totals because data are not presented for all races. Persons whose ethnicity is identified as Hispanic or Latino may be of any race. Updated population controls are introduced annually with the release of January data.

SOURCE: "24. Unemployed Persons by Marital Status, Race, Hispanic or Latino Ethnicity, Age, and Sex," in *Household Data Annual Averages*, Bureau of Labor Statistics, 2007, http://www.bls.gov/cps/cpsaat24.pdf (accessed January 11, 2009)

mental illness or injury that may cause his or her death, or if the condition lasts for 12 months or longer. Those who met earlier state Aid to the Permanently Disabled requirements may also qualify for assistance.

Unmarried children under the age of 18 (or age 22 if a full-time student) may qualify for SSI if they have a medically determinable physical or mental impairment that substantially reduces their ability to function independently or to engage in age-appropriate activities. This impairment must be expected to last for a continuous period of more than 12 months or to result in death.

Because SSI is a means-tested benefit, a person's income and property must be counted before he or she can receive benefits. In *Green Book*, the Committee on Ways and Means indicates that in 2008 individuals and couples receiving Social Security benefits could not earn more than $657 and $976 per month, respectively. In addition, a person could have no more than $2,000 worth of property, and a couple could have no more than $3,000 worth of property (mainly in savings accounts or stocks and bonds). Not included in countable resources are the person's home, as well as household goods and personal

TABLE 3.11

Federal minimum wage rates under the Fair Labor Standards Act, 1938–2009

Effective date	1938 Act[a]	1961 Amendments[b]	1966 & Subsequent amendments[c]	
			Nonfarm	Farm
Oct. 24, 1938	$0.25			
Oct. 24, 1939	$0.30			
Oct. 24, 1945	$0.40			
Jan. 25, 1950	$0.75			
Mar. 1, 1956	$1.00			
Sept. 3, 1961	$1.15	$1.00		
Sept. 3, 1963	$1.25			
Sept. 3, 1964		$1.15		
Sept. 3, 1965		$1.25		
Feb. 1, 1967	$1.40	$1.40	$1.00	$1.00
Feb. 1, 1968	$1.60	$1.60	$1.15	$1.15
Feb. 1, 1969			$1.30	$1.30
Feb. 1, 1970			$1.45	
Feb. 1, 1971			$1.60	
May 1, 1974	$2.00	$2.00	$1.90	$1.60
Jan. 1, 1975	$2.10	$2.10	$2.00	$1.80
Jan. 1, 1976	$2.30	$2.30	$2.20	$2.00
Jan. 1, 1977			$2.30	$2.20
Jan. 1, 1978	$2.65 for all covered, nonexempt workers			
Jan. 1, 1979	$2.90 for all covered, nonexempt workers			
Jan. 1, 1980	$3.10 for all covered, nonexempt workers			
Jan. 1, 1981	$3.35 for all covered, nonexempt workers			
Apr. 1, 1990[d]	$3.80 for all covered, nonexempt workers			
Apr. 1, 1991	$4.25 for all covered, nonexempt workers			
Oct. 1, 1996[e]	$4.75 for all covered, nonexempt workers			
Sept. 1, 1997	$5.15 for all covered, nonexempt workers			
Jul. 24, 2007	$5.85 for all covered, nonexempt workers			
Jul. 24, 2008	$6.55 for all covered, nonexempt woikers			
Jul. 24, 2009	$7.25 for all covered, nonexempt workers			

[a]The 1938 Act was applicable generally to employees engaged in interstate commerce or in the production of goods for interstate commerce.
[b]The 1961 Amendments extended coverage primarily to employees in large retail and service enterprises as well as to local transit, construction, and gasoline service station employees.
[c]The 1966 Amendments extended coverage to state and local government employees of hospitals, nursing homes, and schools, and to laundries, dry cleaners, and large hotels, motels, restaurants, and farms. Subsequent amendments extended coverage to the remaining federal, state and local government employees who were not protected in 1966, to certain workers in retail and service trades previously exempted, and to certain domestic workers in private household employment.
[d]Grandfather Clause: Employees who do not meet the tests for individual coverage, and whose employers were covered by the FLSA, on March 31, 1990, and fail to meet the increased annual dollar volume (ADV) test for enterprise coverage, must continue to receive at least $3.35 an hour.
[e]A subminimum wage—$4.25 an hour—is established for employees under 20 years of age during their first 90 consecutive calendar days of employment with an employer.

SOURCE: "Federal Minimum Wage Rates under the Fair Labor Standards Act," U.S. Department for Labor, Employment Standards Administration, 2007, http://www.dol.gov/esa/minwage/chart.pdf (accessed January 11, 2009)

effects worth less than $2,000. A car is not counted if a member of the household uses it to go to and from work or to medical treatments or if it has been adapted for a disabled person. Someone applying for SSI may have life insurance with a cash value of $1,500 or less and/or a burial policy up to the same value.

RECIPIENTS OF SSI BENEFITS. In December 2007, 7.4 million people received SSI payments. Of these, 83% were disabled, 16% were elderly, and 1% were blind. (See Figure 3.5.) Most of those receiving SSI were between the ages of 18 and 64 (57%). Table 3.13 shows the annual amount of payments by source of payment and category

from 1974 to 2006. About 48.4% of SSI recipients in 2006 were female, and 51.6% were male. (See Table 3.14.)

Tax Relief for the Poor

Both conservatives and liberals hailed the Tax Reform Act of 1986 as a major step toward relieving the tax burden of low-income families, one group of Americans whose wages and benefits have been eroding since 1979. The law enlarged and inflation-proofed the Earned Income Tax Credit (EITC), which provides a refundable tax credit that both offsets taxes and often operates as a wage supplement. Only those who work can qualify. The amount is determined, in part, by how much each qualified individual or family earns. It is also adjusted to the size of the family. To be eligible for the family EITC, workers must live with their children, who must be under 19 years old or full-time students under 24 years old.

The maximum credit for 2008 was $2,917 for taxpayers with one child, $4,824 for taxpayers with more than one child, and $438 for people with no children. (See Figure 3.6.) Families received less if their income was low because they were also eligible for public assistance. A family of four received the maximum benefit if its earnings were slightly below the poverty line, but many families well above the poverty line received some credit. Single-parent families with one child were eligible for some credit up to an income of $33,995, and single-parent families with at least two children were eligible for some credit up to an income of $38,646. Benefits phased down gradually when income surpassed $15,740 and phased out entirely for married-couple families with two or more children that earned more than $41,646.

The largest EITC benefits go to families that no longer need welfare. The gradual phaseout and availability of the EITC at above-poverty income levels help stabilize a parent's employment by providing additional money to cover expenses associated with working, such as child care and transportation. Research finds that the EITC has been an effective work incentive and has significantly increased work participation among single mothers. The Urban Institute states in "Government Work Supports and Low-Income Families" that eight out of 10 low-income working families are eligible to receive the tax credit and that the EITC is the support program with the highest participation rate.

Those who do not owe income tax, or who owe an amount smaller than the credit, receive a check directly from the Internal Revenue Service for the credit due them. Most recipients claim the credit when they file an income tax form.

Even though the Tax Reform Act of 1986 has helped ease the burden of federal taxes, most of the poor still pay a substantial share of their income in state and local taxes. The State EITC Online Resource Center (2009, http://www.stateeitc.com/map/index.asp) notes that as of April 2009, 23 states and the District of Columbia had enacted a

TABLE 3.12

Workers paid hourly rates at or below minimum wage, by selected characteristics, 2007

	Number of workers (in thousands)				Percent distribution				Percent of workers paid hourly rates		
	Total paid hourly rates	At or below minimum wage			Total paid hourly rates	At or below minimum wage			Total	At or below minimum wage	
Characteristic		Total	At minimum wage	Below minimum wage		Total	At minimum wage	Below minimum wage		At minimum wage	Below minimum wage
Age and sex											
Total, 16 years and over	75,873	1,729	267	1,462	100.0	100.0	100.0	100.0	2.3	0.4	1.9
16 to 24 years	16,275	814	145	669	21.5	47.1	54.3	45.8	5.0	0.9	4.1
16 to 19 years	5,434	373	93	280	7.2	21.6	34.8	19.2	6.9	1.7	5.2
25 years and over	59,597	915	122	793	78.5	52.9	45.7	54.2	1.5	0.2	1.3
Men, 16 years and over	37,790	546	86	460	49.8	31.6	32.2	31.5	1.4	0.2	1.2
16 to 24 years	8,314	242	52	190	11.0	14.0	19.5	13.0	2.9	0.6	2.3
16 to 19 years	2,652	136	37	99	3.5	7.9	13.9	6.8	5.1	1.4	3.7
25 years and over	29,476	304	34	270	38.8	17.6	12.7	18.5	1.0	0.1	0.9
Women, 16 years and over	38,082	1,183	181	1,002	50.2	68.4	67.8	68.5	3.1	0.5	2.6
16 to 24 years	7,961	572	93	479	10.5	33.1	34.8	32.8	7.2	1.2	6.0
16 to 19 years	2,782	238	56	182	3.7	13.8	21.0	12.4	8.6	2.0	6.5
25 years and over	30,121	611	88	523	39.7	35.3	33.0	35.8	2.0	0.3	1.7
Race, sex, and Hispanic or Latino ethnicity											
White[a]	61,061	1,420	204	1,216	80.5	82.1	76.4	83.2	2.3	0.3	2.0
Men	30,944	471	73	398	40.8	27.2	27.3	27.2	1.5	0.2	1.3
Women	30,117	949	131	818	39.7	54.9	49.1	56.0	3.2	0.4	2.7
Black or African American[a]	9,965	205	55	150	13.1	11.9	20.6	10.3	2.1	0.6	1.5
Men	4,482	49	10	39	5.9	2.8	3.7	2.7	1.1	0.2	0.9
Women	5,483	156	45	111	7.2	9.0	16.9	7.6	2.8	0.8	2.0
Asian[a]	2,730	51	1	50	3.6	2.9	0.4	3.4	1.9	0.0	1.8
Men	1,260	14	—	14	1.7	0.8	—	1.0	1.1	—	1.1
Women	1,469	37	1	36	1.9	2.1	0.4	2.5	2.5	0.1	2.5
Hispanic or Latino[a]	13,168	246	41	205	17.4	14.2	15.4	14.0	1.9	0.3	1.6
Men	7,796	114	19	95	10.3	6.6	7.1	6.5	1.5	0.2	1.2
Women	5,372	132	22	110	7.1	7.6	8.2	7.5	2.5	0.4	2.0
Full-and-part-time status and sex											
Full-time workers[b]	57,745	752	94	658	76.1	43.5	35.2	45.0	1.3	0.2	1.1
Men	32,003	283	30	253	42.2	16.4	11.2	17.3	0.9	0.1	0.8
Women	25,743	469	64	405	33.9	27.1	24.0	27.7	1.8	0.2	1.6
Part-time workers[b]	17,997	971	172	799	23.7	56.2	64.4	54.7	5.4	1.0	4.4
Men	5,721	260	56	204	7.5	15.0	21.0	14.0	4.5	1.0	3.6
Women	12,276	711	117	594	16.2	41.1	43.8	40.6	5.8	1.0	4.8

[a]Estimates for the above race groups (white, black or African American, and Asian) do not sum to totals because data are not presented for all races. Persons whose ethnicity is identified as Hispanic or Latino may be of any race.

[b]The distinction between full- and part-time workers is based on hours usually worked. These data will not sum to totals because full- or part-time status on the principal job is not identifiable for a small number of multiple jobholders.

Note: Data exclude all self-employed persons regardless of whether or not their businesses are incorporated. Dash indicates no data or data that do not meet publication criteria.

SOURCE: "Table 1. Employed Wage and Salary Workers Paid Hourly Rates with Earnings at or below the Prevailing Federal Minimum Wage by Selected Characteristics, 2007 Annual Averages," in *Characteristics of Minimum Wage Workers: 2007*, U.S. Department of Labor, Bureau of Labor Statistics, March 2008, http://www.bls.gov/cps/minwage2007.pdf (accessed January 11, 2009)

FIGURE 3.5

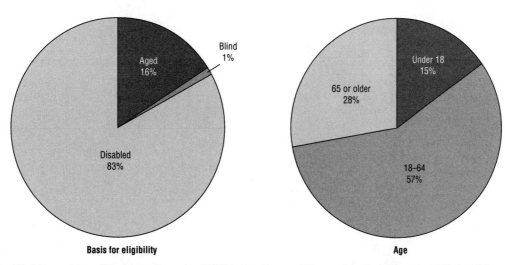

Supplemental Security Income (SSI) recipients, by basis of eligibility and age, December 2007

Basis for eligibility

Age

SOURCE: "Basis for Eligibility and Age of Recipients, December 2007," in *Fast Facts and Figures about Social Security, 2008*, Social Security Administration, Office of Retirement and Disability Policy, Office of Research, Evaluation, and Statistics, August 2008, http://www.ssa.gov/policy/docs/chartbooks/fast_facts/2008/fast_facts08.pdf (accessed January 11, 2009)

state EITC to supplement the federal credit. These state programs boost the income of families that move from welfare to work and prevent states from taxing poor families deeper into poverty.

OVERLAPPING SERVICES

Not surprisingly, poor households that receive one form of social welfare assistance are likely to qualify for and receive others. For example, the Committee on Ways and Means notes in *The Green Book* (2004, http://waysandmeans.house.gov/media/pdf/greenbook2003/15OVERVIEW.pdf.) that during 2002 (the most recent year for which data are available as of mid-2009), 37.6% of households receiving TANF also received housing assistance, 62.3% received free or reduced-price school meals, 80.8% received food stamps, and 99.6% were on Medicaid. Similarly, among households receiving SSI, 17.7% received free or reduced-price school meals, 22.9% lived in public or subsidized rental housing, 40.2% received food stamps, and 96.4% were on Medicaid. About 18.2% of those receiving Social Security and 17.8% of people receiving Medicare were also on Medicaid. Among households receiving food stamps, 16.2% received TANF, 26% were on Medicare, 30.2% received SSI, and 30.5% received Social Security. (These figures do not add up to 100% because some people received more than one benefit.) About 10.8% of those receiving WIC also received TANF benefits.

Data from 2004 also show substantial overlap in individuals participating in public assistance programs. In that year, 15.1% of mothers who had a birth in the last year participated in one public assistance program, 11.2% participated in two programs, 5.2% participated in three programs, and 2.7% participated in four to six programs. (See Figure 3.2.) Mothers who had not had a birth in the last year had lower participation rates. Nearly one out of 10 (9.5%) participated in one government assistance program, 6.5% participated in two programs, 3.2% participated in three programs, and 0.8% participated in four to eight programs.

In "Government Work Supports and Low-Income Families," the Urban Institute points out how important the "package of supports" could be to working, low-income families. The package could include Medicaid, food stamps, child care subsidies, and the EITC. According to the Urban Institute, in 2002 a single parent with two children working full time and earning $10,000 (the minimum wage in 2002) could receive about $23,600 in work supports. However, most working families did not receive all the supports they could have; in fact, only 7% of families with incomes below the federal poverty level received all four supports in 2002.

TABLE 3.13

Total annual amount of SSI payments by eligibility category, selected years 1974–2006

[In thousands of dollars]

Year	Total	Federal SSI	Federally administered state supplementation
All recipients			
1974	5,096,813	3,833,161	1,263,652
1975	5,716,072	4,313,538	1,402,534
1980	7,714,640	5,866,354	1,848,286
1985	10,749,938	8,777,341	1,972,597
1990	16,132,959	12,893,805	3,239,154
1995	27,037,280	23,919,430	3,117,850
2000	30,671,699	27,290,248	3,381,451
2001	32,165,856	28,705,503	3,460,353
2002	33,718,999	29,898,765	3,820,234
2003	34,693,278	30,688,029	4,005,249
2004	36,065,358	31,886,509	4,178,849
2005	37,235,843	33,058,056	4,177,787
2006	38,888,961	34,736,088	4,152,873
Aged			
1974	2,414,034	1,782,742	631,292
1975	2,516,515	1,842,980	673,535
1980	2,617,023	1,860,194	756,829
1985	2,896,671	2,202,557	694,114
1990	3,559,388	2,521,382	1,038,006
1995	4,239,222	3,374,772	864,450
2000	4,540,045	3,597,516	942,530
2001	4,664,076	3,708,527	955,549
2002	4,802,792	3,751,491	1,051,301
2003	4,856,875	3,758,070	1,098,805
2004	4,894,070	3,773,901	1,133,324
2005	4,964,627	3,836,625	1,128,002
2006	5,115,911	3,953,106	1,162,804
Blind			
1974	125,791	91,308	34,483
1975	127,240	92,427	34,813
1980	185,827	131,506	54,321
1985	259,840	195,183	64,657
1990	328,949	238,415	90,534
1995	367,441	298,238	69,203
2000	385,927	312,238	73,688
2001	398,624	323,895	74,729
2002	416,454	335,405	81,049
2003	409,293	325,878	83,415
2004	412,414	327,446	85,364
2005	414,147	330,591	83,556
2006	409,287	326,230	83,057
Disabled			
1974	2,556,988	1,959,112	597,876
1975	3,072,317	2,378,131	694,186
1980	4,911,792	3,874,655	1,037,137
1985	7,593,427	6,379,601	1,213,826
1990	12,244,622	10,134,007	2,110,615
1995	22,430,612	20,246,415	2,184,197
2000	25,745,710	23,380,477	2,365,233
2001	27,125,707	24,695,630	2,430,077
2002	28,499,771	25,811,887	2,687,884
2003	29,429,428	26,606,400	2,823,028
2004	30,745,406	27,785,246	2,960,160
2005	31,857,069	28,890,840	2,966,229
2006	33,363,762	30,456,751	2,907,011

Note: Totals do not necessarily equal the sum of rounded components.
SSI = Supplemental Security Income.

SOURCE: "Table 7.A4. Total Federally Administered Payments, by Eligibility Category, Selected Years 1974–2006," in *Annual Statistical Supplement, 2007*, Social Security Administration, April 2008, http://www.ssa.gov/policy/docs/statcomps/supplement/2007/7a.pdf (accessed January 11, 2009)

TABLE 3.14

Number and percentage distribution of federally administered awards, by sex, age, and eligibility category, 2006

Sex and age	Adults				Blind and disabled children[a]
	Total	Aged	Blind	Disabled	
All persons					
Number	838,448	110,264	3,531	548,527	176,126
Percent	100.0	100.0	100.0	100.0	100.0
Percentage distribution by sex					
Male	51.6	38.2	52.5	50.2	64.2
Female	48.4	61.8	47.5	49.8	35.8
Percentage distribution by age					
Under 5	8.5	—	—	—	40.4
5–9	5.6	—	—	—	26.8
10–14	4.4	—	—	—	20.7
15–17	1.9	—	—	—	8.8
18–21	5.3	—	15.2	7.0	3.2
22–29	6.0	—	10.0	9.0	—
30–39	9.6	—	14.7	14.5	—
40–49	17.6	—	21.6	26.7	—
50–59	22.2	—	28.2	33.8	—
60–64	5.6	—	7.3	8.6	—
65–69	7.3	54.3	0.9	0.3	—
70–74	2.7	20.8	0.8	b	—
75–79	1.6	12.3	0.5	b	—
80 or older	1.7	12.7	0.9	b	—
Male					
Number	432,361	42,124	1,853	275,329	113,055
Percent	100.0	100.0	100.0	100.0	100.0
Under 5	9.9	—	—	—	38.0
5–9	7.7	—	—	—	29.6
10–14	5.6	—	—	—	21.5
15–17	2.1	—	—	—	8.0
18–21	5.9	—	15.7	8.0	2.9
22–29	6.2	—	11.2	9.6	—
30–39	9.0	—	15.2	14.0	—
40–49	16.9	—	23.2	26.4	—
50–59	21.5	—	27.0	33.5	—
60–64	5.3	—	6.1	8.2	—
65–69	5.6	56.4	0.5	0.2	—
70–74	2.2	22.4	0.3	b	—
75–79	1.2	11.9	0.3	b	—
80 or older	0.9	9.2	0.4	b	—
Female					
Number	406,087	68,140	1,678	273,198	63,071
Percent	100.0	100.0	100.0	100.0	100.0
Under 5	7.0	—	—	—	44.8
5–9	3.4	—	—	—	21.7
10–14	3.0	—	—	—	19.3
15–17	1.6	—	0.1	—	10.3
18–21	4.7	—	14.7	6.0	3.9
22–29	5.7	—	8.7	8.4	—
30–39	10.2	—	14.1	15.0	—
40–49	18.3	—	19.8	27.1	—
50–59	23.1	—	29.4	34.1	—
60–64	6.1	—	8.5	9.0	—
65–69	9.1	52.9	1.4	0.3	—
70–74	3.3	19.8	1.3	b	—
75–79	2.1	12.5	0.7	b	—
80 or older	2.5	14.8	1.4	b	—

Notes: Totals do not necessarily equal the sum of rounded components.
— = Not applicable.
[a]Includes students aged 18–21.
[b]Less than 0.05 percent.

SOURCE: "Table 7.E2. Percentage Distribution of Federally Administered Awards, by Sex, Age, and Eligibility Category, 2006," in *Annual Statistical Supplement, 2007*, Social Security Administration, April 2008, http://www.ssa.gov/policy/docs/statcomps/supplement/2007/7e.pdf (accessed January 11, 2009)

FIGURE 3.6

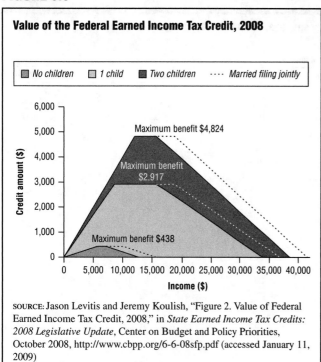

Value of the Federal Earned Income Tax Credit, 2008

SOURCE: Jason Levitis and Jeremy Koulish, "Figure 2. Value of Federal Earned Income Tax Credit, 2008," in *State Earned Income Tax Credits: 2008 Legislative Update*, Center on Budget and Policy Priorities, October 2008, http://www.cbpp.org/6-6-08sfp.pdf (accessed January 11, 2009)

CHAPTER 4
CHARACTERISTICS OF THE HOMELESS

AUTHORITATIVE ESTIMATES OF HOMELESSNESS

The Facts Are Hard to Determine

Broad national assessments of homelessness were undertaken by several agencies and organizations during the 1980s and mid-1990s, including *A Report to the Secretary on the Homeless and Emergency Shelters* (1984) by the U.S. Department of Housing and Urban Development (HUD), Martha R. Burt and Barbara Cohen's *America's Homeless: Numbers, Characteristics, and Programs that Serve Them* (1989), and Martha R. Burt et al.'s *Homelessness: Programs and the People They Serve* (December 1999, http://www.urban.org/UploadedPDF/homelessness.pdf). In 2002 Burt et al. summarized in *Evaluation of Continuums of Care for Homeless People* (May 2002, http://www.huduser.org/publications/pdf/continuums_of_care.pdf) the difficulty of addressing homelessness without a continuing census or other governmental program to track the homeless population.

In 2001 Congress directed HUD to begin collecting nationwide data on homelessness. In July 2008 HUD released *The Third Annual Homeless Assessment Report to Congress* (http://www.hudhre.info/documents/3rdHomelessAssessmentReport.pdf). This was the first HUD report that included both a point-in-time count of the homeless and data on sheltered homeless people over a 12-month period. Both of these counts were nationally representative samples, rather than full counts. Regardless, they are the most accurate recent counts of the homeless population available.

Several other organizations periodically collect data on the homeless population. The National Alliance to End Homelessness has collected more recent information that can be used to measure homelessness over time. In 2007 the organization compiled data from 461 local Continuum of Care point-in-time counts from across the nation and published an estimate of the national homeless population in *Homelessness Counts: Changes in Homelessness from 2005 to 2007* (January 2009, http://www.endhomelessness.org/content/article/detail/2158). The alliance estimates that in 2007, 671,859 people experienced homelessness. (See Table 4.1.) Of these, 391,399 (58.3%) were sheltered and 280,460 (41.7%) were unsheltered. Nearly two-thirds (423,348, or 63%) were homeless individuals and 248,511 (37%) were members of homeless families. Nearly one out of five (123,790, or 18.4%) of homeless people were chronically homeless—in other words, they had been homeless repeatedly or for a long period of time. The number of homeless people had dropped 10% since 2005, although in some groups there were more dramatic drops. The number of chronically homeless people dropped 28%, and the number of people in homeless families dropped 18%. However, the alliance cautions that point-in-time estimates tell only how many people are homeless at a given time and that, in reality, many more people experience homeless at some point in a given year.

How Numbers Are Used

When hearing reports about the homeless, the ordinary citizen envisions people, including children, who live on the street permanently and sleep in cardboard boxes under bridges or in cars. There are, of course, people in this category, but they are the minority among the homeless. The National Alliance to End Homelessness labels such people the chronically homeless and estimates their number at 123,790. (See Table 4.1.) Most of the homeless (82%) are not chronically homeless but are temporarily without a residence. After some period of homelessness, they find permanent shelter or move in with relatives; however, people who have moved in with family as well as people who are doubled up are also counted as homeless by some programs and homeless advocates.

A more accurate definition of the homeless population is the group of people who are, on any day, without proper shelter. When agencies or the media cite numbers in the 600,000 to 800,000 range, they mean the size of the homeless

TABLE 4.1

Homeless point-in-time estimates by type, 2005 and 2007

	2005 estimate	2007 estimate	Change	% change
Total homeless	**744,313**	**671,859**	**−72,454**	**−10%**
Individuals	437,710	423,348	−14,362	−3%
Chronically homeless	171,192	123,790	−47,402	−28%
Persons in families	303,524	248,511	−55,013	−18%
Family households	98,452	83,935	−14,517	−15%
Unsheltered	322,082	280,460	−41,622	−13%
Sheltered	407,813	391,399	−16,414	−4%

Notes: The 2005 numbers are an adjusted tabulation of 2005 CoC point-in-time estimates. These data were adjusted and corrected for data entry errors, summation errors, and outliers that were based on unscientific extrapolations or states that did not follow Department of Housing and Urban Development's (HUD) guidance for counting homeless people.

SOURCE: "Table 1. Changes in CoC Homelessness Estimates: 2005 to 2007," in *Homelessness Counts: Changes in Homelessness from 2005 to 2007*, National Alliance to End Homelessness, January 2009, http://www.end homelessness.org/content/article/detail/2158 (accessed February 10, 2009)

TABLE 4.2

Number likely to be homeless at least once during the year, 1996

	New homeless spells begun in last week	Average week estimate	Annual projection
	A	B	C
February 1996	52,000	842,000	3.5 million
October 1996	36,900	444,000	2.3 million

Note: The projection is developed by taking column A times 51 weeks and adding the result to column B. Column B represents the estimated constant population of homeless in any one week. The assumption is that a population of the size shown in column A is continuously passing into and also out of homeless status throughout the year. Data for February were based on the estimates of homeless program employees, data for October on interviews with the homeless.

SOURCE: "Number Likely to Be Homeless at Least Once in a Given Year," in *America's Homeless II: Populations and Services*, Urban Institute, February 2000, http://www.urban.org/UploadedPDF/900344_AmericasHomelessII.pdf (accessed January 14, 2009)

TABLE 4.3

Homeless children and youth enrolled in school during the 2003–04 school year

Grades	Number enrolled
K–5	338,982
6–8	153,500
9–12	110,086
Total all grades	**602,568**

SOURCE: "Table 1. Homeless Children and Youth Enrolled in School during the 2003–04 School Year," in *Report to the President and Congress on the Implementation of the Education for Homeless Children and Youth Program under the McKinney-Vento Homeless Assistance Act*, U.S. Department of Education, April 2006, http://www.ed.gov/programs/homeless/rpt2006.doc (accessed January 14, 2009)

population at any one point in time. Individuals are continuously joining this population, and others are leaving it. If all people who are homeless at some point during a given year were counted, the number would reach between 2.5 million and 3.5 million individuals, as indicated by Burt et al. in *Evaluation of Continuums of Care for Homeless People.*

The manner in which the annual projections for 1996 were derived is shown in Table 4.2. The data for October, which are projected from counts of homeless services seekers, show that an estimated 36,900 individuals began spells of homelessness during the week surveyed, whereas the total number of people in the homeless population in any one week was estimated to be 444,000. The annual projection assumed that each week 36,900 became homeless and an equal number phased out of the homeless status. Multiplying 36,900 by the 51 weeks remaining in the year, and then adding that total to the average homeless population in a week produced the 2.3 million count of people who were homeless at least once in 1996. This number does not mean that there were 2.3 million homeless during the entire span of 1996.

In the *Third Annual Homeless Assessment Report to Congress*, HUD notes that in it conducted a count of all homeless individuals who used a shelter during a 12-month period. Over half a million (1,589,000) individuals, or one out of every 200 U.S. residents, used an emergency shelter or transitional housing. This count underrepresents the number of women, because the residents of domestic violence shelters are not reported. It also does not include the unsheltered homeless population.

Counting Homeless Children

Under the McKinney-Vento Homeless Assistance Act of 1987, the U.S. Department of Education is required to file a report on homeless children served by the act. The

Department of Education obtains the data from school districts; however, school districts use different methods of estimation. In *Report to the President and Congress on the Implementation of the Education for Homeless Children and Youth Program under the McKinney-Vento Homeless Assistance Act* (2006, http://www.ed.gov/programs/homeless/rpt2006.doc), the Department of Education states that 602,568 children who experienced homelessness at some point during the year were enrolled during the 2003–04 school year. (See Table 4.3.) This number is almost certainly much lower than the number of children who actually experienced homelessness during that period, as the homeless status of children does not always come to the attention of school officials and many homeless children are not enrolled in school.

The most recent data on homeless children was released in 2009 by the National Center on Family Homelessness in *America's Youngest Outcasts: State Report Card on Child Homelessness* (March 2009, http://www.homelesschildren america.org/pdf/rc_full_report.pdf). The organization uses data collected by 12,550 local education agencies as mandated by the McKinney-Vento Homeless Assistance Act to estimate that 1.5 million children experience homelessness each year. It further notes that one out of 50 American children was homeless at some point during the 2005–06 school year. In Louisiana 18.7% of all children were homeless, which was by far the worst state in the nation. Few homeless children lived without shelter—56% of homeless children lived doubled-up, 24% lived in shelters, 7% lived in hotels/motels, and 3% were unsheltered.

PROFILES OF THE HOMELESS

Gender and Race

Studies of homeless people and surveys of officials knowledgeable about homeless clients conducted since the 1990s show similar patterns of gender and racial data for the homeless, although the percentages vary from study to study.

Data collected by the U.S. Conference of Mayors show that in almost all cities surveyed in 2007, single males greatly outnumbered single females among the homeless; 67.5% of singles and unaccompanied youth were male, and 32.5% were female. (See Table 4.4.) However, among members of homeless families, 65% were female and 35% were male, reflecting that homeless families are most often headed by women.

African-Americans are overrepresented among the homeless population. In 2007, 47% of the homeless population in surveyed cities was white and 47% was African-American. (See Table 4.4.) About 24% of the homeless population was Hispanic.

The Association of Gospel Rescue Missions (AGRM) regularly surveys the homeless population at more than a hundred missions serving inner cities. AGRM surveys are based on large numbers of homeless served. For example, in *Women with Children Hit Hardest by Slow Economy* (November 2008, http://www.agrm.org/pdf/snapshot_natio nal_2008.pdf), the AGRM states that 22,000 individuals were surveyed at rescue missions around the country in 2008. Its data show that men made up 74% of the homeless population in 2008. (See Table 1.8 in Chapter 1.)

According to the AGRM, in *Survey of 14,000 Homeless: Most Are New to the Streets; One in Four Is under 25* (November 21, 1996, http://www.agrm.org/statistics/snap96 .html), the racial and ethnic composition of the homeless population it served in 1995 was 37% white, 45% African-American, 13% Hispanic, 2% Asian-American, and 3% Native American. By 2008 the proportion of white homeless people had risen to 46%; the African-American proportion had dropped to 35%; the Hispanic proportion decreased to 11%; the Asian-American proportion remained unchanged; and the Native American proportion had increased to 5%. (See Table 1.8 in Chapter 1.) There is also a noticeable

TABLE 4.4

Demographic characteristics of sheltered homeless persons as reported by cities, 2007

Characteristic	% members of households with children*	% singles and unaccompanied youth*
Age		
Under 5	25.4%	<1%
5–17	35.2%	1.3%
18–34	23.5%	24.8%
35–61	15.7%	68.2%
62 and over	1.6%	5.4%
Gender (adults only)		
Male	35.0%	67.5%
Female	65.0%	32.5%
Ethnicity		
Non-Hispanic/Latino	76.0%	87.2%
Hispanic/Latino	24.0%	12.8%
Race		
American Indian or Alaska Native	4.0%	2.5%
Asian	2.0%	1.6%
Black or African-American	47.0%	45.7%
Native Hawaiian or other Pacific Islander	1.0%	<1%
White	47.0%	50.0%
Employed persons (adults only)	17.4%	13.0%
Veterans (adults only)	2.8%	16.9%
Victims of domestic violence (adults only)	12.1%	7.2%
Disability status (adults only)		
Mental health	7.9%	22.4%
Substance abuse	9.6%	37.1%
Persons with HIV/AIDS	<1%	1.6%
Physical disability	3.9%	11.9%
Developmental disability	0.8%	3.7%

Notes: The number of cities reporting data on each of the characteristics presented in the exhibit was not consistent. For members of households with children, 12 cities reported age, 16 cities reported gender, 15 cities reported ethnicity, 16 cities reported race, 15 cities reported employment and Veterans status, 14 cities reported victims of domestic violence, and 14 cities reported disability status. For singles and unaccompanied youth, 14 cities reported age, 16 cities reported gender, 16 cities reported ethnicity, 16 cities reported race, 15 cities reported employment and Veterans status, 14 cities reported victims of domestic violence, and 15 cities reported disability status.
*Totals may exceed 100 percent due to rounding. For race, several cities reported clients in multiple categories and therefore the totals exceed 100 percent.

SOURCE: "Exhibit 2.4. Demographic Characteristics of Sheltered Homeless Persons As Reported by Cities," in *Hunger and Homelessness Survey: A Status Report on Hunger and Homelessness in America's Cities, A 23-City Survey*, U.S. Conference of Mayors—Sodexho, December 2007, http://www.usmayors.org/HHSurvey2007/hhsurvey07.pdf (accessed January 14, 2009)

increase in the proportion of homeless women—they had risen from 19% in 1995 to 26% in 2008.

The AGRM's numbers are similar to Burt et al.'s *Homelessness*. In 1996, 68% of the homeless population was male and 32% was female. Forty-one percent of the homeless were white, 40% black, 11% Hispanic, 8% Native American, and 1% of other races.

The surveys thus exhibit similar patterns. More of the homeless were male than female, but these proportions have been gradually changing. In all surveys, African-Americans are greatly overrepresented among the homeless—most surveys state that African-Americans make up about 40% of the homeless population, whereas the U.S. Census Bureau reports that they made up only about 14% (40.7

TABLE 4.5

Estimates of the population by sex, race, and Hispanic origin, 2000 and 2007

Sex, race, and hispanic origin	Population estimates		April 1, 2000	
	July 1, 2007	July 1, 2000	Estimates base	Census
Both sexes	**301,621,157**	**282,194,308**	**281,424,602**	**281,421,906**
One race	296,765,021	278,266,300	277,526,880	277,524,226
White	241,166,890	228,622,981	228,106,500	228,104,485
Black	38,756,452	35,812,983	35,704,871	35,704,124
AIAN	2,938,436	2,673,312	2,663,851	2,663,818
Asian	13,366,154	10,692,156	10,589,122	10,589,265
NHPI	537,089	464,868	462,536	462,534
Two or more races	4,856,136	3,928,008	3,897,722	3,897,680
Race alone or in combination*				
White	245,373,882	231,980,517	231,436,438	231,434,388
Black	40,744,132	37,231,316	37,105,009	37,104,248
AIAN	4,536,857	4,236,189	4,225,121	4,225,058
Asian	15,165,186	12,121,675	12,006,747	12,006,894
NHPI	1,019,301	910,595	906,797	906,785
Not Hispanic	**256,116,846**	**246,545,323**	**246,118,224**	**246,116,088**
One race	251,912,205	243,113,878	242,711,940	242,709,840
White	199,091,567	195,769,808	195,576,996	195,575,485
Black	37,037,204	34,413,175	34,313,716	34,313,007
AIAN	2,286,734	2,103,896	2,097,464	2,097,440
Asian	13,079,642	10,458,204	10,356,661	10,356,804
NHPI	417,058	368,795	367,103	367,104
Two or more races	4,204,641	3,431,445	3,406,284	3,406,248
Race alone or in combination*				
White	202,719,711	198,692,789	198,477,136	198,475,591
Black	38,716,774	35,613,659	35,498,895	35,498,173
AIAN	3,657,920	3,462,740	3,455,577	3,455,525
Asian	14,687,894	11,743,712	11,631,783	11,631,935
NHPI	831,723	754,679	751,849	751,844
Hispanic	**45,504,311**	**35,648,985**	**35,306,378**	**35,305,818**
One race	44,852,816	35,152,422	34,814,940	34,814,386
White	42,075,323	32,853,173	32,529,504	32,529,000
Black	1,719,248	1,399,808	1,391,155	1,391,117
AIAN	651,702	569,416	566,387	566,378
Asian	286,512	233,952	232,461	232,461
NHPI	120,031	96,073	95,433	95,430
Two or more races	651,495	496,563	491,438	491,432
Race alone or in combination*				
White	42,654,171	33,287,728	32,959,302	32,958,797
Black	2,027,358	1,617,657	1,606,114	1,606,075
AIAN	878,937	773,449	769,544	769,533
Asian	477,292	377,963	374,964	374,959
NHPI	187,578	155,916	154,948	154,941

*'In combination' means in combination with one or more other races. The sum of the five race groups adds to more than the total population because individuals may report more than one race.

Note: The April 1, 2000 Population Estimates base reflects changes to the Census 2000 population from the Count Question Resolution program. The original race data from Census 2000 are modified to eliminate the "some other race" category. This modification is used for all Census Bureau estimates products. Hispanic origin is considered an ethnicity, not a race. Hispanics may be of any race.

Abbreviations
Black = Black or African American
AIAN = American Indian and Alaska Native
NHPI = Native Hawaiian and other Pacific Islander

SOURCE: Adapted from "Table 3. Annual Estimates of the Population by Sex, Race, and Hispanic Origin for the United States: April 1, 2000 to July 1, 2007," U.S. Census Bureau, April 2008, http://www.census.gov/popest/national/asrh/NC-EST2007-srh.html (accessed January 14, 2009)

million out of 301.6 million) of the U.S. population in 2007. (See Table 4.5.) Hispanics' representation among the homeless was near their share of the total U.S. population (45.5 million, or 15%).

Family Structure

According to Burt et al., in *Homelessness*, 62% of homeless men and 16% of homeless women were single in 1996—meaning they were homeless without a spouse or children. In *Homelessness Counts*, the National Alliance to End Homelessness finds that 248,511 individuals were members of 83,935 families in 2007; this represented 37% of the total homeless population. (See Table 4.1.) The number of families among the homeless population had declined 15% from two years before. The Conference of Mayors notes that in 2007, 65% of homeless women and 35% of homeless men were members of households with children. (See Table 4.4.)

In *Homelessness Counts*, the National Alliance to End Homelessness does not specify gender in its count of the 2007 homeless population by gender, but it does break the count down into individuals (423,348, or 63%) and people in families (248,511, or 37%). (See Table 4.1.) The AGRM survey for 2008 presents data about the family structure of homeless families. (See Table 1.8 in Chapter 1.) The organization speculates that the economic crisis that began in 2008 will hit single women with children harder than any other group, as demonstrated by the fact that women with children made up 66% of homeless families counted in 2008, a jump from 55% the year before. The National Center on Family Homelessness states in *America's Youngest Outcasts*, "With the current economic downturn and the staggering increase in housing foreclosures, more and more families are likely to become homeless."

Age

Burt et al. find in *Homelessness* that in 1996, 25% of the homeless were between 25 and 34 years of age, 35% were between 35 and 44, and 17% were between 45 and 54. The AGRM survey for 2008 shows that 18% of the homeless were between 26 and 35 years of age, 26% were between 36 and 45, and 31% were between 46 and 65. (See Table 1.8 in Chapter 1.)

CHILDREN AND YOUTHS. Homeless children and youths have always received special attention from the public and from welfare agencies. In the terminology of the nineteenth century, children are considered "worthy" poor, because if they are homeless, they did nothing to deserve this status.

Estimates provided by the Conference of Mayors give some indication of the proportion of children and runaway teens (unaccompanied youth) among the homeless population. (See Table 4.6.) On an average night, the vast majority of people living on the streets in 2008 were single adults (12,679, or 94%), and only 4% (543) were people in families and 2% (268) were unaccompanied youth. Homeless families were much more likely to be living in permanent supportive housing or transitional housing. In 2008, 9,930 (29%) people in families were living in emergency shelters on an average night, 10,710 (40%) were living in permanent supportive housing, and 12,862 (56%) were living in transitional housing. Unaccompanied youth were most often found in emergency shelters.

The Department of Education collects estimates of homeless children from selected school district records and reports the date in *Report to the President and Congress.* The data exclude infants but include some children of preschool age. The department's tallies show a total of 602,568 children and youth of school age and another 19,343 children of preschool age that had been served during the 2003–04 school year. Of these children, about half (50.3%) lived doubled-up with relatives or friends, a quarter (25.3%) lived in shelters, 9.9% lived in hotels or motels, and 2.6% were

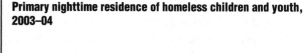

TABLE 4.6

Total number of persons homeless or in permanent supportive housing on an average night in 2008

[23 cities responding]

	Persons in families	Single adults	Unaccompanied youth
Living on the streets	543	12,679	268
Emergency shelter	9,930	23,566	352
Transitional housing	12,862	10,007	243
Permanent supportive housing	10,710	16,257	140

SOURCE: "Exhibit 2.2. Total Number of Persons Homeless or in Permanent Supportive Housing on an Average Night in 2008," in *Hunger and Homelessness Survey: A Status Report on Hunger and Homelessness in America's Cities, A 25-City Survey*, U.S. Conference of Mayors, December 2008, http://www.usmayors.org/pressreleases/documents/hungerhomeless nessreport_121208.pdf (accessed January 4, 2009)

FIGURE 4.1

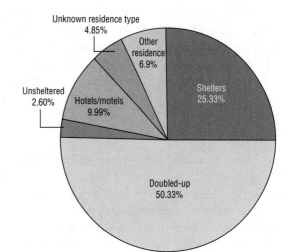

Primary nighttime residence of homeless children and youth, 2003–04

Unknown residence type 4.85%

Other residence 6.9%

Unsheltered 2.60%

Hotels/motels 9.99%

Shelters 25.33%

Doubled-up 50.33%

SOURCE: "Chart 1. Primary Nighttime Residence of Homeless Children and Youth, 2003–04," in *Report to the President and Congress on the Implementation of the Education for Homeless Children and Youth Program under the McKinney-Vento Homeless Assistance Act*, U.S. Department of Education, April 2006, http://www.ed.gov/programs/homeless/rpt2006.doc (accessed January 14, 2009)

unsheltered—in other words, sleeping outside, in vehicles, or in abandoned buildings. (See Figure 4.1.)

Even though the Department of Education's 2006 report omits estimates of the total number of homeless children in the population, *Education for Homeless Children and Youth Program, Report to Congress, Fiscal Year 2000* (2001, www.ed.gov/programs/homeless/rpt2000.doc) does include this information. The department finds that of total children estimated by school districts to be homeless in 2000, only a portion were enrolled and even a smaller number attended school regularly. Among the estimated 343,340 homeless elementary students, 305,920 (89%) were enrolled and 271,906 (79%) attended regularly. However, Arun Venugopal indicates in "Advocates Say City Undercounts Homeless Kids" (September 14, 2006, http://www.wnyc.org/news/articles/64264) that the Department of Education undercounts the number of homeless kids, which would place the number of homeless kids not enrolled in or attending school even higher. For example, in *2007 Greater Los Angeles Homeless Count* (2007, http://www.lahsa.org/docs/homelesscount/2007/LAHSA.pdf), a survey of homeless respondents in Los Angeles, California, the Los Angeles Homeless Services Authority finds that 11% of homeless families with school-age children stated their children were not attending school in 2007. When homeless children do attend school, they have less than optimal conditions for educational achievement.

In *America's Youngest Outcasts: State Report Card on Child Homelessness* (2009, http://www.homelesschildren america.org/pdf/rc_full_report.pdf), the National Center on Family Homelessness indicates that during the 2005–06 school year homeless children had lower proficiency scores when compared to all students. At the elementary school level, the math and reading proficiency scores for all students were 39.6% and 33.8%, respectively; for homeless children, their scores were 21.5% and 24.4%, respectively. At the high school level, the math proficiency scores for all students were 32.2% and for homeless children, 11.4%; and the reading proficiency scores for all students were 30.9% and for homeless children, 14.6%.

The poor educational achievement of homeless youth puts them at an increased risk for homelessness in their adulthood. The National Center on Family Homelessness explains that "poverty traps poor students who need a good education to better their living standards. But in a classic Catch 22, poor children are more likely to do worse than nonpoor children on measures of school achievement. They are twice as likely as their nonpoor counterparts to have repeated a grade, to have been expelled or suspended from school, or to have dropped out of high school." The result is that fewer than a quarter of homeless children graduate from high school. Furthermore, the center notes that "82% of children whose parents have less than a high school diploma live in poverty."

Military Background

Burt et al. report in *Homelessness* that in 1996, 23% of the homeless were veterans, whereas 13% of the general population were veterans. Among men, 33% of the homeless men were veterans and 31% of men in the general population were veterans. The U.S. Department of Veterans Affairs reports in "Overview of Homelessness" (January 16, 2009, http://www1.va.gov/homeless/page.cfm?pg=1) that approximately 154,000 veterans were homeless on any given day, and up to 308,000 experienced homelessness annually. The Conference of Mayors reports that in 2007, 16.9% of homeless adults who were not part of family groups were veterans. (See Table 4.4.)

Citing Department of Veterans Affairs sources, the National Coalition for Homeless Veterans (NCHV) states in "Background and Statistics" (2005, http://www.nchv.org/background.cfm) that of homeless veterans, 96% are male and 4% are female. Almost half (47%) served during the Vietnam War (1955–1975); two-thirds (67%) served for three years or more and one-third (33%) were stationed in a war zone. Seventy-six percent of homeless veterans have problems with alcohol, drugs, or mental health.

In "Survey Confirms 'War on Terror' Veterans Are Seeking Homeless Assistance" (January 12, 2005, http://www.nchv.org/news_article.cfm?id=101), a small survey of 19 homeless veteran service providers to determine the effects of the wars in Iraq and Afghanistan on homeless veteran numbers, the NCHV finds that those service providers had served 67 veterans from these wars. Linda Boone, the executive director of the NCHV, states that these veterans are likely to request assistance sooner and in greater numbers than veterans of previous foreign wars.

President Barack Obama (1961–) responded to the crisis of homelessness among veterans by allocating $1.5 billion to the Homelessness Prevention Fund in the American Recovery and Reinvestment Act, signed into law on February 17, 2009. According to HUD, in "Homelessness Prevention Fund (Formula)" (March 30, 2009, http://www.hud.gov/recovery/homeless-prevention.cfm), "The Homelessness Prevention Fund will provide financial assistance and services to prevent individuals and families from becoming homeless and help those who are experiencing homelessness to be quickly re-housed and stabilized." Obama's proposed 2010 budget would expand the services offered by the Department of Veterans Affairs to include providing supportive services and helping veterans maintain stable housing.

DURATION AND RECURRENCE OF HOMELESSNESS

Most homeless people will become homeless again. In *Homelessness*, Burt et al. note that 51% of all homeless people surveyed in 1996 had been homeless before. The AGRM finds in its 2008 survey that 67% of the homeless had been homeless before—24% had been homeless only once before. Thirty-nine percent of the homeless studied by Burt et al. had been homeless less than six months; six out of 10 (61%) had been homeless for more than half a year. Six out of 10 (60%) of those surveyed by the AGRM in 2008 had been homeless for less than a year.

These studies confirm that homelessness is usually a recurring experience and lasts for months at a time, sug-

TABLE 4.7

Population in emergency and transitional shelters, 1990 and 2000

Area	Population in shelters				Total 2000 U.S. population Percent
	1990		2000		
	Number	Percent	Number	Percent	
United States	178,638	100.0	170,706	100.0	100.0
Region					
Northeast	60,077	33.6	52,369	30.7	19.0
Midwest	27,245	15.3	28,438	16.7	22.9
South	42,407	23.7	42,471	24.9	35.6
West	48,909	27.4	47,428	27.8	22.5

SOURCE: Annetta C. Smith and Denise I. Smith, "Table 1. Population in Emergency and Transitional Shelters for the United States, Regions, States, and Puerto Rico: 1990 and 2000," in *Emergency and Transitional Shelter Population: 2000*, U.S. Census Bureau, October 2001, http://www.census.gov/prod/2001pubs/censr01-2.pdf (accessed January 14, 2009)

gesting that programs that help the homeless do not uniformly help clients solve the fundamental problems that can lead to life on the streets.

WHERE THE HOMELESS LIVE

Homelessness varies, in both the numbers of homeless people and the number of sheltered homeless people. Table 4.7 shows the regional breakdowns of the sheltered homeless population as enumerated in the 1990 and 2000 census counts. In 2000, 30.7% of the sheltered population was found in the Northeast, a region with 19% of the total U.S. population. The West also had a disproportionate share of homeless people in shelters—27.8% of the sheltered were found in the region, yet it had only 22.5% of the total population. The Midwest and the South had smaller shares of the sheltered than of their total populations, which might suggest that a greater proportion of people on the coasts were homeless than people in the middle of the country or that a greater proportion of homeless people on the coasts were sheltered.

Rural Homelessness

Most studies on the homeless have been focused on urban areas, leaving the impression that this problem exists only on city sidewalks. Homelessness is more common in the cities, where the bulk of the population resides, but many areas of rural America also experience the phenomenon. In "Fact Checker: Rural Homelessness" (April 17, 2007, http://www.endhomelessness.org/content/article/detail/1613), the National Alliance to End Homelessness reports that rural communities have higher poverty rates than do urban areas. Furthermore, rural communities have fewer official shelters and fewer public places (e.g., heating grates, subways, or train stations) where the homeless can find temporary shelter. Therefore, they are more likely to live in a car or camper, or with relatives in overcrowded or rundown housing. Therefore, finding the rural homeless is more difficult for investigators of the problem.

The National Coalition for the Homeless (NCH) reports in the fact sheet "Rural Homelessness" (June 2008, http://www.nationalhomeless.org/publications/facts/Rural.pdf) that the rural homeless are more likely to be white, female, married, and currently working than are the urban homeless. They are also more likely to be homeless for the first time and generally experience homelessness for a shorter period of time than the urban homeless. Furthermore, the NCH notes that domestic violence is more likely to be a cause of homelessness in rural areas and that alcohol and substance abuse is less likely to be a cause. The odds of being poor are higher in rural areas than in urban areas, which sometimes results in homelessness. In addition, those living in rural areas have fewer employment opportunities, typically earn lower wages, and remain unemployed for longer periods of time than do people living in metropolitan areas.

Burt et al. determine in *Homelessness* that in 1996, 21% of all homeless people in their study lived in suburban areas and 9% lived in rural communities. The rural homeless surveyed were more likely to be working, or to have worked recently, than the urban homeless—65% of the rural homeless had worked for pay in the last month. Homeless people living in rural areas were also more likely to be experiencing their first spell of homelessness (60%). In 55% of the cases the homeless period lasted three months or less.

In *Hard to Reach: Rural Homelessness and Health Care* (January 2002, http://www.nhchc.org/Publications/RuralHomeless.pdf), Patricia A. Post of the National Health Care for the Homeless Council argues that rural residents typically deal with a lack of permanent housing not by sleeping on the streets, like their urban counterparts, but by first moving in with a series of friends; second moving into abandoned shacks, cars, or campgrounds; and finally moving to cities in search of employment. They also differ from urban homeless people in many ways: They have less education, typically hold temporary jobs with no benefits, are less likely to receive government assistance or have health insurance, and are more likely to have been incarcerated.

Several types of rural areas generate higher-than-average levels of homelessness, including regions that:

- Are primarily agricultural—residents often lose their livelihood because of either a reduced demand for farm labor or a shrinking service sector

- Depend on declining extractive industries, such as mining or timber

- Are experiencing economic growth—new or expanding industrial plants often attract more job seekers than what can be absorbed

- Have persistent poverty, such as Appalachia and the rural South, where the young and able-bodied may have to relocate before they can find work

According to Brian Dabson of the Rural Policy Research Institute, in "The President's Budget FY 2010: What's in It for Rural America?" (March 2, 2009, http://www.rupri.org/Forms/Budget2010.pdf), the Obama administration offered several proposals to address the housing crisis in rural areas within its first months in office. The proposed 2010 budget would provide $4.5 billion to the Community Development Block Grant Program as well as reform the program to better address the needs of distressed rural communities. The Homeless Emergency Assistance and Rapid Transition to Housing Act was introduced into Congress on April 2, 2009, to reauthorize the McKinney-Vento Homeless Assistance Grants Program. The National Alliance to End Homelessness explains in "Highlights of the HEARTH Act" (April 10, 2009, http://www.endhomelessness.org/content/article/detail/2241) that passage of the bill would improve homeless assistance programs in rural communities by allowing these communities greater flexibility to respond to the particular needs of rural homeless people and by permitting some funds to be used for construction to house those at risk of becoming homeless.

TRENDS IN HOMELESSNESS

Poverty Estimates

There is an undeniable connection between homelessness and poverty. People in poverty live from day to day with little or no safety net for times when unforeseen expenses arise. If a family's resources are small, expenditures on necessities such as food, shelter, and health care have to be carefully decided and sometimes sacrificed. Should one spend money on food, a visit to the doctor, buying necessary medicines, or paying the rent? In 2009 a full-time job paying minimum wage for 40 hours per week provided an income under the poverty line for a family of three. (See Chapter 3.) Being poor often means that an illness, an accident, or a missed paycheck could be enough to cause homelessness.

Housing costs for such a family may be out of reach. According to the Joint Center for Housing Studies of Harvard University, in "America's Rental Housing—The Key to a Balanced National Policy" (2008, http://www.jchs.harvard.edu/publications/rental/rh08_americas_rental_housing/rh08_intro.pdf), the foreclosure crisis in 2007 and 2008 pushed previous homeowners into the rental market, who then competed for the limited number of affordable housing units. The organization points out that "no single minimum-wage earner working 40 hours a week, 52 weeks a year, earns enough to cover the cost of a modest rental anywhere in the country." Low income and high-rent payments often result in substandard housing accommodation, doubled-up living, or living on the street or in a public shelter. The necessity of basic sustenance and medical care usually leaves little money left to meet housing needs. People in poverty have further difficulties finding housing if they have previously defaulted on their rent or mortgage, with the result of homelessness.

After large decreases in the poverty rate in the 1960s and 1970s, the poverty rate increased in the 1990s to a high of 15.1% in 1993. (See Table 1.2 in Chapter 1.) Steady gains in decreasing the proportion of people living below the poverty threshold were made between 1994 and 2001. However, between 2001 and 2007 the poverty rate once again rose, to a high of 12.7% in 2004. It had decreased slightly to 12.5% by 2007; 37.3 million people lived below the poverty level that year. In fact, the number of homeless people continued to increase between 1987 and 2007, whereas the poverty level declined only slightly during this 20-year period. (See Table 1.2 in Chapter 1.)

No strong correlation between poverty and homelessness can be seen in these data; however, there is a definite relationship between homelessness and poverty. The NCH suggests in *Foreclosure to Homelessness: The Forgotten Victims of the Subprime Crisis* (April 15, 2008, http://www.nationalhomeless.org/housing/foreclosure_report.pdf) that the economic downturn that began in 2008 and the rise in foreclosures will lead to increasing numbers of homeless people.

Trends Profiled in Cities

In *Hunger and Homelessness Survey: A Status Report on Hunger and Homelessness in America's Cities, a 25-City Survey, December 2008* (December 2008, http://www.usmayors.org/pressreleases/documents/hungerhomelessnessreport_121208.pdf), the Conference of Mayors reports that homelessness increased in 19 of 25 cities. (See Figure 4.2.) On average, cities reported a 12% increase in homelessness, but some cities experienced increases of up to 50%. Sixteen cities reported that family homelessness in particular was on the increase. Mayors attributed the rise in the homeless population to the economic climate, high unemployment, and a lack of affordable housing.

In 2007 the National League of Cities surveyed a random sample of the nation's elected municipal officials regarding issues and problems they faced in governing U.S. cities. (See Table 4.8.) When asked about whether various conditions were a problem in their city, 17% said homelessness was a major problem, 43% said it was a moderate problem, and 40% said it was a minor problem or no problem. General housing affordability was reported to be a major problem in 32% of cities and a moderate problem in 49% of cities—only one out of five (20%) municipal officials reported that housing affordability was either a minor problem or no problem.

Municipal officials highlighted that in 2007 foreclosures were a problem, especially in urban areas. Foreclosures were thought to be a major problem in 15% of cities and a moderate problem in 36% of cities surveyed. (See Table 4.8.) Over three-quarters (78%) of officials surveyed

FIGURE 4.2

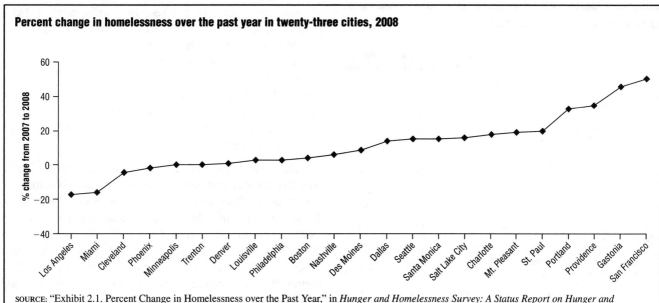

Percent change in homelessness over the past year in twenty-three cities, 2008

SOURCE: "Exhibit 2.1. Percent Change in Homelessness over the Past Year," in *Hunger and Homelessness Survey: A Status Report on Hunger and Homelessness in America's Cities, A 25-City Survey*, U.S. Conference of Mayors, December 2008, http://www.usmayors.org/pressreleases/documents/hungerhomelessnessreport_121208.pdf (accessed January 4, 2009)

from large-core cities said the foreclosure problem had worsened during the past year; 68% of officials from developed suburban areas stated foreclosures had worsened; 57% of officials from outer developing suburbs said the problem had worsened; and 54% of smaller or midsized regions said foreclosures had worsened. (See Table 4.9.) Few officials said that foreclosures had improved within the last year in their area.

EMPLOYMENT AND THE HOMELESS

It is extremely difficult for people to escape homelessness without a job. Yet, it is equally difficult for homeless people to find and keep good jobs. The NCH lists in the fact sheet "Employment and Homelessness" (June 2008, http://www.nationalhomeless.org/publications/facts/Employment.pdf) the following barriers to employment for homeless people:

- Lack of education

- Lack of competitive work skills

- Lack of transportation

- Lack of day care

- Disabling conditions

In addition, the homeless, like other workers, are subject to the state of the labor market. The availability of jobs and the wages and benefits paid for those available jobs often determine whether or not people can remove themselves from homelessness. Many homeless are underemployed—that is, they would like to work full time but have been unsuccessful at finding full-time work.

Burt et al. indicate in *Homelessness* that in 1996, 44% of homeless respondents reported working in the previous month. Two percent earned income as self-employed entrepreneurs—by peddling or selling belongings. Forty-two percent of the homeless respondents worked for, and were paid by, an employer. The Conference of Mayors finds that in 2007, 17.4% of members of homeless families and 13% of homeless singles and unaccompanied youth were employed at the time of the survey. (See Table 4.4.)

According to the NCH, advocates for the homeless are concerned that this dependency on wages, combined with the unfavorable labor market conditions, actually supports continued homelessness. Because most homeless people do not have more than a high school education, and because a majority of the low paying jobs go to those with at least a high school education, advocates worry that the available job opportunities for homeless people provide an insufficient base for exiting homelessness.

It costs money to live. Even homeless people have needs that can only be met with money. From needing something as simple as a toothbrush or a meal, to money for a newspaper or a phone call to a job prospect, homeless people need money to begin to improve their lives. Out of the need to survive, homeless people have come up with a number of ways to earn money.

Day Labor

Regular work, characterized by a permanent and ongoing relationship between employer and employee, does not figure significantly in the lives and routines of most

TABLE 4.8

Indicators of local housing condition, 2007

	Major problem	Moderate problem	Minor/ no problem
a. General housing affordability	32%	49%	20%
b. Equitable distribution of affordable housing throughout region/metro area	32%	42%	26%
c. Absentee landlords	30%	42%	29%
d. Vacant and abandoned properties	23%	32%	45%
e. Availability of transitional housing	21%	42%	37%
f. Opportunities for homeownership for lower income residents/renters	32%	51%	17%
g. Availability of rental housing stock	18%	42%	40%
h. Predatory lending	18%	34%	48%
i. Foreclosures	15%	36%	49%
j. Homelessness	17%	43%	40%
k. Sprawl	12%	33%	55%
l. Deteriorating housing stock	25%	40%	35%
m. Availability of subsidized rental stock	20%	47%	33%
n. Over-crowding in homes	11%	37%	52%
o. Neighborhoods with high disinvestment	16%	31%	53%
p. Property tax increases making housing unaffordable	13%	31%	54%
q. Need for home repairs among elderly and low-income families	26%	52%	23%
r. Opposition to density	15%	38%	47%
s. Links between housing and essential supportive services	13%	40%	48%
t. Proximity of public transportation to low income housing	16%	36%	48%
u. Zoning/land use standards for development of a variety of housing	5%	35%	60%
v. Homes not built to fit community character	5%	24%	72%
w. High property turnover	5%	22%	72%
x. Housing market discrimination	4%	20%	76%
y. Racial segregation in housing	5%	24%	72%
z. Housing for aging population	11%	46%	43%
aa. Sufficient infrastructure to support new development	16%	37%	47%
bb. Environmental/health issues (mold, asbestos, and lead)	9%	33%	58%
cc. Crime	16%	39%	45%
dd. Housing for immigrants	8%	33%	59%

SOURCE: Christiana McFarland, Casey Dawkins, and C. Theodore Koebel, "Appendix A: Indicators of Local Housing Condition," in *The State of America's Cities 2007, Local Housing Conditions and Contexts: A Framework for Policy Making*, National League of Cities, 2007, http://www.nlc.org/ASSETS/29106477103E49EBB9BEFD49588362E5/PAR2007SoACHousingrpt.pdf (accessed January 14, 2009)

TABLE 4.9

Change in foreclosures during the past year, by city type, 2008

	Worsened	Improved	No change
Core city of a larger region (n=45)	78%	0%	22%
Core city of a smaller/mid-sized region (n=75)	54%	4%	41%
Inner ring or developed suburb (68)	68%	2%	31%
Developing or outer suburbs (n=59)	57%	0%	43%
Core city/town of a rural region (n=75)	36%	1%	63%
Rural city/town (n=42)	42%	0%	59%

Notes: n = Sample size.

SOURCE: Christiana McFarland, "Change in Foreclosures during the Past Year, by City Type," in *2008 State of America's Cities: Annual Opinion Survey of Municipal Officials*, National League of Cities, December 2008, http://www.nlc.org/ASSETS/43A4BDCCFDAE4D029D66719CE63F43DA/StateofAmericasCities2008.pdf (accessed January 14, 2009)

homeless, as it is usually unavailable or inaccessible. Homelessness makes getting and keeping regular work difficult because of the lack of a fixed address, communication, and, in many cases, the inability to get a good night's sleep, clean up, and dress appropriately. Studies find that the longer a person is homeless, the less likely he or she is to pursue wage labor and the more likely he or she is to engage in some other form of work. For those who do participate in regular jobs, in most cases, the wages received are not sufficient to escape living on the street.

Day labor (wage labor secured on a day-to-day basis, typically at lower wages and changing locations) is somewhat easier for the homeless to secure. Tim Bartley and Wade T. Roberts state in "Relational Exploitation: The Informal Organization of Day Labor Agencies" (*WorkingUSA: The Journal of Labor and Society*, vol. 9, March 2006) that "popular and scholarly depictions of homelessness have often portrayed homeless individuals as disconnected from the world of work—implicitly or explicitly equating homelessness with joblessness.... Yet ... homeless persons engage in far more paid work than usually assumed." In fact, between 25% and 50% of homeless people engage in some form of wage work, often day labor.

Day labor may involve unloading trucks, cleaning up warehouses, cutting grass, or washing windows. Day labor often fits the abilities of the homeless because transportation may be provided to the worksite, and appearance, work history, and references are less important than in regular employment. Equally attractive to a homeless person, day labor usually pays cash at quitting time, thus providing immediate pocket money. Day labor jobs are, however, by definition, without a future, and Bartley and Roberts point out the exploitation that many day laborers face. Because of the growth of day labor, agencies have sprung up to profit from making these informal arrangements more formal. Many of these agencies do not pay workers for time they wait until being assigned or charge fees for equipment or check-cashing. Such jobs might provide for daily survival on the street but are not generally sufficient to get a person off the street. Consequently, many homeless turn to shadow work.

Shadow Work

Shadow work refers to methods of getting money that are outside the normal economy, some of them illegal. David Levinson, the editor of *Encyclopedia of Homelessness* (2004), explains that these methods include panhandling, scavenging, selling possessions, picking up aluminum cans and selling them, selling one's blood or plasma, theft, or peddling illegal goods, drugs, or services. A homeless person seldom engages in all these activities consistently but may turn to some of them as needed. Researchers estimate that 60% of homeless people engage in some shadow work. Shadow work is more common for homeless men than for homeless women. Theft is more common for younger homeless people.

In "Buddy, Can You Spare a Dime?: Homelessness, Panhandling, and the Public" (*Urban Affairs Review*, vol. 38, no. 3, 2003), Barrett A. Lee and Chad R. Farrell of Pennsylvania State University note that a mixture of institutionalized assistance, wage labor, and shadow work is typical of those who live on the streets. Studies find that many homeless people are resourceful in surviving the rigors of street life and recommend that this resourcefulness be somehow channeled into training that can lead to jobs paying a living wage. However, the NCH reports in "Employment and Homelessness" that some observers suggest that homeless people who have adapted to street life may likely need transitional socialization programs as much as programs that teach them a marketable skill.

Institutionalized Assistance

According to Levinson, a certain proportion of homeless people receive some form of institutionalized assistance. This would include institutionalized labor, such as that provided by soup kitchens, shelters, and rehabilitation programs that sometimes pay the homeless for work related to facility operation. The number of people employed by these agencies is a small percentage of the homeless population. In addition, the pay—room, board, and a small stipend—tends to tie the homeless to the organization rather than providing the means to get off the street.

Institutionalized assistance also includes income supplements provided by the government, family, and friends. Snow et al. indicate that even though a considerable number of the homeless may receive some financial help from family or friends, it is usually small. Women seem to receive more help from family and friends and to remain on the streets for shorter periods than men. Cash from family and friends seems to decline with the amount of time spent on the street and with age.

Street Newspapers: Bootstrap Initiatives

In the United States, as well as overseas, homeless people are writing, publishing, and selling their own newspapers. Many street newspaper publishers belong to the North American Street Newspaper Association (NASNA), which was organized in Chicago in 1996. The NASNA holds an annual conference, offers business advice and services, and supports street newspaper publishers in the same way that any professional organization supports its membership. It also lobbies the government on homeless issues. The NASNA (http://www.nasna.org/about.html) had 27 members in January 2009, up from 19 members just 2 years before. Its members had a combined monthly circulation of 287,000.

Generally, the street newspapers are loaned on credit to homeless vendors who then sell them for $1 each. At the end of the workday, the vendor pays the publisher the agreed-on price and pockets the remainder as profit. For example, Boston's *Spare Change* newspaper publishes 9,000 copies every 2 weeks. Vendors purchase newspapers for $0.25 each and resell them for $1.00, pocketing $0.75 for each paper sold. Some street newspapers charge vendors nothing at all. California's *Street Spirit* and *Street Sheet* both make their papers free to vendors.

This cooperative arrangement among publishers, vendors, and consumers has many benefits:

- Creation of jobs
- Supports the work ethic
- Accommodates the mobility of homeless people
- Provides reliable employment despite crisis living conditions
- Informs the public about homelessness
- Erases stereotypes of the drunken, illiterate, and "unworthy" homeless person
- Gives the writers and vendors a sense of accomplishment
- Provides immediate cash to people who desperately need it

Most of the homeless newspaper vendors have not been able to earn enough just from selling newspapers to move themselves from homelessness, but as the quality and availability of these publications grow, homeless people envision the street newspaper industry becoming a means of moving tens of thousands from homelessness.

EXITING HOMELESSNESS

According to Burt et al., in *Homelessness*, homeless people said in 1996 that the primary reason they could not exit homelessness is insufficient income. Of those clients surveyed, 54% mentioned employment-related reasons for why they remained homeless—30% cited insufficient income and 24% cited lack of a job.

Data used by Burt et al. show how little income the homeless earned in 1996. Eighty-one percent of the "currently" homeless had incomes of less than $700 in the 30 days before the study; the average monthly income was $367. Most of the homeless in the study were receiving their income from Aid to Families with Dependent Children (now Temporary Assistance for Needy Families). Of the formerly homeless people surveyed, the median (the middle value—half are higher and half are lower) monthly income of $470 would amount to an annual income of $5,640, an amount well below the poverty level for a single person ($7,740 in 1996).

In *2007 Greater Los Angeles Homeless Count*, the Los Angeles Homeless Services Authority reports that homeless people mentioned a variety of reasons for their continued homelessness. Among the top five reasons for being homelessness, 37% cited health issues (such as having an illness, mental health issues, or problems with alcohol or drugs), 19% cited social issues (such as experiencing domestic violence, familial conflict, or divorce), 17% cited economic issues (such as losing a job, being evicted, or failing to pay rent), 15% cited youth-related issues (such as aging out of foster care or running away from home), and 13% cited external issues (such as losing a home to a fire, flood, or other type of natural disaster).

These findings clearly demonstrate the financial difficulty a homeless person encounters when trying to permanently exit homelessness or poverty. However, exiting homelessness—especially by the chronically homeless—requires more than income. Persistent medical assistance, sometimes for an entire lifetime, has to be available for the mentally ill or for people with addiction and substance abuse problems. Furthermore, without programs such as job training, assistance with general education, help with socialization skills, and counseling, the maintenance of a degree of independent life for the long term can be difficult for the chronically homeless.

CHAPTER 5
THE HOUSING PROBLEM

At one time a home was defined as a place where a family resided, but as American society changed, so did the definition of the word *home*. A home is now considered a place where one or more people live together, a private place to which they have legal right and where strangers may be excluded. It is the place where people keep their belongings and where they feel safe from the outside world. For housing to be considered a home, it should be permanent with an address. Furthermore, in the best of circumstances a home should not be substandard but should still be affordable. Many people would agree that a place to call home is a basic human right.

Those people who have no fixed address and no private space of their own are the homeless. The obvious solution to homelessness would be to find a home for everyone who needs one. There is enough housing available in the United States; as such, the problem lies in the affordability of that housing. Most of the housing in the United States costs far more than poor people can afford to rent or buy.

HIGH HOUSING COSTS AND HOMELESSNESS

According to Mary Cunningham and Sharon McDonald, in *Promising Strategies to End Family Homelessness* (June 2006, http://www.hoopsforthehomeless.org/docs/hoopspaperfinal.pdf), research indicates that the primary cause of most homelessness is the inability to pay for housing, which is caused by some combination of low income and high housing costs. Even though many other factors may contribute to homelessness, such as a low level of educational achievement or mental illness, addressing these problems will seldom bring someone out of homelessness by itself. The underlying issue of not being able to afford housing will still need to be addressed.

Furthermore, the National Alliance to End Homelessness notes that, in the main, homeless people are no different from housed people. The alliance argues in *Policy Book 2006* (August 17, 2006, http://www.endhomelessness.org/content/article/detail/586) that 80% of homeless people

"have similar rates of mental illness, substance abuse disorders, physical ailments, and domestic violence experience. They have similar education levels and numbers of children." This group only needs affordable housing. The other 20% of homeless people can be characterized as chronically homeless, and they do differ substantially from the general population of poor people: they have higher rates of chronic disabilities, substance abuse disorders, physical disabilities, human immunodeficiency virus (HIV), and acquired immunodeficiency syndrome (AIDS). These people need housing linked to other supportive services to help them move out of homelessness.

Veterans make up a disproportionate number of homeless people; a main cause of homelessness among this population is the high cost of housing. In *Vital Mission: Ending Homelessness among Veterans* (November 2007, http://www.endhomelessness.org/content/article/detail/1837), Mary Cunningham, Meghan Henry, and Webb Lyons explain that some veterans are at a high risk of homelessness due to severe rent burdens. They write, "Lack of affordable housing is the primary driver of homelessness.... There is a subset of veterans who have severe housing cost burden." Cunningham, Henry, and Lyons explain that there is a pressing need to target veterans in homelessness prevention programs. The National Alliance to End Homelessness notes in the press release "President's 2010 Budget Proposal Boosts Affordable Housing and Homelessness Assistance" (February 26, 2009, http://www.endhomelessness.org/content/article/detail/2182) that President Barack Obama's (1961–) 2010 budget proposal will expand services offered by the U.S. Department of Veterans Affairs to help maintain stable housing and other supportive services for veterans at risk for homelessness.

HOUSING THE POOR

When 30% or more of a meager income is spent on housing, hardship is the result. For that reason the federal government's official standard for low-income housing is that rent and utilities should cost no more than 30% of the annual income of someone in poverty. Low-income housing is housing that is affordable to those in poverty based on that formula. In 2009 a family of two with an annual income of less than $14,000 was in poverty; a family of four was in poverty if their income was less than $21,200. (See Table 1.1 in Chapter 1.) Thus, in 2009 housing for a family of two at the poverty line should cost no more than 30% of $14,000 annually, or no more than $350 a month; for a family of four, housing should cost no more than one-third of $21,200 annually, or no more than $530 a month.

However, the price of rental units has been on the rise since 1975, at the same time that the real income of renters

has been declining. The Joint Center for Housing Studies (JCHS) of Harvard University finds in *The State of the Nation's Housing, 2008* (2008, http://www.jchs.harvard .edu/publications/markets/son2008/son2008.pdf) that in 2007 dollars renters in 1975 had a median (the middle value—half are higher and half are lower) income of $2,690 per month and a median gross rent (including rent and utilities) of $708. (See Table 5.1.) By 2007 gross rent had risen while income had declined. In that year, renters had a median income of $2,615 per month and a median gross rent of $775.

According to the U.S. Census Bureau, the median monthly gross rent for renter-occupied housing units was $789 in 2007. (See Table 5.2.) As a result of such high

TABLE 5.1

Income and housing costs for owners and renters, 1975–2007

[2007 dollars]

| | | | | | | | | | Cost as percent of income | | | |
| | Monthly income | | | | Owner costs | | Renter costs | | Owners | | Renters | |
Year	Owner	Renter	Home price	Mortgage rate (%)	Before-tax mortgage payment	After-tax mortgage payment	Contract rent	Gross rent	Before-tax mortgage payment	After-tax mortgage payment	Contract rent	Gross rent
1975	4,522	2,690	124,969	8.9	899	769	654	708	19.9	17.0	24.3	26.3
1976	4,661	2,697	127,387	8.9	912	784	654	710	19.6	16.8	24.2	26.3
1977	4,676	2,714	132,334	8.8	943	868	653	712	20.2	18.6	24.0	26.2
1978	4,726	2,750	140,372	9.4	1,050	934	651	711	22.2	19.8	23.7	25.9
1979	4,733	2,691	141,458	10.6	1,173	1,025	629	688	24.8	21.7	23.4	25.6
1980	4,444	2,551	134,913	12.5	1,292	1,100	605	666	29.1	24.7	23.7	26.1
1981	4,316	2,517	129,320	14.4	1,415	1,183	597	660	32.8	27.4	23.7	26.2
1982	4,323	2,542	125,505	14.7	1,404	1,189	607	675	32.5	27.5	23.9	26.5
1983	4,420	2,536	125,284	12.3	1,182	1,008	625	696	26.8	22.8	24.6	27.4
1984	4,536	2,614	125,019	12.0	1,157	991	632	703	25.5	21.8	24.2	26.9
1985	4,656	2,652	126,688	11.2	1,101	945	650	720	23.6	20.3	24.5	27.1
1986	4,821	2,683	133,038	9.8	1,032	891	677	745	21.4	18.5	25.2	27.8
1987	4,851	2,657	137,348	9.0	990	884	680	745	20.4	18.2	25.6	28.0
1988	4,878	2,737	140,093	9.0	1,013	927	678	741	20.8	19.0	24.8	27.1
1989	4,943	2,828	142,008	9.8	1,104	1,001	672	734	22.3	20.3	23.8	25.9
1990	4,798	2,739	139,186	9.7	1,075	978	664	724	22.4	20.4	24.3	26.4
1991	4,726	2,625	136,086	9.1	992	909	660	719	21.0	19.2	25.1	27.4
1992	4,690	2,553	135,689	7.8	882	821	657	716	18.8	17.5	25.7	28.0
1993	4,651	2,526	134,538	6.9	800	755	653	712	17.2	16.2	25.8	28.2
1994	4,697	2,510	134,549	7.3	831	785	652	710	17.7	16.7	26.0	28.3
1995	4,742	2,558	135,138	7.7	866	814	650	706	18.3	17.2	25.4	27.6
1996	4,822	2,580	136,600	7.6	866	813	648	704	18.0	16.9	25.1	27.3
1997	4,932	2,639	138,847	7.5	875	821	652	708	17.8	16.6	24.7	26.8
1998	5,079	2,691	143,920	7.0	859	809	662	717	16.9	15.9	24.6	26.6
1999	5,191	2,788	148,067	7.1	899	841	668	722	17.3	16.2	24.0	25.9
2000	5,138	2,805	153,283	7.9	999	922	670	724	19.4	17.9	23.9	25.8
2001	5,033	2,781	160,837	6.9	957	890	681	739	19.0	17.7	24.5	26.6
2002	5,004	2,677	168,951	6.4	955	892	696	751	19.1	17.8	26.0	28.1
2003	5,031	2,588	176,239	5.7	918	884	701	758	18.2	17.6	27.1	29.3
2004	4,994	2,551	189,753	5.7	989	944	701	759	19.8	18.9	27.5	29.7
2005	5,041	2,568	207,010	5.9	1,099	1,035	698	760	21.8	20.5	27.2	29.6
2006	5,115	2,639	218,485	6.5	1,246	1,155	701	766	24.4	22.6	26.5	29.0
2007	5,107	2,615	217,900	6.4	1,230	1,144	710	775	24.1	22.4	27.2	29.6

Notes: All dollar amounts are expressed in 2007 constant dollars using the Consumer Price Index (CPI-U) for all items. Renters exclude those paying no cash rent. 2007 income is based on Moody's Economy.com estimate for all households, adjusted by the three-year average ratio of CPS owner and renter incomes to all household incomes. Home price is the 2007 median sales price of existing single-family homes determined by the National Association of Realtors® indexed by the Freddie Mac Conventional Mortgage Home Price Index. Mortgage rates are from the Federal Housing Finance Board, Monthly Interest Rate Survey; 2007 and 2006 values are the average of monthly rates. Mortgage payments assume a 30-year mortgage with 10% down. After-tax mortgage payment equals mortgage payment less tax savings of homeownership. Tax savings are based on the excess of housing (mortgage interest and real-estate taxes) plus non-housing deductions over the standard deduction. Non-housing deductions are set at 5% of income through 1986, 4.25% from 1987 to 1993, and 3.5% from 1994 on. Contract rent equals median 2005 contract rent from the American Housing Survey, indexed by the CPI residential rent index with adjustments for depreciation in the stock before 1987. Gross rent is equal to contract rent plus fuel and utilities.

SOURCE: "Table A-1. Income and Housing Costs, U.S. Totals: 1975–2007," in *The State of the Nation's Housing, 2008*, Joint Center for Housing Studies of Harvard University, 2008, http://www.jchs.harvard.edu/publications/markets/son2008/son2008.pdf (accessed January 14, 2009)

TABLE 5.2

Median monthly housing costs for renter-occupied housing units by state, 2007

Rank	State	Median
1	Hawaii	1,194
2	California	1,078
3	New Jersey	1,026
4	Maryland	1,000
5	Nevada	980
6	Massachusetts	946
7	District of Columbia	934
8	Connecticut	931
9	Florida	925
10	Alaska	918
11	Delaware	910
12	New York	907
13	New Hampshire	892
13	Virginia	892
15	Rhode Island	830
16	Arizona	819
17	Washington	816
	United States	**789**
18	Colorado	788
19	Illinois	783
20	Georgia	768
21	Vermont	756
22	Oregon	743
23	Texas	734
24	Utah	733
25	Minnesota	711
26	Pennsylvania	685
27	Michigan	683
28	North Carolina	678
29	Wisconsin	673
30	Idaho	654
31	Louisiana	651
32	Maine	650
33	South Carolina	645
34	Ohio	643
35	Indiana	638
36	New Mexico	637
37	Wyoming	636
38	Tennessee	634
39	Kansas	623
40	Missouri	618
41	Nebraska	614
42	Mississippi	609
43	Alabama	601
44	Oklahoma	588
45	Montana	579
46	Arkansas	573
47	Iowa	567
48	Kentucky	563
49	South Dakota	526
50	West Virginia	525
51	North Dakota	516
	Puerto Rico	392

SOURCE: Adapted from "R2514. Median Monthly Housing Costs for Renter-Occupied Housing Units," in *2007 American Community Survey*, U.S. Census Bureau, 2008, http://factfinder.census.gov/servlet/GRTTable?_bm=y&-geo_id01000US&-_box_head_nbrR2514&-ds_nameACS_2007_1YR_G00_&-redoLog false&-formatUS-30&-mt_nameACS_2005_EST_G00_R2514_US30&-CONTEXTgrt (accessed January15, 2009)

TABLE 5.3

Percent of renter-occupied units spending 30% or more of household income on rent and utilities by state, 2007

Rank	State	Percent
1	Florida	52.7
2	California	51.2
3	New Jersey	48.5
4	Michigan	48
5	Hawaii	47.9
6	Nevada	47.7
7	New York	47.6
8	Connecticut	47.5
9	Massachusetts	47.2
10	Rhode Island	47.1
11	Arizona	46.8
12	Illinois	46.6
13	Delaware	46.5
14	Maryland	46.3
15	Colorado	46.2
16	District of Columbia	45.8
	United States	**45.6**
17	Ohio	45.1
17	Oregon	45.1
19	Vermont	45
20	Georgia	44.8
20	Washington	44.8
22	Minnesota	43.9
23	Texas	43.5
24	Pennsylvania	43.3
25	Missouri	42.9
26	North Carolina	42.7
26	Virginia	42.7
28	Louisiana	42.4
28	Mississippi	42.4
30	New Hampshire	42.2
31	Maine	42.1
31	New Mexico	42.1
33	Indiana	41.8
33	Wisconsin	41.8
35	Arkansas	41.6
36	Tennessee	40.8
37	Alabama	40.6
38	Kentucky	39.5
39	Utah	39.4
40	South Carolina	39.2
41	Idaho	38.8
41	Oklahoma	38.8
43	Iowa	38.4
44	Nebraska	38.3
45	Kansas	37.8
46	Alaska	37.2
47	North Dakota	36.9
48	West Virginia	36.5
49	Montana	36.4
50	South Dakota	34.4
51	Wyoming	28.3
	Puerto Rico	32.3

SOURCE: Adapted from "R2515. Percent of Renter-Occupied Units Spending 30 Percent or More of Household Income on Rent and Utilities: 2007," in *2007 Community Survey*, U.S. Census Bureau, 2008, http://factfinder.census.gov/servlet/GRTTable?_bm=y&-geo_id=01000US&-_box_head_nbr=R2515&-ds_name=ACS_2007_1YR_G00_&-redoLog=false&- format=US-30&-mt_name=ACS_2005_EST_G00_R2515_US30&-CONTEXT=grt (accessed January 15, 2009)

rents, across the nation 45.6% of households in rental property spent 30% or more of their household income on rent. (See Table 5.3.) Renters in California faced particularly difficult circumstances. The median monthly rent there was the highest in the continental United States ($1,078) and more than half (51.2%) of renters spent 30% or more of their household income on housing.

Homeownership is also well beyond the reach of most low-income families. The National Association of Realtors reports in the news release "4th Quarter Metro Area Home Prices down as Buyers Purchase Distressed Property" (February 12, 2009, http://www.realtor.org/press_room/news_releases/2009/02/4th_quarter_metro_area_home_prices _down) that the median price for existing single-family homes was $180,100 in the fourth quarter of 2008, 12.4% lower than a year earlier, reflecting the high percentage of distressed sales (sales of foreclosed houses and sales of homes below market value). Nearly half (45%) of all homes sold in the fourth quarter were distressed sales. Even though the median price of homes fell, they were still out of reach of low-income families because of the uncertain economy and credit crunch that began 2008.

Not Enough Affordable Units Available

Researchers agree that the number of housing units that are affordable to the poor is insufficient to meet needs. The JCHS finds in *State of the Nation's Housing, 2008* that there were 3 million more lowest-income renter households than there were affordable units available. (See Figure 5.1.) Higher income renters occupied approximately half of the affordable rental units, so 6 million lowest-income renter households did not have affordable housing.

In December 2000 Congress established the bipartisan Millennial Housing Commission to examine the role of the federal government in meeting the nation's housing needs. In *Meeting Our Nation's Housing Challenges* (May 30, 2002, http://permanent.access.gpo.gov/lps19766/www.mhc.gov/

mhcfinal.pdf), the commission states that "there is simply not enough affordable housing. The inadequacy of supply increases dramatically as one moves down the ladder of family earnings. The challenge is most acute for rental housing in high-cost areas, and the most egregious problem is for the very poor."

The limited availability of affordable housing is a problem across the nation. According to Christiana McFarland, Casey Dawkins, and C. Theodore Koebel, in *The State of America's Cities 2007, Local Housing Conditions and Contexts: A Framework for Policy Making* (2007, http://www.nlc.org/ASSETS/29106477103E49EBB9BEFD49588362E5/PAR2007SoACHousingrpt.pdf), 32% of city officials believed general housing affordability was a major problem in their area, and another 49% believed it was a moderate problem. The JCHS notes that between 1995 and 2005, 930,000 units that cost under $399 per month had been lost from the housing stock and 530,000 units that cost between $400 and $599 had been lost. (See Figure 5.2.) By contrast, 110,000 units that cost between $800 and $999 per month had been lost during this period.

At Risk of Becoming Homeless

The severe shortage of affordable housing means that many low-income people and families constantly face the threat of homelessness, and the problem is not getting better. In May 2007 the U.S. Department of Housing and Urban Development (HUD) released the results of an in-depth study, *Affordable Housing Needs 2005: Report to Congress* (http://www.huduser.org/Publications/pdf/AffHsgNeeds.pdf).

FIGURE 5.1

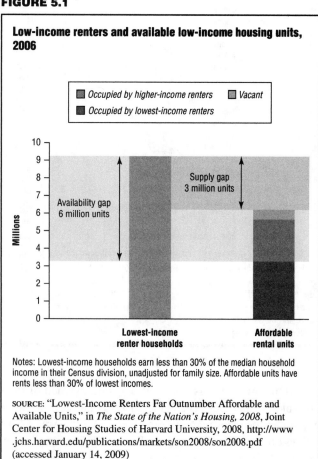

Low-income renters and available low-income housing units, 2006

Notes: Lowest-income households earn less than 30% of the median household income in their Census division, unadjusted for family size. Affordable units have rents less than 30% of lowest incomes.

SOURCE: "Lowest-Income Renters Far Outnumber Affordable and Available Units," in *The State of the Nation's Housing, 2008*, Joint Center for Housing Studies of Harvard University, 2008, http://www.jchs.harvard.edu/publications/markets/son2008/son2008.pdf (accessed January 14, 2009)

FIGURE 5.2

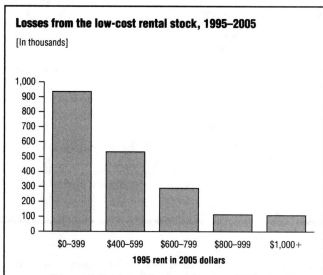

Losses from the low-cost rental stock, 1995–2005

SOURCE: "Figure 15. Twice As Many Low-Cost Rental Units Have Been Lost Than of All Other Units Combined," in *America's Rental Housing: The Key to a Balanced National Policy*, Joint Center for Housing Studies of Harvard University, 2008, http://www.jchs.harvard.edu/publications/rental/rh08_americas_rental_housing/rh08_americas_rental_housing.pdf (accessed February 1, 2009)

FIGURE 5.3

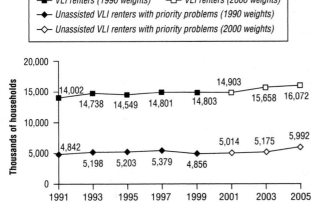

Trend in the number of very low-income (VLI) renters and those with worst-case needs, 1991–2005

SOURCE: "Exhibit 2-4. Overall Trend in the Number of Very Low-Income Renters and Those with Worst Case Needs, 1991–2005," in *Affordable Housing Needs 2005: Report to Congress*, U.S. Department of Housing and Urban Development, Office of Policy Development and Research, May 2007, http://www.huduser.org/Publications/pdf/AffHsgNeeds.pdf (accessed January 15, 2009)

FIGURE 5.4

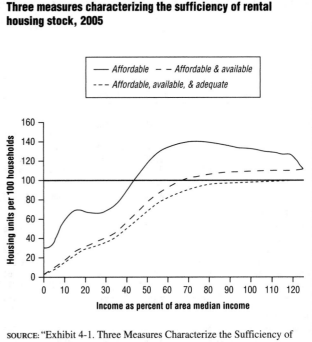

Three measures characterizing the sufficiency of rental housing stock, 2005

SOURCE: "Exhibit 4-1. Three Measures Characterize the Sufficiency of the U.S. Rental Housing Stock, 2005," in *Affordable Housing Needs 2005: Report to Congress*, U.S. Department of Housing and Urban Development, Office of Policy Development and Research, May 2007, http://www.huduser.org/Publications/pdf/AffHsgNeeds.pdf (accessed January 15, 2009)

The report finds that the number of low-income households paying more than 30% of their income in rent or living in substandard housing rose from 5.2 million in 2003 to 6 million in 2005, an increase of 16%. (See Figure 5.3.) Approximately 5.5% of U.S. households experienced in that year what HUD called worst-case needs. HUD defines families with worst-case needs as those who:

- Are renters

- Do not receive housing assistance from federal, state, or local government programs

- Have incomes below 50% of their local area median family income, as determined by HUD

- Pay more than half of their income for rent and utilities, or live in severely substandard housing

In other words, these are extremely impoverished people who do not own their housing and can barely afford to pay their housing costs or can only afford to stay in the worst housing. Of all housed people, they are the ones closest to being forced into homelessness. HUD reports that in 2005, 11.4 million people in 6 million households had worst-case housing needs. Of these households, 2.3 million were families with children and 1.3 million were elderly households. These households had an average income of $648 per month and an average gross monthly rent of $647—a rent burden of nearly 100%.

HUD also indicates that in 2005 there was an adequate number of rental housing units to provide affordable housing to households with incomes above 45% of the area median income, but that there were far fewer adequate housing units available to the poorest households, especially in urban areas. In addition, some higher-income households occupied housing units that cost less than 30% of their income, restricting the units available to lower-income households. Some of the housing available was substandard as well. Furthermore, the housing stock affordable to low-income people is continually shrinking. (See Figure 5.4.) The Joint Center for Housing Studies of Harvard University explains in "America's Rental Housing—The Key to a Balanced National Policy" (2008, http://www.jchs.harvard.edu/publications/rental/rh08_americas_rental_housing/rh08_intro.pdf) that the soaring foreclosure rates in 2007 and 2008 only increased pressure on the affordable housing stock, as previous homeowners began looking for rental housing.

For as long as worst-case needs have been reported by HUD, affordability rather than housing quality has been the main problem facing renters. A household that spends more than 50% of its income on housing is considered severely cost burdened. According to the JCHS, in *State of the Nation's Housing, 2008*, the number of households with severe cost burdens—in other words, that paid more than half their income for housing—increased by 3.8 million between 2001 and 2006 to a record 17.7 million households. (See Table 5.4.) Almost half (13.2 million households, or 47%) of households in the bottom income quartile were severely cost burdened in 2006.

TABLE 5.4

Housing cost-burdened households by tenure and income, 2001 and 2006

[In thousands]

Tenure and income	2001				2006				Percent change 2001–2006			
	No burden	Moderate burden	Severe burden	Total	No burden	Moderate burden	Severe burden	Total	No burden	Moderate burden	Severe burden	Total
Owners												
Bottom decile	771	709	2,506	3,986	653	672	2,714	4,039	−15.3	-5.2	8.3	1.3
Bottom quintile	3,381	1,906	3,921	9,208	2,958	1,956	4,481	9,395	−12.5	2.6	14.3	2.0
Bottom quartile	5,065	2,549	4,428	12,042	4,510	2,654	5,168	12,331	−11.0	4.1	16.7	2.4
Lower-middle quartile	10,695	3,630	1,456	15,781	10,389	4,358	2,346	17,092	−2.9	20.1	61.1	8.3
Upper-middle quartile	16,015	2,882	465	19,362	15,924	4,111	1,003	21,037	−0.6	42.6	115.9	8.7
Top quartile	21,457	1,208	137	22,802	22,102	2,221	292	24,614	3.0	83.8	113.3	7.9
Total	**53,231**	**10,270**	**6,485**	**69,986**	**52,924**	**13,343**	**8,808**	**75,075**	**−0.6**	**29.9**	**35.8**	**7.3**
Renters												
Bottom decile	1,309	789	4,559	6,657	1,335	792	4,996	7,122	2.0	0.4	9.6	7.0
Bottom quintile	2,731	2,798	6,550	12,079	2,652	2,764	7,512	12,928	−2.9	-1.2	14.7	7.0
Bottom quartile	3,705	3,962	6,901	14,567	3,527	3,966	8,079	15,573	−4.8	0.1	17.1	6.9
Lower-middle quartile	7,698	2,710	419	10,828	6,864	3,233	716	10,812	−10.8	19.3	70.6	−0.1
Upper-middle quartile	6,771	437	39	7,247	6,161	641	65	6,868	−9.0	46.8	65.9	−5.2
Top quartile	3,735	71	2	3,807	3,217	72	1	3,290	−13.9	1.4	−51.8	−13.6
Total	**21,908**	**7,180**	**7,361**	**36,449**	**19,769**	**7,912**	**8,861**	**36,542**	**−9.8**	**10.2**	**20.4**	**0.3**
All households												
Bottom decile	2,080	1,498	7,065	10,643	1,988	1,464	7,710	11,162	−4.4	−2.3	9.1	4.9
Bottom quintile	6,112	4,704	10,472	21,287	5,610	4,720	11,993	22,323	−8.2	0.4	14.5	4.9
Bottom quartile	8,769	6,511	11,328	26,609	8,037	6,620	13,247	27,904	−8.4	1.7	16.9	4.9
Lower-middle quartile	18,393	6,340	1,876	26,609	17,252	7,591	3,061	27,904	−6.2	19.7	63.2	4.9
Upper-middle quartile	22,786	3,319	504	26,609	22,084	4,752	1,068	27,904	−3.1	43.2	111.9	4.9
Top quartile	25,191	1,280	138	26,609	25,319	2,293	292	27,904	0.5	79.2	111.4	4.9
Total	**75,140**	**17,450**	**13,846**	**106,436**	**72,692**	**21,256**	**17,669**	**111,617**	**−3.3**	**21.8**	**27.6**	**4.9**

Notes: Income deciles/quintiles/quartiles are equal tenths/fifths/fourths of all households sorted by pre-tax income. Moderate (severe) burdens are defined as housing costs of 30–50% (more than 50%) of household income.

SOURCE: "Table A-7. Housing Cost-Burdened Households by Tenure and Income: 2001 and 2006," in *The State of the Nation's Housing, 2008*, Joint Center for Housing Studies of Harvard University, 2008, http://www.jchs.harvard.edu/publications/markets/son2008/son2008.pdf (accessed January 14, 2009)

Working Families Struggle to Keep Up

In *Out of Reach, 2007–2008* (2008, http://www.nlihc.org/oor/oor2008/), the National Low Income Housing Coalition (NLIHC) analyzes the fair market rent (FMR)—HUD's estimate of what a household seeking modest rental housing must expect to pay for rent and utilities—for a two-bedroom rental unit to the median hourly wage. In 2008 the hourly wage needed to pay the FMR for a two-bedroom apartment spending no more than 30% of one's income on rent was $17.32. However, the median hourly wage in the United States was under $16.00, the average renter earned $13.94 per hour, and the federal minimum wage was $5.85. The NLIHC states that besides minimum-wage workers not being able to find affordable two-bedroom apartments, "there is no county in the country where an individual can work 40 hours per week at the minimum wage and afford even a one-bedroom apartment at the local FMR." In most cities in the nation, the housing wage was at least twice the federal minimum wage. In other words, to afford the FMR for a two-bedroom apartment, a household must have two or three minimum-wage workers working full time. Figure 5.5 provides a graphic representation of the wage needed to afford a two-bedroom apartment at the FMR across the nation.

FEDERALLY SUBSIDIZED HOUSING

The national effort to provide housing for those in need is far more massive than would be indicated by the fiscal year (FY) 2009 expenditure of about $1.6 billion on assistance grants to the homeless. (See Table 5.5.) HUD's expenditures on public and Native American housing were projected to be $23 billion in FY 2009. If these funds are added to projected expenditures on homeless grant programs, the total spending on subsidized housing in FY 2009 would be $24.6 billion. Of this total, 6.7% is allocated to helping the homeless and 93.3% to ensuring that people do not become homeless. To help people stay housed, the government has housing programs that help poor and low-income people.

Most government housing programs are targeted to poor or low-income households. For this reason subsidized housing is means-tested, meaning that the income of those receiving help must be below a certain threshold. The qualifying income level—much like the definition of poverty—changes over time. Beneficiaries of housing assistance never receive cash outright. The benefits are therefore labeled "means-tested noncash benefits." In 2006, 10.3 million people, or 3.5% of the population, lived in subsidized housing. (See Table 5.6.)

FIGURE 5.5

Housing wage by area of the country, 2008

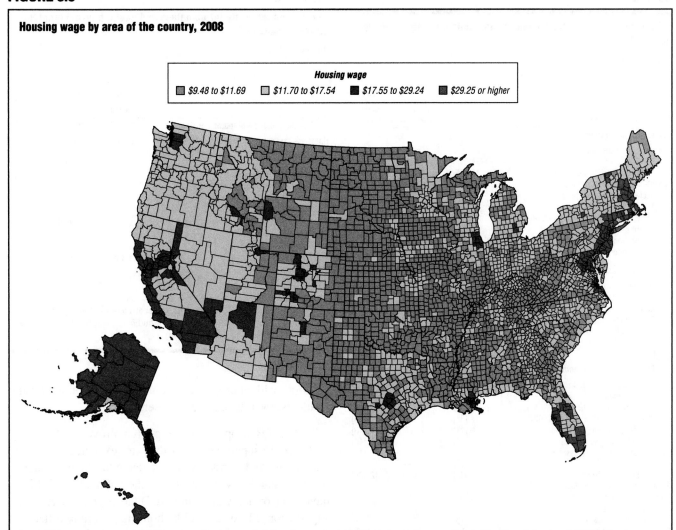

Notes: Minimum wage is currently $5.85 per hour. Housing wage is the hourly wage needed to afford a two-bedroom apartment at the fair market rent, paying 30% of pre-tax income and working 40 hours a week for 50 weeks. Analysis is based on methodology developed by Cushing N. Dolbeare and the National Low Income Housing Coalition.

SOURCE: "Figure 31. The Housing Wage across the Country Exceeds the Federal Minimum Wage of $5.85 per Hour," in *The State of the Nation's Housing, 2008*, Joint Center for Housing Studies of Harvard University, 2008, http://www.jchs.harvard.edu/publications/markets/son2008/son2008.pdf (accessed January 14, 2009)

HUD operates many different kinds of housing programs, but these can be classified under three headings: public housing owned by the government, tenant-based programs that provide people vouchers to subsidize rent, and project-based programs that underwrite the costs of private owners who, in turn, pledge to house low-income people.

Public housing and voucher programs account for roughly equal proportions of subsidized units. Project-based programs, also known as private subsidized projects, account for the most units, but these private subsidies take many forms, some quite complicated. A look at the major programs follows.

Public Housing

HUD's FY 2009 budget appropriated $23 billion for public and Native American housing (see Table 5.5); the

American Recovery and Reinvestment Act of 2009 allocated an additional $3 billion to make significant improvements in the quality of public housing nationwide. In FY 2009, $2 billion was allocated to the capital fund to finance major repairs and modernize units. No money was appropriated for the now-defunct HOPE VI grant program to help public housing authorities replace and revitalize the most severely distressed public housing and implement community service and supportive service improvements in those projects, but HUD indicates in the press release "HUD Speeds Nearly $3 Billion to Nation's Public Housing Authorities to Improve Housing" (March 24, 2009, http://www.hud.gov/recovery/2009/03/24/comms/pr09-027.cfm?CFID=19343186&CFTOKEN=38492949) that an additional $3 billion would be made available to the 3,122 public housing authorities in the United States, Puerto Rico, and the U.S. Virgin Islands to fund capital improvement projects.

TABLE 5.5

HUD budget authority for homeless and public housing programs, 2007–09

[Dollars in millions]

Discretionary programs	2007 Enacted	2008 Enacted	2009 Budget request
Public and Indian Housing			
Housing certificate fund			
Rescission	($1,255)	($1,250)	—
Total, housing certificate fund	(1,255)	(1,250)	0
Tenant-based rental assistance:			
Section 8 contract renewals	14,479	14,705	$14,319
Administrative fees	1,246	1,340	1,400
Family self-sufficiency coordinators	48	49	48
Tenant protection vouchers	148	200	150
Advanced appropriation for FY 2007	[4,200]		
Advanced appropriation for FY 2008	[(4,193)]	[4,193]	
Advanced appropriation for FY 2009	—	[(4,158)]	[4,158]
Advanced appropriation for FY 2010	—	—	[(4,000)]
Transfer to working capital fund	6	6	8
Exigencies/portability	[100]	[50]	[100]
Non-elderly disabled	—	30	—
Family unification program	—	20	—
Disaster displacement assistance program	—	—	39
Veterans affairs supportive housing	—	75	75
Rescission	(40)	(723)	—
Total, tenant-based rental assistance	**15,887**	**15,702**	**16,039**
Public housing capital fund	2,439	2,439	2,024
Modernization TA	[11]	[12]	[7]
Emergency cap needs	[17]	[19]	[...]
ROSS (within CDBG until FY 2003)	[38]	[40]	[38]
Transfer to working capital fund	[11]	[17]	[15]
Administrative receivership	[9]	[9]	[10]
Financial and physical assessment support	0	[15]	[15]
Rescission	(8)	—	—
Subtotal, PIH capital fund	[2,431]	[2,439]	[2,024]
Revitalization of severely distressed public housing projects	99	100	0
Technical assistance	[2]	[2]	[...]
HOPE VI rescission	(3)	—	—
Public housing operating fund	3,864	4,200	4,300
Asset-based management transition fund	0	[6]	[6]
Native American housing block grants	624	630	627
Technical assistance	[4]	[4]	[4]
National American Indian housing council	[...]	[2]	[...]
Title VI federal guarantees for tribal housing activities			
Program account	[2]	[2]	[2]
Administrative expenses	[[0.1]]	[[...]]	[[...]]
Loan guarantee limitation	[[18]]	[[17]]	[[17]]
Indian housing loan guarantee fund			
Program account	$6	$7	$9
Administrative expenses	[0.3]	[...]	[...]
Loan guarantee contracts	[...]	[...]	[0.8]
Limitation level	[251]	[367]	[420]
Native Hawaiian loan guarantee fund			
Program account	1	1	—
Limitation level	[36]	[42]	[...]
Native Hawaiian housing block grants	9	9	6
Native Hawaiian housing block grants technical assistance	[0.3]	[0.3]	[0.3]

The management of public housing is handled by housing agencies (sometimes called authorities) established by local governments to administer HUD housing programs. The Housing Act of 1937 required that public housing agencies (PHAs) submit annual plans to HUD but also declared it to be the policy of the United States "to vest in public housing agencies that perform well, the maximum amount of responsibility and flexibility in program admin-

	2007 Enacted	2008 Enacted	2009 Budget request
Subtotal, public and Indian housing	**21,663**	**21,838**	**23,005**
Homeless assistance grants	$1,442	$1,586	$1,636
Demonstration program of rapid re-housing of families	[...]	[25]	[...]
Evaluation of demonstration	[...]	[[1]]	[3]
Transfer to working capital fund	[1]	[2]	[3]
Technical assistance and management information systems	[8]	[8]	[8]
Shelter plus care (renewals)	[285]	[320]	[365]
Samaritan	[...]	[...]	[50]
Rescission	(7)		
Total, homeless	**[1,442]**	**[1,586]**	**[1,636]**

Note: Totals may differ from President's Budget due to rounding.

SOURCE: Adapted from "Appendix A. Budget Authority by Program," in *Fiscal Year 2009 Budget Summary*, U.S. Department of Housing and Urban Development, February 2008, http://www.hud.gov/about/budget/fy09/fy09budget.pdf (accessed January 15, 2009)

istration, with appropriate accountability to public housing residents, localities, and the general public."

Thus, PHAs operate under plans approved by HUD and under HUD supervision, but they are expected to operate with some independence accountable to their residents, local (or state) governments, and the public. Not all PHAs have "performed well," and HUD has been accused of lax supervision. PHAs and public housing generally reflect the distressed economic conditions of the population living in government-owned housing. Many PHAs have been charged with neglecting maintenance, with tolerating unsafe living conditions for tenants, and with fraudulent or careless financial practices.

Troubled housing refers to low-income projects that are badly deteriorated, are located in unsafe neighborhoods, or are in danger of being lost to market-rate housing conversion or foreclosure. In an effort to improve its accountability for the conditions of low-income housing, HUD began to implement a Public Housing Assessment System (PHAS) in January 2000. The PHAS is used to measure the performance of PHAs. Four primary components of the assessment system are designed to ensure, through physical inspection, that PHAs meet the minimum standard of being decent, safe, sanitary, and in good repair; to oversee the finances of PHAs; to evaluate the effectiveness of the management of PHAs; and to receive feedback from PHA residents on housing conditions.

In *Public Housing: New Assessment System Holds Potential for Evaluating Performance* (March 2002, http://www.gao.gov/new.items/d02282.pdf), the U.S. General Accounting Office (GAO; now the U.S. Government

TABLE 5.6

Persons living in households receiving selected noncash benefits, 2006

[In thousands (296,450 represents 296,450,000), except percent]

Age, sex, and race	Total	In household that received means-tested assistance[a]		In household that received means-tested cash assistance		In household that received food stamps		In household in which one or more persons were covered by Medicaid		Lived in public or authorized housing	
		Number	Percent	Number	Percent	Number	Percent	Number	Percent	Number	Percent
Total	296,450	77,058	26.0	17,056	5.8	21,780	7.3	60,453	20.4	10,250	3.5
Under 18 years	73,727	28,988	39.3	5,111	6.9	9,421	12.8	22,638	30.7	3,773	5.1
18 to 24 years	28,405	7,706	27.1	1,605	5.7	2,275	8.0	6,331	22.3	1,095	3.9
25 to 34 years	39,868	10,948	27.5	1,977	5.0	3,186	8.0	8,778	22.0	1,283	3.2
35 to 44 years	42,762	10,149	23.7	2,093	4.9	2,502	5.9	7,663	17.9	1,000	2.3
45 to 54 years	43,461	8,000	18.4	2,342	5.4	1,879	4.3	6,311	14.5	931	2.1
55 to 59 years	18,221	2,812	15.4	1,074	5.9	711	3.9	2,222	12.2	353	1.9
60 to 64 years	13,970	2,235	16.0	907	6.5	566	4.1	1,814	13.0	370	2.7
65 years and over	36,035	6,221	17.3	1,947	5.4	1,241	3.4	4,696	13.0	1,444	4.0
65 to 74 years	18,998	3,253	17.1	1,033	5.4	684	3.6	2,551	13.4	644	3.4
75 years and over	17,037	2,968	17.4	914	5.4	557	3.3	2,145	12.6	800	4.7
Male	145,486	35,475	24.4	7,535	5.2	9,347	6.4	27,888	19.2	4,053	2.8
Female	150,964	41,582	27.5	9,521	6.3	12,433	8.2	32,566	21.6	6,197	4.1
White alone[b]	237,619	54,388	22.9	10,773	4.5	13,312	5.6	43,043	18.1	5,120	2.2
Black alone[b]	37,306	16,257	43.6	4,658	12.5	6,794	18.2	12,248	32.8	4,218	11.3
Asian alone[b]	13,177	3,075	23.3	729	5.5	416	3.2	2,526	19.2	368	2.8
Hispanic[c]	44,784	21,145	47.2	3,239	7.2	4,824	10.8	16,390	36.6	1,943	4.3
White alone, Non-Hispanic[b]	196,049	34,926	17.8	7,957	4.1	9,080	4.6	28,047	14.3	3,543	1.8

[a]Means-tested assistance includes means-tested cash assistance, food stamps, Medicaid, and public or authorized housing.
[b]Refers to people who reported specific race and did not report any other race category.
[c]People of Hispanic origin may be of any race.
Notes: Persons, as of March 2007, who lived with someone (a nonrelative or a relative) who received aid. Not every person tallied here received the aid themselves. Persons living in households receiving more than one type of aid are counted only once. Excludes members of the Armed Forces except those living off post or with their families on post. Population controls for 2007 based on Census 2000 and an expanded sample of households. Based on Current Population Survey.

SOURCE: "Table 524. Persons Living in Households Receiving Selected Noncash Benefits: 2006," in *The 2009 Statistical Abstract*, U.S. Census Bureau, December 2008, http://www.census.gov/compendia/statab/tables/09s0524.pdf (accessed January 4, 2009)

Accountability Office) examines the implementation of the PHAS and its progress. The GAO finds that HUD had also formed the Public and Indian Housing Information Center, a database that collects additional information not addressed by the PHAS, such as compliance and funding. The findings indicate that HUD was only looking at one of its four criteria—the effectiveness of management—when determining if a PHA was troubled. The other three criteria were not being considered at that time, but plans called for them to be incorporated into future evaluations. In FY 2001, of the existing 3,167 authorities investigated, 532 (17%) PHAs were troubled overall or in one area, 827 (26%) were high performers, and 1,808 (57%) were standard performers.

The GAO confirms in "Major Management Challenges at the Department of Housing and Urban Development" (2005, http://www.gao.gov/pas/2005/hud.htm) that HUD continued to have major problems. According to the GAO, HUD had made some progress in addressing management problems. However, because "some of HUD's corrective actions are still in the early stages of implementation and additional steps are needed to resolve ongoing problems," its rental housing assistance programs remain "high risk." David G. Wood of the Financial Markets and Community Investments notes in *Public Housing: Informa-* *tion on the Roles of HUD, Public Housing Agencies, Capital Markets, and Service Organizations* (February 15, 2006, http://www.gao.gov/new.items/d06419t.pdf) that in many cases, HUD's enforcement actions against troubled PHAs—such as technical assistance and training or sanctions such as withholding of funding—resulted in some improvements.

Vouchers

Voucher programs pay a portion of the rent for qualifying families. Only low-income families are eligible, specifically those with incomes lower than half of an area's median income. Under some circumstances, families with up to 80% of the local median income may also qualify; such cases may involve, for instance, families displaced by public housing demolition. The family pays 30% of its income in rent. Vouchers are issued by the Public Housing Agency, which executes assistance contracts with the landlord, who must also qualify.

Two major voucher programs are available: tenant based and project based. In tenant-based programs, the voucher "follows" the tenant when the tenant moves to another qualifying unit. In project-based programs, the voucher "attaches" to a project. Families are directed to participating projects after they qualify. Tenants cannot automatically transfer their voucher in a project-based dwelling to another—but they may qualify for tenant-based vouchers after they move.

Besides these two basic programs, HUD also has five other voucher programs. Conversion vouchers are used to help tenants relocate when public housing is demolished. Family unification vouchers are used to help families stay together. Homeownership vouchers assist families in purchasing a first home or another home if the family has not lived in a house in the past three years. Participants must be employed and have an income of at least minimum wage. Vouchers for people with disabilities and welfare-to-work vouchers assist the elderly or nonelderly disabled and families transitioning from welfare to work.

The homeownership voucher program, begun in 2002, provides vouchers to participants in the tenant-voucher programs who meet income and eligibility requirements to help them buy their first home. HUD reports in *Annual Performance Plan, Fiscal Year 2009* (February 2008, http://www.hud.gov/offices/cfo/reports/pdfs/app2009.pdf) that the program will assist over 13,000 families during FY 2009.

In all these programs, the housing supplied is privately owned and operated and the rents paid are at or below FMR. HUD determines the FMR in every locality of the nation by an annual survey of new rental contracts signed in the past 15 months. The FMR is set as the 40th percentile of rents paid, meaning that 40% paid a lower rent and 60% paid a higher rent. HUD has chosen the 40th percentile to increase housing choices while keeping budgets at reasonable levels. Table 5.7 presents FMRs used by HUD in a sample of cities around the country in 2008. Rents in certain cities are calculated at the 50th percentile under new HUD rules that went into effect in 2001 for 39 markets, which resulted in a raise in the FMR in these localities.

Of the cities shown in Table 5.7, the highest FMR for a two-bedroom unit in the continental United States for 2008 was in San Francisco, California ($1,592 per month). The lowest FMR was in Bismarck, North Dakota ($532 per month).

As shown in Table 5.8, the amount of subsidized housing and the number of Section 8 housing vouchers declined across all categories between 2003 and 2005. Project-based Section 8 housing has declined dramatically because funding for new construction stopped in 1983 with some minor exceptions (including construction/rehabilitation aimed at supporting homeless programs). Support of housing in such units continues, but the housing stock is going out of use through demolitions and conversions. Thus, in 2005 the vast majority of Section 8 housing

TABLE 5.7

Fair market rental rates for selected metropolitan areas, 2008

Area definition	Fair market rental rate				
	0 bedroom	1 bedroom	2 bedroom	3 bedroom	4 bedroom
Bismarck, ND	$409	$428	$532	$770	$792
San Juan-Guaynabo, PR	$429	$465	$517	$685	$810
Lexington-Fayette, KY	$461	$554	$683	$918	$947
Cincinnati-Middletown, OH-KY-IN	$473	$560	$726	$972	$1,009
Albuquerque, NM	$511	$602	$760	$1,107	$1,327
Gulfport-Biloxi, MS	$546	$579	$676	$881	$905
Kansas City, MO-KS	$547	$657	$754	$1,020	$1,073
Salt Lake City, UT	$575	$625	$754	$1,061	$1,235
Minneapolis-St.Paul-Bloomington, MN-WI	$593	$699	$848	$1,110	$1,247
Memphis, TN-MS-AR	$615	$669	$743	$990	$1,021
Charlotte-Gastonia-Concord, NC-SC	$615	$667	$740	$932	$1,085
Dallas, TX	$645	$718	$871	$1,156	$1,401
Anchorage, AK	$652	$741	$930	$1,339	$1,631
Portland, ME	$673	$800	$1,036	$1,305	$1,399
Philadelphia-Camden-Wilmington, PA-NJ-DE-MD	$682	$781	$932	$1,116	$1,327
Atlanta-Sandy Springs-Marietta, BA	$684	$741	$824	$1,003	$1,094
Seattle-Bellevue, WA	$687	$783	$942	$1,331	$1,626
Ann Arbor, MI	$690	$774	$942	$1,185	$1,220
Las Vegas-Paradise, NV	$719	$843	$996	$1,382	$1,680
Chicago-Naperville-Joliet, IL	$734	$840	$944	$1,154	$1,304
Orlando-Kissimmee, FL	$737	$801	$915	$1,146	$1,349
Baltimore-Towson, MD	$747	$844	$1,013	$1,301	$1,607
Flagstaff, AZ	$753	$896	$1,012	$1,301	$1,641
New Orleans-Metairie-Kenner, LA	$764	$846	$990	$1,271	$1,314
Los Angeles-Long Beach, CA	$863	$1,041	$1,300	$1,746	$2,101
Washington-Arlington-Alexandria, DC-VA-MD	$1,025	$1,168	$1,324	$1,708	$2,235
San Francisco, CA	$1,035	$1,272	$1,592	$2,125	$2,246
Boston-Cambridge-Quincy, MA-NH	$1,086	$1,153	$1,353	$1,618	$1,778
New York, NY	$1,095	$1,185	$1,318	$1,621	$1,823
Honolulu, HI	$1,131	$1,348	$1,630	$2,377	$2,799

SOURCE: Adapted from "SCHEDULE B. FY 2008 Final Fair Market Rents for Existing Housing," U.S. Department of Housing and Urban Development, January 5, 2009, http://www.huduser.org/datasets/fmr/fmr2008f/FY2008_FMR_SCHEDULEB.pdf (accessed January 5, 2009)

TABLE 5.8

Subsidized units available under public housing and voucher programs, 1998, 2003, and 2005

	1998	2003	2005
Public housing	1,300,493	1,241,466	1,220,937
Section 8 tenant vouchers	1,391,526	2,077,336	1,803,013
Section 8 project-based vouchers/certificates	1,001,939	817,274	9,833

SOURCE: Adapted from "Basic Counts," in *A Picture of Subsidized Households in 1998*, U.S. Department of Housing and Urban Development, August 28, 1998, http://www.huduser.org/datasets/assthsg/statedata98/index.html, and *Resident Characteristics Report*, U.S. Department of Housing and Urban Development, March 2005, http://www.hud.gov/offices/pih/systems/pic/50058/rcr/index.cfm (accessed April 11, 2005)

TABLE 5.9

Selected characteristics of subsidized housing populations, 2005

	Public housing	Tenant vouchers
Average income	$10,725	$11,080
Percent with income of		
$0	5	4
$1–5,000	16	13
$5,001–10,000	41	39
$10,001–15,000	18	20
$15,001–20,000	9	12
$20,001–25,000	5	6
Above $25,000	7	6
Percent below 30% of median income	56	66
Average monthly payment	$243	$253
Race		
White	50	52
Black	46	44
American Indian/Alaska Native	1	1
Asian	2	3
Ethnicity		
Hispanic	21	17
Not-Hispanic	79	83
Average household size	2.2	2.6
Percent with 4 or more people	18	25
Percent with 2 bedrooms	30	37

SOURCE: Adapted from *Resident Characteristics Report*, U.S. Department of Housing and Urban Development, March 2005, http://www.hud.gov/offices/pih/systems/pic/50058/rcr/index.cfm (accessed April 11, 2005)

vouchers were tenant based. Even though tenant-voucher residents have a fractionally higher average household income than public housing residents, they also have a larger family size. Therefore, two-thirds (66%) of voucher users and a little more than half (56%) of public housing residents have an extremely low income for their family size. (See Table 5.9.) The shift of the subsidized population from public housing toward voucher housing represents not an improvement so much as a shift in policy, whereby the provision of housing in the future appears to be headed for privatization. Tenant-based voucher programs give low-income people choices in housing, which can help poor families be more flexible and move to areas with better job opportunities and transportation options, as well as help reverse the trend of the concentration of poverty in certain urban areas.

Other Housing Assistance Programs

The two biggest low-income housing programs in the United States are public housing and the Section 8 voucher programs. Section 8 funds are distributed under HUD's Housing Certificate Fund. Other HUD programs fund housing for people living with AIDS, elderly people, Native Americans and Native Hawaiians, and people with disabilities. A new 2005 program, the Prisoner Reentry Initiative, helps former prisoners find housing as well as with job training and other services.

The Self-Help Homeownership Opportunity Program supports the construction of new homes for low-income people. Homebuyers must help construct or rehabilitate the property. In *Fiscal Year 2009 Budget Summary* (February 2008, http://www.hud.gov/about/budget/fy09/fy09budget.pdf), HUD notes that the FY 2009 HUD budget requested $40 million for the program. Other HUD programs aim to increase privately owned low-income housing stock. HUD explains in *Annual Performance Plan, Fiscal Year 2009* (February 2008, http://www.hud.gov/offices/cfo/reports/pdfs/app2009.pdf) that the Federal Housing Administration (FHA) provides mortgage insurance for multifamily proj-

ects, tax credits to housing developers who provide a portion of their projects at low rents, and a Community Development Block Grant program to promote homeownership in some minority communities.

HUD maintains demographic and income data only on participants in the major programs. For that reason, information on the characteristics of participants in many other HUD subsidy programs aimed at low-income people is unavailable. The previously cited programs do not include mortgage insurance and other FHA programs aimed to assist the more affluent general population to own a home.

Rural Housing Programs

A variety of rural housing programs are administered by the Rural Housing Service (RHS), a division of the U.S. Department of Agriculture. (See Table 5.10.) These programs make federal money available for housing in rural areas, which are considered places with populations of 50,000 or less. Eligibility for rural housing programs is similar to that of subsidized urban programs. The requirements vary from region to region, and applicants must meet minimum and maximum income guidelines. The subsidies come in the form of grants or low-interest loans to repair substandard housing, subsidized mortgages for low-income home ownership, and grants to cover down payment and purchasing costs of low-income homes.

Table 5.10 shows the various programs that were available under RHS funding in millions of dollars. In 2007, $5.7 billion was appropriated for rural housing programs;

TABLE 5.10

Funding for selected rural housing programs, fiscal years 1980–2007, in millions of dollars

[Dollars in millions]

Rural housing program	Total dollars spent, fiscal year 1987	Total dollars spent, fiscal year 1997	Total dollars requested, fiscal year 2007	Type of assistance
Single-family housing direct loans (sec. 502)	1,144.2	706.4	1,237.5	Loans subsidized as low as 1% interest
Single-family housing guaranteed loans (sec. 502)	NA	2,000.0	3,564.2	No money down, no monthly mortgage insurance loans
Single-family home repair grants and loans (sec. 504)	18.4	48.5	66.2	Grants for elderly and loans subsidized as low as 1% interest
Single-family housing mutual self-help grants (sec. 523)	7.6	26.2	37.6	Grants to nonprofit and public entities to provide technical assistance
Multifamily direct rural rental housing loans (sec. 515)	554.9	152.5	0	Loans to developers subsidized as low as 1% interest
Multifamily housing guaranteed loans (sec. 538)	NA	51.8	198.0	Guaranteed loans for developing moderate-income apartments
Multifamily housing farm labor grants and loans (secs. 516/514)	17.8	23.4	55.5	Grants and loans subsidized at 1% interest
Multifamily housing preservation grants (sec. 533)	19.1	7.6	9.9	Grants to nonprofit organizations, local governments, and Native American tribes, usually leveraged with outside funding
Multifamily housing rental assistance (sec. 521)	275.3	520.2	486.3	Rental assistance to about one-half the residents in RHS rental and farm labor units

SOURCE: Adapted from Bruce E. Foote, "Table 1a. Funding for Selected Rural Housing Programs, FY1980–FY2007," and "Table 1b. Funding for Selected Rural Housing Programs, FY1980–FY2007," in *USDA Rural Housing Programs: An Overview*, Congressional Research Service, July 27, 2007, http://www .nationalaglawcenter.org/assets/crs/RL33421.pdf (accessed January 5, 2009)

of that, $4.9 billion subsidized single-family home loans (Sections 502, 504, and 523) and $486 million provided rental assistance to families (Section 521).

Much of the rural low-income housing where renters, migrant workers, and a large population of minorities live is substandard. There are four major areas affected by housing inadequacies: the Mississippi Delta, Native American trust lands, the colonias (poor neighborhoods) bordering Mexico, and Appalachia.

The RHS, like HUD, has been plagued by accusations of mismanagement. William B. Shear finds in *Rural Housing Service: Opportunity to Improve Management* (June 19, 2003, http://www.gao.gov/new.items/d03911t.pdf) that the RHS could be improved by reducing costs and centralizing administration. The GAO indicates in *Rural Housing Service: Agency Has Overestimated Its Rental Assistance Budget Needs over the Life of the Program* (May 2004, http://www.gao.gov/new.items/d04752.pdf) that the RHS had consistently overestimated its budget needs. In *Rural Housing Service: Overview of Program Issues* (March 10, 2005, http://www.gao.gov/highlights/d05382thigh.pdf), the GAO states that "several issues prevent the agency from making the best use of resources," including the policy of grandfathering communities, which inhibits an accurate determination of metropolitan versus rural areas; the consistent overestimation of the RHS's rental assistance budget needs and insufficiently monitoring the use of the agency's funds; and inaccurate data collection methods.

Reasons for the Lack of Low-Income Housing

The JCHS notes in *States of the Nation's Housing, 2008* that between 1997 and 2007 funding for housing assistance programs fell from 10% to 8% of the nation's domestic discretionary spending. This highlights one of the major reasons for the lack of low-income housing: declining federal support. Other reasons that low-income housing is diminishing are bureaucratic red tape, fraud, and waste, and a variety of local factors that affect new construction.

DECLINING FEDERAL SUPPORT. The poor essentially have two rental options: low-income housing units operated by local public housing authorities and privately owned housing, whose owners accept Section 8 rental assistance vouchers (also called Housing Choice vouchers). The vouchers pay the difference between 30% of the renter's income and the fair market value of the rental. However, concern exists that HUD is not committed to keeping private owners in the Section 8 program. The GAO indicates in *Project-Based Rental Assistance: HUD Should Update Its Policies and Procedures to Keep Pace with the Changing Housing Market* (April 2007, http://www.gao .gov/new.items/d07290.pdf) that between 2001 and 2005 only 92% of Section 8 rental assistance contracts were renewed, and even among those contracts that were renewed, there were 5% fewer units covered. Individuals who left Section 8 did so to "seek higher rents in the private market or to convert their units into condominiums." According to the GAO, rents permitted under the voucher program have not kept pace with actual rents in many markets. HUD policies, such as the one-for-one replacement policy that does not allow owners to reduce the total number of units in a property when a contract is renewed and therefore does not allow them to reconfigure a property and offer larger units, compel some private owners to leave the program. In addition, adjustments to rent are slow, administrative costs are high, and subsidy payments are often late, forcing some owners to leave the program. The GAO recommends that HUD modify some of its policies and address other concerns of private owners in the program to preserve Section 8 rental stock.

Low-income people hoping for housing assistance from the federal government face formidable obstacles. In *Federal Programs for Addressing Low-Income Housing Needs* (December 2008, http://www.urban.org/Uploaded PDF/411798_low-income_housing.pdf), Margery Austin Turner and G. Thomas Kingsley of the Urban Institute report that only about one out of four eligible households receive federal housing assistance. Section 8 waiting lists and conventional public housing waiting lists are long and often closed in surveyed cities. For example, in the fact sheet "About NYCHA" (December 15, 2008, http://www.nyc.gov/html/nycha/downloads/pdf/factsheet.pdf), the New York City Housing Authority indicates that it had not processed applicants for Section 8 housing since the wait list was reopened for two months in early 2007. As of November 2008, 130,638 families were on the Section 8 wait list, and another 131,792 families were on the wait list for conventional public housing units. In another example, Brandt Williams reports in "Long Waiting List for Public Housing Gets Longer" (June 12, 2008, http://minnesota.publicradio.org/display/web/2008/06/12/housingvoucher/) that in Minneapolis, Minnesota, officials expected more than 15,000 people to apply for Section 8 vouchers when they allowed them to apply for the first time in five years in June 2008. There was little hope any new applicants would get vouchers soon—some people on the waiting list had already waited 10 years.

According to HUD, in "The U.S. Department of Housing and Urban Development 2010 Budget" (March 2009, http://www.whitehouse.gov/omb/assets/fy2010_factsheets/fy10_housing_urban_development.pdf), President Obama's 2010 budget proposal asked for substantially more money to bolster affordable housing programs. If adopted, the proposal would increase HUD funding by 18%, from $40.1 billion in FY 2009 to $47.5 billion in FY 2010. To provide funding to impoverished neighborhoods, President Obama asked for increased funding for the Housing Choice Voucher Program and the Project-Based Rental Assistance Program, requested full funding for the Community Development Block Grant program, and created a new Choice Neighborhoods Initiative. The proposed budget also included

$1 billion to establish a National Housing Trust Fund, which would rehabilitate and preserve affordable housing for extremely low-income people.

LOW PROFIT MARGINS BRING NEGLECT. HUD contracts with private owners limit profits and often limit the monies put back into the property for repairs. The existing housing available to renters at the lowest income levels often suffers from a lack of upkeep. Neglected maintenance results in deterioration and sometimes removal from the housing inventory altogether.

The JCHS notes in *The State of the Nation's Housing, 2003* (2003, http://www.jchs.harvard.edu/publications/markets/son2003.pdf) that about 705,000 tenants receiving government housing assistance in 2003 lived in substandard conditions. HUD data show that in 2003 an affordable unit existed for every household that earned 40% of the area medium income. However, as Figure 5.4 shows, housing units were only both affordable and available for households earning 70% of the area medium income. It also shows a significant proportion of those housing units are substandard, or inadequate. In fact, there is not enough affordable, available, and adequate housing available to house all low-income households.

FACTORS THAT INHIBIT CONSTRUCTION. Construction of low-income units has been hampered by community resistance, by regulations that increase the cost of construction, and by limits on federal tax credits that make new construction unprofitable.

In his "Dissenting Statement to the Report of the Millennial Housing Commission" (May 31, 2002, http://www.heritage.org/Research/Welfare/WM102.cfm), Robert Rector of the Heritage Foundation complains, "It is a simple fact that those cities that have the greatest 'affordability' problem are those that have 'smart growth' or other regulatory policies that severely limit new housing growth. Policies such as restrictive zoning, antiquated building codes, and high impact fees for new construction reduce housing supply and greatly increase costs for everyone in a community."

These regulatory policies are put in place in part because, to many people, the prospect of low-income subsidized housing is synonymous with rising crime, falling property values, and overcrowded classrooms, and it is cause for protest. Resistance to the construction of low-income housing is said to be evidence of a "not in my backyard" (NIMBY) way of thinking. However, in *From NIMBY to Good Neighbors: Recent Studies Reinforce That Apartments Are Good for a Community* (May 1, 2006, http://www.nmhc.org/Content/ServeFile.cfm?FileID=5408), the National Multi Housing Council summarizes research showing that smart growth (long-term goals for managing the growth of a community) may depend on the development of more high-density housing, such as apartments. The council states, "The good news is that there is an ever-increasing body of research that indicates that apartments (including affordable apartments) are not a threat to local property values and are a net plus to communities."

However, developers complain that there is no profit to be made from building and operating low-income housing. To provide incentives to developers, the 1986 Low-Income Housing Tax Credit program gave the states $1.25 per capita (per person) in tax credits toward the private development of low-income housing. In "A New Era for Affordable Housing" (*National Real Estate Investor*, March 1, 2003), H. Lee Murphy reports on the National Council of State Housing Agencies' data indicating that construction hit a high in 1994, when 117,100 apartment units were built with the credits. Skyrocketing construction costs brought a decline in new construction, which reached a low of 66,900 units in 2000. In 2001 Congress raised the per capita allotment to $1.75 and provided that the formula would rise each year with inflation. The tax credits financed the construction of 75,000 new units in 2001. Stan Luxenberg reports in "Affordable Housing Shortage" (*National Real Estate Investor*, September 1, 2006) that between 2002 and 2006 tax credits subsidized the construction of about 125,000 units per year. However, this rate of construction still did not keep pace with the number of affordable housing units that are demolished each year.

Habitat for Humanity

One group dedicated to solving the housing problem one house at a time was the brainchild of Millard Fuller (1935–2009) and Linda Fuller, who formed Habitat for Humanity International with a group of supporters in 1976. The purpose of this worldwide Christian service organization is to provide simple housing for the needy, built by volunteers and assisted by the future homeowner. The homeowner assumes an interest-free, 20- to 30-year mortgage, and materials are funded through donations and fund-raising activities. The idea is to give people assistance accompanied by responsibility.

Habitat for Humanity International indicates in "Habitat for Humanity Fact Sheet" (2009, http://www.habitat .org/how/factsheet.aspx) that by early 2009 it had built more than 300,000 houses that sheltered over 1.5 million people worldwide. According to the organization, homes in developing countries may cost as little as $800 to build, whereas the average house in the United States can cost nearly $60,000. Not all houses are new; the organization also restores older homes. Many volunteers travel to other countries to build homes. The most famous volunteers, the former president Jimmy Carter (1924–) and his wife, Rosalynn (1927–), made their first work trip in 1984 to New York City, sparking widespread interest in the movement. An annual event since that time, the week-long Carter Work Project in June 2008 built about 250 homes in areas of the Gulf Coast that were devastated by Hurricane Katrina in 2005.

WHERE THE HOMELESS LIVE

When faced with high rents and low housing availability, many poor people become homeless. What happens to them? Where do they live? Research shows that after becoming homeless, many people move around, staying in one place for a while, then moving on to another place. Many homeless people take advantage of homeless shelters at some point. Such shelters may be funded by the federal government, by religious organizations, or by other private homeless advocates.

Emergency Housing: Shelters and Transitional Housing

Typically, a homeless shelter provides dormitory-style sleeping accommodations and bathing facilities, with varying services for laundry, telephone calls, and other needs. Residents are often limited in the length of their stay and must leave the shelter during the day under most circumstances. By contrast, transitional housing is intended to bridge the gap between the shelter or street and permanent housing, with appropriate services to move the homeless into independent living. It may be a room in a hotel or motel, or it may be a subsidized apartment. HUD indicates in *The Third Annual Homeless Assessment Report to Congress* (July 2008, http://www.hudhre.info/documents/3rd HomelessAssessmentReport.pdf) that in 2007 there were 211,451 beds available in year-round emergency shelters and another 21,025 available seasonal beds; there were 211,205 beds in transitional housing available.

Illegal Occupancy

Poor neighborhoods are often full of abandoned buildings. Even the best-intentioned landlords cannot afford to maintain their properties in these areas. Many have let their buildings deteriorate or have simply walked away, leaving the fate of the building and its residents in the hands of the government. Despite overcrowding and unsafe conditions, many homeless people move into these dilapidated buildings illegally, glad for what shelter they can find. Municipal governments, overwhelmed by long waiting lists for public housing, by a lack of funds and personnel, and by an inadequate supply of emergency shelter beds, are often unable or unwilling to strictly enforce housing laws, allowing the homeless to become squatters rather than forcing them into the streets. Some deliberately turn a blind eye to the problem, knowing they have no better solution for the homeless.

The result is a multitude of housing units with deplorable living conditions—tenants bedding down in illegal boiler basements, sharing beds with children or in-laws, or sharing bathrooms with strangers. The buildings may have leaks and rot, rusted fire escapes, and rat and roach infestations. Given the alternative, many homeless people feel lucky to be sheltered at all.

Some homeless people are turning to foreclosed homes in their search for shelter. As a result of the housing crisis that began in 2008, foreclosures are dramatically on the rise. According to the article "Some Homeless Turn to Foreclosed Homes" (Associated Press, February 17, 2008), many homeless are turning to these vacant homes and becoming squatters. The article notes that "foreclosed homes often have an advantage over boarded-up and dilapidated houses that have been abandoned because of rundown conditions: Sometimes the heat, lights and water are still working." The article "Activist Moves Homeless into Foreclosures" (Associated Press, December 1, 2008) explains that homeless people are squatting in foreclosed homes in southern Florida with the help of an organization called Take Back the Land. Taryn Wobbema reports in "City Foreclosures Open Space for Squatters" (MNDaily.com, March 4, 2009) that in Minneapolis, the Poor People's Economic Human Rights Campaign actually places homeless people in empty homes illegally. Similar actions are taking place around the country.

CHAPTER 6
DEALING WITH THE PROBLEM OF HOMELESSNESS

FEDERAL GOVERNMENT AID FOR THE HOMELESS

What should the role of the government be in combating homelessness? Some people believe it is the duty of the government to take care of all citizens in times of need. Others point out that government help has often been misdirected or inadequate; in some instances, it has even added to the problem. Some people assert that people in trouble should solve their problems themselves. Federal programs for the homeless reflect a consensus that limited government help is important and necessary, but that homeless people also need to help themselves.

Since 1860 the federal government has been actively involved with the housing industry, specifically the low-income housing industry. In 1860 the government conducted the first partial census of housing—by counting slave dwellings. Twenty years later the U.S. census focused on the living quarters of the rest of the population by conducting a full housing census. Since then the federal government has played an increasingly larger role in combating housing problems in the United States:

- 1937—the U.S. Housing Act established the Public Housing Administration (which was later merged into the Federal Housing Administration [FHA] and the U.S. Department of Housing and Urban Development [HUD]) to create low-rent housing programs across the country through the establishment of local public housing agencies.

- 1949—the Housing Act set the goals of "a decent home and a suitable environment" for every family and authorized an 810,000-unit public housing program over the next six years. Title I of the act created the Urban Renewal Program, and Title V created the basic rural housing program under the FHA, which put the federal government directly into the mortgage business.

- 1965—Congress established HUD. Its goal was to create a new rent supplement program for low-income households in private housing.

- 1974—the Housing and Community Development Act created a new leased-housing program that included a certificate (voucher) program, expanding housing choices for low-income tenants. The voucher program soon became known as Section 8, after the section of the act that established it.

THE MCKINNEY-VENTO HOMELESS ASSISTANCE ACT

Widespread public outcry over the plight of the homeless in the early 1980s prompted Congress to pass the Stewart B. McKinney Homeless Assistance Act of 1987. Congress renamed the act the McKinney-Vento Homeless Assistance Act in 2000 to honor Representative Bruce Vento's (1940–2000; D-MN) service to the homeless. The range and reach of the act has broadened over the years. Most of the money authorized by the act went, initially, toward the funding of homeless shelters. The program also funded a Supportive Housing Program, a Shelter Plus Care Program, and the Single-Room Occupancy Program besides the Emergency Shelter Grant Program. Amendments to the act later enabled funding and other services to support permanent housing and other programs to help the homeless. HUD administers most McKinney-Vento funds.

In 2009 programs administered under the McKinney-Vento Homeless Assistance Act fell into three distinct categories. A cluster of activities known as the Continuum of Care programs provided competitive grants intended to help communities and organizations provide comprehensive services to the homeless. The Emergency Shelter Grants Program, a noncompetitive formula grant program, provided funds for emergency shelters to states, large cities, urban counties, and U.S. territories. The Title V program freed properties for use to house the homeless.

Continuum of Care

According to HUD, in *Homeless Assistance Programs* (March 21, 2008, http://www.hud.gov/offices/cpd/home

less/programs/index.cfm), the concept behind Continuum of Care programs is as follows: "A continuum of care system is designed to address the critical problem of homelessness through a coordinated community-based process of identifying needs and building a system to address those needs. The approach is predicated on the understanding that homelessness is not caused merely by a lack of shelter, but involves a variety of underlying, unmet needs—physical, economic, and social."

Nonprofit groups and local government entities applying for funds under these programs are expected to survey and assess local needs and to write a comprehensive plan for combating homelessness and meeting needs. Grant recipients are required to assess their clients' progress and make changes in the program in response to ongoing evaluation. Three major programs and some additional demonstration and rural efforts have developed over the years.

Supportive Housing Program

The aim of the Supportive Housing Program (SHP) is to provide housing and services that will enable homeless clients to achieve economic independence and control over their life. In *Supportive Housing Program Desk Guide* (2008, http://hudhre.info/documents/SHPDeskguide.pdf), HUD explains that the SHP provides matching funds for the construction of new buildings for housing homeless people; it also provides funding for the acquisition or refurbishing of existing buildings. The program underwrites 75% of the operating cost, including administration, and up to 80% of the cost of support programs. These programs must help clients achieve independence by providing skills training, child care, education, transportation assistance, counseling, and job referrals. Elements of the program include transitional housing for 24 months, permanent housing for the disabled, supportive services without housing, havens for the hard-to-reach and the mentally ill, and other innovative programs to solve problems of homelessness.

Shelter Plus Care

HUD notes in "Shelter Plus Care Program (S+C)" (March 21, 2008, http://www.hud.gov/offices/cpd/home less/programs/splusc/) that the Shelter Plus Care Program helps agencies that specifically target the hardest-to-serve homeless: those with mental and physical disabilities living on the street or in shelters, including drug addicts and acquired immunodeficiency (AIDS) syndrome sufferers. The program provides for rental assistance funded by HUD and other sources. Housing in this program can be in the form of group homes or individual units with supportive services. Grant funds must be matched with local dollars. Subsidies for projects are available for 10 years; assistance to sponsors and tenants is available for 5 years. A range of supportive services for tenants must be funded through other sources. Rental assistance includes four types of contracts:

- Tenant-Based Rental Assistance—direct contract with a low-income tenant

- Project-Based Rental Assistance—building owner contracts

- Sponsor-Based Rental Assistance—contracts with nonprofit organizations

- Single-Room Occupancy–Based Rental Assistance—single-room occupancy contracts provided by public housing authorities

Single-Room Occupancy

According to HUD, in "Single Room Occupancy Program (SRO)" (March 21, 2008, http://www.hud.gov/offices/cpd/homeless/programs/sro/), single-room occupancy housing is housing in a dormitory-style building where each person has his or her own private room but shares kitchens, bathrooms, and lounges. Single Room Occupancy Program housing is generally the cheapest type of housing available. Funding is intended to encourage the establishment and operation of such housing. Subsidy payments fund a project for a period of 10 years in the form of rental assistance in amounts equal to the rent, including utilities, minus the portion of rent payable by the tenants.

Other Program Components

Other programs folded under the Continuum of Care designation by HUD include demonstration programs for safe havens for the homeless and innovative homeless programs as well as rural homeless housing programs.

Emergency Shelter Grants

The Emergency Shelter Grant Program is HUD's formula grant program administered as a part of its community planning and development grant program. In "Emergency Shelter Grants (ESG) Program" (February 7, 2008, http://www.hud.gov/offices/cpd/homeless/pro grams/esg/), HUD explains that this "program provides homeless persons with basic shelter and essential supportive services. It can assist with the operational costs of the shelter facility, and for the administration of the grant. ESG also provides short-term homeless prevention assistance to persons at imminent risk of losing their own housing due to eviction, foreclosure, or utility shutoffs." Recipients of funding are states, large cities, urban counties, and U.S. territories that have filed consolidated community development plans with HUD. The program is called a formula program because the amounts allocated are based in part on population and poverty levels within the planning entities that participate. Grant funds flow from governmental entities to organizations that actually operate shelters and provide services to homeless people or people at risk of becoming homeless.

Money may be used to help individuals avoid homelessness by providing them with emergency funds. All grantees except for state governments must match grant funds dollar for dollar.

Title V

HUD notes in "Title V" (November 30, 2007, http://www.hud.gov/offices/cpd/homeless/programs/t5/) that it maintains information about and publishes listings of federal properties categorized as unutilized, underutilized, in excess, or in surplus. States, local governments, and nonprofit organizations can apply to use such properties to house the homeless. Title V does not provide funding; it provides properties to agencies for housing use. Groups may apply for funding under the Continuum of Care program to modify, refurbish, or adapt such structures for residential uses.

Consolidations, New Initiatives, and Reorganizations

HUD's programs, particularly those under Continuum of Care, have overlapping objectives yet operate under separate rules and requirements. (See Table 6.1.) The U.S. General Accounting Office (GAO; now the U.S.

Government Accountability Office) studied the McKinney programs in 1999 and concluded in *Homelessness: Coordination and Evaluation of Programs Are Essential* (February 1999, http://www.gao.gov/archive/1999/rc99049 .pdf) that the number of programs and the differences between them create barriers to their efficient use. Stanley J. Czerwinski states in *Homelessness: Improving Program Coordination and Client Access to Programs* (March 6, 2002, http://www.gao.gov/new.items/d02485t.pdf) that even though "HUD has taken actions that have improved the coordination of homeless assistance programs within communities and have helped reduce some of the administrative burdens that separate programs cause," consolidating the McKinney-Vento programs could harm homeless people if a system was not first devised to hold mainstream programs accountable for serving the homeless.

HUD's program administrators evidently reached much the same conclusions as the GAO. In 2004 HUD proposed consolidating its three major programs under Continuum of Care, along with the demonstration and rural assistance programs, into a single Homeless Assistance Grants Program. The GAO believed this consolidation would facilitate comprehensive delivery of services

TABLE 6.1

Requirements of four HUD McKinney-Vento programs

Program requirement	Emergency shelter grants	Supportive housing program	Shelter plus care	Single-room occupancy
Type of grants	Formula grant	Competitive grant	Competitive grant	Competitive grant
Eligible applicants	States Metropolitan cities Urban counties Territories	States Local governments Other governmental agencies Private nonprofit organizations Community mental health centers that are public nonprofit organizations	States Local governments Public housing authorities	Public housing authorities Private nonprofit organizations
Eligible program services	Emergency shelter Essential social services	Transitional housing Permanent housing for people with disabilities Supportive services only Safe havens Innovative supportive housing	Tenant based rental assistance Sponsor based rental assistance Project based rental assistance Single-room occupancy based rental assistance	Single-room occupancy housing
Eligible activities	Renovation/conversion Major rehabilitation Supportive service Operating costs Homelessness prevention activities	Acquisition Rehabilitation New construction Leasing Operating and administrative costs Supportive services only	Rental assistance	Rental assistance
Eligible population	Homeless individuals and families People at risk of becoming homeless	Homeless individuals and families for transitional housing and supportive services Disabled homeless individuals for permanent housing Hard-to-reach mentally ill homeless individuals for safe havens	Disabled homeless individuals and their families	Homeless individuals
Initial term of assistance	1 year	Up to 3 years	5 or 10 years	10 years
Matching funds	States: no match for first $100,000 and dollar-for-dollar match for rest of funds. Local governments: dollar-for-dollar match for all funds.	Dollar-for-dollar match for acquisition, rehabilitation, and new construction grants. Operating costs must be shared by 25 percent in the first 2 years and 50 percent in the third year. A 25-percent match for supportive service grants No match for grants used for leasing or administrative costs.	Dollar-for-dollar match of the federal shelter grant to pay for supportive services	No match required

SOURCE: Stanley J. Czerwinski, "Table 3. Requirements of Four HUD McKinney-Vento Programs," in *Homelessness: Improving Program Coordination and Client Access to Programs*, U.S. General Accounting Office, March 2002, http://www.gao.gov/new.items/d02485t.pdf (accessed January 11, 2009)

while reducing administrative expenses, both at HUD and on the part of grant recipients. In *Annual Performance Plan, Fiscal Year 2009* (February 2008, http://www.hud.gov/offices/cfo/reports/pdfs/app2009.pdf), HUD continues to propose "to legislatively consolidate the number of homeless assistance grants and reduce the administrative burden on jurisdictions to administer multiple programs." In fiscal year (FY) 2009 HUD's proposed budget for programs to help the homeless was a record $1.6 billion, a $50 million increase over FY 2008. (See Table 5.5 in Chapter 5.)

Beginning in 2004 HUD proposed in its annual budget request that Congress fund a new program called the Samaritan Initiative. The new program targeted an estimated 150,000 individuals HUD considers "chronically homeless." The FY 2009 HUD budget proposed setting aside up to $50 million for programs to help end chronic homelessness. (See Table 5.5 in Chapter 5.)

In February 2007 the Homeless Emergency Assistance and Rapid Transition to Housing (HEARTH) Act was introduced in the U.S. House of Representatives to reauthorize the McKinney-Vento Homeless Assistance Programs; it was reintroduced in September 2008. The National Policy and Advocacy Council on Homelessness explains in "HEARTH Act Amends HUD Definition of Homelessness and Improves Support for All Homeless Populations" (February 16, 2007, http://npach.org/HEARTH/2007/02/hearth_act_special_section.html) that this act would more closely align the HUD definition of homelessness with the definition of other government agencies, expand resources for supportive services, including shelters, emphasize the prevention of homelessness, and provide for greater decision-making power and flexibility at the local level. The bill was passed in the House in October 2008 and was introduced in the U.S. Senate on April 7, 2009. Senator Jack Reed (1949–; D-RI) explains in the press release "Reed Unveils New Approach to Preventing and Reducing Homelessness" (April 7, 2009, http://reed.senate.gov/newsroom/details.cfm?id=311261) that if passed, the bill will provide $2.2 billion for targeted homelessness assistance programs as well as expand the definition of homelessness.

Education for Homeless Children and Youth

In response to reports that over 50% of homeless children were not attending school regularly, Congress enacted the McKinney-Vento Homeless Assistance Act's Education for Homeless Children and Youth program in 1987. The program ensures that homeless children and youth have equal access to the same free, appropriate education, including preschool education, provided to other children. Education for Homeless Children and Youth also provides funding for state and local school districts to implement the law. States are required to

report estimated numbers of homeless children and the problems encountered in serving them. The act includes the following guidelines:

- Homeless children cannot be segregated.

- Transportation has to be provided to and from schools of origin if requested (a school of origin is the school the student attended when permanently housed, or the school in which the student was last enrolled).

- In case of a placement dispute, immediate enrollment is required pending the outcome.

- Local education agencies must put the "best interest of the child" first in determining the feasibility of keeping children in their school of origin.

- Local education agencies must designate a local liaison for homeless children and youth.

- States have to subgrant 50% to 75% of their allotments under Education for Homeless Children and Youth competitively to local education agencies.

At the time the McKinney-Vento Homeless Assistance Act was passed, only an estimated 57% of homeless children were enrolled in school. By 2000 the percentage had increased to 88%. In the 2003–04 school season more homeless children were enrolled in elementary school than in middle school or high school. (See Table 4.3 in Chapter 4.) Even though the data appear inconclusive because elementary school children may be more likely to be homeless, thus accounting for their greater numbers, the data seem to suggest that older homeless children may be less likely to be enrolled in school than elementary school-age children.

However, in implementing the legislation, school districts found that barriers arose in areas such as residency, guardian requirements, incomplete or missing documentation (including immunization records and birth certificates), and transportation. Consequently, some school districts established separate schools for homeless children. In 2001 there were an estimated 40 separate schools for the homeless in 19 states, according to Kristen Kreisher in "Educating Homeless Children" (*Children's Voice*, September–October 2002), and even though separate schools were outlawed with the 2002 reauthorization of the McKinney-Vento Homeless Assistance Act, those schools that already existed were allowed to remain.

Transportation became an issue for school districts providing education to homeless students. Nicole Brode reports in "New York's School Choice Leaves More Homeless Children with Hour-Plus Commutes" (*Knight-Ridder/Tribune Business News*, February 10, 2003) that 34% of the 226 students in one New York homeless shelter faced commutes of longer than an hour because their parents had opted to keep their children in the same schools they had attended before they became homeless, a right guaranteed by the new law. In 2005 the Thomas J. Pappas schools for the homeless in Phoenix and Tempe, Arizona, reported that 12 buses traveled more than 1,000 miles (1,609 km) each morning to transport children to school. In "Homeless Kids Lack School to Call Home" (*Chicago Tribune*, February 13, 2009), Carlos Sadovi notes that homeless children must either change schools often or face commutes of up to several hours. According to Kathleen Kingsbury, in "Keeping Homeless Kids in School" (*Time*, March 12, 2009), in March 2009, when nearly one out of 10 children in Minneapolis, Minnesota, was homeless, children faced commutes of an hour or more.

In the fact sheet "Education of Homeless Children and Youth" (June 2008, http://www.nationalhomeless .org/publications/facts/education.html), the National Coalition for the Homeless (NCH) indicates that funding for the Education for Homeless Children and Youth program has been insufficient to meet the needs of homeless children. The National Association for the Education of Homeless Children and Youth states in "Legislative Update" (March 24, 2009, http://www.naehcy.org/update .html) that in FY 2008 the program received $64 million. Six percent of school districts nationwide received funds under the program in 2006–07; however, most homeless children reside in school districts that received no grant money. The American Recovery and Reinvestment Act signed into law by President Barack Obama (1961–) in February 2009 included $70 million in additional funding for the Education for Homeless Children and Youth Program to be distributed by states to local school districts. The McKinney-Vento Homeless Education Act is scheduled to be considered for reauthorization in 2009.

RESTRICTIVE ORDINANCES

According to Tom Wetzel, in "What Is Gentrification?" (2004, http://www.uncanny.net/~wetzel/gentry .htm), the process of renewal and rebuilding that accompanies an influx of middle-class or affluent people into deteriorating areas is called gentrification. It typically displaces earlier—and usually poorer—residents and often destroys ethnic communities. Even though gentrification has positive aspects—reduced crime, new investment in the community, and increased economic activity—these benefits are generally enjoyed by the newcomers while the existing residents are marginalized. When a neighborhood is gentrified, the visible homeless come to be seen as a blight on the quality of life of the new residents. The presence of homeless people can drive away tourists and frustrate the proprietors of area businesses. The widening gap between the haves and the have-nots in American society is evident in the plight of homeless people. As more and more privately owned, federally subsidized apartment buildings and former "skid rows" were gentrified during

the economic boom of the 1990s, more of the poorest people were forced into homelessness.

In recent years there has been an increase in the enactment of laws and ordinances intended to regulate the activities of homeless people. Moreover, in some areas homeless children even found themselves placed outside the regular public school system and segregated in special schools for the homeless. Advocates for the homeless contend that such practices deny the homeless their most basic human, legal, and political rights.

Some local ordinances prevent homeless people from sleeping on the streets or in parks, even though there may not be enough shelter beds to accommodate every homeless person every night. The homeless may be turned out of shelters to fend for themselves during the day, yet local ordinances prevent them from loitering in public places or resting in bus stations, libraries, or public buildings. Begging or picking up cans for recycling may help the homeless to support themselves, yet often there are restrictions against panhandling (begging) or limits on the number of cans they can redeem. To see the homeless bathe or use the toilet in public makes people uncomfortable; consequently, laws are passed to prohibit such activities.

Are homeless people targeted by these laws and consequently denied their civil rights? Do such ordinances criminalize homelessness by singling out the minority (the unhoused) but not the majority (the housed)? For example, drinking alcoholic beverages in public is illegal, but the police may selectively enforce the law against street people while ignoring other drinkers, such as tourists. Ordinances disallowing life-sustaining activities performed by homeless individuals may be said to exclude the homeless from equal protection under the law.

Most measures regulating the behavior of homeless people are enacted at the community level. Sometimes the most restrictive of these laws have been challenged in federal court on the grounds that they violate the rights of the homeless people they seek to regulate. For example, a federal court may be asked to determine whether begging or panhandling is considered protected conduct under the First Amendment (freedom of speech).

Criminalizing Homelessness

Homeless people live in and move about public spaces, and many Americans believe society has a right to control or regulate what homeless people can do in these shared spaces. A city or town may introduce local ordinances or policies designed to restrict homeless people's activities, remove their belongings, or destroy their nontraditional living places. In many cities municipal use of criminal sanctions to protect public spaces has come into conflict with efforts by civil rights and homeless advocates to prevent the criminalization of the necessary activities of the homeless population.

TABLE 6.2

Prohibited conduct in selected cities, 2005

	Begging in public places city-wide	Begging in particular public places	"Aggressive" panhandling	Sleeping in public city-side	Sleeping in particular public places	Sitting/lying in particular public places	Loitering, loafing, vagrancy city-wide	Obstruction of sidewalks or other public places
Atlanta, GA		X	X	X	X	X		X
Baltimore, MD		X	X				X	X
Boston, MA		X	X	X		X		X
Chicago, IL		X	X					
Cincinnati, OH		X	X			X		X
Dallas, TX		X	X	X				X
Detroit, MI	X						X	X
Las Vegas, NV		X	X		X			X
Los Angeles, CA		X	X		X	X		X
Miami, FL			X	X				X
New York								
Philadelphia, PA		X	X			X		X
Phoenix, AZ		X	X	X		X		X
Portland, OR		X				X		X
San Francisco, CA		X	X		X			X
Seattle, WA			X			X		X
Trenton, NJ		X	X	X		X		X
Washington, D.C.		X	X			X	X	X

SOURCE: Adapted from "Prohibited Conduct Chart," in *A Dream Denied: The Criminalization of Homelessness in U.S. Cities*, The National Coalition for the Homeless and The National Law Center on Homelessness and Poverty, January 2006, http://www.nationalhomeless.org/publications/crimreport/chart.pdf (accessed January 5, 2009)

There have been other approaches. Several cities have proposed or created community courts specifically to handle "public nuisance" crimes. Other cities have implemented plans to privatize public property as a way of restricting the access of homeless people to certain areas.

Other localities pass ordinances that target homeless people in the hopes of driving them from the community. According to the NCH, in *A Dream Denied: The Criminalization of Homelessness in U.S. Cities* (January 2006, http://www.nationalhomeless.org/publications/crimreport/report.pdf), of 224 cities surveyed in 2006, 27% prohibited sitting or lying in some public places; 28% prohibited camping in some places and 16% prohibited it citywide; 39% prohibited loitering in some places and 16% prohibited it citywide; and 43% prohibited begging in some places, 45% prohibited aggressive panhandling, and 21% had citywide prohibitions. The number of laws prohibiting sitting or lying, begging, and aggressive panhandling in some public places had all increased from the previous survey by over 10%.

Violating Human Rights

In *A Dream Denied*, the NCH states that, as successful lawsuits have shown, "many of the practices and policies that punish the public performance of life-sustaining activities by homeless persons violate the constitutional rights of homeless persons." The NCH notes that nearly all the communities surveyed lacked sufficient shelter space to accommodate the homeless and suggests that the effort and money spent on bringing the homeless into the courthouse might better be directed toward addressing the nation's lack of affordable housing.

Table 6.2 illustrates the antihomeless laws that existed in some of the cities surveyed for the 2006 report. Prohibited or restricted behaviors fell under the categories of sanitation, begging, sleeping/camping, sitting/lying, loitering/loafing, and vagrancy.

The NCH names Sarasota, Florida; Lawrence, Kansas; Little Rock, Arkansas; Atlanta, Georgia; and Las Vegas, Nevada, as the five "meanest cities" based on the number of antihomeless laws passed or pending, the enforcement and severity of their laws, the local support for the "meanest" designation, and the "general political climate" with regard to the homeless, among other criteria. Two examples of the practices of these cities follow.

Sarasota tried a third time to criminalize homelessness after two previous antilodging laws were overturned as unconstitutional by Florida courts. The latest law explicitly targeted homeless people—to be arrested under the law, a person must have "no other place to live."

Even though Las Vegas lacks an adequate number of shelter beds, police regularly sweep homeless encampments and repeat misdemeanor offenders face extended jail time. The city considered making parks private to enable owners to kick out unwanted people. According to the NCH, Mayor Oscar Goodman said, "I don't want them there. They're not going to be there. I'm not going to let it happen. They think I'm mean now; wait until the homeless try to go over there."

The Rationale for Restrictive Ordinances

Local officials often restrict homeless people's use of public space to protect public health and safety—either of the general public, the homeless themselves, or both. Dangers to the public have included tripping over people and objects on sidewalks, intimidation of passersby caused by aggressive begging, and the spreading of diseases. Many people believe the very presence of the homeless is unsightly and their removal improves the appearance of public spaces. Other laws are based on the need to prevent crime. New York's campaign is based on the broken windows theory of the criminologists James Q. Wilson (1931–1997) and George Walton Kelling (1944–), who discuss this theory in "Broken Windows" (*Atlantic Monthly*, March 1982). They argue that allowing indications of disorder, such as a broken window or street people, to remain unaddressed, shows a loss of public order and control, as well as apathy in a neighborhood, which breeds more serious criminal activity. Therefore, keeping a city neat and orderly should help prevent crime.

All these are legitimate concerns to some degree. The problem, critics say, is that rather than trying to eliminate or reduce homelessness by helping the homeless find housing and jobs, most local laws try to change the behavior of the homeless by punishing them. They target the homeless with legal action, ignoring the fact that many would gladly stop living in the streets and panhandling if they had any feasible alternatives. Even though these laws may be effective in the sense that the shanties are gone and homeless people are not allowed to bed down in subway tunnels or doorways, the fact remains that homelessness has not been eradicated. Homeless people have simply been forced to move to a different part of town, have hidden themselves, or have been imprisoned. Furthermore, many of these laws have been challenged in court as violating the legal rights of the homeless people they target.

Alternative Strategies

In *A Dream Denied*, the NCH argues that criminalization does nothing to address the problem and that local government, police officials, and business groups should work with advocates and providers for the homeless to come up with solutions that prevent and end homelessness. For example, more resources should be made available for affordable housing projects and homeless shelters and other services. The NCH states that business groups can put resources toward solutions to end homelessness rather than toward lobbying for criminalization methods. The NCH contends that "as criminalization measures move people away from services, make it more difficult for people to move out of homelessness, and cost more due to incarceration and law enforcement costs than more constructive approaches, cities would be wise to seek constructive alternatives to criminalization. When cities work with homeless persons and advocates toward solutions to homelessness, instead of punishing those who are homeless or poor, everyone can benefit."

Alternatives to criminalizing homeless behavior can be implemented with help from community leadership and homeless advocates, who have intimate knowledge from close contact with homelessness. The NCH details in *A Dream Denied* the innovative programs that some cities have put in place to better deal with the problem of homelessness.

A key element of most successful programs is the partnering of governmental and police organizations with advocacy organizations. For example, in Broward County, Florida, the Taskforce for Ending Homelessness partnered with the Fort Lauderdale police department to create an outreach team that includes not only police officers but also a civilian advocate who was formerly homeless. After five years of operation, the team had over 23,000 contacts with homeless individuals and had prevented an estimated 2,400 arrests each year. In Columbus, Cleveland, and Cincinnati, Ohio, teams of trained workers visit homeless encampments at nontraditional hours to assist homeless people. Key to the success of the program is that they do not put many restrictions on the assistance they offer. In Washington, D.C., the downtown business community created a community day center for homeless people to provide services when shelters are closed. The center serves up to 260 people per day, providing them with laundry services and showers, as well as a morning meal.

CONSTITUTIONAL RIGHTS OF THE HOMELESS

The U.S. Constitution and its amendments, especially the Bill of Rights, guarantee certain freedoms and rights to all U.S. citizens, including the homeless. As more and more cities move to deal with homelessness by aggressively enforcing public place restrictions, the restrictions are increasingly being challenged in court as unconstitutional. Sometimes a city ordinance has been declared unconstitutional; at other times the courts have found that there were special circumstances that allowed the ordinance to stand.

There are many ways in which ordinances affecting the homeless can violate their rights. Many court challenges claim that the law in question is unconstitutionally broad or vague. Others claim that a particular law denies the homeless equal protection under the law or violates their right to due process, as guaranteed by the Fifth and Fourteenth amendments. There are also cases based on a person's right to travel, and others that claim restrictions on the homeless constitute "cruel and unusual punishment," which is prohibited by the Eighth Amendment. Many cities have ordinances against panhandling, but charitable organizations freely solicit in public places. As a result, according to those challenging the ordinances, the right to free expression under the First Amendment is available to organizations but denied to the homeless.

The appearance of poverty should not deny an individual's right to be free from unreasonable search and seizure, as guaranteed by the Fourth Amendment. Often, homeless people's property has been confiscated or destroyed (such as camping gear or personal possessions) without warning because they were found on public property. The state of homelessness is such that even the most personal living activities have to be performed in public. Denying activities that are necessary for survival may infringe on an individual's rights under the Eighth Amendment.

The Fourteenth Amendment's right to equal protection under the law may be at issue when the homeless are cited for sleeping in the park, but others lying on the grass sunning themselves or taking a nap during a picnic, for instance, are not.

Testing the Constitutionality of Laws in Court

Some court cases test the law through civil suits, and others challenge the law by appealing convictions in criminal cases. Many advocates for the homeless, or the homeless themselves, challenge laws that they believe infringe on the rights of homeless people. The NCH argues that antipanhandling laws may infringe on the First Amendment's right of free speech; that anticamping laws penalize people when no shelter space is available and violate the Eighth Amendment's right to be free from cruel and unusual punishment; that antiloitering laws are often unconstitutionally vague and violate the Due Process Clause of the Fourteenth Amendment; and that sweeps targeted toward cleaning public areas may violate the Fourth Amendment's right to be free from unreasonable searches and seizures.

NO BED, NO ARREST. The concept of "no bed, no arrest" first arose out of a 1988 class action suit filed by the Miami Chapter of the American Civil Liberties Union on behalf of about 6,000 homeless people living in Miami, Florida. The city had a practice of sweeping the homeless from the areas where the Orange Bowl Parade and other related activities were held. The complaint in *Pottinger v. City of Miami* (S.D.Fla. 810 F. Supp. 1551 [1992]) alleged that the city had "a custom, practice and policy of arresting, harassing and otherwise interfering with homeless people for engaging in basic activities of daily life—including sleeping and eating—in the public places where they are forced to live. Plaintiffs further claim that the City has arrested thousands of homeless people for such life-sustaining conduct under various City of Miami ordinances and Florida Statutes. In addition, plaintiffs assert that the city routinely seizes and destroys their property and has failed to follow its own inventory procedures regarding the seized personal property of homeless arrestees and homeless persons in general."

The U.S. District Court for the Southern District of Florida ruled in *Pottinger* that the city's practices were cruel and unusual, in violation of the Eighth Amendment's ban against punishment based on status (only the homeless were being arrested). Furthermore, the court found the police practices of taking or destroying the property of the homeless to be in violation of the Fourth and Fifth amendments' rights of freedom from unreasonable seizure and confiscation of property.

The city appealed the district court's judgment. Ultimately, a settlement was reached in which Miami agreed that a homeless person observed committing a "life-sustaining conduct" misdemeanor may be warned to stop, but if there is no available shelter, no warning is to be given. If there is an available shelter, the homeless person is to be told of its availability. If the homeless person accepts assistance, no arrest is to take place.

In *In re Eichorn* (81 Cal. Rptr. 2d 535 [Cal. App. Dep't. Super. Ct. 2000]), James Eichorn challenged his arrest for sleeping outside a county office building in Santa Ana, California. He attempted to prove, per the "no bed, no arrest" policy, that on the night he was arrested there were no shelter beds available. However, the court would not allow a jury to consider the "necessity" defense, and Eichorn was subsequently convicted and lost his appeal. Eichorn's lawyer then filed a writ of habeas corpus. The appeals court found in that case that Eichorn should have been allowed to present his necessity defense, and the conviction was set aside and remanded back to the municipal court. In that case, the district attorney decided not to retry him. In essence, the case reaffirmed the "no bed, no arrest" policy.

SLEEPING OUTDOORS. Sarasota, Florida, passed a series of ordinances after 2000 that were designed to criminalize sleeping outdoors; two were overturned by state courts. A third ordinance made it illegal to sleep outdoors on either private or public property without permission of the property owner or the city manager if one of the following conditions existed: many personal objects were present (indicating the person is homeless), the person is cooking or maintaining a fire, the person is digging, or the person states he or she is homeless. This law survived the constitutionality test in *City of Sarasota v. McGinnis* (No. 2005 MO 16411 NC [Fla. Cir. Ct. 2005]). However, Sarasota's ordinance against sleeping outdoors was found unconstitutional in *City of Sarasota v. Nipper* (No. 2005 MO 4369 NC [Fla. Cir. Ct. 2005]), in which the court found that the law punished innocent conduct and left too much discretion in the hands of police.

LOITERING OR WANDERING. In 2000 homeless street dwellers and shelter residents of the Skid Row area (the plaintiffs) sought a temporary restraining order (TRO) against the Los Angeles Police Department (the defendant), claiming that their First and Fourth amendment rights were being violated. The plaintiffs alleged that they were being stopped without cause and their identification demanded on threat of arrest; that they were being ordered to "move along" even though they were not in anyone's way; that their belongings were being confiscated; and that they were being ticketed for loitering. In *Justin v. City of Los Angeles* (No. CV-00-12352 LGB, 2000 U.S. Dist. Lexis 17881 [C.D. Cal. December 5, 2000]), Judge Lourdes G. Baird (1935–) denied a TRO that would have prevented the defendant from asking the plaintiffs to "move along." The TRO was granted with reference to the following actions when in the Skid Row area:

- Detention without reasonable suspicion

- Demand of identification on threat of arrest

- Searches without probable cause

- Removal from sidewalks unless free passage of pedestrians was obstructed

- Confiscation of personal property that was not abandoned

- Citation of those who may "annoy or molest" if interference was reasonable and free passage of pedestrians was not impeded

LIVING IN AN ENCAMPMENT. In 1996 advocates for the homeless sought an injunction against a Tucson, Arizona, resolution barring homeless encampments from city-owned property on Eighth Amendment and equal protection grounds. The court, in *Davidson v. City of Tucson* (924 F. Supp. 989), held that the plaintiffs did not have standing to raise a cruel and unusual punishment claim, as they had not been convicted of a crime and no one had been arrested under the ordinance. The equal protection claim failed because the court did not consider homeless people a suspect class and the right to travel did not include the right to ignore trespass laws or remain on property without regard to ownership.

A Sarasota, Florida, law prohibited camping on public or private property between sunset and sunrise. Five homeless people challenged the law; their lawyer argued that it punished innocent conduct and was unconstitutionally vague. The circuit court found in *City of Sarasota v. Tillman* (No. 2003 CA 15645 NC [Fla. Cir. Ct. 2004]) that the law unconstitutional for criminalizing the non-criminal act of sleeping.

LOITERING IN A TRAIN STATION. In 1995 plaintiffs challenged Amtrak's policy of arresting or ejecting people who appeared to be homeless or loitering in Penn Station in New York City, even though the individuals were not apparently committing crimes. The district court, in *Streetwatch v. National R.R. Passenger Corp.* (875 F. Supp. 1055), determined that Amtrak's rules of conduct were unacceptably vague and that their enforcement impinged on the plaintiffs' rights to freedom of movement and due process.

PANHANDLING. One of the notable court cases addressing panhandling involved Jennifer Loper, who moved from her parents' suburban New York home to beg on the streets of New York City. From time to time she and her friend William Kaye were ordered by police to move on, in accordance with the city ordinance, which stated: "A person is guilty of loitering when he: '(1) Loiters, remains or wanders about in a public place for the purpose of begging.'" In 1992 Loper and Kaye sued the city, claiming that their free speech rights had been violated and that the ordinance was unconstitutional. A district court declared the ordinance unconstitutional on First Amendment grounds. On appeal, the police department argued that begging has no expressive element that is protected by the First Amendment. In *Loper v. New York City Police Department* (999 F.2d 699 [2d Cir. 1993]), the U.S. Court of Appeals, Second Circuit, declared the city's ban on begging invalid, noting that the regulations applied to sidewalks, which have historically been acknowledged to be a public forum. The court agreed that the ban deprived beggars of all means to express their message. Even if a panhandler does not speak, "the presence of an unkempt and disheveled person holding out his or her hand or a cup to receive a donation itself conveys a message of need for support and assistance."

ZONING THE HOMELESS OUT OF DOWNTOWN. In 1998 Alan Mason, a homeless man, sought an injunction, damages, and relief against the city of Tucson and the city police for zoning homeless people. The suit alleged that homeless people were arrested without cause, were charged with misdemeanors, and were then released only if they agreed to stay away from the area where they had been arrested. Mason himself had been restricted from certain downtown areas, such as federal, state, and local courts (including the court in which his case was tried); voter registration facilities; a soup kitchen; places of worship; and many social and transportation agencies.

The plaintiff argued that such restrictions violated his constitutional right to travel, deprived him of liberty without due process in violation of the Fifth Amendment, and implicated the equal protection clause of the Fourteenth Amendment. In *Mason v. Tucson* (D. Arizona, 1998), the district court granted a temporary injunction against enforcing the law, saying the zone restrictions were overbroad. The case was subsequently settled out of court.

SLEEPING ON SIDEWALKS. In 2006 a federal appeals court in Pasadena, California, ruled that ordinances against homeless people "sitting, lying, or sleeping" on sidewalks are unconstitutional. In *Jones v. City of Los Angeles* (444 F.3d 1118 [9th Cir.]), the court ruled that Los Angeles enforced the law only against homeless people, therefore criminalizing "the status of homelessness," which violated the Eight Amendment. It was the first time in more than a decade that a law criminalizing homelessness had been struck down in court.

CHAPTER 7
HEALTH AND HUNGER

HEALTH OF POOR PEOPLE
Connection between Poor Health and Poverty

The National Center for Health Statistics (NCHS) points out in *Health, United States, 2008* (2009, http://www.cdc .gov/nchs/data/hus/hus08.pdf) that poverty causes poor health due to its connection with a nutritionally poor diet, substandard housing, exposure to the elements and environmental hazards, unhealthy lifestyle, and decreased access to and use of health care services. Jane Knitzer (http:// www.nccp.org/publications/pdf/text_705.pdf), the director of the National Center for Children in Poverty, testified before the House Committee on Ways and Means on January 24, 2007, that economic hardship in childhood is linked to poor health and that poor health adversely affects educational attainment and future productivity, leading to a cycle of poverty.

Poor people are more likely to suffer from chronic (long-term) conditions that limit their activities. According to the NCHS, 11.6% of the population had such conditions in 2006. However, over one out of five (22.1%) people living below the poverty line suffered from chronic health complaints, compared to 16.4% of those whose household incomes were 100% to 199% of the poverty level and 8.7% of those whose incomes were 200% or more of the poverty level. In addition, 14.2% of adults with incomes below the poverty line had difficulty seeing even with corrective lenses, compared to 12.2% of people with incomes 100% to 199% of the poverty line and 8.1% of those with incomes 200% of the poverty line or higher.

The NCHS also reports that poor respondents were much more likely to rate their health as only fair or poor, compared to their more affluent peers. In 2006 more than one out of five (20.3%) people with incomes below the poverty level rated their health as fair or poor, compared to 14.4% of people with incomes 100% to 199% of the poverty level and only 6.1% of people with higher incomes.

According to the NCHS, poor people also have more mental health problems. In 2006 only 1.7% of people with incomes 200% of the poverty level or higher reported they suffered from serious psychological distress within the past 30 days. However, 5.2% of people with incomes 100% to 199% of the poverty line and 7.6% of people with incomes below the poverty level reported such psychological distress.

Poverty and Access to Health Care

The NCHS notes in *Health, United States, 2008* that poor and near-poor people have reduced access to medical care. In 2006, 10.6% of those living below the poverty level reported not receiving care because of cost and 12.2% reported delaying receiving health care because of cost in the previous year. In contrast, of those with incomes 100% to 199% of the poverty level, 9.6% reported not receiving care and 11.8% reported a delay in receiving care, whereas among those with incomes 200% of the poverty level or more, 3.6% reported not receiving care and 5.7% reported a delay in receiving care in the previous year. In addition, 13.7% of people with incomes below the poverty level did not get prescription drugs because of the cost, compared to 11.1% of people with incomes 100% to 199% of the poverty level and only 4.2% of those with higher incomes. The percentage of people unable to get prescription drugs because of their cost has risen markedly in all socioeconomic groups since 1997. Nearly all Americans are affected by skyrocketing health care costs. A Kaiser Family Foundation explains in the press release "More Than Half of Americans Say Family Skimped on Medical Care Because of Cost in Past Year" (February 25, 2009, http://www.kff.org/kaiserpolls/kaiserpolls022509nr .cfm) that more than half of American families postponed or did without medical treatments in 2008 due to the lack of affordable health care.

A higher percentage of poor and low-income children in 2005–06 had not visited the doctor in the previous 12 months than children in higher income families; this was particularly true among Hispanic children. According to the NCHS, one out of five (20%) Hispanic children living in households with incomes below the poverty level or with incomes 100% to 199% of the poverty level (19.1%) had not visited a doctor in the previous year, whereas 13.4% of Hispanic children living in households with incomes 200% or more than the poverty level had not visited a doctor in the past year. Among non-Hispanic white children, only 9.4% of those living below the poverty level, 13.2% of those living at 100% to 199% of the poverty level, and 8.4% of those living at 200% or more of the poverty level had not seen a doctor in the previous year. Among African-American children, 12.1% of those living below the poverty level, 13.1% of those living at 100% to 199% of the poverty level, and 10.2% of those living at 200% or more of the poverty level had failed to see a doctor within the past year.

HEALTH INSURANCE

The scope of health issues regarding the impoverished and homeless in the United States is related in part to the number of uninsured Americans. Figure 7.1 shows that in 2007 the number of uninsured people had declined slightly from the year before, when it had been higher than it had been in decades. At that time, 45.7 million people were uninsured, but as unemployment rose during the economic recession that began in 2008, this number was expected to rise.

In the 2005 to 2007 period, Hispanic people were the most likely to be uninsured. Nearly a third (32.8%) of Hispanics during this period were uninsured, followed by Native Americans (32.1%), Native Hawaiian and other Pacific Islanders (20.5%), and African-Americans (19.6%). (See Table 7.1.) Only 10.6% of non-Hispanic whites lacked health insurance during this period.

Certain demographic factors made it more likely that a person would not have health insurance. The lower a household's income, the more likely a family did not carry health insurance. In 2007, 24.5% of households earning less than $25,000 a year carried health insurance. (See Table 7.2.) In contrast, only 7.8% of households with incomes of $75,000 or more were uninsured. In addition, young adults aged 18 to 24 years old were the most likely group to not have health insurance coverage—over a quarter (28.1%) of this

FIGURE 7.1

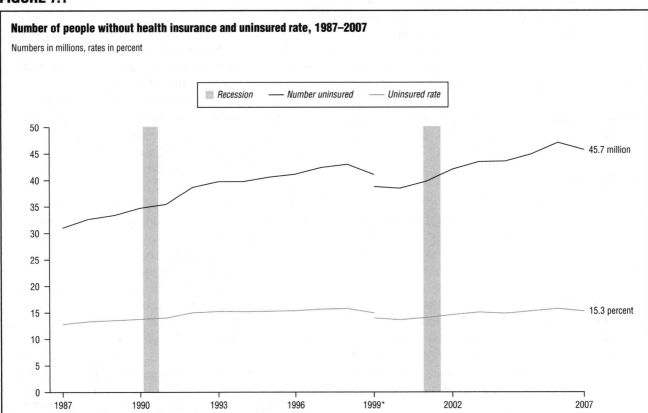

Number of people without health insurance and uninsured rate, 1987–2007

Numbers in millions, rates in percent

*Implementation of Census 2000-based population controls occurred for the 2000 Annual Social and Economic Supplement (ASEC), which collected data for 1999. These estimates also reflect the results of follow-up verification questions that were asked of people who responded "no" to all questions about specific types of health insurance coverage in order to verify whether they were actually uninsured. This change increased the number and percentage of people covered by health insurance, bringing the Current Population Survey (CPS)more in line with estimates from other national surveys.
Note: Respondents were not asked detailed health insurance questions before the 1988 CPS.

SOURCE: Carmen DeNavas-Walt, Bernadette D. Proctor, and Jessica C. Smith, "Figure 6. Number Uninsured and Uninsured Rate: 1987 to 2007," in *Income, Poverty, and Health Insurance Coverage in the United States: 2007*, Current Population Reports, U.S. Census Bureau, August 2008, http://www.census.gov/prod/2008pubs/p60-235.pdf (accessed December 15, 2008)

TABLE 7.1

People without health insurance coverage by race and Hispanic origin, 2004–07

[Numbers in thousands. People as of March of the following year.]

Race[a] and Hispanic origin	3-year average 2005–2007[b] Estimate	2-year average		Change (2006–2007 average less 2004–2005[b] average) Estimate
		2004–2005[b] Estimate	2006–2007 Estimate	
Number uninsured				
All races	45,822	44,156	46,326	2,170
White	34,578	33,484	34,893	1,409
White, not Hispanic	20,873	20,732	20,855	123
Black	7,343	6,935	7,512	577
American Indian and Alaska Native	809	693	869	176
Asian	2,147	2,031	2,139	109
Native Hawaiian and other Pacific Islander	140	139	141	2
Hispanic (any race)	14,673	13,633	15,033	1,400
Percentage uninsured				
All races	15.4	15.1	15.5	0.5
White	14.5	14.2	14.6	0.4
White, not Hispanic	10.6	10.6	10.6	—
Black	19.6	18.9	20.0	1.1
American Indian and Alaska Native	32.1	30.3	32.9	2.6
Asian	16.5	16.3	16.2	−0.2
Native Hawaiian and other Pacific Islander	20.5	22.8	19.5	−3.2
Hispanic (any race)	32.8	32.1	33.1	1.0

—Represents or rounds to zero.

[a]Federal surveys now give respondents the option of reporting more than one race. Therefore, two basic ways of defining a race group are possible. A group such as Asian may be defined as those who reported Asian and no other race (the race-alone or single-race concept) or as those who reported Asian regardless of whether they also reported another race (the race-alone-or-in-combination concept). This table shows data using the first approach (race alone). The use of the single-race population does not imply that it is the preferred method of presenting or analyzing data. The Census Bureau uses a variety of approaches. Information on people who reported more than one race, such as white *and* American Indian and Alaska Native or Asian and black or African American, is available from Census 2000 through American FactFinder. About 2.6 percent of people reported more than one race in Census 2000.
[b]The 2004 and 2005 data were revised in March 2007.

SOURCE: Carmen DeNavas-Walt, Bernadette D. Proctor, and Jessica C. Smith, "Table 7. People without Health Insurance Coverage by Race and Hispanic Origin Using 2- and 3-Year Averages: 2004–2005 and 2006–2007," in *Income, Poverty, and Health Insurance Coverage in the United States: 2007*, Current Population Reports, U.S. Census Bureau, August 2008, http://www.census.gov/prod/2008pubs/p60–235.pdf (accessed December 15, 2008)

group were uninsured. Foreign-born residents were more likely to be uninsured than were native-born citizens (33.2% and 12.7%, respectively).

Figure 7.2 shows the average number of people between 2005 and 2007 who were without health insurance coverage by state. Texas (24.4%) had the highest percentage of uninsured people, whereas Massachusetts (8.3%), Hawaii (8.3%), Minnesota (8.5%), Wisconsin (8.8%), and Iowa (9.4%) had the lowest. Comparisons of two-year averages (2004–05 and 2006–07) show that the percentage of people without health insurance rose in 10 states (Kansas, Kentucky, Louisiana, Mississippi, Nebraska, New Jersey, New Mexico, New York, North Carolina, and Texas) and dropped in only five (Connecticut, Indiana, Massachusetts, West Virginia, and Wisconsin) and the District of Columbia. (See Figure 7.3.)

Children in poverty were much more likely than children in general to be uninsured in 2007 (17.6% and 11%, respectively). (See Figure 7.4.) However, this rate varied greatly by race. Hispanic children (20%) were far more likely to be uninsured than African-American children (12.2%), Asian-American children (11.7%), or non-Hispanic white children (7.3%).

People without insurance are less likely to seek medical care. They also tend to use the emergency room for medical care, leading to skyrocketing health care costs. In "Health Insurance Coverage" (2009, http://www.nchc.org/facts/coverage.shtml), the National Coalition on Health Care indicates that uninsured people are 30% to 50% more likely to be hospitalized for an avoidable condition than are insured people.

At the same time that overall money spent on health care in the United States is growing rapidly, government spending to help the uninsured has remained stagnant or declined. The Kaiser Commission notes in "Covering the Uninsured: Growing Need, Strained Resources" (January 2007, http://www.kff.org/uninsured/upload/7429-02.pdf) that between 2001 and 2004 health care expenses rose by nearly 14%, and federal spending on safety net programs (a network of hospitals, clinics, and health centers that are largely supported by government resources) increased 15.4%, from $19.8 billion in 2001 to $22.8 billion in 2004. However, because the number of uninsured grew by nearly 5 million people over this period, federal spending per uninsured person actually declined, from $546 per person to $498 per person in constant 2004 dollars. The Kaiser Commission concludes, "As critical

TABLE 7.2

People without health insurance coverage by selected characteristics, 2006 and 2007

[Numbers in thousands. People as of March of the following year.]

Characteristic	2006			2007			Change in uninsured (2007 less 2006)[a]	
	Total	Uninsured		Total	Uninsured			
		Number	Percentage		Number	Percentage	Number	Percentage
People								
Total	296,824	46,995	15.8	299,106	45,657	15.3	−1,337	−0.6
Family status								
In families	245,199	36,230	14.8	245,443	34,629	14.1	−1,601	−0.7
Householder	78,454	10,770	13.7	77,908	10,272	13.2	−499	−0.5
Related children under 18	72,609	8,303	11.4	72,792	7,802	10.7	−501	−0.7
Related children under 6	24,204	2,690	11.1	24,543	2,555	10.4	−135	−0.7
In unrelated subfamilies	1,367	341	25.0	1,516	363	23.9	21	−1.0
Unrelated individuals	50,258	10,423	20.7	52,147	10,665	20.5	242	−0.3
Race[b] and Hispanic origin								
White	237,892	35,486	14.9	239,399	34,300	14.3	−1,186	−0.6
White, not Hispanic	196,252	21,162	10.8	196,768	20,548	10.4	−614	−0.3
Black	37,369	7,652	20.5	37,775	7,372	19.5	−280	−1.0
Asian	13,194	2,045	15.5	13,268	2,234	16.8	188	1.3
Hispanic (any race)	44,854	15,296	34.1	46,026	14,770	32.1	−526	−2.0
Age								
Under 18 years	74,101	8,661	11.7	74,403	8,149	11.0	−512	−0.7
18 to 24 years	28,405	8,323	29.3	28,398	7,991	28.1	−332	−1.2
25 to 34 years	39,868	10,713	26.9	40,146	10,329	25.7	−384	−1.1
35 to 44 years	42,762	8,018	18.8	42,132	7,717	18.3	−301	−0.4
45 to 64 years	75,653	10,738	14.2	77,237	10,784	14.0	47	−0.2
65 years and older	36,035	541	1.5	36,790	686	1.9	145	0.4
Nativity								
Native born	259,545	34,380	13.2	261,842	33,269	12.7	−1,111	−0.5
Foreign born	37,279	12,615	33.8	37,264	12,388	33.2	−226	−0.6
Naturalized citizen	14,538	2,384	16.4	15,050	2,651	17.6	267	1.2
Not a citizen	22,741	10,231	45.0	22,214	9,737	43.8	−494	−1.2
Region								
Northeast	54,139	6,648	12.3	54,031	6,143	11.4	−506	−0.9
Midwest	65,491	7,458	11.4	65,480	7,495	11.4	37	0.1
South	108,030	20,486	19.0	109,710	20,210	18.4	−276	−0.5
West	69,163	12,403	17.9	69,883	11,809	16.9	−593	−1.0
Residence								
Inside metropolitan statistical areas	249,391	39,421	15.8	51,363	38,497	15.3	−924	−0.5
Inside principal cities	95,240	18,107	19.0	96,874	17,935	18.5	−172	−0.5
Outside principal cities	154,151	21,314	13.8	154,489	20,563	13.3	−751	−0.5
Outside metropolitan statistical areas[c]	47,433	7,574	16.0	47,743	7,160	15.0	−414	−1.0
Household income								
Less than $25,000	55,856	13,933	24.9	55,267	13,539	24.5	−394	−0.4
$25,000 to $49,999	72,582	15,319	21.1	68,915	14,515	21.1	−804	0.0
$50,000 to $74,999	58,555	8,459	14.4	58,355	8,488	14.5	29	0.1
$75,000 or more	109,831	9,283	8.5	116,568	9,115	7.8	−168	−0.6

to the care of the uninsured as safety net providers are, they are unable to meet all the needs of the uninsured, particularly if resources continue to decrease as the number of uninsured increases."

Diane Rowland of the Kaiser Family Foundation points out in "Health Care and Medicaid—Weathering the Recession" (*New England Journal of Medicine*, vol. 360, no. 13, March 26, 2009) that the economic recession that began in 2008 further jeopardizes Americans' health care. Not only does it mean that more people will rely on Medicaid for health insurance but also many Americans will "fall through the holes"—not meet Medicaid eligibility requirements and not have the resources to continue

paying for employer-sponsored health coverage—and become uninsured. Rowland states, "For every increase of 1 percentage point in the national unemployment rate, it is estimated that an additional 1 million Americans turn to Medicaid for coverage and another 1.1 million go uninsured, while revenues for financing the state's share of Medicaid costs and other state services fall by 3 to 4% as Medicaid expenditures are rising." According to her estimates, the number of uninsured Americans was likely almost 50 million in February 2009.

Barack Obama (1961–) campaigned for the presidency in 2008 with a pledge to reform the health care system to provide accessible health care for all Americans. Accord-

TABLE 7.2

People without health insurance coverage by selected characteristics, 2006 and 2007 [CONTINUED]

[Numbers in thousands. People as of March of the following year.]

Characteristic	2006			2007			Change in uninsured (2007 less 2006)[a]	
		Uninsured			Uninsured			
	Total	Number	Percentage	Total	Number	Percentage	Number	Percentage
Work experience								
Total, 18 to 64 years old	186,688	37,792	20.2	187,913	36,822	19.6	−971	−0.6
Worked during year	147,789	27,627	18.7	148,603	26,840	18.1	−787	−0.6
Worked full-time	123,272	22,010	17.9	123,882	21,060	17.0	−950	−0.9
Worked part-time	24,517	5,618	22.9	24,721	5,780	23.4	163	0.5
Did not work	38,899	10,165	26.1	39,310	9,981	25.4	−184	−0.7

—Represents or rounds to zero.
[a]Details may not sum to totals because of rounding.
[b]Federal surveys now give respondents the option of reporting more than one race. Therefore, two basic ways of defining a race group are possible. A group such as Asian may be defined as those who reported Asian and no other race (the race-alone or single-race concept) or as those who reported Asian regardless of whether they also reported another race (the race-alone-or-in-combination concept). This table shows data using the first approach (race alone). The use of the single-race population does not imply that it is the preferred method of presenting or analyzing data. The Census Bureau uses a variety of approaches. Information on people who reported more than one race, such as white and American Indian and Alaska Native or Asian and black or African American, is available from Census 2000 through American FactFinder. About 2.6 percent of people reported more than one race in Census 2000. Data for American Indians and Alaska Natives, Native Hawaiians and other Pacific Islanders, and those reporting two or more races are not shown separately.
[c]The "outside metropolitan statistical areas" category includes both micropolitan statistical areas and territory outside of metropolitan and micropolitan statistical areas.

SOURCE: Carmen DeNavas-Walt, Bernadette D. Proctor, and Jessica C. Smith, "Table 6. People without Health Insurance Coverage by Selected Characteristics: 2006 and 2007," in *Income, Poverty, and Health Insurance Coverage in the United States: 2007*, Current Population Reports, U.S. Census Bureau, August 2008, http://www.census.gov/prod/2008pubs/p60–235.pdf (accessed December 15, 2008).

ing to the White House, in "Health Care" (2009, http://www.whitehouse.gov/agenda/health_care/), his plan promised that existing health insurance policies would decrease by as much as $2,500 per year, and that uninsured people would "have a choice of new, affordable health insurance options." Obama promised that health insurance companies would be required to cover preexisting conditions and that a new public plan would be created based on the benefits already available to government employees that would allow individuals and small businesses to purchase quality, affordable health insurance.

The Office of Management and Budget notes in "The U.S. Department of Health and Human Services 2010 Budget" (2009, http://www.whitehouse.gov/omb/assets/fy2010_factsheets/fy10_health_human_services.pdf) that once President Obama took office in January 2009, he signed into law the reauthorization of the Children's Health Insurance Program (CHIP), which would provide coverage for an additional 4 million children by 2013. The American Recovery and Reinvestment Act of 2009, signed into law on February 17, 2009, included $1 billion to digitize medical records and provide information on treatments to doctors, measures that the administration believed would reduce health care costs. Obama's proposed 2010 budget would set up a reserve fund of $630 billion over the next decade to finance health reform measures.

Medicaid

Medicaid, which is authorized under Title XIX of the Social Security Act, is a federal-state program that provides medical insurance for low-income people who are aged, blind, disabled, or members of families with dependent children and for certain other pregnant women and children. Within federal guidelines, each state designs and administers its own program. For this reason, there may be considerable differences from state to state as to who is covered, what type of coverage is provided, and how much is paid for medical services. States receive federal matching payments based on their Medicaid expenditures and the state's per capita (per person) income. The federal match ranges from 50% to 80% of Medicaid expenditures. Table 7.3 shows the number of recipients, the amount of payments, and the average payment per recipient for each state or territory in fiscal year 2004.

Even though Medicaid eligibility had been linked to receipt of, or eligibility to receive, benefits under Aid to Families with Dependent Children or Supplemental Security Income, legislation gradually extended coverage in the 1980s and 1990s. Beginning in 1986 benefits were extended to low-income children and pregnant women not on welfare. States must cover children less than six years of age and pregnant women with family incomes below 133% of the federal poverty level. Pregnant women are only covered for medical services related to their pregnancies, and children receive full Medicaid coverage. The states may cover children under one year old and pregnant women with incomes more than 133%, but not more than 185%, of the poverty level. Medicaid also covers aged and disabled people receiving Medicare whose incomes are below 100% of the poverty level.

States may deny Medicaid benefits to adults who lose Temporary Assistance for Needy Families (TANF) benefits because they refuse to work. However, the law exempts poor pregnant women and children from this provision,

FIGURE 7.2

Three-year average percentage of people without health insurance coverage, by state, 2005–07

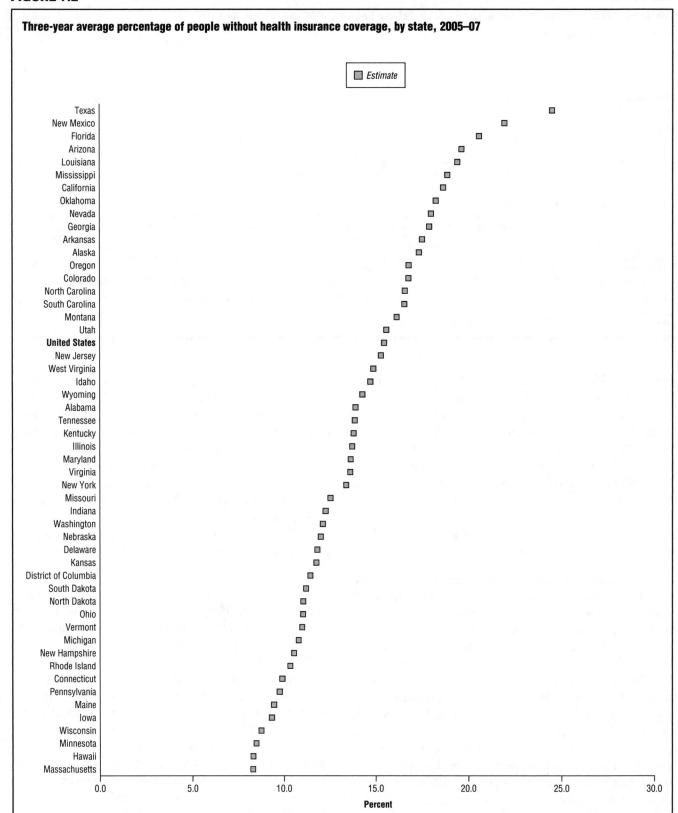

SOURCE: Carmen DeNavas-Walt, Bernadette D. Proctor, and Jessica C. Smith, "Figure D-1. Three-Year-Average Percentage of People without Health Insurance Coverage by State: 2005 to 2007," in *Income, Poverty, and Health Insurance Coverage in the United States: 2007*, Current Population Reports, U.S. Census Bureau, August 2008, http://www.census.gov/prod/2008pubs/p60-235.pdf (accessed December 15, 2008)

FIGURE 7.3

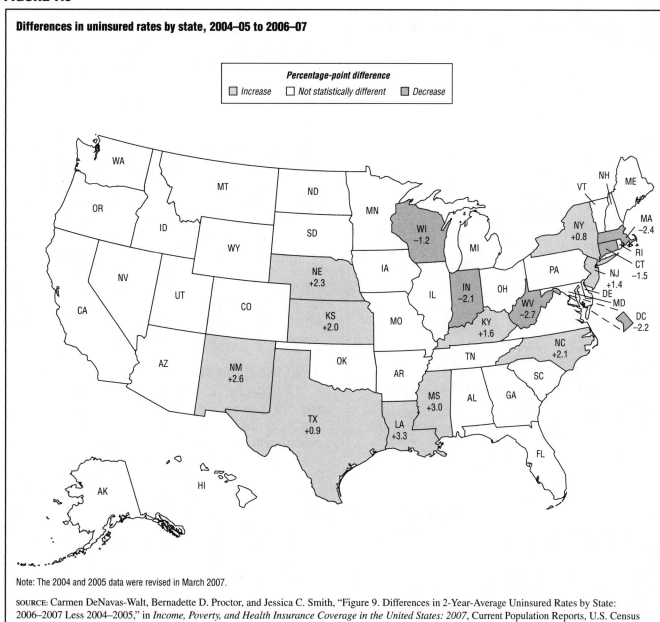

Differences in uninsured rates by state, 2004–05 to 2006–07

Note: The 2004 and 2005 data were revised in March 2007.

SOURCE: Carmen DeNavas-Walt, Bernadette D. Proctor, and Jessica C. Smith, "Figure 9. Differences in 2-Year-Average Uninsured Rates by State: 2006–2007 Less 2004–2005," in *Income, Poverty, and Health Insurance Coverage in the United States: 2007*, Current Population Reports, U.S. Census Bureau, August 2008, http://www.census.gov/prod/2008pubs/p60-235.pdf (accessed December 15, 2008)

requiring their continued Medicaid eligibility. In addition, the welfare law requires state plans to ensure Medicaid for children receiving foster care or adoption assistance.

Carmen DeNavas-Walt, Bernadette D. Proctor, and Jessica C. Smith of the U.S. Census Bureau report in *Income, Poverty, and Health Insurance Coverage in the United States: 2007* (August 2008, http://www.census.gov/prod/2008pubs/p60-235.pdf) that 8.1 million (11%) children are uninsured. In an effort to reach these uninsured children, many states are simplifying the Medicaid application process. In addition, the 1996 welfare law gives states the option to use Medicaid to provide health care coverage to low-income working parents. About half (46%) of poor adults without children, 43% of poor parents, and 20% of poor children were uninsured in 2007. (See Figure 7.5.) Even

though the income of these households is below the federal poverty line, working poor parents have been ineligible for publicly funded health insurance. In addition, low-wage jobs often do not offer affordable employer-sponsored coverage. The number of uninsured working poor parents is likely to grow as welfare recipients move into the workforce, as required under the welfare reform law, unless states expand Medicaid to cover this group. Medicaid accounted for 13.2% of all health coverage in 2007. (See Figure 7.6.)

Of the 57.6 million people enrolled in Medicaid in 2005 (the most recent year for which detailed statistics were available in mid-2009), the majority were dependent children under 21 years of age (26.3 million) and adults in families with dependent children (12.5 million). (See Table 7.4.) The remainder of Medicaid recipients were disabled (8.2 million)

FIGURE 7.4

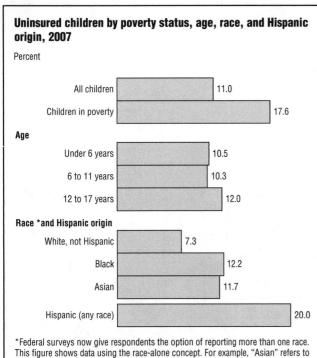

Uninsured children by poverty status, age, race, and Hispanic origin, 2007

Percent

All children — 11.0
Children in poverty — 17.6

Age

Under 6 years — 10.5
6 to 11 years — 10.3
12 to 17 years — 12.0

Race *and Hispanic origin

White, not Hispanic — 7.3
Black — 12.2
Asian — 11.7
Hispanic (any race) — 20.0

*Federal surveys now give respondents the option of reporting more than one race. This figure shows data using the race-alone concept. For example, "Asian" refers to people who reported Asian and no other race.

SOURCE: Carmen DeNavas-Walt, Bernadette D. Proctor, and Jessica C. Smith, "Figure 8. Uninsured Children by Poverty Status, Age, and Race and Hispanic Origin: 2007," in *Income, Poverty, and Health Insurance Coverage in the United States: 2007*, Current Population Reports, U.S. Census Bureau, August 2008, http://www.census.gov/prod/2008pubs/p60-235.pdf (accessed December 15, 2008).

following five years, as well as institute cuts in federal funding of CHIP. As a result of the cuts in January 2007, some medical providers turned away Medicaid and Medicare patients. The American Medical Association reports in "Highlights: H.R. 6331, 'Medicare Improvements for Patients and Providers Act of 2008'" (July 10, 2008, http://www.ama-assn.org/ama1/pub/upload/mm/399/hr6331_highlights.pdf) that on July 9, 2008, a planned 10.6% cut on July 1, 2008, and an additional 5.4% cut on January 1, 2009, were stopped when Congress passed the Medicare Improvements for Patients and Providers Act of 2008, over Bush's veto. This act fixed Medicare payments to physicians for 18 months. The Kaiser Commission on Medicaid Facts notes in "American Recovery and Reinvestment Act: Medicaid and Health Care Provisions" (March 2009, http://www.kff.org/medicaid/upload/7872.pdf) that the American Recovery and Reinvestment Act, signed into law on February 17, 2009, increased the federal share of Medicaid costs by $87 billion and provided another $25 billion for temporary COBRA subsidies of 65% for people who had lost their jobs between September 1, 2009, and December 31, 2009.

State Child Health Insurance Program

The Balanced Budget Act of 1997 set aside $24 billion over five years to fund CHIP in an effort to reach children who were uninsured. This was the nation's largest children's health care investment since the creation of Medicaid in 1965. The Children's Health Insurance Program Reauthorization Act of 2009 was signed into law by President Obama on February 4, 2009, extending and expanding the existing CHIP. CHIP requires states to use the funding to cover uninsured children whose families earn too much for Medicaid but too little to afford private coverage. States may use this money to expand their Medicaid programs, design new child health insurance programs, or create a combination of the two. The expanding legislation is expected to provide coverage to an additional 4 million children by 2013.

States must enroll all children who meet Medicaid eligibility rules in the Medicaid program rather than in CHIP. They are not allowed to use CHIP to replace existing health coverage. In addition, states must decide on what kind of cost-sharing, if any, to require of low-income families without keeping them from accessing the program. The only federal requirement is that cost-sharing cannot exceed 5% of family income. In August 2008 the Bush administration limited the ability of states to expand coverage under CHIP to children living in families that had incomes above 250% of the poverty level. President Obama withdrew this directive in February 2009.

Health Care for the Homeless

In 1987 Congress passed the Stewart B. McKinney Homeless Assistance Act to provide services to the homeless, including job training, emergency shelter, education, and

or elderly (4.4 million). The number receiving Medicaid coverage had more than doubled since 1985, when approximately 21.8 million people were enrolled.

The rapid growth in spending for Medicaid has contributed to the concern over the rising cost of health care. Not accounting for inflation, spending skyrocketed from $37.5 billion in 1985 to $275.6 billion in 2005. (See Table 7.4.) Of the $275.6 billion spent on Medicaid payments in 2005, most went for the disabled ($119.6 billion, or 43.4%) and the elderly ($63.4 billion, or 23%). In addition, considerable amounts were spent on dependent children under the age of 21 ($42 billion, or 15%) and adults in families with dependent children ($32.4 billion, or 12%). On average, in 2005 the Medicaid program spent $14,413 on every elderly recipient, $1,595 on each dependent child under the age of 21, and $14,574 on each disabled person in the program.

Medicare and Medicaid payments to physicians were cut after 2000. In "Bush Seeks Big Medicare and Medicaid Saving, but Faces Hard Fight" (*New York Times*, February 2, 2007), Robert Pear reports that more deep cuts in physician reimbursement in January 2007 were followed by the announcement that the administration of George W. Bush (1946–) planned to ask Congress in February 2007 to cut more than $70 billion from Medicare and Medicaid over the

TABLE 7.3

Number of Medicaid recipients, amount of payments, and average payment, by state, fiscal year 2004

State	Number of recipients	Total payments (millions of dollars)	Average payment (dollars)
United States*	55,002,107	257,748	4,686
Alabama	808,192	3,857	4,772
Alaska	118,005	905	7,665
Arizona	1,070,317	3,888	3,633
Arkansas	707,792	2,358	3,332
California	10,014,373	27,444	2,740
Colorado	503,485	2,399	4,765
Connecticut	500,952	3,696	7,377
Delaware	157,306	800	5,086
District of Columbia	157,650	1,269	8,052
Florida	2,952,363	12,834	4,347
Georgia	1,928,820	6,944	3,600
Hawaii	218,397	862	3,946
Idaho	206,462	990	4,796
Illinois	2,031,777	10,796	5,314
Indiana	946,212	4,343	4,589
Iowa	382,887	2,206	5,760
Kansas	365,078	1,860	5,095
Kentucky	860,508	3,924	4,560
Louisiana	1,108,054	4,039	3,645
Maine	293,966	2,366	8,050
Maryland	750,287	4,594	6,123
Massachusetts	1,074,050	7,776	7,240
Michigan	1,799,058	7,697	4,278
Minnesota	697,929	4,575	6,555
Mississippi	725,637	3,312	4,564
Missouri	1,140,194	4,887	4,286
Montana	112,642	585	5,191
Nebraska	244,275	1,346	5,509
Nevada	237,015	806	3,399
New Hampshire	119,207	822	6,898
New Jersey	959,843	6,623	6,900
New Mexico	474,303	2,278	4,802
New York	4,712,211	37,273	7,910
North Carolina	1,512,608	7,388	4,884
North Dakota	78,324	477	6,096
Ohio	1,896,173	11,375	5,999
Oklahoma	653,777	2,335	3,572
Oregon	559,004	2,153	3,851
Pennsylvania	1,834,651	10,055	5,481
Rhode Island	207,621	1,531	7,374
South Carolina	856,715	4,015	4,686
South Dakota	127,783	580	4,537
Tennessee	1,654,656	6,971	4,213
Texas	3,603,539	13,214	3,667
Utah	307,059	1,356	4,416
Vermont	148,921	744	4,998
Virginia	732,009	3,574	4,883
Washington	1,109,110	4,930	4,445
West Virginia	376,680	2,020	5,361
Wisconsin	896,468	4,314	4,812
Wyoming	67,762	363	5,362

Note: Totals do not necessarily equal the sum of rounded components.
*Excludes recipients in Puerto Rico and the Virgin Islands. Data are not available.

SOURCE: "Table 8.H1. Number of Recipients, Total Payments, and Average Payment, by State, Fiscal Year 2004," in *Annual Statistical Supplement, 2007,* Social Security Administration, April 2008, http://www.ssa.gov/policy/docs/statcomps/supplement/2007/8h.pdf (accessed January 11, 2009)

health care. Title VI of the act funds Health Care for the Homeless (HCH) programs. The National Health Care for the Homeless Council (NHCHC) notes in "Health Care for the Homeless Program" (May 2008, http://www.nhchc.org/Advocacy/HCHFactsheet053008.pdf) that the HCH has become the national umbrella under which most homeless health care initiatives operate. In 2008, 205 programs provided health care to about 700,000 people each year. President Obama's proposed FY 2009 budget asked for $178 million for HCH programs. The U.S. Interagency Council on Homelessness (March 11, 2009, http://www.ich.gov/newsletter/archive/03-11-09_e-newsletter.htm) reports that when President Obama signed the 2009 budget into law on March 11, 2009, it included an increase for the HCH programs.

Nonprofit private organizations and public entities, including state and local government agencies, may apply for grants from the program. The grants may be used to continue to provide services for up to one year to indi-

FIGURE 7.5

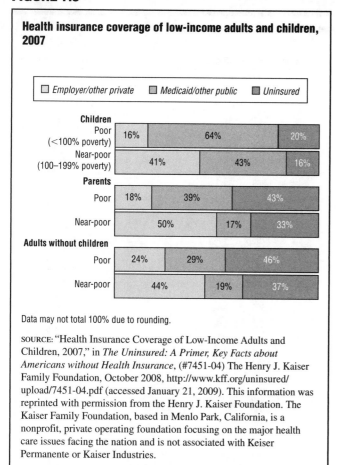

Health insurance coverage of low-income adults and children, 2007

Data may not total 100% due to rounding.

SOURCE: "Health Insurance Coverage of Low-Income Adults and Children, 2007," in *The Uninsured: A Primer, Key Facts about Americans without Health Insurance*, (#7451-04) The Henry J. Kaiser Family Foundation, October 2008, http://www.kff.org/uninsured/upload/7451-04.pdf (accessed January 21, 2009). This information was reprinted with permission from the Henry J. Kaiser Foundation. The Kaiser Family Foundation, based in Menlo Park, California, is a nonprofit, private operating foundation focusing on the major health care issues facing the nation and is not associated with Keiser Permanente or Kaiser Industries.

FIGURE 7.6

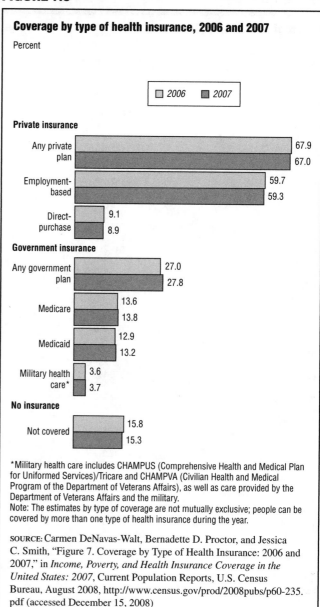

Coverage by type of health insurance, 2006 and 2007

*Military health care includes CHAMPUS (Comprehensive Health and Medical Plan for Uniformed Services)/Tricare and CHAMPVA (Civilian Health and Medical Program of the Department of Veterans Affairs), as well as care provided by the Department of Veterans Affairs and the military.
Note: The estimates by type of coverage are not mutually exclusive; people can be covered by more than one type of health insurance during the year.

SOURCE: Carmen DeNavas-Walt, Bernadette D. Proctor, and Jessica C. Smith, "Figure 7. Coverage by Type of Health Insurance: 2006 and 2007," in *Income, Poverty, and Health Insurance Coverage in the United States: 2007*, Current Population Reports, U.S. Census Bureau, August 2008, http://www.census.gov/prod/2008pubs/p60-235.pdf (accessed December 15, 2008)

viduals who have obtained permanent housing if services were provided to them when they were homeless.

The goal of the HCH programs is to improve the health of homeless individuals and families by improving access to primary health care and substance abuse services. The HCH provides outreach, counseling to clients explaining available services, case management, and linkages to services such as mental health treatment, housing, benefits, and other critical supports. Access to around-the-clock emergency services is available, as is help in establishing eligibility for assistance and obtaining services under entitlement programs.

LIVING IN PUBLIC: INCREASED HEALTH PROBLEMS

Poor people can be catapulted into homelessness because of the expenses and missed work caused by poor health. Homelessness itself causes a person's health to deteriorate further. Thus, health problems can both cause and result from homelessness. For example, a health problem that prevents an impoverished person from working can result in a loss of income that leads to homelessness. For those living on the streets, lack of adequate shelter and proper facilities for maintaining personal hygiene can exacerbate illness. Alcoholism, mental illnesses, diabetes, and

depression become visible and more pronounced in homeless people. Other serious illnesses (e.g., tuberculosis [TB]) are almost exclusively associated with the unhealthy living conditions brought on by poverty. In general, experts agree that homeless people suffer from more types of illnesses, for longer periods of time, and with more harmful consequences than housed people. In addition, the NHCHC explains in "Homelessness and Health" (2008, http://www.nhchc.org/Advocacy/PolicyPapers/HomelessnessHealth2008.pdf) that health care delivery is complicated by a patient's homeless status, making management of chronic diseases such as diabetes, human immunodeficiency virus (HIV), and hypertension more difficult. Most Americans suffer illness and disease at some time in their life, but for people experiencing homelessness and poverty, illness often leads to serious health concerns or premature death.

TABLE 7.4

Number of total Medicaid recipients, total vendor payments, and average amounts, by type of eligibility category, 1985–2005

Year	Total	Aged 65 or older	Blind	Permanent and total disability	Dependent children under age 21	Adults in families with dependent children	Other
Number of recipients (thousands)							
1985	21,814	3,061	80	2,937	9,757	5,518	1,214
1986	22,515	3,140	82	3,100	10,029	5,647	1,362
1987	23,109	3,224	85	3,296	10,168	5,599	1,418
1988	22,907	3,159	86	3,401	10,037	5,503	1,343
1989	23,511	3,132	95	3,496	10,318	5,717	1,175
1990	25,255	3,202	83	3,635	11,220	6,010	1,105
1991	28,280	3,359	85	3,983	13,415	6,778	658
1992	30,926	3,742	84	4,378	15,104	6,954	664
1993	33,432	3,863	84	4,932	16,285	7,505	763
1994	35,053	4,035	87	5,372	17,194	7,586	779
1995	36,282	4,119	92	5,767	17,164	7,604	1,537
1996	36,118	4,285	95	6,126	16,739	7,127	1,746
1997	34,872	3,955	—	6,129	15,791	6,803	2,195
1998	40,649	3,964	—	6,638	18,964	7,908	3,176
1999[a]	40,300	4,241	—	7,303	20,119	8,552	846
2000[a]	42,886	4,289	—	7,479	21,086	10,543	862
2001[a]	46,163	4,420	—	7,703	22,533	11,639	869
2002[a, b]	49,329	3,890	—	7,411	22,421	11,253	4,354
2003[a]	51,971	4,041	—	7,669	23,992	11,679	4,591
2004[a]	55,002	4,318	—	7,933	25,613	12,225	4,913
2005[a, c]	57,643	4,396	—	8,210	26,337	12,529	6,171
Total payments (millions of dollars)							
1985	37,508	14,096	249	13,203	4,414	4,746	798
1986	41,005	15,097	277	14,635	5,135	4,880	980
1987	45,050	16,037	309	16,507	5,508	5,592	1,078
1988	48,710	17,135	344	18,250	5,848	5,883	1,198
1989	54,500	18,558	409	20,476	6,892	6,897	1,268
1990	64,859	21,508	434	23,969	9,100	8,590	1,257
1991	77,048	25,453	475	27,798	11,690	10,439	1,193
1992	90,814	29,078	530	33,326	14,491	12,185	1,204
1993	101,709	31,554	589	38,065	16,504	13,605	1,391
1994	108,270	33,618	644	41,654	17,302	13,585	1,467
1995	120,141	36,527	848	48,570	17,976	13,511	2,708
1996	121,685	36,947	869	51,196	17,544	12,275	2,853
1997	124,430	37,721	—	54,130	17,544	12,307	2,727
1998	142,318	40,602	—	60,375	22,806	14,833	3,702
1999[a]	147,372	40,470	—	63,028	20,765	15,141	7,966
2000[a]	168,442	44,560	—	72,772	23,490	17,671	9,948
2001[a]	186,913	48,431	—	80,493	26,770	20,096	11,121
2002[a, b]	213,497	52,012	—	92,414	31,595	23,525	13,950
2003[a]	233,206	55,271	—	102,014	35,079	26,689	14,153
2004[a]	257,748	59,541	—	111,614	39,194	30,522	16,877
2005[a, c]	275,569	63,358	—	119,647	42,012	32,385	18,167
Average payment (dollars)							
1985	1,719	4,605	3,104	4,496	452	860	658
1986	1,821	4,808	3,401	4,721	512	864	719
1987	1,949	4,975	3,644	5,008	542	999	761
1988	2,126	5,425	4,005	5,366	583	1,069	891
1989	2,318	5,926	4,317	5,858	668	1,206	1,079
1990	2,568	6,717	5,212	6,595	811	1,429	1,138
1991	2,725	7,577	5,572	6,979	871	1,540	1,813
1992	2,936	7,770	6,298	7,612	959	1,752	1,813
1993	3,042	8,168	7,036	7,717	1,013	1,813	1,824
1994	3,089	8,331	7,412	7,755	1,006	1,791	1,884
1995	3,311	8,868	9,256	8,422	1,047	1,777	1,762
1996	3,369	8,622	9,143	8,357	1,048	1,722	1,635
1997	3,568	9,538	—	8,832	1,111	1,809	3,597
1998	3,501	10,242	—	9,095	1,203	1,876	1,166

There is a growing belief in the health care field that homelessness must be considered in epidemic terms—that massive increases in homelessness may result in a hastened spread of illness and disease, overwhelming the health care system. John Lozier writes in *The Health Care of Homeless Persons* (2004) that "primary care clinics for indigent people generally operate beyond their capacity, are not well-located to serve people staying in shelters, and are not prepared to deal with the complex conditions often presented by homeless people." He conveys the sense of many public health officials that the health care system is facing a crisis because of homelessness when he states, "The public health system, which made great strides in the 20th century by eliminating unhealthy living conditions,

TABLE 7.4

Number of total Medicaid recipients, total vendor payments, and average amounts, by type of eligibility category, 1985–2005 [CONTINUED]

Year	Total	Aged 65 or older	Blind	Permanent and total disability	Dependent children under age 21	Adults in families with dependent children	Other
1999[a]	3,657	9,541	—	8,630	1,032	1,770	9,407
2000[a]	3,928	10,388	—	9,729	1,114	1,676	11,536
2001[a]	4,049	10,957	—	10,449	1,188	1,727	12,792
2002[a, b]	4,328	13,370	—	12,470	1,409	2,091	3,204
2003[a]	4,487	13,677	—	13,303	1,462	2,285	3,083
2004[a]	4,686	13,790	—	14,070	1,530	2,497	3,435
2005[a, c]	4,781	14,413	—	14,574	1,595	2,585	2,944

Notes: Totals do not necessarily equal the sum of rounded components.
Beginning in 1997, "Disability" data includes blindness. "Children" includes foster care children, and "other" are "unknowns." In 1999 and 2000, "other" includes foster care children and "unknowns." In 2001 and 2002, "other" includes foster care children, "unknowns," and individuals covered under the Breast and Cervical Cancer Prevention and Treatment Act of 2000.
— = Not applicable.
[a]Excludes recipients in Puerto Rico and the Virgin Islands. Data are not available.
[b]Revised data.
[c]Fiscal year 2005 data are not available for Maine. Fiscal year 2004 data has been substituted.

SOURCE: "Table 8.E2. Unduplicated Number of Recipients, Total Vendor Payments, and Average Payment, by Type of Eligibility Category, Fiscal Years, 1985–2005," in *Annual Statistical Supplement, 2007*, Social Security Administration, April 2008, http://www.ssa.gov/policy/docs/statcomps/supplement/2007/8e.pdf (accessed January 11, 2009)

seems ill-equipped to contend with the teeming shelters that are a throwback to the 19th century."

The rates of both chronic and acute (short-term) health problems are disproportionately high among the homeless population. Except for obesity, strokes, and cancer, homeless people are far more likely than the housed to suffer from every category of chronic health problems. Conditions that require regular, uninterrupted treatment, such as TB, HIV, acquired immunodeficiency syndrome (AIDS), diabetes, hypertension, malnutrition, severe dental problems, addictive disorders, and mental disorders, are extremely difficult to treat or control among those without adequate housing.

Street living comes with a set of health conditions that living in a home does not. Homeless people fall prey to parasites, frostbite, leg ulcers, and infections. They are also at greater risk of physical and psychological trauma resulting from muggings, beatings, and rape. With no safe place to store belongings, the proper storage or administration of medications becomes difficult. In addition, some homeless people with mental disorders may use drugs or alcohol to self-medicate, and those with addictive disorders are more susceptible to HIV and other communicable diseases.

Homeless people may also lack the ability to access some of the basic rituals of self-care: bed rest, good nutrition, and good personal hygiene. For example, the luxury of taking it easy for a day or two is almost impossible for homeless people; they must often keep walking or remain standing all day to avoid criminal charges.

Unwell homeless people also remain untreated longer than their sheltered counterparts because obtaining food and shelter takes priority over health care. As a result, relatively minor illnesses go untreated until they develop into major emergencies, requiring expensive acute care treatment and long-term recovery.

At least one study suggests that the health of homeless people may be getting worse. In "A Comparison of the Health and Mental Health Status of Homeless Mothers in Worcester, Mass: 1993 and 2003" (*American Journal of Public Health*, vol. 96, no. 8, August 2006), Linda F. Weinreb et al. report that between 1993 and 2003 homeless women and their families exhibited more acute and chronic mental health problems, especially major depression and post-traumatic stress disorder, their overall health declined, and their physical functioning became more limited. Their social functioning also became more impaired because of all of these factors. In addition, homeless women and their families were poorer in 2003 than in 1993 when inflation was taken into account. Weinreb et al. speculate that cuts in welfare spending and the decrease in the availability of affordable housing might be responsible for this trend.

Mortality Rates

Various studies have examined why homeless living can lead to a premature death. They cite various factors, including: exposure to extremes of weather and temperature (both cold and hot); the spread of communicable diseases such as TB and pneumonia, which increases when people live in crowded shelters; violence; substance abuse; prevalence of medical and psychiatric illnesses; poor nutrition; poor access to health care; lack of a family support system; etc. Stephen W. Hwang et al. find in "Health Care Utilization among Homeless Adults Prior to Death" (*Journal of Health Care for the Poor and Underserved*, vol. 12, no. 1, February 2001) that of 558 deaths among the homeless population in Boston in 2001, within one year before death 27% of homeless people had no outpatient visits, emergency department visits, or hospitalizations. Hwang et al. conclude that even homeless people at high risk of death are underutilizing health care services.

In *King County 2003: Homeless Death Review* (November 2004, http://www.kingcounty.gov/), a 2003 study of homeless deaths in King County (Seattle), Washington, the Health Care for the Homeless Network identifies 77 people who had died while being homeless in the county that year. Major causes of death included acute intoxication (26%), cardiovascular disease (17%), and homicide (9%). Most of the homeless deaths involved people who had several illnesses; on average, those who died had three health conditions.

In "The Risk of Death among Homeless Women: A Cohort Study and Review of the Literature" (*Canadian Medical Association Journal*, vol. 170, no. 8, April 13, 2004), a study of deaths among homeless women in Toronto, Canada, Angela M. Cheung and Stephen W. Hwang of the University of Toronto find that homeless women aged 18 to 44 were 10 times more likely to die than women in the general population of Toronto. Another key finding of the study is that the risk of death among young homeless women was nearly the same as the risk of death among homeless men of the same age.

Other studies also find that homelessness increases the risk of death. O'Connell reviews in *Premature Mortality in Homeless Populations: A Review of the Literature* (December 2005, http://www.nhchc.org/PrematureMortalityFinal.pdf) the literature concerning the connection between homelessness and mortality. He finds that "a remarkable consistency that transcends borders, cultures and oceans: homeless persons are 3–4 times more likely to die than the general population." In addition, he notes that the average age of death of homeless people in the studies reviewed was between 42 and 52 years, despite a life expectancy of around 80 years in the United States. These premature deaths were highly associated with the coexistence of acute and chronic medical conditions with either mental illness or substance abuse. In "Homelessness as an Independent Risk Factor for Mortality: Results from a Retrospective Cohort Study" (*International Journal of Epidemiology*, March 21, 2009), David S. Morrison concludes that homelessness itself is an independent risk factor for deaths; it appeared to substantially increase mortality risk from specific causes.

Access to Care

Martha R. Burt et al. analyze in *Homelessness: Programs and the People They Serve* (December 1999, http://www.urban.org/UploadedPDF/homelessness.pdf) the results of the 1996 National Survey of Homeless Assistance Providers and Clients, the only survey of its kind (studies of the homeless tend to focus on local populations). The researchers note that in the year preceding the survey, 25% of the clients studied had needed medical attention but were not able to see a doctor or a nurse. They also reveal that newly housed people were even less likely to receive medical help when needed.

Burt et al. attribute the higher rate of health problems among newly housed people to several factors, including:

• The loss of convenient health care in centers or shelters

• The habit of enduring untreated ailments

• A lack of health care benefits (common among people below the poverty level)

In "The Behavioral Model for Vulnerable Populations: Application to Medical Care Use and Outcomes for Homeless People" (*Health Services Research*, vol. 34, no. 6, February 2000), Lillian Gelberg, Ronald M. Andersen, and Barbara D. Leake report the results of a study on the prevalence of certain disease conditions among homeless adults, which revealed that 37% suffered from functional vision impairment; 36% from skin, leg, and foot problems; and 31% tested positive for TB. The researchers indicate that homeless people who had a community clinic or private physician as a regular source of care exhibited better health outcomes. Gelberg, Andersen, and Leake also suggest that clinical treatment of the homeless be accompanied by efforts to help them find permanent housing.

To fully understand why health care may not be readily available to the homeless population, one must look at the U.S health care system in general. In "U.S. Health-Care System Faces Cost and Insurance Crises: Rising Costs, Growing Numbers of Uninsured and Quality Gaps Trouble World's Most Expensive Health-Care System" (*Lancet*, vol. 362, no. 9381, August 2, 2003), Michael McCarthy describes a system "lurching towards crisis." Health care costs continue to rise, as do the numbers of people who do not have insurance. McCarthy notes that even though most hospitals are required by law to provide care for the indigent, in reality an uninsured patient is less likely to receive any care at all and, if hospitalized, is less likely to receive a high quality of care than an insured patient. He cites *Care without Coverage: Too Little, Too Late* (2002), a study by the U.S. National Academy of Sciences Institute of Medicine. The study finds that "uninsured patients who are hospitalized for a range of conditions are more likely to die in the hospital, to receive fewer services when admitted, and to experience substandard care and resultant injury than are insured patients."

Ailments of Homeless People

Connecticut Counts 2008: Point-in-Time Homeless Count (July 25, 2008, http://www.hartfordinfo.org/issues/wsd/homelessness/pointintimereport08.pdf), a 2008 Connecticut count of homeless people, finds that health issues were prevalent among the homeless population. A large proportion of people had been hospitalized for mental health, including 60% of unsheltered adults living in families, 37% of sheltered single adults, 33% of unsheltered single adults, and 17% of sheltered adults in families. Over half of sheltered single adults (52%), unsheltered single adults (61%), and sheltered adults in families (60%) had been in detox or rehab for substance abuse. Four out of 10 (41%) sheltered single adults, 50% of unsheltered single adults, and 40% of unsheltered adults living in families had a chronic, limiting health condition. Seven percent of sheltered single adults, 3% of sheltered adults living in families, and 6% of unsheltered single adults had HIV or AIDS. According to Tara L. McLaughlin, Irene Glasser, and Rose Maljanian, in *Homelessness in Hartford 2002: A Combined Report on the Census of the Homeless of Hartford and the Hartford Homeless Health Survey* (2002, http://www.hartfordinfo.org/issues/wsd/homelessness/Homeless AssessRpt02.pdf), over half of all homeless people reported in 2002 suffering from depression and a drug abuse problem. Alcohol abuse was also commonly reported (43.2%), as were chronic back problems (37.9%), severe headaches (33.5%), chronic allergies or sinus trouble (30.6%), trouble seeing (29.6%), and other mental health problems (29.6%).

In "2007 San Mateo County Homeless Census and Survey" (May 2007, http://www.redwoodcityhousing.org/pdf/2007_SMCO_Homeless_Census_and_Survey.pdf), a 2007 survey of homeless people in San Mateo County, California, Housing Our People Effectively finds that both psychological and physical problems were prevalent among the homeless population. Over half (57%) of respondents reported being depressed, 35% reported having a mental illness, 33% said they abused drugs, 31% reported they abused alcohol, and 26% reported experiencing post-traumatic stress disorder. A third (35%) reported having a physical disability, 28% reported chronic physical health problems, and 2% reported having HIV/AIDS.

Gillian Silver and Rea Pañares summarize in *The Health of Homeless Women: Information for State Mental and Child Health Programs* (2000, http://www.jhsph.edu/WCHPC/Publications/homeless.PDF) one study's findings regarding the health problems faced by homeless women, who made up about one-third (32%) of the homeless population. This group was prone to the same physical ailments reported by the general homeless population in Hartford but also reported high rates of gastrointestinal problems, neurological disorders, chronic obstructive pulmonary disease, and peripheral vascular disease. (See Table 7.5.)

Physical Disorders and Diseases

The following is a description of a few of the chronic problems suffered by homeless people.

TUBERCULOSIS. Several kinds of acute, nonspecific respiratory diseases are common among homeless people. These diseases are easily spread through group living in overcrowded shelters without adequate nutrition. TB, a disease at one time almost eliminated from the general American population, has become a major health problem among the homeless. This disease is associated with exposure, poor diet, alcoholism, intravenous drug use, HIV, and other illnesses that lower the body's resistance to infection. TB is spread by long personal contact, making it a potential hazard not only to shelter residents but also to the general public.

According to the Centers for Disease Control and Prevention (CDC), in *Reported Tuberculosis in the United States, 2007* (September 2008, http://www.cdc.gov/tb/surv/2007/pdf/fullreport.pdf), between 1953 and 1985 the United States experienced a decrease of 74% in the number of reported TB cases. However, in 1986 the number of TB cases began to rise, reaching 26,673 cases in 1992. The CDC notes that rising homelessness and poverty account, in part, for the resurgence of TB. Poor ventilation systems in shelters and impoverished homes, as well as the inability to quarantine poor or transient victims, contribute to the rise. The CDC finds that by 2007 the number of TB cases had dropped to 12,518; 5.7% of those infected with TB were homeless, a much higher rate of infection than among the general population. (See Table 7.6.) State-by-state breakdowns showing high rates of infection among the homeless populations of some states give one indication of the contagious nature of the disease. In 2007, for example, Alaska reported that 23.9% of those testing positive for TB were homeless, and South Dakota reported that 30.8% of those testing positive were homeless, whereas Delaware, Maine, New Hampshire, North Dakota, Rhode Island, Vermont, and Wyoming had no cases of TB among their homeless populations.

Clinical data from the federally funded HCH programs find prevalence rates for TB to be 100 to 300 times higher among the homeless than among the overall population. Maryam B. Haddad et al. report in "Tuberculosis and Homelessness in the United States, 1994–2003" (*Journal of the American Medical Association*, vol. 293, no. 22, June 8, 2005) that many of the risk factors for TB in the United States overlap with the risk factors associated with homelessness, including having a history of incarceration or substance abuse. An additional contributing factor was the emergence of drug-resistant strains of TB. Experts report that to control the spread of TB, the homeless population must receive frequent screenings for TB and the infected must get long-term care and rest.

A campaign for increased public awareness, particularly among members of the medical community, was launched in 1990 to identify and screen those at the greatest risk for TB. Some researchers, such as Po-Marn Kong et al. in "Skin-Test Screening and Tuberculosis Transmission among the Homeless" (*Emerging Infectious Diseases*, vol. 8, no. 11, November 2002) and Mary Lashley of Towson University in "A

TABLE 7.5

Health problems faced by homeless women

Health issue	Key findings
Chronic disease	• The most common chronic physical conditions (excluding substance abuse) are hypertension, gastrointestinal problems, neurological disorders, arthritis and other musculoskeletal disorders, chronic obstructive pulmonary disease, and peripheral vascular disease.
Infectious disease	• The most common infectious diseases reported were chest infection, cold, cough, and bronchitis; reporting was the same for those formerly homeless, currently homeless, and other service users.
	• Homeless patients with tuberculosis (TB) were more likely to present with a more progressed form than nonhomeless.
	• Widespread screening for TB in shelters may miss most homeless persons because many do not live in the shelter, and instead present in emergency departments.
STDs/HIV/AIDS	• A mobile women's health unit in Chicago reported that of 104 female homeless clients, 30 percent had abnormal Pap smears—14 percent with atypia and 10 percent with inflammation; the incidence of chlamydia was 3 percent, gonorrhea 6 percent, and trichomoniasis 26 percent.
	• HIV infection was found to be 2.35 times more prevalent in homeless, drug-abusing women than homeless, drug-abusing men.
Stress	• Homeless mothers reported higher levels of stress, depression, and avoidant and anti-cognitive coping strategies than low-income, housed mothers.
Nutrition	• Currently and formerly homeless clients are more likely to report not getting enough to eat (28 and 25 percent respectively) than among all U.S. households (4 percent) and among poor households (12 percent).
	• Contrary to their opinions, homeless women and their dependents were consuming less than 50 percent of the 1989 recommended daily allowance for iron, magnesium, zinc, folic acid, and calcium.
	• Subjects of all ages consumed higher than desirable quantities of fats.
	• The health risk factors of iron deficiency anemia, obesity, and hypercholesterolemia were prevalent.
Smoking	• More than half of both homeless mothers and low-income housed mothers were current smokers, compared with 22.6 percent of female adults 18 years and over.
Violence	• Poor women are at higher risk for violence than women overall; poverty increases stress and lowers the ability to cope with the environment and live safely.
	• In a study of 436 sheltered homeless and poor housed women: 84 percent of these women had been severely assaulted at some point in their lives; 63 percent had been severely assaulted by parental caretakers while growing up; 40 percent had been sexually molested at least once before reaching adulthood; 60 percent had experienced severe physical attacks by a male intimate partner, and 33 percent had been assaulted by their current or most recent partner.
	• A study of 53 women homeless for at least three months in the past year demonstrated that this group is at a very high risk of battery and rape, with 91 percent exposed to battery and 56 percent exposed to rape.
Substance abuse	• Homeless women comprise a subpopulation at high risk for substance abuse; rates of substance use disorder range from 16 percent to 67 percent. There exists an imbalance between treatment need and treatment access.
	• Some homeless people with mental disorders may use drugs or alcohol to self-medicate.
Mental health/depression	• A case-control study of 100 homeless women with schizophrenia and 100 nonhomeless women with schizophrenia found that homeless women had higher rates of a concurrent diagnosis of alcohol abuse, drug abuse, antisocial personality disorder, and also had less adequate family support.
	• Many homeless women with serious mental illness are not receiving care; this is due to lack of perception of a mental health problem and lack of services designed to meet the needs of homeless women.

SOURCE: Gillian Silver and Rea Pañares, "Table 2. Summary of Study Findings Related to Health Problems Faced by Homeless Women," in *The Health of Homeless Women: Information for State Mental and Child Health Programs*, Women's and Children's Health Policy Center, Johns Hopkins Bloomberg School for Public Health, 2000, http://www.jhsph.edu/WCHPC/Publications/homeless.PDF (accessed January 11, 2009)

Targeted Testing Program for Tuberculosis Control and Prevention among Baltimore City's Homeless Population" (*Public Health Nursing*, vol. 24, no. 1, 2007), tested pilot programs to better identify and treat homeless people infected with TB. Other studies, such as Jacqueline Peterson Tulsky et al. in "Can the Poor Adhere? Incentives for Adherence to TB Prevention in Homeless Adults" (*International Journal of Tuberculosis and Lung Disease*, January 2004) and Adeline Nyamathi et al. in "Efficacy of Nurse Case-Managed Intervention for Latent Tuberculosis among Homeless Subsamples" (*Nursing Research*, vol. 57, no. 1, January–February 2008), investigated how best to help homeless adults adhere to treatment for latent TB infection. The CDC notes in *Reported Tuberculosis in the United States, 2007* that the number of reported TB cases in the United States declined from 13,754 in 2006 to 12,518 in 2007, a decrease of 8.9%.

SKIN AND BLOOD VESSEL DISORDERS. Frequent exposure to severe weather, insect bites, and other infestations make skin lesions fairly common among the homeless. Being forced to sit or stand for extended periods results in many homeless people being plagued with edema (swelling of the feet and legs), varicose veins, and skin ulcerations. This population is more prone to conditions that can lead to chronic phlebitis (inflammation of the veins). A homeless person with circulatory problems who sleeps sitting up in a doorway or a bus station can develop open lacerations that may become infected or maggot-infested if left untreated.

Regular baths and showers are luxuries to most homeless people, so many suffer from various forms of dermatitis (inflammation of the skin), often due to infestations of lice or scabies (a contagious skin disease caused by a parasitic mite that burrows under the skin to deposit eggs, causing intense itching). The lack of bathing increases the opportunity for infection to develop in cuts and other lacerations.

HIV/AIDS. The CDC notes in *HIV/AIDS Surveillance Report: Cases of HIV Infection and AIDS in the United States and Dependent Areas, 2007* (2009, http://www.cdc.gov/Hiv/topics/surveillance/resources/reports/2007report/pdf/2007SurveillanceReport.pdf) that in 2006, 56,300 new

TABLE 7.6

Tuberculosis (TB) cases by homeless status, 2007

Reporting area	Total cases	Cases with information on homeless status[a]		Cases reported as being homeless[a]	
		No.	(%)	No.	(%)
United States	**12,518**	**12,364**	**(98.8)**	**705**	**(5.7)**
Alabama	168	167	(99.4)	7	(4.2)
Alaska	47	46	(97.9)	11	(23.9)
Arizona	278	262	(94.2)	25	(9.5)
Arkansas	95	95	(100.0)	2	(2.1)
California	2,592	2,570	(99.2)	155	(6.0)
Colorado	104	104	(100.0)	6	(5.8)
Connecticut	105	104	(99.0)	6	(5.8)
Delaware	18	18	(100.0)	0	(0.0)
District of Columbia	58	58	(100.0)	4	(6.9)
Florida	928	921	(99.2)	70	(7.6)
Georgia	437	434	(99.3)	36	(8.3)
Hawaii	119	118	(99.2)	2	(1.7)
Idaho	9	8	(88.9)	1	(12.5)
Illinois	504	481	(95.4)	34	(7.1)
Indiana	123	122	(99.2)	10	(8.2)
Iowa	42	42	(100.0)	3	(7.1)
Kansas	55	55	(100.0)	3	(5.5)
Kentucky	116	116	(100.0)	11	(9.5)
Louisiana	207	203	(98.1)	14	(6.9)
Maine	17	17	(100.0)	0	(0.0)
Maryland	257	257	(100.0)	18	(7.0)
Massachusetts	209	207	(99.0)	6	(2.9)
Michigan	205	195	(95.1)	5	(2.6)
Minnesota	216	215	(99.5)	6	(2.8)
Mississippi	128	125	(97.7)	9	(7.2)
Missouri	115	115	(100.0)	7	(6.1)
Montana	11	11	(100.0)	1	(9.1)
Nebraska	23	23	(100.0)	1	(4.3)
Nevada	93	92	(98.9)	7	(7.6)
New Hampshire	11	9	(81.8)	0	(0.0)
New Jersey	437	437	(100.0)	7	(1.6)
New Mexico	49	49	(100.0)	5	(10.2)
New York state[b]	245	234	(95.5)	7	(3.0)
New York City	888	864	(97.3)	42	(4.9)
North Carolina	320	320	(100.0)	15	(4.7)
North Dakota	7	7	(100.0)	0	(0.0)
Ohio	239	239	(100.0)	16	(6.7)
Oklahoma	128	121	(94.5)	6	(5.0)
Oregon	87	84	(96.6)	5	(6.0)
Pennsylvania	249	240	(96.4)	11	(4.6)
Rhode Island	37	37	(100.0)	0	(0.0)
South Carolina	205	205	(100.0)	7	(3.4)
South Dakota	13	13	(100.0)	4	(30.8)
Tennessee	224	224	(100.0)	19	(8.5)
Texas	1,406	1,406	(100.0)	63	(4.5)
Utah	37	37	(100.0)	5	(13.5)
Vermont	3	3	(100.0)	0	(0.0)
Virginia	291	291	(100.0)	7	(2.4)
Washington	269	269	(100.0)	21	(7.8)
West Virginia	24	24	(100.0)	1	(4.2)
Wisconsin	68	68	(100.0)	4	(5.9)
Wyoming	2	2	(100.0)	0	(0.0)
American Samoa[c]	3	3	(100.0)	0	(0.0)
Fed. States of Micronesia[c]	49	45	(91.8)	0	(0.0)
Guam[c]	61	58	(95.1)	0	(0.0)
Marshall Islands[c]	93	91	(97.8)	1	(1.1)
N. Mariana Islands[c]	41	24	(58.5)	–	–
Puerto Rico[c]	94	94	(100.0)	4	(4.3)
Republic of Palau[c]	11	11	(100.0)	0	(0.0)
U.S. Virgin Islands[c]	—	—		—	

[a]Homeless within past 12 months of TB diagnosis. Percentage based on 52 reporting areas (50 states, New York City, and the District of Columbia). Counts and percentages shown only for reporting areas with information reported for ≥75% of cases.
[b]Excludes New York City.
[c]Not included in U.S. totals.
Note: Ellipses indicate data not available.

SOURCE: "Table 30. Tuberculosis Cases and Percentages by Homeless Status, Age > or = 15: Reporting Areas, 2007," in *Reported Tuberculosis in the United States, 2007*, U.S. Department of Health and Human Services, Centers for Disease Control and Prevention, September 2008, http://www.cdc.gov/tb/surv/2007/pdf/table30.pdf (accessed January 25, 2009)

cases of HIV infection were reported. It also notes that 14,561 people with AIDS died in 2007. Since the beginning of the epidemic, 328,103 HIV cases that had not since progressed to full-blown AIDS had been reported. In addition, at the end of 2007, 455,636 people were living with AIDS in the United States. Between 2003 and 2007 the number of HIV/AIDS cases increased by 22%.

According to the press release "FDA Approves New Rapid HIV Test Kit" (November 7, 2002, http://www.fda .gov/bbs/topics/NEWS/2002/NEW00852.html), in November 2002 the U.S. Food and Drug Administration approved a rapid test for HIV infection that can provide results in 20 minutes. The U.S. Secretary of Health and Human Services Tommy G. Thompson (1941–) explained the significance of the test: "Each year, 8,000 HIV-infected people who come to public clinics for HIV testing do not return a week later to receive their test results.... With this new test, in less than a half an hour they can learn preliminary information about their HIV status, allowing them to get the care they need to slow the progression of their disease and to take precautionary measures to help prevent the spread of this deadly virus."

The CDC estimates that up to one-fourth of people infected with HIV are not aware of their condition. The CDC is working with health officials to make the rapid test widely available, particularly in places where likely victims reside, such as homeless shelters, drug treatment centers, and jails.

According to "Study: Disparity between Rich and Poor Mortality: Poor, Disadvantaged People Develop AIDS Faster" (*AIDS Alert*, vol. 18, no. 8, August 2003), a study of AIDS patients in San Francisco, California, poor people die sooner from AIDS. Within five years of diagnosis, fewer than 70% of people living in the city's poorest neighborhoods were still alive, compared to more than 85% of people who lived in the richest neighborhoods. Poor people with HIV usually have a number of co-occurring disorders, such as drug dependence, mental illness, and unstable housing arrangements. The lack of affordable and appropriate housing can be an acute crisis for these individuals, who need a safe shelter that provides protection and comfort, as well as a base from which to receive services, care, and support.

The National Alliance to End Homelessness points out in the fact sheet "Homelessness and HIV/AIDS" (August 10, 2006, http://www.endhomelessness.org/content/general/ detail/1073) that HIV/AIDS is more prevalent in homeless populations. As many as 3.4% of homeless people are HIV positive, a rate that is three times higher than that of the general population. The high costs of medical care may even put individuals with HIV/AIDS at a greater risk of homelessness. Furthermore, the homeless life poses a grave threat to the health of those with HIV/AIDS, whose immune systems are compromised by the disease. Shelter conditions expose people to dangerous infections, and exposure to the

elements and malnutrition exacerbate chronic illness. In addition, homeless people have difficulty obtaining and using common HIV/AIDS medications.

Mental Health and Substance Abuse

Before the 1960s people with chronic mental illness were often committed involuntarily to state psychiatric hospitals. The development of medications that could control the symptoms of mental illness coincided with a growing belief that involuntary hospitalization was warranted only when a mentally ill person posed a threat to him- or herself or to others. Gradually, large numbers of mentally ill people were discharged from hospitals and other treatment facilities. Because the community-based treatment centers that were supposed to take the place of state hospitals were often either inadequate or nonexistent, many of these people ended up living on the streets.

In "Prevalence and Risk Factors for Homelessness and Utilization of Mental Health Services among 10,340 Patients with Serious Mental Illness in a Large Public Mental Health System" (*American Journal of Psychiatry*, vol. 162, no. 2, February 2005), David P. Folsom et al. find that 15% of patients treated for serious mental illness were homeless at some point during a one-year period. Twenty percent of patients with schizophrenia, 17% of patients with bipolar disorder, and 9% of patients with depression were homeless. Folsom et al. find that mentally ill people are at a much higher risk of homelessness than the general population. They emphasize that homelessness among the mentally ill was associated with two other factors: substance use disorders and a lack of Medicaid insurance. Folsom et al. state, "Although it would be naïve to assume that treatment for substance abuse disorders and provision of Medicaid insurance could solve the problem of homelessness among persons with serious mental illness, further research is warranted to test the effect of interventions designed to treat patients with dual diagnoses and to assist homeless persons with serious mental illness in obtaining and maintaining entitlement benefits."

Table 7.5 shows the results of a study of 100 homeless women with schizophrenia and 100 nonhomeless women with schizophrenia. The study, which is summarized by Silver and Pañares, finds that homeless schizophrenic women had higher rates of co-occurring disorders, including alcohol and/or drug abuse and antisocial personality disorder.

Silver and Pañares note that families with children make up about 40% of the total homeless population and that the vast majority (about 90%) are female-headed. They also report on a study of 436 sheltered homeless and low-income housed mothers. The study found that 84% of these women had a history of having been severely assaulted at some point in their life. Research shows that mothers with a history of abuse are more likely to have children with mental health problems.

PREVALENCE AND TREATMENT. Experts debate the rate of mental disorders among homeless populations, but they generally agree that it is greater among the homeless than the general population. In "The Prevalence of Mental Disorders among the Homeless in Western Countries" (*PLoS Medline*, vol. 5, no. 12, December 2, 2008), Seena Fazel et al. analyze data from 29 surveys of the homeless in Western countries to find the prevalence of mental disorders in this population. The researchers find that the most common mental disorders were alcohol and drug dependence. The prevalence rates of psychosis and depression ranged from 2.8% to 42.3%. Fazel et al. conclude that the prevalence of substance abuse disorder, psychotic disorders, and depression are higher among the homeless population than among the general population.

Mentally ill homeless people present special problems for health care workers. They may not be as cooperative and motivated as other patients. Because of their limited resources, they may have difficulty getting transportation to treatment centers. They frequently forget to show up for appointments or take medications. The addition of drug abuse can make them unruly or unresponsive. Among people with severe mental disorders, those at greatest risk of homelessness are both the most severely ill and the most difficult to help.

The National Alliance on Mental Illness states in "Dual Diagnosis and Integrated Treatment of Mental Illness and Substance Abuse Disorder" (2003, http://www.nami.org/) that mental illness and substance abuse frequently occur together; clinicians call this dual diagnosis. Experts explain that in the absence of appropriate treatment, people with mental illness often resort to self-medication—that is, using alcohol or drugs to silence the voices or calm the fears that torment them. Approximately 50% of individuals with severe mental disorders also abuse drugs or alcohol. Homeless people with dual diagnoses are frequently excluded from mental health programs because of treatment problems created by their substance abuse and are excluded from substance abuse programs due to problems in treating their mental illness. Experts note that the lack of an integrated system of care plays a major role in these people's recurrent homelessness and stress that transitional or assisted housing initiatives for homeless substance abusers must realistically address the issue of abstinence and design measures for handling relapses that do not place people back on the streets.

THE HEALTH OF HOMELESS CHILDREN

In "Are There Different Types of Homeless Families? A Typology of Homeless Families Based on Cluster Analysis" (*Family Relations*, vol. 47, no. 2, April 1998), Evangeline R. Danseco and E. Wayne Holden seek to identify different types of homeless families and to examine children from these families. The researchers studied 180 families, with a total of 348 children, participating in a comprehensive health care program for children of homeless families. The results show that homeless children consistently exhibited greater behavior problems and showed a trend of poorer cognitive, academic, and adaptive behaviors than children in the general population.

The American Academy of Pediatrics reviews in "Policy Statement: Providing Care for Immigrant, Homeless, and Migrant Children" (*Pediatrics*, vol. 115, no. 4, April 2005) the literature on the health of homeless children. The policy statement enumerates many health effects of homelessness, including that homeless children are more likely to experience poor health or fair health than are other children. In particular, they have more trauma-related injuries, a greater incidence of sinus infections, anemia, asthma, eczema, visual and neurologic deficits, and digestive disorders. In addition, obesity and hunger are common. Unaccompanied youth as well as children in families living on the streets are at a higher risk of experiencing violence or victimization.

John C. Buckner of the Harvard Medical School summarizes the results of several studies of homeless children's mental and physical health in "Understanding the Impact of Homelessness on Children: Challenges and Future Research Directions" (*American Behavioral Scientist*, vol. 51, no. 6, February 2008). He finds that both homeless and low-income housed children have higher rates of physical and mental health problems than do other children. He also notes that most studies find that homeless children evidence greater health problems than do low-income housed children. However, he calls for more research to investigate these probable differences.

VICTIMS OF VIOLENCE
Violence toward Homeless Women

Homeless women are at a high risk of interpersonal violence. According to Ellen Bassuk, Ree Dawson, and Nicholas Huntington, in "Intimate Violence in Extremely Poor Women: Longitudinal Patterns and Risk Markers" (*Journal of Family Violence*, vol. 21, no. 6, August 2006), almost two-thirds of 280 homeless and extremely poor housed women had experienced intimate partner violence in their lifetime. Women who had been molested in childhood, who had inadequate emotional support from professionals, or who had poor self-esteem were the most likely to have experienced intimate partner violence in the past 12 months. In "Relative Contributions of Parent Substance Use and Childhood Maltreatment to Chronic Homelessness, Depression, and Substance Abuse Problems among Homeless Women: Mediating Roles of Self-Esteem and Abuse in Adulthood" (*Child Abuse and Neglect*, vol. 26, no. 10, October 2002), Judith A. Stein, Michelle Burden Leslie, and Adeline Nyuamathi note that recent intimate partner violence actually contributes to a greater likelihood of chronic homelessness among women.

A study by Suzanne L. Wenzel et al. find in "Sexual Risk among Impoverished Women: Understanding the Role of Housing Status" (*AIDS and Behavior*, vol. 11, supplement 6, November 2007) that impoverished women who are homeless or have been recently victimized are also more likely to engage in risky sexual behavior that can lead to HIV infection. The researchers indicate that homeless African-American and Hispanic women had from two to five times greater odds of engaging in risky sexual behavior than women who were housed.

Hate Crimes

The National Coalition for the Homeless (NCH) reports in *Hate, Violence, and Death on Main Street USA: A Report on Hate Crimes and Violence against People Experiencing Homelessness 2007* (April 2008, http://www.nationalhomeless.org/getinvolved/projects/hatecrimes/hatecrimes2007.pdf), "In 2007, homeless individuals in America faced another year of brutality that ranged from assault to killings." The NCH identifies 217 deaths and 557 nonlethal attacks on homeless people between 1999 and 2007—160 attacks in 2007 alone. The crimes occurred in 235 cities in 45 states and in Puerto Rico.

The NCH recommends the following actions to address the problem of violence against homeless individuals:

- A public statement by the U.S. Department of Justice that identifies attacks on homeless people as hate crimes.

- The creation of a Department of Justice database to track hate crimes perpetrated against homeless people.

- Training for local police in investigating crimes and working with people experiencing homelessness.

- Legislation at the state level to better protect people experiencing homelessness from violence.

- A U.S. Government Accountability Office study of the scope of the problem.

Homeless advocates have demanded that crimes against homeless people be defined as hate crimes, which may result in harsher penalties in federal courts. However, determining how many of these crimes occur is difficult. Some factors that affect the accuracy of the count are:

- The bodies of the victims are not always discovered.

- Bodies may be badly decomposed when found, preventing accurate identification of the cause of death.

- Local authorities may rule causes of death other than violence.

- Survivors do not always report crimes, and murdered victims cannot tell their own stories.

HUNGER
The Extent of the Problem

During the 1980s a number of studies found that some Americans, especially children, were suffering from hunger. Many observers did not believe these reports or thought they had been exaggerated. In 1984 a Task Force on Food Assistance appointed by President Ronald Reagan (1911–2004) found that it could not find evidence on the extent of hunger because there was no agreed-on way to measure hunger.

In response, the Food Research and Action Center (FRAC), an advocacy group for the poor, launched the Community Childhood Hunger Identification Project (CCHIP) to determine the extent of hunger in the United States. The first FRAC survey conducted interviews in 2,335 households with incomes at or below 185% of the poverty level and with at least one child under 12 years of age. The results of this survey, as reported by Cheryl A. Wehler et al. in *Community Childhood Hunger Identification Project: A Survey of Childhood Hunger in the United States* (1991), indicated that 32% of U.S. households with incomes at or below 185% of the poverty level experienced hunger. At least one child out of every eight under 12 years of age suffered from hunger. Another 40% of low-income children were at risk for hunger.

Between 1992 and 1994 FRAC sponsored a second round of CCHIP surveys in nine states and the District of Columbia (5,282 low-income families with at least one child aged 12 and younger). For the purposes of its report, FRAC defined hunger as food insufficiency—skipping meals, eating less, or running out of food—that occurred because of limited household resources. The results were reported by Cheryl A. Wehler et al. in *Community Childhood Hunger Identification Project: A Survey of Childhood Hunger in the United States* (1995). FRAC concluded in the 1995 CCHIP survey that about 4 million children aged 12 and younger experienced hunger for one or more months during the previous year. Another 9.6 million children were at risk of becoming hungry.

The 1995 CCHIP survey studied one child in each household (the child with the most recent birthday) and found that, in comparison with nonhungry children, hungry children were:

- More than three times as likely to suffer from unwanted weight loss

- More than four times as likely to suffer from fatigue

- Almost three times as likely to suffer from irritability

- More than three times as likely to have frequent headaches

- Almost one and a half times as likely to have frequent ear infections

- Four times as likely to suffer from concentration problems
- Almost twice as likely to have frequent colds

Based on the findings from the 1991 and 1995 CCHIP surveys, FRAC concluded that even though federal food programs are targeted to households most in need, a common barrier to program participation is a lack of information, particularly about eligibility guidelines. FRAC contended that if federal, state, and local governments made a greater effort to ensure that possible recipients were aware of their eligibility for food programs, such as Special Supplemental Food Program for Women, Infants, and Children (WIC) and the School Breakfast Program, there would be a large drop in hunger in the United States.

In 1997 the Urban Institute conducted the National Survey of American Families (NSAF; 2006, http://www.urban.org/center/anf/snapshots.cfm). Nearly half of low-income families (those with family incomes up to 200% of the federal poverty line) who were interviewed in 1997 reported that the food they purchased ran out before they got money to buy more or they worried they would run out of food. Four out of five of these families with food problems reported suffering actual food shortages, and one out of five worried about food shortages. More children than adults lived in families that worried about or had trouble affording food—54% of low-income children experienced this problem. The NSAF was repeated in 1999, and families reported fewer problems affording food than in 1997. Four out of ten low-income families were either concerned about or had difficulty affording food, down 10% from 1997. However, approximately half of all low-income children still lived in families with difficulties affording food or concern about lack of food.

A third NSAF was conducted in 2002, and the results were released in 2004. According to Sandi Nelson of the Urban Institute, in "Trends in Parents' Economic Hardship" (March 2004, http://www.urban.org/UploadedPDF/310970_snapshots3_no21.pdf), the 2002 report showed that 51.3% of low-income parents faced food hardship, 59.4% of single parents experienced food hardship, and the gains between 1997 and 1999 had been all but erased.

Since 1995 the Food and Nutrition Service (FNS) and the Census Bureau have conducted annual surveys of food security, low food security (or food insecurity), and very low food insecurity (previously called hunger). (Food-secure households are those that have access at all times to enough food for an active, healthy life. Low-food-security households are uncertain of having, or unable to acquire, enough food to meet basic needs at all times during the year.) According to Mark Nord, Margaret Andrews, and Steven Carlson of the Economic Research Service, in *Household Food Security in the*

United States, 2007 (November 2008, http://www.ers.usda.gov/publications/ERR66/ERR66.pdf), the survey is based on an 18-item scale:

1. Worried food would run out before (I/we) got money to buy more
2. Food bought didn't last and (I/we) didn't have money to get more
3. Couldn't afford to eat balanced meals
4. Adult(s) cut size of meals or skipped meals
5. Respondent ate less than felt he/she should
6. Adult(s) cut size or skipped meals in 3 or more months
7. Respondent hungry but didn't eat because couldn't afford
8. Respondent lost weight
9. Adult(s) did not eat for whole day
10. Adult(s) did not eat for whole day in 3 or more months
11. Relied on few kinds of low-cost food to feed child(ren)
12. Couldn't feed child(ren) balanced meals
13. Child(ren) were not eating enough
14. Cut size of child(ren)'s meals
15. Child(ren) were hungry
16. Child(ren) skipped meals
17. Child(ren) skipped meals in 3 or more months
18. Child(ren) did not eat for whole day

Figure 7.7 shows that levels of food insecurity steadily rose from 1999 to 2004, but dropped in 2005 to 1995 levels before rising again. The prevalence rate of very low food security rose between 1999 and 2007. (Households with very low food security often worry that their food will run out, report that their food does run out before they have money to get more, cannot afford to eat balanced meals, often have adults who skip meals because there is not enough money for food, and report that they eat less than they should because of lack of money.) In 2007, 11.1% of households reported low food security at some time during the year, and 4.1% reported being very low food security. (See Figure 7.8.)

Poor and low-income households were more likely to experience food insecurity and very low food security during the year than were households with higher incomes. Nord, Andrews, and Carlson indicate that in 2007, 22.8% of households with an income below the poverty line reported low food security and 14.9% of these households reported very low food security. In comparison, 17.5% of households with an income-to-poverty ratio under 1.85 experienced low food security and 11.2% of these households experienced very low food security. Only 3.7% of house-

FIGURE 7.7

Trends in prevalence of household food insecurity, 1995–2007

——— Food insecurity, data as collected (unadjusted) *
- - - Food insecurity, adjusted for comparability in all years
——— Very low food security, data as collected (unadjusted)[1]
········· Very low food security, adjusted for comparability in all years

Percent of households (y-axis: 0, 2, 4, 6, 8, 10, 12, 14)

(x-axis: 1995, 97, 99, 2001, 03, 05, 07)

*Data as collected in 1995–97 are not directly comparable with data collected in 1998–2007.

SOURCE: Mark Nord, Margaret Andrews, and Steven Carlson, "Figure 2. Trends in the Prevalence of Food Insecurity in U.S. Households, 1995–2007," in *Household Food Security in the United States, 2007*, U.S. Department of Agriculture, Economic Research Service, November 2008, http://www.ers.usda.gov/Publications/ERR66/ERR66 .pdf (accessed January 21, 2009)

FIGURE 7.8

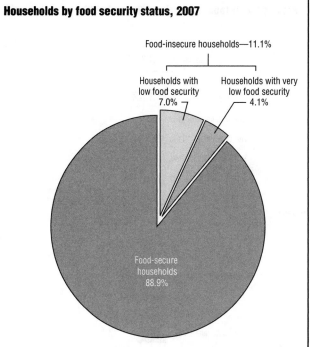

Households by food security status, 2007

Food-insecure households—11.1%

Households with low food security 7.0%

Households with very low food security 4.1%

Food-secure households 88.9%

SOURCE: Mark Nord, Margaret Andrews, and Steven Carlson, "Figure 1. U.S. Households by Food Security Status, 2007," in *Household Food Security in the United States, 2007,* U.S. Department of Agriculture, Economic Research Service, November 2008, http://www.ers.usda.gov/ Publications/ERR66/ERR66.pdf (accessed January 21, 2009)

holds with higher incomes experienced low food security. The prevalence of food insecurity had risen in all categories from the year before. (See Figure 7.9 and Figure 7.10.)

Among the children, 16.9% experienced low food security in 2007, and 0.9% experienced very low food security. (See Table 7.7.) The poorest families experienced low food security the most often; only 57.1% of households with an income-to-poverty ratio under 1.00 were food secure, compared to 58.8% of families with income-to-poverty ratios under 1.30, 64.6% of families with income-to-poverty ratios under 1.85, and 93.1% of families with income-to-poverty ratios of 1.85 and over. Families headed by married couples are much less likely to experience low food security than families headed by single females; only 11.8% of married-couple households reported low food security in 2007, compared to 31.8% of female-headed households. Low food security was also more prevalent among African-American families, 26.1% of whom experienced low food security, and Hispanic families, 26.7% of whom experienced low food security, than among non-Hispanic whites, 11.9% of whom experienced low food security.

Emergency Food Assistance

Feeding America (2009, http://feedingamerica.org/ about-us.aspx) is the nation's largest charitable hunger-relief organization, serving over 25 million people per year. In

Hunger in America 2006 (March 2006, http://www.hunger inamerica.org/export/sites/hungerinamerica/about_the _study/A2HNationalReport.pdf), a study based on 52,878 interviews with clients and 31,342 questionnaires from Feeding America agencies, the organization finds the following characteristics of recipients of emergency food assistance:

- More than a third (36.4%) of the members of households served by the national network were children; and 8% were children under the age of five.

- More than a third (36%) of all emergency client households had at least one member working.

- More than two-thirds (68%) of the households had incomes below the poverty level.

- More than one out of 10 (12%) clients were homeless.

- About a third (35%) of client households also received Food Stamp Program benefits; 51% of families with young children participated in the WIC program, and 62% of households with school-age children participated in school lunch programs.

- About 40% of recipients at all program sites were non-Hispanic whites, 38% were African-American, and 17% were Hispanic.

- Twenty-nine percent reported that at least one household member was in poor health.

FIGURE 7.9

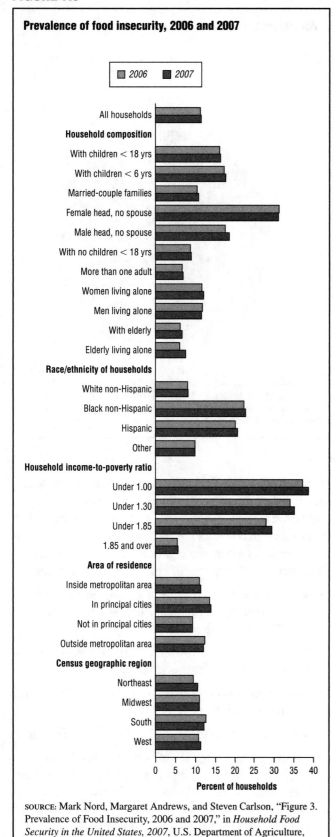

Prevalence of food insecurity, 2006 and 2007

☐ 2006   ■ 2007

Percent of households

SOURCE: Mark Nord, Margaret Andrews, and Steven Carlson, "Figure 3. Prevalence of Food Insecurity, 2006 and 2007," in *Household Food Security in the United States, 2007*, U.S. Department of Agriculture, Economic Research Service, November 2008, http://www.ers.usda.gov/Publications/ERR66/ERR66.pdf (accessed January 21, 2009)

FIGURE 7.10

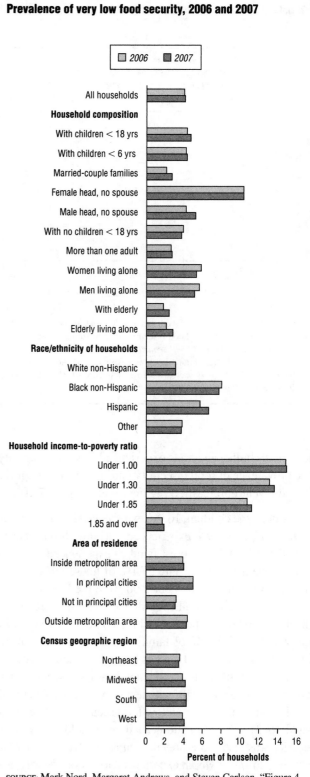

Prevalence of very low food security, 2006 and 2007

☐ 2006   ■ 2007

Percent of households

SOURCE: Mark Nord, Margaret Andrews, and Steven Carlson, "Figure 4. Prevalence of Very Low Food Security, 2006 and 2007," in *Household Food Security in the United States, 2007*, U.S. Department of Agriculture, Economic Research Service, November 2008, http://www.ers.usda.gov/Publications/ERR66/ERR66.pdf (accessed January 21, 2009)

TABLE 7.7

Number of children by food security status of households and selected household characteristics, 2007

Category	Total[a] 1,000	In food-secure households 1,000	Percent	In food-insecure households[b] 1,000	Percent	In households with very low food security among children 1,000	Percent
All children	73,575	61,140	83.1	12,435	16.9	691	0.9
Household composition							
With children <6 yrs	37,139	30,132	81.1	7,007	18.9	292	.8
Married-couple families	51,733	45,639	88.2	6,094	11.8	315	.6
Female head, no spouse	16,921	11,541	68.2	5,380	31.8	346	2.0
Male head, no spouse	3,896	3,098	79.5	798	20.5	25	.6
Other household with child[c]	1,026	863	84.1	163	15.9	4	.4
Race/ethnicity of households							
White non-Hispanic	44,117	38,866	88.1	5,251	11.9	201	.5
Black non-Hispanic	10,615	7,840	73.9	2,775	26.1	192	1.8
Hispanic[d]	14,433	10,581	73.3	3,852	26.7	277	1.9
Other	4,409	3,851	87.3	558	12.7	22	.5
Household income-to-poverty ratio							
Under 1.00	12,080	6,895	57.1	5,185	42.9	359	3.0
Under 1.30	15,852	9,323	58.8	6,529	41.2	439	2.8
Under 1.85	24,571	15,877	64.6	8,694	35.4	518	2.1
1.85 and over	37,483	34,883	93.1	2,600	6.9	85	.2
Income unknown	11,521	10,380	90.1	1,141	9.9	88	.8
Area of residence[e]							
Inside metropolitan area	61,415	51,123	83.2	10,292	16.8	625	1.0
In principal cities[f]	19,996	15,748	78.8	4,248	21.2	305	1.5
Not in principal cities	31,784	27,351	86.1	4,433	13.9	181	.6
Outside metropolitan area	12,160	10,018	82.4	2,142	17.6	65	.5
Census geographic region							
Northeast	12,328	10,526	85.4	1,802	14.6	84	.7
Midwest	15,936	13,477	84.6	2,459	15.4	150	.9
South	27,375	22,375	81.7	5,000	18.3	234	.9
West	17,935	14,762	82.3	3,173	17.7	222	1.2

[a]Totals exclude children in households whose food security status is unknown because they did not give a valid response to any of the questions in the food security scale. In 2007, these represented 419,000 children (0.6 percent).
[b]Food-insecure households are those with low or very low food security among adults or children.
[c]Households with children in complex living arrangements, e.g., children of other relatives or unrelated roommate or boarder.
[d]Hispanics may be of any race.
[e]Metropolitan area residence is based on 2003 Office of Management and Budget delineation. Prevalence rates by area of residence are comparable with those for 2004 and later years, but are not precisely comparable with those of earlier years.
[f]Households within incorporated areas of the largest cities in each metropolitan area. Residence inside or outside of principal cities is not identified for about 16 percent of children living in metropolitan statistical areas.

SOURCE: Mark Nord, Margaret Andrews, and Steven Carlson,"Table 6. Number of Children by Food Security Status of Households and Selected Household Characteristics, 2007," in *Household Food Security in the United States, 2007*, U.S. Department of Agriculture, Economic Research Service, November 2008, http://www.ers.usda.gov/Publications/ERR66/ERR66.pdf (accessed January 21, 2009)

- A significant proportion of clients had to choose between food and other necessities; 42% reported having to choose between paying for food and paying for utilities, 35% had to choose between paying for food and paying their rent or mortgage, and 32% had to choose between paying for food and paying for medical care.

Malnutrition among the Homeless

Homeless people face a daily challenge to fulfill their basic need for food. They often go hungry. This is borne out by Burt et al. Clients of homeless assistance programs were found to have higher levels of food problems than poor people in general; 28% reported not getting enough to eat sometimes or often, compared to 12% of poor American adults. Close to four out of 10 (39%) of the homeless clients had been hungry in the past 30 days but did not eat because

they had no money for food, and 40% reported going at least one whole day without eating. Undernourishment and vitamin deficiency can cause or aggravate other physical conditions.

Meg Wilson of the University of Saint Francis finds in "Health-Promoting Behaviors of Sheltered Homeless Women" (*Family and Community Health*, vol. 28, no. 1, January–March 2005) that despite being homeless, many homeless women practiced "health-promoting behaviors." However, because of their homelessness, they had difficulty getting adequate nutrition.

The diet of homeless people, even those who live in shelters or cheap motels, is generally not balanced or of good quality. Homeless people often rely on ready-cooked meals, fast-food restaurants, garbage cans, and the sometimes infrequent meal schedules of free food sources, such as shelters, soup kitchens, and drop-in centers. However, many soup kitchens serve only one meal per day, and many shelters that serve meals—and not all of them do—serve only two meals per day.

In *Hunger and Homelessness Survey: A Status Report on Hunger and Homelessness in America's Cities, a 25-City Survey, December 2008* (December 2008, http://www .usmayors.org/pressreleases/documents/hungerhomeless nessreport_121208.pdf), the U.S. Conference of Mayors indicates that 95% of cities surveyed in 2008 reported an increase in requests for emergency food assistance over the course of the year by an average of 18%. The majority (59%) of people requesting emergency food assistance were in families. Eighty percent of the cities reported that the demand for food assistance was larger than the supply. Officials cited poverty (83%), unemployment or under-employment (74%), high housing costs (57%), and an increase in food prices (39%) as major causes of hunger in their cities.

As part of the American Recovery and Reinvestment Act of 2009, the food and shelter programs authorized under the McKinney-Vento Homeless Assistance Act received an additional $100 million.

GOVERNMENT PROGRAMS TO COMBAT HUNGER

Supplemental Nutrition Assistance Program

The Supplemental Nutrition Assistance Program (SNAP; previously called the Food Stamp Program), administered by the U.S. Department of Agriculture (USDA), is the largest food assistance program in the United States. The SNAP program is designed to help low-income families purchase a nutritionally adequate, low-cost diet. Generally, SNAP may only be used to buy food to be prepared at home. It cannot be used for alcohol, tobacco, or hot foods intended to be consumed immediately, such as restaurant or delicatessen food.

The typical U.S. household spends 30% of its monthly income on food purchases. The program calculates 30% of the family's earnings and then issues enough food stamps to make up the difference between that amount and the amount needed to buy an adequate diet. These monthly allotments are usually provided electronically through an electronic benefit transfer, a debit card that is similar to a bank card.

The cash value of these benefits is based on the size of the household and how much the family earns. Households without an elderly or disabled member generally must have a monthly total (gross) cash income at or below 130% of the poverty level and may not have liquid assets (cash, savings, or other assets that can be easily sold) of more than $2,000. (If the household has a member aged 60 and older, the asset limit is $3,000.) The net

TABLE 7.8

Income chart for eligibility to receive food stamps, 2008–09

People in household	Gross monthly income*	Net monthly income
1	$1,127	$867
2	$1,517	$1,167
3	$1,907	$1,467
4	$2,297	$1,767
5	$2,687	$2,067
6	$3,077	$2,367
7	$3,467	$2,667
8	$3,857	$2,967
Each additional person	+$390	+$300

*Larger households can have more income. Amounts are higher in Alaska and Hawaii. People who receive Supplemental Security Income (SSI) in California are not eligible.

SOURCE: "Is My Income under the Limit?" in *Food Stamps Make America Stronger*, U.S. Department of Agriculture, Food and Nutrition Service, September 2007, http://www.fns.usda.gov/FSP/outreach/Translations/ English/313Brochure-08.pdf (accessed January 25, 2009)

monthly income limit (gross income minus any approved deductions for child care, some housing costs, and other expenses) must be 100% or less of the poverty level, or $1,767 per month for a family of four between October 2008 and September 2009. (See Table 7.8.)

With some exceptions, SNAP is automatically available to Supplemental Security Income and TANF recipients. SNAP benefits are higher in states with lower TANF benefits because those benefits are considered a part of a family's countable income. To receive SNAP, certain household members must register for work, accept suitable job offers, or fulfill work or training requirements (such as looking or training for a job).

Even though the federal government sets guidelines and provides funding, SNAP is actually administered by the states. State agencies certify eligibility as well as calculate and issue benefit allotments. Most often, the welfare agency and staff that administer the TANF and Medicaid programs also run SNAP. The program operates in all 50 states, the District of Columbia, Guam, and the Virgin Islands. (Puerto Rico is covered under a separate nutrition-assistance program.)

Except for some small differences in Alaska, Hawaii, and the territories, the program is run the same way throughout the United States. The states pay 50% of the administrative costs, and the federal government pays 100% of SNAP benefits and the other 50% of the administrative costs. In 2001 the federal government paid only $15.5 billion in SNAP benefits, but by 2007 it paid $34.6 billion in SNAP benefits, or an estimated average monthly benefit of $101.53 per recipient. (See Table 7.9.)

SNAP participation decreased significantly after the Personal Responsibility and Work Opportunity Reconciliation Act of 1996 went into force, from a high of 27.5 million program participants in 1994 to a low of 17.2

TABLE 7.9

Supplemental Nutrition Assistance Program participation and costs, 1969–2008

Fiscal year	Average participation	Average benefit per person[a]	Total benefits	All other costs[b]	Total costs
	Thousands	Dollars	Millions of dollars		
1969	2,878	6.63	228.8	21.7	250.5
1970	4,340	10.55	549.7	27.2	576.9
1971	9,368	13.55	1,522.7	53.2	1,575.9
1972	11,109	13.48	1,797.3	69.4	1,866.7
1973	12,166	14.60	2,131.4	76.0	2,207.4
1974	12,862	17.61	2,718.3	119.2	2,837.5
1975	17,064	21.40	4,385.5	233.2	4,618.7
1976	18,549	23.93	5,326.5	359.0	5,685.5
1977	17,077	24.71	5,067.0	394.0	5,461.0
1978	16,001	26.77	5,139.2	380.5	5,519.7
1979	17,653	30.59	6,480.2	459.6	6,939.8
1980	21,082	34.47	8,720.9	485.6	9,206.5
1981	22,430	39.49	10,629.9	595.4	11,225.2
1982[c]	21,717	39.17	10,208.3	628.4	10,836.7
1983	21,625	42.98	11,152.3	694.8	11,847.1
1984	20,854	42.74	10,696.1	882.6	11,578.8
1985	19,899	44.99	10,743.6	959.6	11,703.2
1986	19,429	45.49	10,605.2	1,033.2	11,638.4
1987	19,113	45.78	10,500.3	1,103.9	11,604.2
1988	18,645	49.83	11,149.1	1,167.7	12,316.8
1989	18,806	51.85	11,669.8	1,231.8	12,901.6
1990	20,049	58.96	14,142.8	1,304.5	15,447.3
1991	22,625	63.87	17,315.8	1,431.5	18,747.3
1992	25,407	68.57	20,905.7	1,556.6	22,462.3
1993	26,987	67.95	22,006.0	1,647.0	23,653.0
1994	27,474	69.00	22,748.6	1,744.8	24,493.4
1995	26,619	71.27	22,764.1	1,856.3	24,620.4
1996	25,543	73.21	22,440.1	1,890.8	24,330.9
1997	22,858	71.27	19,548.9	1,958.6	21,507.5
1998	19,791	71.12	16,890.5	2,097.8	18,988.3
1999	18,183	72.27	15,769.4	2,051.5	17,820.9
2000	17,194	72.62	14,983.3	2,070.7	17,054.0
2001	17,318	74.81	15,547.4	2,242.0	17,789.4
2002	19,096	79.67	18,256.2	2,380.9	20,637.1
2003	21,259	83.90	21,404.3	2,412.1	23,816.4
2004	23,858	85.99	24,618.9	2,480.3	27,099.2
2005	25,718	92.57	28,567.9	2,504.9	31,072.8
2006	26,672	94.32	30,187.3	2,725.0	32,912.3
2007	26,468	95.63	30,373.3	2,824.2	33,197.5
2008	28,408	101.53	34,611.1	3,044.7	37,655.8

Fiscal year 2008 data are preliminary; all data are subject to revision.
[a]Represents average monthly benefits per person.
[b]Includes the federal share of state administrative expenses and employment and training programs. Also includes other federal costs (e.g., printing and processing of stamps; anti-fraud funding; program evaluation).
[c]Puerto Rico initiated food stamp operations during fiscal year 1975 and participated through June of fiscal year 1982. A separate Nutrition Assistance Grant was begun in July 1982.

SOURCE: "Supplemental Nutrition Assistance Program Participation and Costs," U.S. Department of Agriculture, Food and Nutrition Service, January 2009, http://www.fns.usda.gov/pd/SNAPsummary.htm (accessed February 5, 2009)

million in 2000. (See Table 7.9.) However, with the worsening economy at the start of the twenty-first century, participation rates steadily increased then surpassed 1994 levels in 2008. In that year, 28.4 million people participated in the program.

The SNAP program is the nation's largest source of food assistance, helping about 26.5 million Americans in an average month in 2007. The FNS notes in "Characteristics of Food Stamp Households: Fiscal Year 2007—Summary" (September 2008, http://www.fns.usda.gov/ora/MENU/Published/snap/FILES/Participation/2007CharacteristicsSummary.pdf) that in 2007, 49% of the participants were children and 9% were 60 years old and older. Four out of ten (41%) SNAP recipients lived in a household with earnings as the primary source of income, and most SNAP households did not receive cash welfare benefits—only 12% received TANF. Most SNAP households were poor; only 13% of households had incomes above the poverty level and 39% had incomes at or below half the poverty line.

The average household receiving SNAP benefits received a monthly benefit of $212 in 2007. Table 7.10 shows the maximum monthly food stamp allotments between 2008 and 2009 for households of varying sizes within the continental United States. During this period the maximum monthly benefit for a four-person household was $588.

Because funds provided to nutritional assistance programs are extremely likely to be spent, such funds are considered economic stimulus. On February 17, 2009, President Obama signed the American Recovery and Reinvestment Act into law in response to the severe economic recession that began in 2008. The legislation provided an additional $500 million to support participation in the program. The act also authorized an increase in benefits of up to 113.6% of the value of the Thrifty Food Plan (a plan that serves as the basis for maximum food stamp allotments).

National School Lunch and School Breakfast Programs

The National School Lunch Program (NSLP) and the School Breakfast Program (SBP) provide federal cash and commodity support to participating public and private schools and to nonprofit residential institutions that serve meals to children. Children from households with incomes at or below 130% of the poverty line receive free meals. Children from households with incomes between 130% and 185% of the poverty level receive meals at a reduced price (no more than $0.40). Table 7.11 shows the income eligibility guidelines, based on the poverty guidelines, effective from July 1, 2008, to June 30, 2009. The levels are higher for Alaska and Hawaii than in the 48 contiguous states, the District of Columbia, Guam, and other U.S. territories.

TABLE 7.10

Maximum food stamp allotments, 2008–09

People in household	Maximum monthly benefits*
1	$176
2	$323
3	$463
4	$588
5	$698
6	$838
7	$926
8	$1,058
Each additional person	+$132

*Amounts are higher in Alaska and Hawaii. People who receive Supplemental Security Income (SSI) in California are not eligible.

SOURCE: "If I Am Eligible, What Is the Most I Can Get?" in *Food Stamps Make America Stronger*, U.S. Department of Agriculture, Food and Nutrition Service, September 2007, http://www.fns.usda.gov/FSP/outreach/Translations/English/313Brochure-08.pdf (accessed January 25, 2009)

TABLE 7.11

Income eligibility guidelines for free or reduced-price meals, 2008–09

Household size	Federal poverty guidelines Annual	Reduced price meals—185% Annual	Monthly	Twice per month	Every two weeks	Weekly	Free meals—130% Annual	Monthly	Twice per month	Twice two weeks	Weekly
48 contiguous States, District of Columbia, Guam, and Territories											
1	10,400	19,240	1,604	802	740	370	13,520	1,127	564	520	260
2	14,000	25,900	2,159	1,080	997	499	18,200	1,517	759	700	350
3	17,600	32,560	2,714	1357	1,253	627	22,880	1,907	954	880	440
4	21,200	39,220	3,269	1,635	1,509	755	27,560	2,297	1,149	1,060	530
5	24,800	45,880	3,824	1,912	1,765	883	32,240	2,687	1,344	1,240	620
6	28,400	52,540	4,379	2,190	2,021	1,011	36,920	3,077	1,539	1,420	710
7	32,000	59,200	4,934	2,467	2,277	1,139	41,600	3,467	1,734	1,600	800
8	35,600	65,860	5,489	2,745	2,534	1,267	46,280	3,857	1,929	1,780	890
For each add'l family member, add	3,600	6,660	555	278	257	129	4,680	390	195	180	90
Alaska											
1	13,000	24,050	2,005	1,003	925	463	16,900	1,409	705	650	325
2	17,500	32,375	2,698	1,349	1,246	623	22,750	1,896	948	875	438
3	22,000	40,700	3,392	1,696	1,566	783	28,600	2,384	1,192	1,100	550
4	26,500	49,025	4,086	2,043	1,886	943	34,450	2,871	1,436	1,325	663
5	31,000	57,350	4,780	2,390	2,206	1,103	40,300	3,359	1,680	1,550	775
6	35,500	65,675	5,473	2,737	2,526	1,263	46,150	3,846	1,923	1,775	888
7	40,000	74,000	6,167	3,084	2,847	1,424	52,000	4,334	2,167	2,000	1,000
8	44,500	82,325	6,861	3,431	3,167	1,584	57,850	4,821	2,411	2,225	1,113
For each add'l family member, add	4,500	8,325	694	347	321	161	5,850	488	244	225	113
Hawaii											
1	11,960	22,126	1,844	922	851	426	15,548	1,296	648	598	299
2	16,100	29,785	2,483	1,242	1,146	573	20,930	1,745	873	805	403
3	20,240	37,444	3,121	1,561	1,441	721	26,312	2,193	1,097	1,012	506
4	24,380	45,103	3,759	1,880	1,735	868	31,694	2,642	1,321	1,219	610
5	28,520	52,762	4,397	2,199	2,030	1,015	37,076	3,090	1,545	1,426	713
6	32,660	60,421	5,036	2,518	2,324	1,162	42,458	3,539	1,770	1,633	817
7	36,800	68,080	5,674	2,837	2,619	1,310	47,840	3,987	1,994	1,840	920
8	40,940	75,739	6,312	3,156	2,914	1,457	53,222	4,436	2,218	2,047	1,024
For each add'l family member, add	4,140	7,659	639	320	295	148	5,382	449	225	207	104

SOURCE: "Income Eligibility Guidelines," in "Child Nutrition Programs—Income Eligibility Guidelines," *Federal Register*, vol. 73, no. 69, April 9, 2008, http://www.fns.usda.gov/cnd/Governance/notices/iegs/IEGs08–09.pdf (accessed February 1, 2009)

Children in TANF families are automatically eligible to receive free breakfasts and lunches. Almost 90% of federal funding for the NSLP is used to subsidize free and reduced-price lunches for low-income children.

The NSLP, created in 1946 under the National School Lunch Act, supplies subsidized lunches to children in almost all schools and in 6,000 residential and day care institutions. During the 1996–97 school year, the USDA changed certain policies so that school meals would meet the recommendations of the Dietary Guidelines for America, the federal standards for what constitutes a healthy diet. About 31 million children, or 60.1% of all children served lunch, received free or reduced-price lunches in 2008. (See Table 7.12.)

The SBP, created under the Child Nutrition Act of 1966, serves far fewer students than does the NSLP. The SBP also differs from the NSLP in that most schools offering the program are in low-income areas, and the children who participate in the program are mainly from low- and moderate-income families. In 2008 about 10.6 million students, or about 80.6% of all children served breakfast, participated. (See Table 7.13.) The total federal cost of school food programs was estimated at $10.6 billion.

As part of the American Recovery and Reinvestment Act (2009), the NSLP received an addition $100 million to distribute to states to pay for equipment needed by the program.

TABLE 7.12

National school lunch program participation and lunches served, 1969–2008

Fiscal year	Average participation				Total lunches served	Percent Free/RP of total
	Free	Reduced price	Full price	Total		
	Millions					%
1969	2.9	*	16.5	19.4	3,368.2	15.1
1970	4.6	*	17.8	22.4	3,565.1	20.7
1971	5.8	0.5	17.8	24.1	3,848.3	26.1
1972	7.3	0.5	16.6	24.4	3,972.1	32.4
1973	8.1	0.5	16.1	24.7	4,008.8	35.0
1974	8.6	0.5	15.5	24.6	3,981.6	37.1
1975	9.4	0.6	14.9	24.9	4,063.0	40.3
1976	10.2	0.8	14.6	25.6	4,147.9	43.1
1977	10.5	1.3	14.5	26.2	4,250.0	44.8
1978	10.3	1.5	14.9	26.7	4,294.1	44.4
1979	10.0	1.7	15.3	27.0	4,357.4	43.6
1980	10.0	1.9	14.7	26.6	4,387.0	45.1
1981	10.6	1.9	13.3	25.8	4,210.6	48.6
1982	9.8	1.6	11.5	22.9	3,755.0	50.2
1983	10.3	1.5	11.2	23.0	3,803.3	51.7
1984	10.3	1.5	11.5	23.4	3,826.2	51.0
1985	9.9	1.6	12.1	23.6	3,890.1	49.1
1986	10.0	1.6	12.2	23.7	3,942.5	49.1
1987	10.0	1.6	12.4	23.9	3,939.9	48.6
1988	9.8	1.6	12.8	24.2	4,032.9	47.4
1989	9.7	1.6	12.9	24.2	4,004.9	47.2
1990	9.8	1.7	12.6	24.1	4,009.0	48.3
1991	10.3	1.8	12.2	24.2	4,050.7	50.4
1992	11.2	1.7	11.7	24.6	4,101.3	53.1
1993	11.7	1.7	11.4	24.9	4,137.7	54.8
1994	12.2	1.8	11.3	25.3	4,201.6	55.9
1995	12.4	1.9	11.4	25.7	4,253.3	56.4
1996	12.6	2.0	11.3	25.9	4,313.2	56.9
1997	12.9	2.1	11.3	26.3	4,409.0	57.6
1998	13.0	2.2	11.4	26.6	4,425.0	57.8
1999	13.0	2.4	11.6	27.0	4,513.6	57.6
2000	13.0	2.5	11.9	27.3	4,575.2	57.1
2001	12.9	2.6	12.0	27.5	4,585.2	56.8
2002	13.3	2.6	12.0	28.0	4,716.6	57.6
2003	13.7	2.7	11.9	28.4	4,762.9	58.5
2004	14.1	2.8	12.0	29.0	4,842.3	59.1
2005	14.6	2.9	12.2	29.6	4,976.4	59.4
2006	14.8	2.9	12.4	30.1	5,029.0	59.3
2007	14.9	3.0	12.6	30.5	5,071.7	59.3
2008	15.4	3.1	12.5	31.0	5,207.0	60.1

Fiscal year 2008 data are preliminary; all data are subject to revision.
Participation data are 9 month averages (summer months are excluded).
*Included with free meals.

SOURCE: "National School Lunch Program: Participation and Lunches Served," U.S. Department of Agriculture, Food and Nutrition Service, January 2009, http://www.fns.usda.gov/pd/slsummar.htm (accessed February 5, 2009)

TABLE 7.13

National school breakfast program participation and meals served, 1969–2008

Fiscal years	Total participation[a]				Meals served	Free/RP of total meals
	Free	Red. price	Paid	Total		
	Millions					Percent
1969	—	—	—	0.22	39.7	71
1970	—	—	—	0.45	71.8	71.5
1971	0.6	[b]	0.2	0.8	125.5	76.3
1972	0.81	[b]	0.23	1.04	169.3	78.5
1973	0.99	[b]	0.2	1.19	194.1	83.4
1974	1.14	[b]	0.24	1.37	226.7	82.8
1975	1.45	0.04	0.33	1.82	294.7	82.1
1976	1.76	0.06	0.37	2.2	353.6	84.2
1977	2.02	0.11	0.36	2.49	434.3	85.7
1978	2.23	0.16	0.42	2.8	478.8	85.3
1979	2.56	0.21	0.54	3.32	565.6	84.1
1980	2.79	0.25	0.56	3.6	619.9	85.2
1981	3.05	0.25	0.51	3.81	644.2	86.9
1982	2.8	0.16	0.36	3.32	567.4	89.3
1983	2.87	0.15	0.34	3.36	580.7	90.3
1984	2.91	0.15	0.37	3.43	589.2	89.7
1985	2.88	0.16	0.4	3.44	594.9	88.6
1986	2.93	0.16	0.41	3.5	610.6	88.7
1987	3.01	0.17	0.43	3.61	621.5	88.4
1988	3.03	0.18	0.47	3.68	642.5	87.5
1989	3.11	0.19	0.51	3.81	658.4	86.8
1990	3.3	0.22	0.55	4.07	707.5	86.7
1991	3.61	0.25	0.58	4.44	771.9	87.3
1992	4.05	0.26	0.61	4.92	852.4	88
1993	4.41	0.28	0.66	5.36	923.6	87.9
1994	4.76	0.32	0.75	5.83	1,001.50	87.4
1995	5.1	0.37	0.85	6.32	1,078.90	86.8
1996	5.27	0.41	0.9	6.58	1,125.70	86.5
1997	5.52	0.45	0.95	6.92	1,191.20	86.5
1998	5.64	0.5	1.01	7.14	1,220.90	86.1
1999	5.72	0.56	1.09	7.37	1,267.60	85.4
2000	5.73	0.61	1.21	7.55	1,303.40	84.2
2001	5.8	0.67	1.32	7.79	1,334.50	83.2
2002	6.03	0.7	1.41	8.15	1,404.80	82.9
2003	6.22	0.74	1.47	8.43	1,447.90	82.8
2004	6.52	0.8	1.58	8.9	1,524.90	82.4
2005	6.8	0.86	1.7	9.36	1,603.90	82.1
2006	6.99	0.92	1.86	9.77	1,663.90	81.2
2007	7.24	0.99	2.02	10.12	1,714.90	80.6
2008	7.48	1.04	2.09	10.61	1,812.20	80.6

Fiscal year 2008 data are preliminary; all data are subject to revision.
[a]Nine month average: October–May plus September.
[b]Included with free participation.

SOURCE: "School Breakfast Program Participation and Meals Served," U.S. Department of Agriculture, Food and Nutrition Service, January 2009, http://www.fns.usda.gov/pd/sbsummar.htm (accessed February 5, 2009)

Special Supplemental Food Program for Women, Infants, and Children

The Special Supplemental Food Program for Women, Infants, and Children (WIC) program provides food assistance as well as nutrition counseling and health services to low-income pregnant women, to women who have just given birth and their babies, and to low-income children up to five years old. Participants in the program must have incomes at or below 185% of the poverty level (all but five states use this cutoff level) and must be nutritionally at risk.

As explained by the Child Nutrition Act of 1966, nutritional risk includes abnormal nutritional conditions, medical conditions related to nutrition, health-impairing dietary deficiencies, or conditions that might predispose a person to these conditions. Pregnant women may receive benefits throughout their pregnancies and for up to six months after childbirth or up to one year for nursing mothers.

Those receiving WIC benefits get supplemental food each month in the form of actual food items or, more commonly, vouchers (coupons) for the purchase of specific items at the store. Permitted foods contain high amounts of protein, iron, calcium, vitamin A, and vitamin C. Items that may be purchased include milk, cheese, eggs, infant formula, cereals, and fruit or vegetable juices. Mothers participating in WIC are encouraged to breastfeed their infants if possible, but state WIC agencies will provide formula for mothers who choose to use it.

The USDA estimates that the national average monthly cost of a WIC food package in 2008 was $43.42 per

TABLE 7.14

Special Supplemental Food Program for Women, Infants, and Children (WIC) program participation and costs, 1974–2008

Fiscal year	Total participation[a]	Food	NSA	Total[b]	Average monthly food cost per person
	(Thousands)	(Millions of dollars)			(Dollars)
1974	88	8.2	2.2	10.4	15.68
1975	344	76.7	12.6	89.3	18.58
1976	520	122.3	20.3	142.6	19.6
1977	848	211.7	44.2	255.9	20.8
1978	1,181	311.5	68.1	379.6	21.99
1979	1,483	428.6	96.8	525.4	24.09
1980	1,914	584.1	140.5	727.7	25.43
1981	2,119	708	160.6	871.6	27.84
1982	2,189	757.6	190.5	948.8	28.83
1983	2,537	901.8	221.3	1,126.00	29.62
1984	3,045	1,117.30	268.8	1,388.10	30.58
1985	3,138	1,193.20	294.4	1,489.30	31.69
1986	3,312	1,264.40	316.4	1,582.90	31.82
1987	3,429	1,344.70	333.1	1,679.60	32.68
1988	3,593	1,434.80	360.6	1,797.50	33.28
1989	4,119	1,489.40	416.5	1,910.90	30.14
1990	4,517	1,636.80	478.7	2,122.40	30.2
1991	4,893	1,751.90	544	2,301.00	29.84
1992	5,403	1,960.50	632.7	2,600.60	30.24
1993	5,921	2,115.10	705.6	2,828.60	29.77
1994	6,477	2,325.20	834.4	3,169.30	29.92
1995	6,894	2,511.60	904.6	3,436.20	30.36
1996	7,186	2,689.90	985.1	3,695.40	31.2
1997	7,407	2,815.50	1,008.20	3,843.80	31.68
1998	7,367	2,808.10	1,061.40	3,890.40	31.76
1999	7,311	2,851.60	1,063.90	3,938.10	32.5
2000	7,192	2,853.10	1,102.60	3,982.10	33.06
2001	7,306	3,007.90	1,110.60	4,153.30	34.31
2002	7,491	3,129.70	1,182.30	4,339.80	34.82
2003	7,631	3,230.30	1,260.00	4,524.40	35.28
2004	7,904	3,562.00	1,272.50	4,887.30	37.55
2005	8,023	3,602.70	1,335.50	4,993.90	37.42
2006	8,088	3,598.40	1,402.60	5,075.50	37.08
2007	8,285	3,880.00	1,479.10	5,411.80	39.03
2008	8,704	4,534.80	1,630.30	6,211.30	43.42

[a]Participation data are annual averages (6 months in FY 1974; 12 months all subsequent years).
[b]In addition to food and NSA costs, total expenditures includes funds for program evaluation, Farmers' Market Nutrition Program (FY 1989 onward), special projects and infrastructure. NSA = Nutrition Services and Administrative costs. Nutrition Services includes nutrition education, preventative and coordination services (such as health care), and promotion of breastfeeding and immunization.
Fiscal year 2008 data are preliminary; all data are subject to revision.

SOURCE: "WIC Program Participation and Costs," U.S. Department of Agriculture, Food and Nutrition Service, January 2009, http://www.fns.usda.gov/pd/wisummary.htm (accessed February 5, 2009)

participant, including food and administrative costs. (See Table 7.14.) In fiscal year 2008 the estimated federal costs for the WIC program were $6.2 billion, and the program served approximately 8.7 million women, infants, and children. WIC works in conjunction with the Farmers' Market Nutrition Program, established in 1992, to provide WIC recipients with increased access, in the form of vouchers, to fresh fruits and vegetables.

WIC is not an entitlement program. That is, the number of participants is limited by the amount of funds available rather than by eligibility. Susan Bartlett et al. indicate in *WIC Participant and Program Characteristics 2006* (December 2007, http://www.fns.usda.gov/ora/menu/Published/WIC/FILES/pc2006.pdf) that of the approximately 8.8 million participants in 2006 (the latest year for which detailed data are available as of mid-2009), 49% were children and 26% were infants. (See Figure 7.11.) In that

year, 25% of WIC participants were women—11% were pregnant, 7% were breastfeeding, and 7% were postpartum.

Bartlett et al. find that in 2006, 67.4% of WIC participants had household incomes at or below the poverty level, compared to 12.6% of the general population. (See Figure 7.12.) Nearly two-thirds (66.2%) of WIC participants received benefits from at least one other public assistance program. Nearly one out of 10 (9.3%) WIC recipients was also receiving TANF, 21.8% were also receiving food stamps, and 63.2% were also covered by Medicaid.

Bartlett et al. also note that the ethnic composition of WIC recipients has been changing since 1992 as the percentage of Hispanic enrollees has risen and the percentage of non-Hispanic white and African-American enrollees has declined. In 2006, 41.2% of all WIC participants were Hispanic, 55.3% were white (Hispanic or non-Hispanic), and 19.6% were African-American.

FIGURE 7.11

Distribution of individuals enrolled in the WIC program, 2006

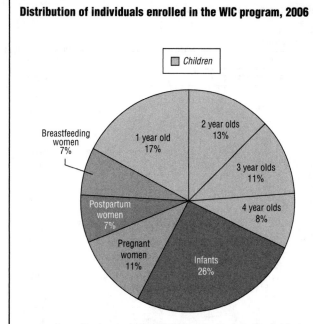

SOURCE: Susan Bartlett et al., "Exhibit E.2. Distribution of Individuals Enrolled in the WIC Program," in *WIC Participant and Program Characteristics 2006*, U.S. Department of Agriculture, Food and Nutrition Service, Office of Analysis, Nutrition and Evaluation, December 2007, http://www.fns.usda.gov/ora/menu/Published/WIC/FILES/pc2006.pdf (accessed February 5, 2009)

FIGURE 7.12

Poverty levels of WIC participants compared to the U.S. population, 2006

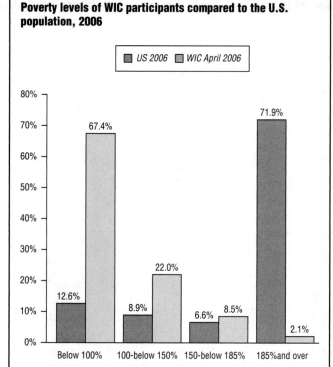

Note: WIC is Women, Infants and Children.

SOURCE: Susan Bartlett et al., "Exhibit E.3. Comparison of Poverty Levels of WIC Participants Reporting Income to Persons in the U.S. Population," in *WIC Participant and Program Characteristics 2006*, U.S. Department of Agriculture, Food and Nutrition Service, Office of Analysis, Nutrition and Evaluation, December 2007, http://www.fns.usda.gov/ora/menu/Published/WIC/FILES/pc2006.pdf (accessed February 5, 2009)

IMPORTANT NAMES
AND ADDRESSES

**American Public Human Services
Association**
1133 19th St. NW, Ste. 400
Washington, DC 20036
(202) 682-0100
FAX: (202) 289-6555
URL: http://www.aphsa.org/

**Association of Gospel Rescue
Missions**
1045 Swift St.
Kansas City, MO 64116-4127
1-800-624-5156
FAX: (816) 471-3718
URL: http://www.agrm.org/

Center on Budget and Policy Priorities
820 First St. NE, Ste. 510
Washington, DC 20002
(202) 408-1080
FAX: (202) 408-1056
E-mail: center@cbpp.org
URL: http://www.cbpp.org/

Center for Law and Social Policy
1015 15th St. NW, Ste. 400
Washington, DC 20005
(202) 906-8000
FAX: (202) 842-2885
URL: http://www.clasp.org/

Center for the Study of Social Policy
1575 Eye St. NW, Ste. 500
Washington, DC 20005
(202) 371-1565
FAX: (202) 371-1472
URL: http://www.cssp.org/

Children's Defense Fund
25 E St. NW
Washington, DC 20001
1-800-233-1200
E-mail: cdfinfo@childrensdefense.org
URL: http://www.childrensdefense.org/

**Child Welfare League of
America**
2345 Crystal Dr., Ste. 250
Arlington, VA 22202
(703) 412-2400
FAX: (703) 412-2401
URL: http://www.cwla.org/

Feeding America
35 E. Wacker Dr., Ste. 2000
Chicago, IL 60601
1-800-771-2303
FAX: (312) 263-5626
URL: http://www.feedingamerica.org/

**Food Research and Action
Center**
1875 Connecticut Ave. NW, Ste. 540
Washington, DC 20009
(202) 986-2200
FAX: (202) 986-2525
URL: http://www.frac.org/

Habitat for Humanity International
121 Habitat St.
Americus, GA 31709-3498
1-800-422-4828
URL: http://www.habitat.org/

Homes for the Homeless
50 Cooper Square, 4th Floor
New York, NY 10003
(212) 529-5252
FAX: (212) 529-7698
E-mail: info@hfhnyc.org
URL: http://www.homes
forthehomeless.com/

Housing Assistance Council
1025 Vermont Ave. NW, Ste. 606
Washington, DC 20005
(202) 842-8600
FAX: (202) 347-3441
E-mail: hac@ruralhome.org
URL: http://www.ruralhome.org/

**Institute for Research on Poverty
University of Wisconsin, Madison**
1180 Observatory Dr.
3412 Social Science Bldg.
Madison, WI 53706-1393
(608) 262-6358
FAX: (608) 265-3119
E-mail: djohnson@ssc.wisc.edu
URL: http://www.irp.wisc.edu/

**Joint Center for Housing Studies
Harvard University**
1033 Massachusetts Ave., Fifth Floor
Cambridge, MA 02138
(617) 495-7908
FAX: (617) 496-9957
URL: http://www.jchs.harvard.edu/
index.htm

Kaiser Family Foundation
2400 Sand Hill Rd.
Menlo Park, CA 94025
(650) 854-9400
FAX: (650) 854-4800
URL: http://www.kff.org/

National Alliance to End Homelessness
1518 K St. NW, Ste. 410
Washington, DC 20005
(202) 638-1526
FAX: (202) 638-4664
E-mail: naeh@naeh.org
URL: http://www.endhomelessness.org/

National Alliance of HUD Tenants
42 Seaverns Ave.
Boston, MA 02130
(617) 267-9564
FAX: (617) 522-4857
E-mail: naht@saveourhomes.org
URL: http://www.saveourhomes.org/

National Alliance on Mental Illness
Colonial Place Three
2107 Wilson Blvd., Ste. 300
Arlington, VA 22201-3042

(703) 524-7600
FAX: (703) 524-9094
URL: http://www.nami.org/
Hometemplate.cfm

National Association for the Education of Homeless Children and Youth
PO Box 26274
Minneapolis, MN 55426
(866) 862-2562
FAX: (763) 545-9499
E-mail: info@naehcy.org
URL: http://www.naehcy.org/

National Center for Children in Poverty
215 W. 125th St., Third Floor
New York, NY 10027
(646) 284-9600
FAX: (646) 284-9623
E-mail: info@nccp.org
URL: http://www.nccp.org/

National Coalition for the Homeless
2201 P St. NW
Washington, DC 20037
(202) 462-4822
FAX: (202) 462-4823
E-mail: info@nationalhomeless.org
URL: http://www.nationalhomeless.org/

National Coalition for Homeless Veterans
333 ½ Pennsylvania Ave. SE
Washington, DC 20003-1148
(202) 546-1969
1-800-838-4357
FAX: (202) 546-2063
E-mail: nchv@nchv.org
URL: http://www.nchv.org/

National Health Care for the Homeless Council
PO Box 60427
Nashville, TN 37206-0427
(615) 226-2292
FAX: (615) 226-1656

E-mail: council@nhchc.org
URL: http://www.nhchc.org/

National Housing Conference
1801 K St. NW, Ste. M-100
Washington, DC 20006-1301
(202) 466-2121
FAX: (202) 466-2122
E-mail: manapol@nhc.org
URL: http://www.nhc.org/

National Housing Law Project
614 Grand Ave., Ste. 320
Oakland, CA 94610
(510) 251-9400
FAX: (510) 451-2300
E-mail: nhlp@nhlp.org
URL: http://www.nhlp.org/

National Law Center for Children and Families
225 N. Fairfax St.
Alexandria, VA 22314
(703) 548-5522
FAX: (703) 548-5544
URL: http://www.nationallawcenter.org/

National Law Center on Homelessness and Poverty
1411 K St. NW, Ste. 1400
Washington, DC 20005
(202) 638-2535
FAX: (202) 628-2737
URL: http://www.nlchp.org/

National League of Cities
1301 Pennsylvania Ave. NW, Ste. 550
Washington, DC 20004
(202) 626-3000
FAX: (202) 626-3043
E-mail: info@nlc.org
URL: http://www.nlc.org/

National Low Income Housing Coalition
727 15th St. NW, Sixth Floor
Washington, DC 20005

(202) 662-1530
FAX: (202) 393-1973
URL: http://www.nlihc.org/

National Rural Housing Coalition
1331 G St. NW, 10th Floor
Washington, DC 20005
(202) 393-5229
FAX: (202) 393-3034
URL: http://www.nrhcweb.org/

National Women's Law Center
11 Dupont Circle NW, Ste. 800
Washington, DC 20036
(202) 588-5180
FAX: (202) 588-5185
URL: http://nwlc.org/

Rural Policy Research Institute University of Missouri
214 Middlebush Hall
Columbia, MO 65211
(573) 882-0316
URL: http://www.rupri.org/

Urban Institute
2100 M St. NW
Washington, DC 20037
(202) 833-7200
URL: http://www.urban.org/

U.S. Conference of Mayors
1620 Eye St. NW
Washington, DC 20006
(202) 293-7330
FAX: (202) 293-2352
E-mail: info@usmayors.org
URL: http://www.usmayors.org/

U.S. Interagency Council on Homelessness
Federal Center SW
409 Third St. SW, Ste. 310
Washington, DC 20024
(202) 708-4663
FAX: (202) 708-1216
E-mail: usich@usich.gov
URL: http://www.ich.gov/

RESOURCES

The federal government remains the premier source of facts on many issues, including poverty, employment, welfare, and housing. Some particularly excellent sources of information from the U.S. Census Bureau are *The 2009 Statistical Abstract* (December 2008), *Income, Earnings, and Poverty Data from the 2007 American Community Survey* (August 2008, Alemayehu Bishaw and Jessica Semega), *Income, Poverty, and Health Insurance Coverage in the United States: 2007* (August 2008, Carmen DeNavas-Walt, Bernadette D. Proctor, and Jessica C. Smith), *America's Families and Living Arrangements: 2007* (July 2008), *Participation of Mothers in Government Assistance Programs: 2004* (May 2008, Jane Lawler Dye), *2007 Community Survey* (2008), *Custodial Mothers and Fathers and Their Child Support: 2005* (August 2007, Timothy S. Grall), *Dynamics of Economic Well-Being: Participation in Government Programs, 2001 through 2003, Who Gets Assistance?* (October 2006, Tracy A. Loveless and Jan Tin), *America's Families and Living Arrangements: 2003* (November 2004, Jason Fields), and *Emergency and Transitional Shelter Population: 2000* (October 2001, Annetta C. Smith and Denise I. Smith).

The monthly *Employment and Earnings* of the Bureau of Labor Statistics (BLS) provides data on wages and work patterns, and the annual *A Profile of the Working Poor, 2006* (August 2008) details labor information about low-income workers. Many of the BLS data are published in the *Monthly Labor Review*. Other material used in preparing this book comes from the BLS's *Characteristics of Minimum Wage Workers: 2007* (March 2008) and *Household Data Annual Averages* (2007).

Other publications of the federal government used in this book include the U.S. Department of Housing and Urban Development's *The Third Annual Homeless Assessment Report to Congress* (July 2008), *The Second Annual Homeless Assessment Report to Congress* (March 2008), *Fiscal Year 2007 Budget Summary* (February 2008), and *Affordable Housing Needs 2005: Report to Congress* (May

2007). The U.S. Department of Education published the *Report to the President and Congress on the Implementation of the Education for Homeless Children and Youth Program under the McKinney-Vento Homeless Assistance Act* (2006). The Social Security Administration publishes the quarterly *Social Security Bulletin* and the *Annual Statistical Supplement to the Social Security Bulletin*, which provide a statistical overview of major welfare programs. The Administration for Children and Families publishes the *Annual Report to Congress*, which describes the Temporary Assistance for Needy Families program.

The National Center for Health Statistics, which issues periodic reports such as *Health, United States, 2008* (2009), as well as vital statistics on birth rates, marital status, and health status, is a part of the Centers for Disease Control and Prevention (CDC). Reports from the CDC used in this book include *Births: Final Data for 2006* (January 2009, Joyce A. Martin et al.), *HIV/AIDS Surveillance Report: Cases of HIV Infection and AIDS in the United States and Dependent Areas, 2007* (2009), and *Reported Tuberculosis in the United States, 2007* (September 2008).

The U.S. Department of Agriculture's Food and Nutrition Service provides detailed tables about the National School Lunch Program, the School Breakfast Program, the Supplemental Nutrition Assistance Program, and the Special Supplemental Food Program for Women, Infants, and Children, as well as data from *Household Food Security in the United States, 2007* (November 2008, Mark Nord, Margaret Andrews, and Steven Carlson), *WIC Participant and Program Characteristics 2006* (December 2007, Susan Bartlett et al.), and *Food Stamps Make America Stronger* (September 2007).

The U.S. Government Accountability Office (GAO) investigates topics as requested by Congress. The GAO publications used in this book include *Project-Based Rental Assistance: HUD Should Update Its Policies and*

Procedures to Keep Pace with the Changing Housing Market (April 2007), *Public Housing: Information on the Roles of HUD, Public Housing Agencies, Capital Markets, and Service Organizations* (February 2006, David G. Wood), *Rural Housing Service: Overview of Program Issues* (March 2005), "Major Management Challenges at the Department of Housing and Urban Development" (2005), *Rural Housing Service: Agency Has Overestimated Its Rental Assistance Budget Needs over the Life of the Program* (May 2004), *Rural Housing Service: Opportunity to Improve Management* (June 2003, William B. Shear), and *Homelessness: Improving Program Coordination and Client Access to Programs* (March 2002, Stanley J. Czerwinski).

The periodically published *The Green Book: Background Material and Data on the Programs within the Jurisdiction of the Committee on Ways and Means* by the U.S. House of Representatives provides the most complete information on the U.S. welfare system in a single source. The annual *State Expenditure Report* of the National Association of State Budget Officers shows how the states and territories spend their welfare funds.

Many different organizations study the poor and homeless. Notable among them for their many large studies on homelessness is the Urban Institute. This organization's ongoing studies of the homeless are among the largest and most comprehensive in the United States. Its publications were a major source of information for this volume, especially *The Changing Role of Welfare in the Lives of Low-Income Families with Children* (August 2006, Pamela Loprest and Sheila Zedlewski), "Government Work Supports and Low-Income Families: Facts and Figures" (July 2006), "A Decade of Welfare Reform: Facts and Figures—Assessing the New Federalism" (June 2006), "Trends in Parents' Economic Hardship" (March 2004, Sandi Nelson), *America's Homeless II: Populations and Services* (February 2000), and *Homelessness: Programs and the People They Serve* (December 1999, Martha R. Burt et al.).

The Center on Budget and Policy Priorities is an advocacy organization that releases reports, papers, updates, and studies on welfare. Its publications include "Policy Basics: An Introduction to TANF" (March 2009, Liz Schott), "Despite Critics' Over-heated Rhetoric, the Economic Recovery Bill Does Not Undermine Welfare Reform" (Feb-

ruary 2009, Sharon Parrott), *Recession Could Cause Large Increases in Poverty and Push Millions into Deep Poverty* (November 2008, Sharon Parrott), "Average Income in 2006 up $60,000 for Top 1 Percent of Households, Just $430 for Bottom 90 Percent" (October 2008, Chye-Ching Huang and Chad Stone), *State Earned Income Tax Credits: 2008 Legislative Update* (October 2008, Jason Levitis and Jeremy Koulish), and "TANF at 10: Program Results Are More Mixed Than Often Understood" (August 2006, Sharon Parrott and Arloc Sherman). Feeding America, a charitable hunger-relief organization, prepared *Hunger in America 2006* (March 2006).

Three other excellent sources of information on the national homeless population are the National League of Cities, the U.S. Conference of Mayors, and the Association of Gospel Rescue Missions. The National League of Cities publication *The State of America's Cities 2007, Local Housing Conditions and Contexts: A Framework for Policy Making* (2007, Christiana McFarland, Casey Dawkins, and C. Theodore Koebel) contains valuable data on the scope of urban homelessness and how cities and regions try to deal with it. *Hunger and Homelessness Survey: A Status Report on Hunger and Homelessness in America's Cities, a 25-City Survey, December 2008* (December 2008) by the Conference of Mayors and *Women with Children Hit Hardest by Slow Economy* (November 2008) by the Association of Gospel Rescue Missions also provide a great deal of information on the homeless population.

The many organizations that advocate for the homeless and their issues are also crucial sources for this book. The National Coalition for the Homeless is certainly one of the most important of these organizations. Its publication *A Dream Denied: The Criminalization of Homelessness in U.S. Cities* (January 2006) is particularly recommended. The Applied Survey Research, the Economic Policy Institute, the Joint Center for Housing Studies of Harvard University, Health Care for the Homeless, the National Coalition for Homeless Veterans, the Millennial Housing Commission, the National Multi Housing Council, the Kaiser Family Foundation, and the National Law Center on Homelessness and Poverty all provide extensive coverage of important aspects of the housing and homelessness issues.

INDEX

Page references in italics refer to photographs. References with the letter t following them indicate the presence of a table. The letter f indicates a figure. If more than one table or figure appears on a particular page, the exact item number for the table or figure being referenced is provided.

A

Abandoned buildings, 108–109
Abstinence-only education programs, 66
Access to health care, 121–122, 133
Affordable housing. *See* Housing
African-Americans
    median household income, 29t
    poverty, 21
AGRM (Association of Gospel Rescue Missions), 12–13, 85, 87, 88
Aid to Families with Dependent Children, 71
AIDS, 135, 136
American Recovery and Reinvestment Act
    food and shelter program funding, 144
    health care, 125
    homeless veterans program funding, 88
    Homelessness Prevention Fund, 16
    Medicaid funding, 128
    public housing funding, 101
    school lunch program, 60, 147
    unemployment compensation expansion, 72
    welfare assistance funding, 39
Amtrak, 119
Antipanhandling laws, 118
Assets and liabilities, 6
Association of Gospel Rescue Missions (AGRM), 12–13, 85, 87, 88

B

Baird, Lourdes G., 119
Balanced Budget Act, 59
Birth rates
    unmarried teens, 65–66
    unmarried women, 71f
Blank, Rebecca M., 5
Blindness, 75
Blood vessel disorders among homeless persons, 135
"Broken Windows" theory, 117
Bush, George W.
    abstinence-only education programs, 66
    Deficit Reduction Act, 61
    Medicare and Medicaid cuts, 128
    State Child Health Insurance Program, 128

C

Camping ordinances, 119
Capital gains, 6
Carter, Jimmy and Rosalynn, 108
Carter Work Project, 108
Caseload, welfare, 57, 58t
CCDF (Child Care Development Fund), 72–73
CCHIP (Community Childhood Hunger Identification Project), 139–140
Census Bureau
    homeless persons, counting of, 13–14
    income definition, 5–6
    income inequality, 6
Child care, 60, 71–72
Child Care Development Fund (CCDF), 72–73
Child Nutrition Act, 148
Child nutrition programs, 60
Child support, 32, 33t, 40t, 59, 69f
Children
    education for homeless children and youth, 114–115
    food security status, 143t
    health care access, 121–122
    health of homeless children, 138
    homelessness, 13t, 84(t4.3), 87–88, 87f
    hunger, 139–140
    living arrangements, 37t–38t
    Medicaid, 125, 127
    mental health issues of homeless children, 137–138
    National School Lunch and School Breakfast programs, 146–147, 146(t7.11)
    Personal Responsibility and Work Opportunity Reconciliation Act, 59–60
    poverty, 21–23, 24t–28t, 39f
    single-parent family groups, 35t–36t
    Special Supplemental Food Program for Women, Infants, and Children, 148–149, 149t, 150f
    State Child Health Insurance Program, 128
    uninsured children, 123, 128f
    unmarried couples, by presence of biological children, 34t
Children's Defense Fund, 22
Children's Health Insurance Program, 125
Choice Neighborhoods Initiative, 107
Chronic homelessness, 83, 94
Chronic medical conditions, 121, 133
Cities, 23, 90–91
City of Los Angeles, Jones v., 119
City of Los Angeles, Justin v., 119
City of Miami, Pottinger v., 118
City of Sarasota v. McGinnis, 118
City of Sarasota v. Nipper, 118
City of Sarasota v. Tillman, 119
City of Tucson, Davidson v., 119
Civil rights, 116–119
Comic Relief (fund-raising event), 15
Committee on National Statistics, 4
Communities
    homelessness ordinances, 15, 115–119, 116t
    low-income housing, resistance to, 107–108

Community Childhood Hunger Identification Project (CCHIP), 139–140

Constitutional rights of the homeless, 117–119

Construction, housing, 105, 107–108

Consumer expenditures, 4

Continuum of Care, 111–112, 113*t*

Costs
fair market rental rates, 104*t*
health care safety net programs, 123–124
housing cost-burdened households, by tenure and income, 100*t*
Medicaid, 128
public housing programs budget, 102*t*
rental housing affordability, 99
rural housing programs funding, 106*t*
school food programs, 147
Supplemental Nutrition Assistance Program, 145*t*

Court cases
City of Sarasota v. McGinnis, 118
City of Sarasota v. Nipper, 118
City of Sarasota v. Tillman, 119
Davidson v. City of Tucson, 119
In re Eichorn, 118
Jones v. City of Los Angeles, 119
Justin v. City of Los Angeles, 119
Loper v. New York City Police Department, 119
Mason v. Tucson, 119
Pottinger v. City of Miami, 118
Streetwatch v. National R. R. Passenger Corp., 119

Criminalization of homelessness, 15, 115–116

Crystal, Billy, 15

Custodial parents
child support, 32, 33*t*
by child support award status, payments received, and demographic characteristics, 40*t*
poverty status, 29*f*, 39*f*

D

Data collection. *See* Measurement and data collection

Davidson v. City of Tucson, 119

Day labor, 91–92

Definitions
homelessness, 10, 83–84, 114
income, 5–6
worst-case needs families, 99

Department of Education, U.S., 84–85, 87–88

Department of Health and Human Services, U.S., 1, 2*t*

Department of Housing and Urban Development, U.S.
homeless services, 16
homelessness data collection, 14–15, 83

housing vouchers, 103–105
McKinney-Vento Homeless Assistance Act programs, 111–115, 113*t*
public housing programs, 101–103, 102*t*
Self-Help Home Ownership Opportunity Program, 105
worst-case needs families, 98–99

Disability
federally administered awards distribution, by sex, age, and eligibility category, 81*t*
homelessness, 85*t*
Supplemental Security Income, 75–77, 79*f*
Supplemental Security Insurance, 80*t*
Temporary Assistance for Needy Families program participation rates, 64*t*

Diseases. *See* Health and health care

Domestic violence victims, 138–139

E

Earned Income Tax Credit (EITC), 77, 79, 82*f*

Earnings. *See* Income; Wages and earnings

Economic recession
foreclosure crisis, 90–91
health care impact, 124–125
homelessness, 15
Supplemental Nutrition Assistance Program, 61, 146
unemployment compensation expansion, 72
welfare assistance funding, 39

Education
abstinence-only programs, 66
custodial parents, 40*t*
homeless children and youth, 87–88, 114–115
living arrangements, 37*t*–38*t*
mothers in welfare assistance programs, 68*t*, 69*f*, 70*t*
poverty, 33–34, 50*t*
Temporary Assistance for Needy Families, 63, 64*t*, 65, 68–69
welfare assistance, duration on, 52

Eichorn, James, 118

EITC (Earned Income Tax Credit), 77, 79, 82*f*

Elderly persons, 4, 23

Eligibility
federally administered awards distribution, 81*t*
food stamps, 144*t*
housing vouchers, 103
Medicaid, 125, 127
Temporary Assistance for Needy Families, 61

Emergency food assistance, 141, 143

Emergency Shelter Grant Program, 112–113, 113*t*

Employment
custodial parents, by poverty status, 29*f*
homelessness, 91–93
income inequality, 9–10
institutionalized assistance, 93
Medicaid for working parents, 127
minimum wage, 75, 77*t*, 78*t*
mothers in welfare assistance programs, 69*f*
odds of mothers receiving welfare assistance, 70*t*
poverty status, 33, 41*t*, 49*t*, 51*t*
street newspapers, 93
Supplemental Nutrition Assistance Program requirements, 61
Temporary Assistance for Needy Families, 69–71
Temporary Assistance for Needy Families program participation rates, 64*t*
wages and housing affordability, 100
welfare-to-work requirements, 66–68
working poor, 50–52

Enumeration of homeless population, 13–15

Equal protection rights, 118

F

Fair Labor Standards Act, 75, 77

Fair market rent, 100, 104*t*

Fair market rental rates, 104, 104*t*

Families
child support, 32, 33*t*
custodial parents, 40*t*
employment status, 29*f*
homelessness, 86–87
households, by type and demographic characteristics, 30*t*
living arrangements of children, 37*t*–38*t*
marital status, by sex and race/ethnicity, 31*t*–32*t*
poverty, 23, 29–32
poverty and work experience, 41*t*
poverty likelihood, by family status, 48
poverty status, by presence of related children and work experience, 51*t*
poverty status of custodial parents, 39*f*
single-parent family groups, 35*t*–36*t*
Temporary Assistance for Needy Families program participation rates, 64*t*
uninsured persons, 124*t*–125*t*
unmarried couples, by age, race, marital status, and presence of biological children, 34*t*
welfare assistance, duration on, 52, 54

Farm Bill, 60

Federal government assistance. *See* Welfare assistance

Feeding America, 141

Female-headed households, 62, 64